The Cognitive Basis of Social Interaction Across the Lifespan

The Cognitive Basis of Social Interaction Across the Lifespan

Edited by

HEATHER J. FERGUSON

*Professor in Psychology,
University of Kent, UK*

ELISABETH E. F. BRADFORD

*Lecturer in Psychology,
University of Dundee, UK*

OXFORD
UNIVERSITY PRESS

Great Clarendon Street, Oxford, OX2 6DP,
United Kingdom

Oxford University Press is a department of the University of Oxford.
It furthers the University's objective of excellence in research, scholarship,
and education by publishing worldwide. Oxford is a registered trade mark of
Oxford University Press in the UK and in certain other countries

© Oxford University Press 2021

The moral rights of the authors have been asserted

First Edition published in 2021

Impression: 1

All rights reserved. No part of this publication may be reproduced, stored in
a retrieval system, or transmitted, in any form or by any means, without the
prior permission in writing of Oxford University Press, or as expressly permitted
by law, by licence or under terms agreed with the appropriate reprographics
rights organization. Enquiries concerning reproduction outside the scope of the
above should be sent to the Rights Department, Oxford University Press, at the
address above

You must not circulate this work in any other form
and you must impose this same condition on any acquirer

Published in the United States of America by Oxford University Press
198 Madison Avenue, New York, NY 10016, United States of America

British Library Cataloguing in Publication Data

Data available

Library of Congress Control Number: 2021933317

ISBN 978–0–19–884329–0

DOI: 10.1093/oso/9780198843290.001.0001

Printed and bound by
CPI Group (UK) Ltd, Croydon, CR0 4YY

Oxford University Press makes no representation, express or implied, that the
drug dosages in this book are correct. Readers must therefore always check
the product information and clinical procedures with the most up-to-date
published product information and data sheets provided by the manufacturers
and the most recent codes of conduct and safety regulations. The authors and
the publishers do not accept responsibility or legal liability for any errors in the
text or for the misuse or misapplication of material in this work. Except where
otherwise stated, drug dosages and recommendations are for the non-pregnant
adult who is not breast-feeding

Links to third party websites are provided by Oxford in good faith and
for information only. Oxford disclaims any responsibility for the materials
contained in any third party website referenced in this work.

Acknowledgements

This book was prepared with the support of a European Research Council grant to Heather Ferguson (Ref: CogSoCoAGE; 636458). This grant supported Elisabeth Bradford, Victoria Brunsdon, and Martina de Lillo, the authors of Chapters 6 and 9. For chapter 2, Tobias Schuwerk and Hannes Rakoczy were supported by a grant from the German Research Foundation (RA 2155/7-1 and SCHU 3060/1-1). For Chapter 8, Muireann Irish was supported by an Australian Research Council Future Fellowship (FT160100096), and Siddharth Ramanan by a University of Sydney, Faculty of Science Ph.D. Research Scholarship.

Thanks are due to Camilla Woodrow-Hill for help with proofreading and formatting draft chapters, and to Netanel Weinstein for providing comments on earlier versions of Chapter 4.

Contents

Contributors	ix
Authors' Biographies	xi
1. The Cognitive Basis of Social Interaction Across the Lifespan: An Introduction *Heather J. Ferguson*	1
2. Social Interaction in Infancy *Tobias Schuwerk and Hannes Rakoczy*	27
3. Social Interaction in Early and Middle Childhood: The Role of Theory of Mind *Serena Lecce and Rory T. Devine*	47
4. Development of Social Cognition in Adolescence and the Importance of Mating *Sarah Donaldson and Kathryn Mills*	70
5. Mindreading in Adults: Cognitive Basis, Motivation, and Individual Differences *Ian A. Apperly and J. Jessica Wang*	96
6. Social Interactions in Old Age *Victoria E. A. Brunsdon, Elisabeth E. F. Bradford, and Heather J. Ferguson*	117
7. Understanding Atypical Social Behaviour Using Social Cognitive Theory: Lessons from Autism *Lucy A. Livingston and Francesca Happé*	147
8. The Ageing Brain in Context: Towards a Refined Understanding of Social Cognition in Ageing and Dementia *Muireann Irish and Siddharth Ramanan*	177
9. The Future of Research on Social Interaction *Elisabeth E. F. Bradford, Martina De Lillo, and Heather J. Ferguson*	201
Index	229

Contributors

Ian A. Apperly, Professor of Cognition and Development, School of Psychology, University of Birwmingham, UK

Elisabeth E. F. Bradford, Lecturer in Psychology, School of Social Sciences, University of Dundee, UK

Victoria E. A. Brunsdon, Postdoctoral Research Associate, School of Psychology, University of Kent, UK

Martina De Lillo, Doctoral Student, School of Psychology, University of Kent, UK

Rory T. Devine, Lecturer in Developmental Psychology, School of Psychology, University of Birmingham, UK

Sarah Donaldson, Doctoral Student, Department of Psychology, University of Oregon, USA

Heather J. Ferguson, Professor in Psychology, School of Psychology, University of Kent, UK

Francesca Happé, Professor of Cognitive Neuroscience, Institute of Psychiatry, Psychology & Neuroscience, King's College London, UK

Muireann Irish, Professor of Cognitive Neuroscience, School of Psychology, Brain and Mind Centre, University of Sydney, Australia

Serena Lecce, Associate Professor in Developmental and Educational Psychology, Department of Brain and Behavioral Science, University of Pavia, Italy

Lucy A. Livingston, Lecturer in Psychology, School of Psychology, Cardiff University, UK

Kathryn Mills, Assistant Professor, Department of Psychology, University of Oregon, USA

Hannes Rakoczy, Developmental Psychologist, Department of Developmental Psychology, University of Göttingen, Germany

Siddharth Ramanan, Postdoctoral Research Associate, MRC Cognition and Brain Sciences Unit, University of Cambridge, UK

Tobias Schuwerk, Clinical and Developmental Psychologist, Department of Developmental and Educational Psychology, Ludwig-Maximilians-University of Munich, Germany

J. Jessica Wang, Lecturer in Psychology, Department of Psychology, Lancaster University, UK

Authors' Biographies

Ian A. Apperly
Ian Apperly is a Professor of Cognition and Development in the School of Psychology at the University of Birmingham. He studied natural sciences at Cambridge University and completed his PhD at the University of Birmingham. His main research interest is in 'mindreading'—the ability to take other people's perspectives for communication, cooperation, competition, or deception—and he has built a strong international profile in this area. His work has been supported by funders including the Economic and Social Research Council, Medical Research Council, and Leverhulme Trust, and he authored a book, *Mindreaders: The Cognitive Basis of Theory of Mind*, in 2010. He has received prizes from the British Psychological Society and the Experimental Psychology Society.

Elisabeth E. F. Bradford
Elisabeth Bradford is a Lecturer in Cognitive and Developmental Psychology at the School of Social Sciences, University of Dundee (Scotland, UK). She completed her PhD at the University of St Andrews in 2016. Prior to her lectureship at the University of Dundee, Lizzie worked as a Postdoctoral Research Associate at the University of Kent (England, UK). Her research focuses on social cognition abilities, examining how these capacities change and develop across the lifespan, the impacts of deficits in social cognition abilities, how social cognition may vary across cultures, and the factors that may underlie successful engagement of social cognition abilities at different ages (e.g. executive functions).

Victoria E. A. Brunsdon

Victoria Brunsdon completed her undergraduate degree in Psychology and MSc in Experimental Psychology at the University of Birmingham, before completing a PhD in Cognitive Psychology at King's College London. Following this, Victoria joined the University of Kent as a Postdoctoral Research Associate, working on the 'CogSoCoAGE' project examining the cognitive basis of social interactions across the lifespan. Her research combines cognitive-experimental measures, twin-model fitting, and structural equation modelling to study typical and atypical development.

Martina De Lillo

Martina De Lillo is a doctoral student in the School of Psychology at the University of Kent, where she has been funded by Heather Ferguson's European Research Council grant (for the 'CogSoCoAGE' project) since 2016. Her research explores social and cognitive abilities across the lifespan, and tests whether social skills can be enhanced indirectly through executive function training.

Rory T. Devine

Dr Rory T. Devine is a Lecturer in Developmental Psychology at the University of Birmingham (UK). Dr Devine completed his PhD. at the University of Cambridge in 2013. Prior to taking up his Lectureship at the University of Birmingham, he worked as a Post-Doctoral Research Associate at the Centre for Family Research at the University of Cambridge and held the post of Director of Studies in Psychology and College Research Associate at Clare College, Cambridge. Dr Devine's research uses cutting-edge statistical techniques and longitudinal methods to shed light on the social influences and social outcomes of individual differences in Theory of Mind and executive function in children.

AUTHORS' BIOGRAPHIES xiii

Sarah Donaldson

Sarah Donaldson is a doctoral student in the Department of Psychology at the University of Oregon. She completed her Master's Degree at Oakland University in 2016. Her research examines biological, cognitive, and behavioural underpinnings of romantic relationships during adolescence from an evolutionary perspective.

Heather J. Ferguson

Heather Ferguson is a Professor in Psychology at the University of Kent. She completed her PhD in Cognitive Neuroscience and Psycholinguistics at the University of Glasgow in 2007, followed by a two-year postdoctoral research position at University College London. Her research broadly examines the cognitive basis of social communication. She examines the time-course of integration, the underlying neural mechanisms, and the extent to which constraints from world knowledge and context compete to influence social interaction and pragmatic language comprehension. This work has received generous funding, including a European Research Council grant examining social communication across the lifespan, and Leverhulme Trust grants that link social processing directly to language (including in autism spectrum disorders). Professor Ferguson has been formally recognized through multiple prize awards (e.g. the Psychonomic Early Career Award 2019), and holds key leadership positions in the discipline (e.g. Honorary Secretary to the Experimental Psychology Society).

Francesca Happé

Francesca Happé is Professor of Cognitive Neuroscience at the Institute of Psychiatry, Psychology & Neuroscience, King's College London. Her research focuses on autism. She has explored social cognition and 'mentalizing' difficulties. She is also actively engaged in studies of abilities and assets in autism, and their relation to detail-focused cognitive style. Some of her recent work focuses on mental health on the autism spectrum, and under-researched groups including women and older people on the autism spectrum. She is a Fellow of the British Academy and the Academy of Medical Sciences, a past-President of the International Society for Autism Research, and has received the British Psychological Society (BPS) Spearman Medal and President's Award, Experimental Psychology Society Prize, Royal Society Rosalind Franklin Award and a CBE for services to the study of autism. She is co-author/editor of two recent books—*Autism: A New Introduction to Psychological Theory and Debate* (with Sue Fletcher-Watson), and *Girls and Autism: Educational, Family and Personal Perspectives* (with Barry Carpenter and Jo Egerton).

Muireann Irish

Muireann Irish is an Australian Research Council Future Fellow and Professor of Cognitive Neuroscience at the Brain and Mind Centre, University of Sydney, where she leads the 'Memory and Imagination in Neurological Disorders' (MIND) group. As a cognitive neuroscientist, Muireann's research focuses on the brain mechanisms underpinning complex expressions of memory, and how these processes are compromised in neurodegenerative disorders such as Alzheimer's disease and frontotemporal dementia. To date, Muireann has produced more than a hundred publications exploring such capacities as autobiographical memory, future thinking, Theory of Mind, and daydreaming in dementia. The quality of Muireann's work has resulted in a series of prestigious awards including the 2019 Cognitive Neuroscience Society Young Investigator Award and the 2020 Gottschalk Medal from the Australian Academy of Science.

Serena Lecce

Dr Serena Lecce is an Associate Professor in Developmental and Educational Psychology at the Department of Brain and Behavioral Sciences, University of Pavia (Italy). She arrived at the University of Pavia as a doctoral student in 2001 and received a doctoral degree in 2004. Dr Lecce was appointed as a Lecturer in 2008 and was subsequently promoted to Associate Professor in 2014. She directs the Laboratory of Social Cognition where she conducts investigations of social and emotional functioning, and works closely with practitioners and teachers. Her research explores social and cognitive development across the lifespan. She is particularly interested in examining origins and consequences of individual differences of Theory of Mind for children's social relationships and adjustment to school. A core applied focus of her research is the development and evaluation of training programmes to promote Theory of Mind and support social and emotional competence.

Lucy Anne Livingston

Lucy Anne Livingston is a Lecturer in Psychology at Cardiff University, based within the Centre for Human Developmental Science. She completed her BSc in Psychology at Durham University, followed by a Medical Research Council funded 1+3 MSc + PhD at the Institute of Psychiatry, Psychology and Neuroscience, King's College London. Her PhD investigated heterogeneity in social cognition in autism through the study of compensatory mechanisms, with a particular focus on Theory of Mind. Lucy was awarded the 2020 British Psychological Society Developmental Section Neil O'Connor Award. She is also a visiting researcher at the UK

National Autistic Society and member of Autistica's Physical Health and Ageing in Autism Study Group. Her current research interests include developmental trajectories and diverse outcomes in autism and other neurodevelopmental conditions, as well as a/typical social cognition across the lifespan.

Kathryn Mills

Dr. Kate Mills is an Assistant Professor in the Department of Psychology at the University of Oregon. She completed her doctoral studies at the Institute of Cognitive Neuroscience at University College London in 2015. Her programme of research applies longitudinal research methods to investigate the intertwined social, biological, and cognitive processes that underlie the development of skills needed to navigate the social environment.

Hannes Rakoczy

Hannes Rakoczy is a Developmental Psychologist at the University of Göttingen in Germany. His research focuses on early cognitive development in human ontogeny, with a complementary comparative perspective: which cognitive capacities are evolutionarily more ancient and develop early in human ontogeny in ways parallel to other primates? And which capacities are uniquely human, develop in more protracted ways, and potentially depend on language and culture?

Siddharth Ramanan

Siddharth Ramanan is a postdoctoral Research Associate at the MRC Cognition and Brain Sciences Unit, The University of Cambridge, UK. Siddharth completed his PhD in Psychology in 2020 at The University of Sydney, Australia, exploring inferior parietal lobe contributions to episodic memory in rare neurodegenerative syndromes. Siddharth's research interests focus on understanding the mechanisms of heterogeneous cognitive and behavioural symptoms in neurodegenerative dementia syndromes. As an early career researcher, Siddharth has received numerous competitive awards in recognition of his work including the 2014 Neuropsychology International Fellowship, 2018 BrightFocus Foundation Travel Award, and 2019 Margaret Ethel Jew Award for Dementia Research.

Tobias Schuwerk

Tobias Schuwerk is a Clinical and Developmental Psychologist at Ludwig-Maximilians-University of Munich, Germany. He studies Theory of Mind in children and adults with and without autism. He is particularly interested in its (neuro-)cognitive basis and its development during early childhood. Further, he investigates if–and, if so, how– the cognitive processes underlying Theory of Mind work differently in people with autism. An additional research focus addresses the question of how we use Theory of Mind in our everyday lives.

J. Jessica Wang

Jessica Wang is currently a Lecturer in Psychology at Lancaster University. She previously held a lectureship at Keele University, and research fellowships at the University of Birmingham and Université Catholique de Louvain in Belgium. She completed her PhD and MRes at the University of Birmingham, after graduating with a BSc in Psychology from the National Chung Cheng University in Taiwan. Jessica's primary research interest is in Theory of Mind and communication. She investigates the cognitive, developmental lifespan, social, and cultural factors implicated in the way in which we think about others' perspectives in various contexts. She is also interested in the spontaneous computation of low-level social information, such as eye gaze and visual perspectives.

1
The Cognitive Basis of Social Interaction Across the Lifespan

An Introduction

Heather J. Ferguson

1.1 Introduction

Social interactions form a hugely important aspect of everyday life, and their success (or lack of) has a heavy impact on our well-being. There is a common agreement that social cognition helps us to understand ourselves, others, and our environment through implicit and explicit processes (Moskowitz & Olcaysoy Okten, 2017), and that any cognitive process can reflect social ability if it involves a social agent or interaction. A vital part of successful social interaction is the ability to understand and predict events in terms of other people's mental states, such as their intentions, beliefs, emotions, and desires (termed Theory of Mind [ToM]). In a single day, we might need to infer mental states for a range of individuals (e.g. a long-term partner *versus* a stranger), under various circumstances (e.g. watching a movie *versus* interacting with people), and given differing levels of importance (e.g. believing a friend left your tea in the kitchen rather than the lounge *versus* believing that the white powder a friend put in your tea was sugar rather than poison). Social cognition underlies nearly all aspects of successful interpersonal relations, because people need to keep track of other people's knowledge, beliefs, and desires to understand their actions and intended meaning. Indeed, when we misunderstand another person's meaning or intentions during conversation, this often leads to negative social implications, such as taking offence or restricting further social interactions. This book will focus on the cognitive mechanisms that underlie human social interaction, how these abilities change across the lifespan, from infancy to older age, and in healthy and atypical development/ageing.

To date, research studies of different stages of the lifespan have progressed largely in isolation from each other, with the majority tending to focus on a single, static age group, and with very little cross-talk between developmental stages. This book therefore aims to bring together these diverse pockets of research, presenting a unique, comprehensive picture of the developmental trajectory, and decline, of social interaction capacities, and enabling a unified dynamic exploration of the cognitive basis of social interaction across the lifespan. Over nine chapters, leading researchers in this field provide an overview of the most recent research in this area, contribute to key debates on social phenomena (including their underlying mechanisms, environmental triggers, and neural bases), and outline some innovative avenues for future research. In this introductory chapter, I will start by defining the concepts underlying social interaction and highlighting the importance of a lifespan approach. Then, I will outline some key theories and mechanisms that have been proposed to underlie communicative success, and showcase a range of methodological approaches to this topic, emphasizing the challenges in applying these methods across the lifespan.

1.2 Concepts underlying social interaction

Despite the importance of social interaction and the decades of research that have explored ToM, there remains no consensus on the taxonomy or mechanisms that underlie these abilities. Some researchers have recently begun to examine the factor structure of social cognition, revealing a great deal of variance in the number of components involved, and a lack of consensus on the interdependence between them. For example, Fiske and Taylor (2013) identified 14 domains of social cognition, including more basic abilities such as social memory and social attention, and more complex concepts like social inferences and decision making. Happé and Frith (2014) tested this question using data on atypical social cognition, and identified at least eight distinct components, including mental state attribution, empathy, self-processing, and affiliation. In their review, Happé et al. (2017), focused on several sociocognitive processes including imitation, biological motion, empathy, social learning, and ToM, and discussed the challenges involved in identifying the components of social cognition and understanding the ways in which they may be related (including a lack of agreed lexical terms for sociocognitive processes). More recently, Beaudoin and colleagues (2020) conducted a systematic review of 830 articles and proposed a new 'Abilities in Theory of Mind Space' (ATOMS) framework, which provides a taxonomy of seven mental state categories (emotions, desires, intentions, percepts, knowledge, beliefs, and mentalistic understanding of non-literal communication). For future research, it will be important to consider whether common representational mechanisms are involved when these social skills require a representation of the self versus other.

In addition to these questions about the specific components that make up social cognition, researchers have distinguished broad categories of social behaviour. For example, ToM has been divided into affective and cognitive facets, whereby affective ToM refers to the ability to mentalize another person's emotions, while cognitive ToM requires comprehension of others' beliefs or intentions (Shamay-Tsoory & Aharon-Peretz, 2007). ToM can therefore be seen as distinct from compassion, as well as early implicit representations of mental states, such as joint attention and imitation, and more complex social abilities, such as cooperation or deception.

Finally, perspective-taking is considered as a means through which people can infer others' mental states. It involves adopting someone else's visual or spatial perspective and is typically examined along one of two dimensions: one that simply assesses *what* someone else can see (termed 'Level 1' perspective-taking), and another that assesses *how* that person sees something (termed 'Level 2' perspective-taking). These two types of perspective-taking can be differentiated according to whether or not they require one to mentally rotate into the position of the other person (Michelon & Zacks, 2006; Surtees et al., 2013).

1.3 The importance of a lifespan approach

Until relatively recently, most researchers assumed that adults are fully capable 'mindreaders', having developed the necessary skills for even complex social interaction between the ages of two and seven years old (Wellman et al., 2001). In fact, over 50 years of research have focused on the developmental trajectory of ToM within this narrow age range, demonstrating a 'transitional phase' in ToM ability between ages three and five (e.g. Wimmer & Perner, 1983).

Over the past couple of decades, new paradigms and methodological advances have facilitated an exciting new body of research that has examined social communication in infancy and beyond childhood. This work has ignited debates about whether infants as young as six months old are capable of spontaneously representing and reasoning about the (false) beliefs of others (e.g. Kovács et al., 2010; Kulke & Rakoczy, 2018; Schuwerk et al., 2018; Southgate & Vernetti, 2014). Importantly, it has also demonstrated that social development continues through adolescence and well into our twenties (e.g. Blakemore, 2008; Dumontheil et al., 2010), that even healthy adults can experience difficulties considering another person's point of view when that view conflicts with their own (e.g. Apperly et al., 2008; Birch & Bloom, 2007; Keysar et al., 2000), and that specific impairments in these abilities emerge with increasing age (e.g. Bailey & Henry, 2008; German & Hehman, 2006; Phillips et al., 2011). It is therefore likely that early studies overlooked key stages in the development of social interaction skills that extend beyond the childhood years.

Moreover, research has established the study of social communication in healthy adults as a research topic in its own right, showing a great deal of individual variation in performance (e.g. Bradford et al., 2015; Brown-Schmidt, 2009; Cane et al., 2017; Lin et al., 2010; Rubio-Fernández & Geurts, 2016; Brunyé et al., 2012; Ferguson et al., 2015a; Kessler & Wang, 2012; Nielsen et al., 2015; Converse et al., 2008; Wu & Keysar, 2007), and that even healthy adults might only consider other people's perspectives under specific task demands (Back & Apperly, 2010; Ferguson et al., 2015b). Examining effects in healthy adults is particularly valuable given recent evidence suggesting that some aspects of our social abilities reach their peak and begin to decline in the early thirties (Germine et al., 2011).

Comparatively less research has examined changes in social interaction in older age, though the majority of studies on this topic indicate that ToM abilities are subject to age-related decline (see Moran, 2013, for a review, and Henry et al., 2013, for a meta-analysis). Research has shown that age-related difficulties in ToM mediate a substantial decline in social participation in older adults, which can in turn lead to isolation, loneliness, and poor health (Bailey et al., 2008). Importantly, debate continues regarding the age at which these declines first appear (see Brunsdon et al., 2019; Pardini & Nichelli, 2009; Duval et al., 2011), with some researchers suggesting that social impairments first emerge in middle age and increase rapidly through older age (e.g. Bernstein et al., 2011). In addition, there is uncertainty regarding the task or domain-specificity of age-related social impairments, with affective ToM appearing to be relatively spared in older adults (e.g. Bottiroli et al., 2016; Castelli et al., 2010; Henry et al., 2013; Mahy et al., 2014; Pardini & Nichelli, 2009), and subjective experience of ToM showing no effects of age (which suggests an age-related impairment in metacognition; Duval et al., 2011).

Finally, it is important to note that the typical trajectory of social development is disrupted in various neurodevelopmental and neurodegenerative disorders (e.g. autism and dementia). Research that has interrogated the patterns of behaviour, neural substrates, and co-occurrences in these disorders has provided valuable insights into the mechanisms and connections that exist in the typical development of social interaction.

1.4 Key theories and mechanisms underlying communicative success

Traditional theories of ToM have leaned heavily on philosophy of mind, defining an observers' key task as reasoning about the relationship between an agent's intentions, beliefs, and desires and their actions, either through a framework of concepts about the mind ('theory theory' or 'folk psychology', Churchland, 1991) or through a re-enactment of others' minds in one's own mind ('simulation theory', Davies & Stone, 1995a, b). These models are based on the idea that children learn about social behaviour by observing others interacting in the world or by reflecting on their own intentional behaviour and emotions, and use this experience to develop and revise theories about the connections and behaviours of people in their social world. However, these models focus on the early development of social understanding, and therefore do not make any testable predictions about the developmental trajectory of social abilities beyond childhood, including how and why they might decline in older age.

Over the past decade or so, there has been increasing speculation about the mediating role of cognitive mechanisms in successful social interaction, with the majority of new psychological theories explicitly reflecting on this relationship when explaining social cognitive phenomena. These accounts therefore offer a more promising view on how social interaction might change across the lifespan, because much is known about how cognitive performance changes with age (Diamond, 2002), including the observation that some aspects of age-related cognitive decline begin when adults are in their twenties and thirties (Salthouse, 2009).

Among the first to detail a theoretical framework that links social abilities with cognitive mechanisms, and therefore offers a clear developmental path, is the 'two systems model for mindreading', proposed by Apperly and Butterfill (2009; see also Apperly, 2009). According to this account, two systems exist for belief reasoning: one is automatic, inflexible, and cognitively efficient (and hence reflects animals' and infants' basic ToM, and adults' moment-by-moment social cognition), and the other is more flexible but is cognitively demanding (and therefore more suited for explicit and planned ToM inferences). This two systems model predicts that, while some aspects of ToM performance will correlate with changes in cognitive abilities (e.g. working memory, inhibitory control, belief reasoning, and inferences from language), those that tap into the cognitively efficient system (e.g. emotion reading and visual perspective-taking) should not reveal a comparable change with reduced cognitive abilities. Applied to lifespan development, this model proposes that basic social inferences that do not rely on cognitive abilities are spontaneously activated much earlier than four years old, the age at which children are known to pass explicit tests of false beliefs. The model also proposes that development of more sophisticated forms of social interaction continues through childhood and adolescence as children rely on increasingly complex cognitive mechanisms, which are known to develop over a protracted period into early adulthood (Best & Miller, 2010; De Luca et al., 2003). Finally, the model accounts for a decline in more cognitively demanding social abilities into older age, as age-related declines in cognitive functioning are relatively robust due to changes in the frontal lobes, specifically age-related volume reduction in the prefrontal cortex (Gunning-Dixon & Raz, 2003). Moreover, there is a vast amount of heterogeneity in regards to when cognitive abilities peak and decline throughout the lifespan, which resonates with the high degree of individual variance seen in social abilities.

While the importance of cognitive mechanisms to support some aspects of social interaction has been largely corroborated by empirical evidence, the need to have two separate systems to manage different social situations has been challenged by Carruthers (2016), who suggests that a single mindreading system can account for the need to recruit cognitive resources during some mindreading tasks. Specifically, the one-system account proposes that a single system exists to support ToM. This system operates in a fairly rudimentary way in early infancy, based on a set of conceptual primitives and thought-attributions. It becomes increasingly efficient from infancy to childhood through a continuous period of development, as social and communicative experience grows, cognitive and language mechanisms mature, and the connection between mindreading and cognition strengthens. Importantly, this model predicts that success in social interaction will vary depending on the demands placed on executive function and language, both of which are subject to age-related decline.

A recent account has proposed that social interaction is a key mechanism though which 'cognitive gadgets' (including reasoning, using language, and mindreading) are culturally inherited and learned (Heyes, 2018). Specifically, Heyes argues that infants are born with a huge range of genetically programmed abilities and assumptions about the world (including instincts to attend to the social world around us, learn, and remember), and these skills and beliefs combined with exposure to culture-soaked environments during infancy and childhood prompt the development of a range of cognitive gadgets (e.g. mindreading, empathy, and imitation). According to the model, the nature of cognitive gadgets that are passed on between people will be influenced by the social context they grow up in. For example, changes in technology and family cultures will lead to subtle changes in the cognitive gadgets that children acquire, and if they are successful those new gadgets will be passed on. As such, this model predicts that social abilities change, not only over lifespan development, but will also vary over social and economic environments, and over different generations.

Finally, Conway et al. (2019) have proposed a model that aims to explain the significant variability with which individuals are able to make inferences about others' minds, and the vastly different minds that we need to infer mental states for. Conway and colleagues adopt a 'Mind-Space' framework, in which other people's minds are represented in a multidimensional space that varies on multiple axes (e.g. cognitive abilities, personality traits, and behavioural tendencies). People therefore learn to adapt their behaviour and social interaction style depending on their Mind-Space representation of the other person (e.g. their age or linguistic background; see Ferguson et al., 2018; Grey & Van Hell, 2017). Therefore, this model allows us to make some predictions about how children's accumulating experience with their own and others' minds leads to a better ability to represent Mind-Space and make appropriate inferences about others' mental states. It also helps explain the variability in accuracy of mental state inferences in adulthood. However, it does not set any testable predictions for whether or how this ability might change in later life.

1.5 A special role for executive functions

As can be seen in the models described above, cognitive abilities, including executive functions (EFs), provide a key component of success in social interaction. EF is a commonly used 'umbrella term' to describe the processes that are responsible for higher-level action control (e.g. planning, inhibition, coordination, and control of behaviours), and are necessary to maintain specific goals and resist distraction from alternatives. Indeed, a long tradition of empirical research has demonstrated a robust relationship between the acquisition of EFs and improvements in ToM skills among young children, independent of age and IQ (e.g. Carlson et al., 2004; Perner & Lang, 1999). However, the exact direction of this relationship remains under debate, with some researchers claiming that ToM is needed for EF (Carruthers, 1996; Perner, 1998; Perner & Lang, 1999, 2000), and others arguing that ToM requires EF (Russell, 1996, 1997; Pacherie, 1997). The specific EF skills that have been shown to be strongly correlated with ToM development are working memory (Keenan et al., 1998), inhibitory control (i.e. ignoring irrelevant information; Carlson et al., 2004), and cognitive flexibility (i.e. switching between different tasks; Hughes, 1998). These links make sense given that successful social cognition requires one to hold in mind multiple perspectives (i.e. working memory), suppress irrelevant perspectives (i.e. inhibitory control), and switch between these two perspectives depending on context (i.e. cognitive flexibility).

Neuropsychological research has demonstrated a protracted period of EF development, which begins in early childhood (~2 years old) and continues into young adulthood, with each sub-component of EF developing at its own rate (Diamond, 2002). For example, working memory and planning develop throughout childhood and into adolescence or early adulthood (e.g. Bishop et al., 2001; Gathercole et al., 2004), whereas cognitive flexibility and inhibition are thought to reach adult-like levels by age 12 (e.g. Crone et al., 2006; Van den Wildenberg & Van der Molen, 2004). This neurocognitive development corresponds with children's ability to pass increasingly complex tests of ToM, from implicit awareness of others' perspectives around 18 months old (e.g. Buttelmann et al., 2009; Kovács et al., 2010; Onishi & Baillargeon, 2005; Senju et al., 2011), to first-order false belief tasks around 4 years old (Astington, 1993; Wellman & Bartsch, 1988), and second-order false belief tasks around 7 or 8 years old (Perner & Wimmer, 1985; Sullivan et al., 1994). Moreover, recent research has established that the social brain continues to develop throughout adolescence (Blakemore & Mills, 2014; Dumontheil, 2016), and that these structural changes underlie major developmental progressions in social cognition, which interact with improvements in cognitive control (Humphrey & Dumontheil, 2016; Mills et al., 2015).

Further evidence of the strong developmental relationship between ToM and EFs comes from research on neurodevelopmental disorders, most notably autism spectrum disorder (ASD). ASD is diagnosed behaviourally, based on social-communication impairments, and restricted and repetitive behaviours (American Psychiatric Association, 2013). ASD can also be described in terms of its core cognitive deficits: namely, in ToM and EFs. These core cognitive deficits co-occur in ASD (Pellicano, 2007; Brunsdon et al., 2015) and may underlie its symptom profile (Brunsdon & Happé, 2014). The neurodevelopmental relationship between ToM and EFs in children with ASD has been evidenced in numerous contexts. For example, correlational studies have revealed a positive association (e.g. Bigham, 2010; Colvert et al., 2002; Joseph & Tager-Flusberg, 2004; Ozonoff et al., 1991; Russell et al., 1991; Zelazo et al., 2002), with individual differences in EF significantly predicting ToM ability in ASD once variance due to age, verbal, and non-verbal ability have been accounted for (Pellicano, 2007). Interestingly, proficient EF skills are apparent in these groups even when ToM ability is impaired. Longitudinal studies provide further evidence for the causal relationship between ToM and EFs. Ozonoff and McEvoy (1994) found that ToM and EF develop in parallel over a 3-year time period and hit a comparable developmental ceiling in ASD. Moreover, individual differences in early EF skills are longitudinally predictive of change in ToM ability in ASD, with the two skills becoming functionally indistinguishable by middle childhood (Pellicano, 2010). This work therefore suggests that EF deficits early in life may limit ToM development in ASD. Finally, intervention studies have shown that ToM can be enhanced in ASD children by training ToM directly or indirectly via the underlying EFs (e.g. Fisher & Happé, 2005), suggesting that EFs are causally related to ToM, either as a prerequisite for ToM development or as a crucial component of executive control of action. In sum, previous research in children with ASD seems to support the notion that EF is a prerequisite for the development of ToM, and that impaired EF influences the (poor) development of ToM.

Thus, the link between ToM and EF seems relatively robust in children, where the majority of this research has been concentrated. Research that has empirically tested this relationship in healthy adults has typically adopted one of three key approaches: (i) used neuroimaging methods to detect overlapping brain activation; (ii) employed dual-task designs that attempt to load one or more EF capacity to observe the consequences on ToM ability; or (iii) tested correlations to assess how individual variance on a measure of EF relates to ToM success.

Healthy ageing is associated with cognitive decline, which leads to general deficits in processing speed as well as specific impairments in EF, including working memory (Braver & West, 2008), inhibition (Maylor et al., 2011), and cognitive flexibility (Greenwood, 2007). This age-related decline is manifest across a range of cognitive skills (e.g. learning, reasoning, and language), with some aspects of cognitive decline beginning from 20 to 30 years old, and decreasing at a faster rate with increasing age (Salthouse, 2009; Singh-Manoux et al., 2012).

These age-related changes in EFs mirror the increased difficulties older adults experience with ToM. A meta-analysis investigating six basic ToM tasks across 23 datasets and 1,462 participants found that older adults performed more poorly than younger adults across all ToM measures assessed (Henry et al., 2013). Moran (2013) also reviewed the literature on typical ageing and ToM, and found that the majority of evidence showed that age-related ToM decline is mediated by EFs, but that some aspects of ToM function independently from general cognition. Younger adults outperform older adults on the ToM stories from the Strange Stories task, and performance on these ToM stories was associated with set-shifting, inhibition, and working memory (Cavallini et al., 2013; Maylor et al., 2002; Rakoczy et al., 2012). However, there is mixed evidence for the mediating role of EFs, because some studies show a relation between age-related ToM decline and EFs (specifically inhibition and shifting ability; Rakoczy et al., 2012) and others show none (Cavallini et al., 2013; Maylor et al., 2002).

The link between ToM and EF in healthy ageing is even more speculative given that findings vary depending on the particular ToM task that is employed. Different aspects of ToM may be subject to differing patterns of ageing effects, and these patterns may be related to different aspects of EF. For example, the Strange Stories task has been divided into cognitive versus affective ToM stories (Wang & Su, 2013). An age effect was found for the cognitive ToM stories but not for the affective ToM stories, and this age effect for cognitive ToM was related to inhibition. The Reading the Mind in the Eyes task (RMET) measures affective aspects of social cognition and has been found to be stable across age (Bottiroli et al., 2016; Cabinio et al., 2015; Castelli et al., 2010; Li et al., 2013), possibly due to the minimal involvement of EFs in this task. In contrast, false belief and faux pas understanding decline with age, and this decline is mediated by inhibition, working memory, and processing speed (German & Hehman, 2006; Li et al., 2013; Phillips et al., 2011). More generally, cognitive ToM has been associated with age and various EFs, such as working memory and inhibition (Bottiroli et al., 2016), and shifting, updating, and inhibition (Duval et al., 2011).

1.6 Methodological approaches and challenges in the study of social interaction

A vast number of tasks have been developed to assess social interaction and its underlying processes. Given researchers' initial focus on the development of ToM abilities in early childhood, most of the traditional tasks relied on participants' explicit responses to questions that require an inference about someone else's mental state, and tested success in isolated scenarios. For example, in the false belief task (Baron-Cohen et al., 1985), children hear a story about two girls (Sally and Anne) playing with a ball. Anne hides the ball while Sally is not looking, and children are asked to decide either verbally or by pointing where Sally will look for the ball. In a similar task, children are shown that a tube of Smarties contains pencils rather than sweets, then are asked to decide what their friend will think is inside the Smarties tube (Perner et al., 1987). While these tasks have provided a great deal of valuable insights into the critical 'transitional phase' during early childhood, when children begin to successfully pass tests of ToM, they are limited in many ways. First, given the explicit responding they involve, it is not possible to infer the processing steps that lead to a particular response. Second, because children consistently pass these tests from around 5 years old, a ceiling performance is reached, which means that their application to populations beyond childhood is limited (Perner & Wimmer, 1985; Stone et al., 1998). Third, it has been suggested that the direct questioning of children in these tasks actually disrupts their ability to use perspective (Rubio-Fernández, 2013; Rubio-Fernández & Geurts, 2013).

Over the past couple of decades, researchers have developed more complicated tasks that are suitable to use beyond childhood and assess a wider range of the processes involved in social interaction. For example, false belief tasks have been adapted by including multiple embeddings (as in, 'Lauren thinks that Tara knows that Alison ate the cheese'; Kinderman et al., 1998; Rutherford, 2004), increasing cognitive demands (e.g. with a concurrent memory task; McKinnon & Moscovitch, 2007), or applying more sensitive measures that allow processing to be assessed in real time (e.g. Ferguson et al., 2010; Ferguson & Breheny, 2012; Ferguson et al., 2015a). Other tasks have aimed to disentangle the ability to reason about others' behaviour from conflicting knowledge from the self-perspective (e.g. Ferguson & Breheny, 2011; Bradford et al., 2015). These studies have revealed that even healthy adults experience a disruption in processing when making inferences about others' mental states, and that engaging mentalizing abilities involves more effortful cognitive processes than other inferences.

More broadly, cognitive aspects of social interaction have been assessed using tasks that are applicable to varying age groups and that differ widely in their demands, ostensibly measuring different elements of social understanding. For example, in the faux pas task, children must identify social faux pas (Abu-Akel & Abushua'leh, 2004; Baron-Cohen et al., 1999), while, in the Strange Stories task, participants are presented with scenarios requiring inferences of mental and/or physical states (Happé, 1994). The Cambridge Mindreading Face-Voice Battery (CAM) requires participants to identify emotions and mental states from a series of voices and whole faces (Golan et al., 2006) whereas, in the Awareness of Social Inference Test (TASIT), participants must identify actors' emotions and sarcasm/lies in conversational vignettes. Whereas adults typically pass the explicit response-based tasks that were developed for children, they show some variation in performance when more sensitive measures are used.

Affective aspects of social interaction, including the ability to infer another person's feelings and emotions, have been assessed in many ways, including behavioural measures, eye-tracking, physiological and electrophysiological recordings, and neuroimaging. These methods are typically used alongside a variety of paradigms that require participants to observe others in emotional situations (e.g. in physical pain, exclusion, facial expressions), and assess the degree to which they understand and share the other person's emotional state and thoughts (e.g. Decety & Michalska, 2010; Krach et al., 2011; Meyer et al., 2012; Perry et al.2010; Wesselmann et al., 2009).

A critical issue in research on social interaction arises from the fact that the majority of studies administer only a single task to measure the social competence or behaviour of their participants (e.g., Alvi et al., 2020; Mohammadzadeh et al., 2020; Stack & Romero-Rivas, 2020), yet the distinctiveness of these tasks and the differential social constructs they measure should not be overlooked. In a recent study by Warnell and Redcay (2019), correlations between ToM tasks within various age groups revealed minimal relations between tasks, with Bayesian analysis indicating the null hypothesis was more likely (i.e. no relationship between tasks) once age and verbal IQ were controlled for. Similarly, Morrison et al. (2019) found minimal to moderate correlations between ToM tasks in a typically developing adult population, and Gallant et al. (2020) discovered that many of the relations between ToM tasks disappeared in 4–6-year-olds once language and age were controlled for. A recent study by Navarro and colleagues (2020), employing psychometric modelling, also found only a subtle relationship between two ToM tasks. It is worth noting that each of these studies included different batteries of tasks to assess social abilities and administered these to different age groups, making direct comparison of the evidence difficult. Indeed, very few studies include participants of varying developmental stages (i.e. throughout childhood, adolescence, and adulthood), and those that do have been forced to use different batteries of social tasks for different age groups in order to avoid ceiling effects. This makes it difficult to fully understand whether group differences are affected by task differences or a typical developmental trajectory. However, these studies highlight an important question to resolve in future research—whether the minimal correlations between tasks indicate a lack of convergent validity of ToM tasks, or reinforce the notion that ToM is not a single construct (Gallant et al., 2020; Hayward & Homer, 2017; Schaafsma et al., 2015).

Finally, it is worth considering the appropriateness of these tasks for comparing social interaction processes between typically developing and clinical groups. Tasks that have been shown to be a useful measure of ToM in a clinical group are not necessarily appropriate for matched typically developing controls. For example, Morrison et al. (2019) found higher correlations between ToM tasks in an ASD group compared with a typically developing control group, and identified differential ToM factor structures for each group: the ASD group yielded a two-factor structure (social perception and social appraisal), while the typically developing group produced a three-factor structure (information processing of static faces, higher-order mental state attributions and attributions to dynamic stimuli, and higher-order judgements). The distinctiveness of the results for each group highlights that certain ToM tasks might be more appropriate for clinical versus typically developing groups, and that the construct of ToM could even differ between them.

The undetermined factorial structure of ToM, lack of task coherence, and methodological limitations highlight significant issues in the current literature. These will need to be addressed in future research in order to fully understand the developmental trajectory of social interaction processes.

1.6.1 Implicit Theory of Mind

In recent years, a heated debate has emerged regarding the meaning and reliability of so-called 'implicit ToM'. Implicit ToM refers to ToM processes that operate without direct verbal measures or explicit instructions to keep track of others' mental states. As such, implicit ToM assumes that some aspects of ToM can be activated in spontaneous, automatic, and unconscious ways. This challenges traditional views that these abilities depend upon linguistic and cultural experiences, and domain-general cognitive processes (Wimmer & Perner, 1983). The majority of evidence supporting implicit ToM comes from infants, because anticipatory looking patterns and violation of expectation looking time biases suggest that others' beliefs are automatically encoded (e.g. Buttelmann et al., 2009; Kovács et al., 2010; Onishi & Baillargeon, 2005; Southgate et al., 2010; Rubio-Fernández & Guerts, 2013), and thus some basic inferences about beliefs might be triggered by the mere presence of other people. The robustness of these findings, however, has been challenged recently by systematic, pre-registered studies that have failed to (fully) replicate many of the key effects, despite using original stimuli, procedures, and large sample sizes (e.g. Kulke et al., 2018a; Kulke et al., 2019a; Schuwerk et al., 2018; Kammermeier & Paulus, 2018). Notably, evidence for spontaneous ToM is mixed across the lifespan, with both children and adults showing inconsistent understanding of others' beliefs, and a great deal of variation depending on the measures employed (e.g. Burnside et al., 2018; Kulke et al., 2018b; Kulke et al., 2019b; Schneider et al., 2017). In sum, the existence and robustness of implicit ToM remains controversial.

It is also important to acknowledge the distinction between implicit *measures* and implicit *paradigms*. Implicit measures refer to tasks that employ techniques, such as eye-tracking, electroencephalography (EEG), and physiological responses, that can measure participants' behaviours or biases in real time (i.e. 'online') without having to wait for participants to make an explicit response. Implicit paradigms describe tasks in which an inference about another person's mental state is incidental to the task; no instructions are given to process mental states. Ideally, the task would also be designed to ensure that stimuli do not 'give away' the purpose of the task, and participants are fully debriefed at the end to ensure that they were unaware of the task's aims (as in Schneider et al., 2013). Some researchers have applied implicit eye-tracking measures and shown enhanced ToM processing when participants are actively engaged versus passive observers in a task (e.g. Brown-Schmidt, 2009; Brown-Schmidt et al., 2008; Schneider et al., 2014). Notably, Ferguson et al. (2015b) revealed an important distinction between the ability to *infer* others' perspectives and explicitly *use* this knowledge to predict their actions; inferences about others' perspectives can be activated spontaneously even without an explicit reason to do so, but explicit use of this knowledge is faster and less susceptible to interference from their own perspective when participants are actively engaged in the task. These findings demonstrate that applying an implicit measure does not necessarily mean that participants are unaware of the experimenter's aim to assess mental state attribution, and, as such, inferences about others' beliefs cannot be interpreted as fully unconscious unless the paradigm is designed to ensure this. This is particularly evident in tasks that have assessed visual perspective-taking and found that altercentric interference from an avatar in the scene disrupts the calculation of one's own perspective (e.g. Samson et al., 2010), but only when the avatar's perspective was task-relevant on some trials (e.g. Cole et al., 2016; Conway et al., 2017; Ferguson et al., 2017). An open question relating to both implicit measures and paradigms is how we define what is being measured implicitly when this cannot be corroborated by explicit feedback.

1.6.2 Ecological validity

As can be seen earlier in this chapter, the majority of research examining the development of social interaction has been conducted in relatively tightly controlled lab-based settings, in which individual participants infer other people's mental states by observing their behaviour in stories, static images, or dynamic videos; participants are not physically co-present in a social interaction (De Jaegher et al., 2010; Schilbach, 2014). Although these lab-based designs have strengths in providing experimental control over stimuli, they are limited in ecological validity. Real-world social interaction and everyday use of social cognition is richer in detail and more nuanced than passively presented stimuli are able to convey (Foulsham & Kingstone, 2017; Risko et al., 2012). As such, it is not clear how performance in lab-based tasks relates to behaviour in real-world situations when more complex stimuli and a wider range of response options are available. Moreover, some studies have revealed inconsistencies in social behaviours when they are tested in a typical lab-setting versus an unconstrained real-world social interaction (e.g. Hayward et al., 2017). Over the past decade, technologies have advanced with new methods that allow researchers to assess social interaction in more realistic situations.

One method that has shown great promise in recent years is virtual reality (VR). VR systems are becoming more commercially available and the technology is easier to navigate, meaning that more researchers have begun to take advantage of the high degree of experimental control, reproducibility, and improved ecological validity that it offers to study human social interactions (Pan & Hamilton, 2018). VR allows researchers to immerse participants in social situations in which individual variables, such as a virtual character's eye gaze or in/out-group membership, can be systematically manipulated while other factors are fully controlled. This approach has many advantages over traditional methods of using trained actors as confederates, because it is difficult for actors to behave consistently across multiple 'live' situations (i.e. with different participants; Kuhlen & Brenan, 2013), participants often adjust their behaviour with a confederate (Kuhlen & Brenan, 2013), and some situations are simply not possible (or too dangerous) to test in the real world (e.g., Zanon et al., 2014). Over the past decade, VR has been used successfully to explore social phenomena such as the effects of racial prejudice during joint actions with an avatar (Sacheli et al., 2015), the negative impact of ostracism (Kassner et al., 2012), as an implicit measure of trust (Hale et al., 2018), and to test the relationship between mimicry and rapport (Hale & Hamilton, 2016). Nevertheless, several challenges remain for research using VR to examine human social interaction, including identifying the conditions under which participants fully embody the self in the virtual world (e.g. Strojny et al., 2020) and reliably attribute human characteristics to a computer-generated avatar (e.g. de Borst & de Gelder, 2015), as well as understanding how participants' behaviour might be influenced by an 'audience effect' (i.e. knowing that the experimenter is watching). Importantly, of course, virtual environments and avatars depict artificial social worlds that differ substantially from the complexity and responsiveness of people in real-life social situations. To date, no studies have used VR to examine changes in social interaction across development.

Another method with significant potential to enhance our understanding of social interaction uses mobile eye-tracking technology to examine how participants allocate their visual attention towards social information in real-world interactive situations. For example, Foulsham et al. (2011) recorded participants' gaze while they walked through a busy university campus. Contrary to lab-based studies that have shown a human predisposition to preferentially attend to social information (Birmingham et al., 2009; Emery, 2000; Kingstone, 2009), they reported that relatively few fixations were directed towards people in naturalistic settings (~22%). Other studies have monitored looking behaviours while participants are actively engaged in a one-to-one conversation. Using this design, Freeth and colleagues (2013; see also Vabalas & Freeth, 2016) found a general preference to look at the conversation partner's face; however, this social preference was amplified when participants were listening compared to speaking, and switched to favour the non-social information (i.e. the background) when speaking compared to listening. This pattern suggests that interlocutors found speaking more cognitively demanding than listening, and used gaze aversion as a means of reducing these processing costs to avoid distracting social information in the face. In addition, social attention is sensitive to factors such as the relationship between interlocutors (i.e. familiar conversation partners exhibit more mutual eye gaze; Broz et al., 2012) and the topic of conversation (i.e. more looks to their partner's face when discussing a familiar topic; Barzy et al., in press; Hutchins & Brien; 2016; Nadig et al., 2010). Importantly, given the relatively low cost of mobile eye-tracking technology, the low demands these real-world tasks place on cognitive resources, and the non-invasive headsets, they are particularly well suited for use with children, older adults, and atypical populations (e.g. Doherty-Sneddon et al., 2002; Doherty-Sneddon & Phelps, 2005; Freeth & Bugembe; 2019; Glenberg et al., 1998). Despite this, no research has yet compared social attention across age groups while people are fully immersed in real-world interactive situations, and this remains an exciting opportunity for future research.

1.7 Structure of this book

This book begins with a chapter detailing what is currently known about social interaction in infancy. Tobias Schuwerk and Hannes Rakoczy focus on evidence for very early sensitivity to social information, before the first year of life, with an understanding of shared intentionality emerging during the second year, and more sophisticated abilities for explicit meta-representational ToM developing around the fourth birthday. Reflecting current debates in this field, it includes a critical discussion on the replicability of mentalizing effects in infants, and reviews theoretical debates and empirical evidence that contribute to our understanding of whether infants possess a fully functioning ToM. In Chapter 3, Serena Lecce and Rory Devine present a critical review of research on the development of social interaction during early and middle phases of childhood, and assess the role of ToM in acquiring successful social interaction skills. Notably, it proposes a new framework to explain the relation between ToM and social outcomes, which emphasizes the moderating role of social context and partner-related features in developing this relationship. In Chapter 4, Sarah Donaldson and Kathryn Mills review current evidence on the protracted development of the social brain and biology through adolescence and into young adulthood, and consider the implications of these changes on social interaction and romantic relationships. This chapter therefore provides insights into the neural, hormonal, and cognitive systems that influence changes in social interaction during adolescence, and considers how adolescent social behaviours and mating interactions are shaped by the social environment (e.g. peer relations and motivation).

In Chapter 5, Ian Apperly and Jessica Wang review research that has established the study of social interaction in healthy adults as a research topic in its own right, linking these diverse empirical findings through a cognitive model. It highlights a great deal of individual variation in ability and contextual factors that influence communicative success, and provides a critical analysis of experimental approaches to mindreading, and their generalizability. In Chapter 6, Victoria Brunsdon, Elisabeth Bradford, and I provide a thorough review of evidence for a decline in social functioning in older age. This chapter attempts to define the onset of 'old age' by evaluating evidence from middle-aged adults, considers the different trajectories of change for different components of social interaction, and discusses promising intervention protocols with the potential to reduce social cognitive declines in older age.

In Chapters 7 and 8, we consider how typical developmental trajectories of social interaction are disrupted in clinical conditions. Lucy Livingston and Francesca Happé focus on the acquisition of social interaction skills in individuals with ASD, whose behaviours are characterized by social communication impairments. The authors critically review a number of social cognitive theories that claim to explain atypical social behaviour in ASD, and identify key ongoing debates that offer potential to explain the diverse social difficulties and individual differences observed within the autistic population. Next, Muireann Irish and Siddharth Ramanan discuss how the typical trajectory of changes in social cognition in healthy ageing are affected by neurodegenerative disorders (i.e. dementia). The chapter focuses on identifying the neural substrates that underlie these changes, and proposes empirically grounded mechanisms to explain the disrupted social functioning in dementia.

Finally, in Chapter 9, Elisabeth Bradford, Martina de Lillo, and I draw together key findings from existing research, and outline open questions and innovative avenues for future research in this area. This chapter therefore highlights state-of-the-art advances in methodological development using methods that aim to increase ecological validity, considers how features of individuals and the social context might have differential impacts on social interactions, and evaluates the potential for social communication skills to be enhanced through training or brain stimulation interventions.

References

Abu-Akel, A., & Abushua'leh, K., 2004. '"Theory of mind" in violent and nonviolent patients with paranoid schizophrenia'. *Schizophrenia Research* 69. 1: 45–53.

Alvi, T., Kouros, C. D., Lee, J., Fulford, D., & Tabak, B. A., 2020. 'Social anxiety is negatively associated with theory of mind and empathic accuracy'. *Journal of Abnormal Psychology* 129. 1: 108–113.

American Psychiatric Association. (2013). *Diagnostic and statistical manual of mental disorders* (5th ed.). Arlington, VA: Author.

Apperly, I. A., 2009. 'Alternative routes to perspective-taking: Imagination and rule use may be better than simulation and theorising'. *British Journal of Developmental Psychology* 27. 3: 545.

Apperly, I. A., & Butterfill, S. A., 2009. 'Do humans have two systems to track beliefs and belief-like states?'. *Psychological Review* 116. 4: 953–970.

Apperly, I. A., Back, E., Samson, D., & France, L., 2008. 'The cost of thinking about false beliefs: Evidence from adult performance on a non-inferential theory of mind task'. *Cognition* 106: 1093–1108.Astington, J. W. 1993. *The Child's Discovery of the Mind*. Harvard University Press.

Back, E., & Apperly, I. A., 2010. 'Two sources of evidence on the non-automaticity of true and false belief ascription'. *Cognition* 115. 1: 54–70.

Bailey, P. E., & Henry, J. D., 2008. 'Growing less empathic with age: Disinhibition of the self-perspective'. *The Journals of Gerontology: Series B* 63. 4: 219–226.

Bailey, P. E., Henry, J. D., & Von Hippel, W., 2008. 'Empathy and social functioning in late adulthood'. *Aging & Mental Health* 12. 4: 499–503.

Baron-Cohen, S., Leslie, A. M., & Frith, U., 1985. 'Does the autistic child have a "theory of mind"?'. *Cognition* 21. 1: 37–46.

Baron-Cohen, S., O'Riordan, M., Stone, V., Jones, R., & Plaisted, K., 1999. 'Recognition of faux pas by normally developing children and children with asperger syndrome or high-functioning autism'. *Journal of Autism and Developmental Disorders* 29. 5: 407–418.

Barzy, M., Ferguson, H. J., & Williams, D., 2020. Perspective influences eye movements during real-life conversation: Mentalising about self vs. others in autism. *Autism* 24: 2153–2165.

Beaudoin, C., Leblanc, É., Gagner, C., & Beauchamp, M. H., 2020. 'Systematic review and inventory of theory of mind measures for young children'. *Frontiers in Psychology* 10: 2905.

Bernstein, D. M., Thornton, W. L., & Sommerville, J. A., 2011. 'Theory of mind through the ages: Older and middle-aged adults exhibit more errors than do younger adults on a continuous false belief task'. *Experimental Aging Research* 37. 5: 481–502.

Best, J. R., & Miller, P. H., 2010. 'A developmental perspective on executive function'. *Child Development* 81. 6: 1641–1660.

Bigham, S., 2010. 'Impaired competence for pretense in children with autism: Exploring potential cognitive predictors'. *Journal of Autism and Developmental Disorders* 40. 1: 30–38.

Birch, S. A., & Bloom, P., 2007. 'The curse of knowledge in reasoning about false beliefs'. *Psychological Science* 18. 5: 382–386.

Birmingham, E., Bischof, W. F., & Kingstone, A., 2009. 'Saliency does not account for fixations to eyes within social scenes'. *Vision Research* 49. 24: 2992–3000.

Bishop, D. V. M., Aamodt-Leeper, G., Creswell, C., McGurk, R., & Skuse, D. H., 2001. 'Individual differences in cognitive planning on the Tower of Hanoi task: Neuropsychological maturity or measurement error?'. *Journal of Child Psychology and Psychiatry* 42. 4: 551–556.

Blakemore, S.-J., 2008. 'The social brain in adolescence'. *Nature Reviews Neuroscience* 9. 4: 267–277.

Blakemore, S.-J., & Mills, K. L., 2014. 'Is adolescence a sensitive period for sociocultural processing?'. *Annual Review of Psychology* 65: 187–207.

Bottiroli, S., Cavallini, E., Ceccato, I., Vecchi, T., & Lecce, S., 2016. 'Theory of mind in aging: Comparing cognitive and affective components in the faux pas test'. *Archives of Gerontology and Geriatrics* 62: 152–162.

Bradford, E. E. F., Jentzsch, I., & Gomez, J.-C., 2015. 'From self to social cognition: Theory of Mind mechanisms and their relation to executive functioning'. *Cognition* 138: 21–34.

Braver, T. S., & West, R., 2008. 'Working memory, executive control, and aging'. In *The Handbook of Aging and Cognition*, edited by F. I. M. Craik & T. A. Salthouse. Psychology Press, pp. 311–372.

Brown-Schmidt, S., 2009. 'The role of executive function in perspective taking during online language comprehension'. *Psychonomic Bulletin & Review* 16: 893–900.

Brown-Schmidt, S., Gunlogson, C., & Tanenhaus, M. K., 2008. 'Addressees distinguish shared from private information when interpreting questions during interactive conversation'. *Cognition* 107. 3: 1122–1134.

Broz, F., Lehmann, H., Nehaniv, C. L., & Dautenhahn, K., 2012, March 5. 'Mutual gaze, personality, and familiarity: Dual eye-tracking during conversation'. In *Proceedings of the 'Gaze in Human-Robot Interaction' Workshop at the ACM/IEEE International Conference on Human-Robot Interaction (HRI)*. IEEE Press.

Brunsdon, V. E., & Happé, F., 2014. 'Exploring the "factionation" of autism at the cognitive level'. *Autism* 18. 1: 17–30.

Brunsdon, V. E., Colvert, E., Ames, C., Garnett, T., Gillan, N., Hallett, V., Lietz, S., Woodhouse, E., Bolton, P., & Happé, F., 2015. 'Exploring the cognitive features in children with autism spectrum disorder, their co-twins, and typically developing children within a population-based sample'. *Journal of Child Psychology and Psychiatry* 56. 8: 893–902.

Brunsdon, V. E. A., Bradford, E. E. F., & Ferguson, H., 2019. 'Sensorimotor mu rhythm during action observation changes across the lifespan independently from social cognitive processes'. *Developmental Cognitive Neuroscience* 38: 100659.Brunyé, T. T., Ditman, T., Giles, G. E., Mahoney, C. R., Kessler, K., & Taylor, H. A., 2012. 'Gender and autistic personality traits predict perspective-taking ability in typical adults'. *Personality and Individual Differences* 52. 1: 84–88.

Burnside, K., Ruel, A., Azar, N., & Poulin-Dubois, D., 2018. 'Implicit false belief across the lifespan: Non-replication of an anticipatory looking task'. *Cognitive Development* 46: 4–11.

Buttelmann, D., Carpenter, M., & Tomasello, M., 2009. 'Eighteen-month-old infants show false belief understanding in an active helping paradigm'. *Cognition* 112. 2: 337–342.

Cabinio, M., Rossetto, F., Blasi, V., Savazzi, F., Castelli, I., Massaro, D., Valle, A., Nemni, R., Clerici, M., Marchetti, A., & Baglio, F., 2015. 'Mind-reading ability and structural connectivity changes in aging'. *Frontiers in Psychology* 6: 1808.

Cane, J. E., Ferguson, H. J., & Apperly, I. A., 2017. 'Using perspective to resolve reference: The impact of cognitive load and motivation'. *Journal of Experimental Psychology: Learning, Memory, and Cognition* 43. 4: 591–610.

Carlson, S. M., Mandell, D. J., & Williams, L., 2004. 'Executive function and Theory of Mind: Stability and prediction from ages 2 to 3'. *Developmental Psychology* 40. 6: 1105–1122.

Carruthers, P., 1996. 'Autism as mind-blindness: An elaboration and partial defence'. In *Theories of Theories of Mind*, edited by P. Carruthers & P. K. Smith. Cambridge University Press.

Carruthers, P., 2016. 'Two systems for mindreading?'. *Review of Philosophy and Psychology* 7. 1: 141–162.

Castelli, I., Baglio, F., Blasi, V., Alberoni, M., Falini, A., Liverta-Sempio, O., Nemni, R., & Marchetti, A., 2010. 'Effects of aging on mindreading ability through the eyes: An fMRI study'. *Neuropsychologia* 48. 9: 2586–2594.

Cavallini, E., Lecce, S., Bottiroli, S., Palladino, P., & Pagnin, A., 2013. 'Beyond false belief: Theory of mind in young, young-old, and old-old adults'. *International Journal of Aging and Human Development* 76. 3: 181–198.

Churchland, P. M., 1991. 'Folk psychology and the explanation of human behavior'. In *The Future of Folk Psychology: Intentionality and Cognitive Science*, edited by J. Greenwood. Cambridge University Press.

Cole, G. G., Atkinson, M., Le, A. T., & Smith, D. T., 2016. 'Do humans spontaneously take the perspective of others?'. *Acta Psychologica* 164: 165–168.

Colvert, E., Custance, D., & Swettenham, J., 2002. 'Rule-based reasoning and theory of mind in autism: A commentary on the work of Zelazo, Jacques, Burack and Frye'. *Infant and Child Development: An International Journal of Research and Practice* 11. 2: 197–200.

Converse, B. A., Lin, S., Keysar, B., & Epley, N., 2008. 'In the mood to get over yourself: Mood affects theory-of-mind use'. *Emotion* 8. 5: 725.

Conway, J. R., Catmur, C., & Bird, G., 2019. 'Understanding individual differences in theory of mind via representation of minds, not mental states'. *Psychonomic Bulletin & Review* 26. 3: 798–812.

Conway, J. R., Lee, D., Ojaghi, M., Catmur, C., & Bird, G., 2017. 'Submentalizing or mentalizing in a Level 1 perspective-taking task: A cloak and goggles test'. *Journal of Experimental Psychology: Human Perception and Performance* 43. 3: 454.

Crone, E. A., Donohue, S. E., Honomichi, R., Wendelken, C., & Bunge, S. A., 2006. 'Brain regions mediating flexible rule use during development'. *Journal of Neuroscience* 26. 43: 11239–11247.

Davies, M., & Stone, T. 1995a. *Folk Psychology: The Theory of Mind Debate*. Blackwell.

Davies, M., & Stone, T. 1995b. *Mental Simulation: Evaluations and Applications-Reading in Mind and Language*. Blackwell.

de Borst, A. W., & de Gelder, B., 2015. 'Is it the real deal? Perception of virtual characters versus humans: An affective cognitive neuroscience perspective'. *Frontiers in Psychology* 6: 576.

Decety, J., & Michalska, K. J., 2010. 'Neurodevelopmental changes in the circuits underlying empathy and sympathy from childhood to adulthood'. *Developmental Science* 13: 886–899.

De Jaegher, H., Di Paolo, E., & Gallagher, S., 2010. 'Can social interaction constitute social cognition?'. *Trends in Cognitive Sciences* 14. 10: 441–447.

De Luca, C. R., Wood, S. J., Anderson, V., Buchanan, J. A., Proffitt, T. M., Mahony, K., & Pantelis, C., 2003. 'Normative data from the CANTAB. I: Development of executive function over the lifespan'. *Journal of Clinical and Experimental Neuropsychology* 25. 2: 242–254.

Diamond, A., 2002. 'Normal development of prefrontal cortex from birth to young adulthood: Cognitive functions, anatomy, and biochemistry'. In Principles of Frontal Lobe Function, edited by D. Struss & R. Knight. Oxford University Press.

Doherty-Sneddon, G., & Phelps, F. G., 2005. 'Gaze aversion: A response to cognitive or social difficulty?'. *Memory and Cognition* 33. 4: 727–733.

Doherty-Sneddon, G., Bruce, V., Bonner, L., Longbotham, S., & Doyle, C., 2002. 'Development of gaze aversion as disengagement from visual information'. *Developmental Psychology* 38. 3: 438.

Dumontheil, I., 2016. 'Adolescent brain development'. *Current Opinion in Behavioral Sciences* 10: 39–44.

Dumontheil, I., Apperly, I. A., & Blakemore, S. J., 2010. 'Online usage of theory of mind continues to develop in late adolescence'. *Developmental Science* 13. 2: 331–338.

Duval, C., Piolino, P., Bejanin, A., Eustache, F., & Desgranges, B., 2011. 'Age effects on different components of theory of mind'. *Consciousness and Cognition* 20. 3: 627–642.

Emery, N. J., 2000. 'The eyes have it: The neuroethology, function and evolution of social gaze'. *Neuroscience and Biobehavioral Reviews* 24. 6: 581–604.

Ferguson, H. J., & Breheny, R., 2011. 'Eye movements reveal the time-course of anticipating behaviour based on complex, conflicting desires'. *Cognition* 119. 2: 179–196.

Ferguson, H. J., & Breheny, R., 2012. 'Listeners' eyes reveal spontaneous sensitivity to others' perspectives'. *Journal of Experimental Social Psychology* 48. 1: 257–263.

Ferguson, H. J., Apperly, I., & Cane, J. E., 2017. 'Eye tracking reveals the cost of switching between self and other perspectives in a visual perspective-taking task'. *Quarterly Journal of Experimental Psychology* 70. 8: 1646–1660.

Ferguson, H. J., Brunsdon, V. E., & Bradford, E. E. F., 2018. 'Age of avatar modulates the altercentric bias in a visual perspective-taking task: ERP and behavioral evidence'. *Cognitive, Affective, & Behavioral Neuroscience* 18. 6: 1298–1319.

Ferguson, H. J., Scheepers, C., & Sanford, A. J., 2010. 'Expectations in counterfactual and theory of mind reasoning'. *Language and Cognitive Processes* 25. 3: 297–346.

Ferguson, H. J., Cane, J. E., Douchkov, M., & Wright, D., 2015a. 'Empathy predicts false belief reasoning ability: Evidence from the N400'. *Social Cognitive and Affective Neuroscience* 10. 6: 848–855.

Ferguson, H. J., Apperly, I., Ahmad, J., Bindemann, M., & Cane, J., 2015b. 'Task constraints distinguish perspective inferences from perspective use during discourse interpretation in a false belief task'. *Cognition* 139: 50–70.

Fisher, N., & Happé, F., 2005. 'A training study of theory of mind and executive function in children with autistic spectrum disorders'. *Journal of Autism and Developmental Disorders* 35. 6: 757.

Fiske, S. T., & Taylor, S. E., 2013. *Social Cognition: From Brains to Culture*. London: Sage.

Foulsham, T., & Kingstone, A., 2017. 'Are fixations in static natural scenes a useful predictor of attention in the real world?'. *Canadian Journal of Experimental Psychology/Revue Canadienne de Psychologie Expérimentale* 71. 2: 172.

Foulsham, T., Walker, E., & Kingstone, A., 2011. 'The where, what and when of gaze allocation in the lab and the natural environment'. *Vision Research* 51. 17: 1920–1931.

Freeth, M., & Bugembe, P., 2019. 'Social partner gaze direction and conversational phase; factors affecting social attention during face-to-face conversations in autistic adults?'. *Autism* 23. 2: 503–513.

Freeth, M., Foulsham, T., & Kingstone, A., 2013. 'What affects social attention? Social presence, eye contact and autistic traits'. *PloS One* 8. 1: e53286.

Gallant, C. M. M., Lavis, L., & Mahy, C. E. V., 2020. 'Developing an understanding of others' emotional states: Relations among affective theory of mind and empathy measures in early childhood'. *British Journal of Developmental Psychology* 38. 2: 151–166.

Gathercole, S. E., Pickering, S. J., Ambridge, B., & Wearing, H., 2004. 'The structure of working memory from 4 to 15 years of age'. *Developmental Psychology* 40. 2: 177.

German, T. P., & Hehman, J. A., 2006. 'Representational and executive selection resources in "theory of mind": Evidence from compromised belief-desire reasoning in old age'. *Cognition* 101. 1: 129–152.

Germine, L. T., Duchaine, B., & Nakayama, K., 2011. 'Where cognitive development and aging meet: Face learning ability peaks after age 30'. *Cognition* 118. 2: 201–210.

Glenberg, A. M., Schroeder, J. L., & Robertson, D. A., 1998. 'Averting the gaze disengages the environment and facilitates remembering'. *Memory and Cognition* 26. 4: 651–658.

Golan, O., Baron-Cohen, S., & Hill, J. J., 2006. 'The Cambridge Mindreading (CAM) face-voice battery: Testing complex emotion recognition in adults with and without asperger syndrome'. *Journal of Autism and Developmental Disorders* 36. 2: 169–183.

Greenwood, P. M., 2007. 'Functional plasticity in cognitive aging: Review and hypothesis'. *Neuropsychology* 21. 6: 657.

Grey, S., & van Hell, J. G., 2017. 'Foreign-accented speaker identity affects neural correlates of language comprehension'. *Journal of Neurolinguistics* 42: 93–108.

Gunning-Dixon, F. M., & Raz, N., 2003. 'Neuroanatomical correlates of selected executive functions in middle-aged and older adults: A prospective MRI study'. *Neuropsychologia* 41. 14: 1929–1941.

Hale, J., & Hamilton, A. F. D. C., 2016. 'Cognitive mechanisms for responding to mimicry from others'. *Neuroscience and Biobehavioral Reviews* 63: 106–123.

Hale, J., Payne, M. E., Taylor, K. M., Paoletti, D., & Hamilton, A. F. D. C., 2018. 'The virtual maze: A behavioural tool for measuring trust'. *Quarterly Journal of Experimental Psychology* 71. 4: 989–1008.

Happé, F., 1994. 'An advanced test of theory-of-mind: Understanding of story characters' thoughts and feelings by able autistic, mentally handicapped and normal children and adults'. *Journal of Autism and Developmental Disorders* 24. 2: 129–154.

Happé, F., & Frith, U., 2014. 'Annual research review: Towards a developmental neuroscience of atypical social cognition'. *Journal of Child Psychology and Psychiatry* 55: 553–577.

Happé, F., Cook, J. L., & Bird, G., 2017. 'The structure of social cognition: In (ter) dependence of sociocognitive processes'. *Annual Review of Psychology* 68: 243–267.

Hayward, E. O., & Homer, B. D., 2017. 'Reliability and validity of advanced theory-of-mind measures in middle childhood and adolescence'. *British Journal of Developmental Psychology* 35. 3: 454–462.

Hayward, D. A., Vorhies, W., Morris, J. L., Capozzi, F., & Ristic, J., 2017. 'Staring reality in the face: A comparison of social attention across laboratory and real world measures suggests little common ground'. *Canadian Journal of Experimental Psychology/Revue Canadienne de Psychologie Expérimentale* 71. 3: 212.

Henry, J. D., Phillips, L. H., Ruffman, T., & Bailey, P. E., 2013. 'A meta-analytic review of age differences in theory of mind'. *Psychology and Aging* 28. 3: 826.

Heyes, C., 2018. 'Empathy is not in our genes'. *Neuroscience and Biobehavioral Reviews* 95: 499–507.

Hughes, C., 1998. 'Finding your marbles: Does preschoolers' strategic behavior predict later understanding of mind?' *Developmental Psychology* 34. 6: 1326.

Humphrey, G., & Dumontheil, I., 2016. 'Development of risk-taking, perspective-taking, and inhibitory control during adolescence'. *Developmental Neuropsychology* 41. 1–2: 59–76.

Hutchins, T. L., & Brien, A., 2016. 'Conversational topic moderates social attention in autism spectrum disorder: Talking about emotions is like driving in a snowstorm'. *Research in Autism Spectrum Disorders* 26: 99–110.

Joseph, R. M., & Tager-Flusberg, H., 2004. 'The relationship of theory of mind and executive functions to symptom type and severity in children with autism'. *Development and Psychopathology* 16. 1: 137.

Kammermeier, M., & Paulus, M., 2018. 'Do action-based tasks evidence false-belief understanding in young children?'. *Cognitive Development* 46: 31–39.

Kassner, M. P., Wesselmann, E. D., Law, A. T., & Williams, K. D., 2012. 'Virtually ostracized: Studying ostracism in immersive virtual environments'. *Cyberpsychology, Behavior and Social Networking* 15. 8: 399–403.

Keenan, T., Olson, D. R., & Marini, Z., 1998. 'Working memory and children's developing understanding of mind'. *Australian Journal of Psychology* 50. 2: 76–82.

Kessler, K., & Wang, H., 2012. 'Spatial perspective taking is an embodied process, but not for everyone in the same way: Differences predicted by sex and social skills score'. *Spatial Cognition and Computation* 12. 2–3: 133–158.

Keysar, B., Barr, D. J., Balin, J. A., & Brauner, J. S., 2000. 'Taking perspective in conversation: The role of mutual knowledge in comprehension'. *Psychological Science* 11. 1: 32–38.

Kinderman, P., Dunbar, R., & Bentall, R. P., 1998. 'Theory-of-mind deficits and causal attributions'. *British Journal of Psychology* 89. 2: 191–204.

Kingstone, A., 2009. 'Taking a real look at social attention'. *Current Opinion in Neurobiology* 19. 1: 52–56.

Kovács, Á. M., Téglás, E., & Endress, A. D., 2010. 'The social sense: Susceptibility to others' beliefs in human infants and adults'. *Science* 330: 1830–1834.

Krach, S., Cohrs, J. C., de Echeverría Loebell, N. C., Kircher, T., Sommer, J., Jansen, A., et al. 2011. 'Your flaws are my pain: Linking empathy to vicarious embarrassment'. *PLoS One* 6. 4: e18675.

Kuhlen, A. K., & Brennan, S. E., 2013. 'Language in dialogue: When confederates might be hazardous to your data'. *Psychonomic Bulletin and Review* 20. 1: 54–72.

Kulke, L., Johannsen, J., & Rakoczy, H., 2019b. 'Why can some implicit Theory of Mind tasks be replicated and others cannot? A test of mentalizing versus submentalizing accounts'. *PLoS One* 14. 3: e0213772.

Kulke, L., & Rakoczy, H., 2018. 'Implicit Theory of Mind—An overview of current replications and non-replications'. *Data in Brief* 16: 101–104.

Kulke, L., Reiß, M., Krist, H., & Rakoczy, H., 2018b. 'How robust are anticipatory looking measures of Theory of Mind? Replication attempts across the life span'. *Cognitive Development* 46: 97–111.

Kulke, L., von Duhn, B., Schneider, D., & Rakoczy, H., 2018a. 'Is implicit theory of mind a real and robust phenomenon? Results from a systematic replication study'. *Psychological Science* 29. 6: 888–900.

Kulke, L., Wübker, M., & Rakoczy, H., 2019. 'Is implicit Theory of Mind real but hard to detect? Testing adults with different stimulus materials'. *Royal Society Open Science* 6. 7: 190068.

Li, X., Wang, K., Wang, F., Tao, Q., Xie, Y., & Cheng, Q., 2013. 'Aging of theory of mind: the influence of educational level and cognitive processing'. *International Journal of Psychology* 48. 4: 715–727.

Lin, S., Keysar, B., & Epley, N., 2010. 'Reflexively mindblind: Using theory of mind to interpret behavior requires effortful attention'. *Journal of Experimental Social Psychology* 46. 3: 551–556.

Mahy, C. E. V., Vetter, N., Kühn-Popp, N., Löcher, C., Krautschuk, S., & Kliegel, M., 2014. 'The influence of inhibitory processes on affective theory of mind in young and old adults'. *Aging, Neuropsychology, and Cognition* 21. 2: 129–145.

Maylor, E. A., Birak, K. S., & Schlaghecken, F., 2011. 'Inhibitory motor control in old age: Evidence for de-automatization?'. *Frontiers in Psychology* 2: 132.

Maylor, E. A., Moulson, J. M., Muncer, A. M., & Taylor, L. A., 2002. 'Does performance on theory of mind tasks decline with age?' *British Journal of Psychology* 93. 4: 465–485.

McKinnon M. C., & Moscovitch, M., 2007. 'Domain-general contributions to social reasoning: Theory of mind and deontic reasoning re-explored'. *Cognition* 102: 179–218.

Meyer, M. L., Masten, C. L., Ma, Y., Wang, C., Shi, Z., Eisenberger, N. I., et al., 2012. 'Empathy for the social suffering of friends and strangers recruits distinct patterns of brain activation'. *Social Cognitive Affective Neuroscience* 8: 446–454.

Michelon, P., & Zacks, J. M., 2006. 'Two kinds of visual perspective taking'. *Perception & Psychophysics* 68: 327–337.

Mills, K. L., Dumontheil, I., Speekenbrink, M., & Blakemore, S. J., 2015. 'Multitasking during social interactions in adolescence and early adulthood'. *Royal Society Open Science* 2. 11: 150117.

Mohammadzadeh, A., Khorrami Banaraki, A., Tehrani Doost, M., & Castelli, F., 2020. 'A new semi-nonverbal task glance, moderate role of cognitive flexibility in ADHD children's theory of mind'. *Cognitive Neuropsychiatry* 25. 1: 28–44.

Moran, J. M., 2013. 'Lifespan development: The effects of typical aging on theory of mind'. *Behavioural Brain Research* 237: 32–40.

Morrison, K. E., Pinkham, A. E., Kelsven, S., Ludwig, K., Penn, D. L., & Sasson, N. J., 2019. 'Psychometric evaluation of social cognitive measures for adults with autism'. *Autism Research* 12. 5: 766–778.

Moskowitz, G. B., & Olcaysoy Okten, I., 2017. 'Social cognition'. In Getting grounded in social psychology, edited by T. D. Nelson. New York, NY: Psychology Press, pp. 37–78.

Nadig, A., Lee, I., Singh, L., Bosshart, K., & Ozonoff, S., 2010. 'How does the topic of conversation affect verbal exchange and eye gaze? A comparison between typical development and hgh-functioning autism'. *Neuropsychologia* 48. 9: 2730–2739.

Navarro, E., Goring, S. A., & Conway, A. R. A., 2020. 'The relationship between theory of mind and intelligence: A formative model approach'. *PsyArXiv*: 1–41.

Nielsen, M. K., Slade, L., Levy, J. P., & Holmes, A., 2015. 'Inclined to see it your way: Do altercentric intrusion effects in visual perspective taking reflect an intrinsically social process?' *Quarterly Journal of Experimental Psychology* 68. 10: 1931–1951.

Onishi, K. H., & Baillargeon, R., 2005. 'Do 15-month-old infants understand false beliefs?' *Science* 308. 5719: 255–258.

Ozonoff, S., & McEvoy, R. E., 1994. 'A longitudinal study of executive function and theory of mind development in autism'. *Development and Psychopathology* 6. 3: 415–431.

Ozonoff, S., Pennington, B. F., & Rogers, S. J., 1991. 'Executive function deficits in high-functioning autistic individuals: relationship to theory of mind'. *Journal of Child Psychology and Psychiatry* 32. 7: 1081–1105.

Pacherie, E., 1997. 'Motor-images, self-consciousness, and autism'. In *Autism as an Executive Disorder*, edited by J. Russell. Oxford University Press.

Pan, X., & Hamilton, A., 2018. 'Why and how to use virtual reality to study human social interaction: The challenges of exploring a new research landscape'. *British Journal of Psychology* 109. 3: 395–417.

Pardini, M., & Nichelli, P. F., 2009. 'Age-related decline in mentalizing skills across the life span'. *Experimental Aging Research* 35. 1: 98–106.

Pellicano, E., 2007. 'Links between theory of mind and executive function in young children with autism: Clues to developmental primacy'. *Developmental Psychology* 43. 4: 974.

Pellicano, E., 2010. 'Individual differences in executive function and central coherence predict developmental changes in theory of mind in autism'. *Developmental Psychology* 46. 2: 530.

Perner, J., 1998. 'The meta-intentional nature of executive functions and theory of mind'. In *Language and Thought: Interdisciplinary Themes*, edited by P. Carruthers & J. Boucher. Cambridge University Press.

Perner, J., & Lang, B., 1999. 'Development of theory of mind and executive control'. *Trends in Cognitive Sciences* 3. 9: 337–344.

Perner, J., & Lang, B., 2000. 'Theory of mind and executive function: Is there a developmental relationship?' In *Understanding Other Minds: Perspectives from Developmental Cognitive Neuroscience*, edited by S. Baron-Cohen et al. Oxford University Press.

Perner, J., & Wimmer, H., 1985. '"John thinks that Mary thinks that … " Attribution of second-order beliefs by 5- to 10-year-old children'. *Journal of Experimental Child Psychology* 39. 3: 437–471.

Perner, J., Leekam, S. R., & Wimmer, H., 1987. 'Three year-olds' difficulty with false belief: The case for a conceptual deficit'. *British Journal of Developmental Psychology* 5. 2: 125–137.

Perry, A., Bentin, S., Bartal, I. B., Lamm, C., & Decety, J., 2010. ' "Feeling" the pain of those who are different from us: modulation of EEG in the mu/alpha range'. *Cognitive Affective Behavioural Neuroscience* 10: 493–504.

Phillips, L. H., Bull, R., Allen, R., Insch, P., Burr, K., & Ogg, W., 2011. 'Lifespan aging and belief reasoning: Influences of executive function and social cue decoding'. *Cognition* 120. 2: 236–247.

Rakoczy, H., Harder-Kasten, A., & Sturm, L., 2012. 'The decline of theory of mind in old age is (partly) mediated by developmental changes in domain-general abilities'. *British Journal of Psychology* 103. 1: 58–72.

Risko, E. F., Laidlaw, K. E., Freeth, M., Foulsham, T., & Kingstone, A., 2012. 'Social attention with real versus reel stimuli: Toward an empirical approach to concerns about ecological validity'. *Frontiers in Human Neuroscience* 6: 143.

Rubio-Fernández, P., 2013. 'Perspective tracking in progress: Do not disturb'. *Cognition* 129. 2: 264–272.

Rubio-Fernández, P., & Geurts, B., 2013. 'How to pass the false-belief task before your fourth birthday'. *Psychological Science* 24. 1: 27–33.

Rubio-Fernández, P., & Geurts, B., 2016. 'Don't mention the marble! The role of attentional processes in false-belief tasks'. *Review of Philosophy and Psychology* 7. 4: 835–850.

Russell, J. 1996. *Agency: Its Role In Mental Development*. Erlbaum Taylor & Francis Ltd.

Russell, J., 1997. 'How executive disorders can bring about an inadequate "theory of mind"'. In *Autism As An Executive Disorder*, edited by J. Russell. Oxford University Press.

Russell, J., Mauthner, N., Sharpe, S., & Tidswell, T., 1991. 'The "windows task" as a measure of strategic deception in preschoolers and autistic subjects'. *British Journal of Developmental Psychology* 9. 2: 331–349.

Rutherford, M. D., 2004. 'The effect of social role on theory of mind reasoning'. *British Journal of Psychology* 95. 1: 91–103.

Sacheli, L. M., Christensen, A., Giese, M. A., Taubert, N., Pavone, E. F., Aglioti, S. M., & Candidi, M., 2015. 'Prejudiced interactions: Implicit racial bias reduces predictive simulation during joint action with an out-group avatar'. *Scientific Reports* 5: 8507.

Salthouse, T. A., 2009. 'When does age-related cognitive decline begin?'. *Neurobiology of Aging* 30. 4: 507–514.

Samson, D., Apperly, I. A., Braithwaite, J. J., Andrews, B. J., & Bodley Scott, S. E., 2010. 'Seeing it their way: evidence for rapid and involuntary computation of what other people see'. *Journal of Experimental Psychology: Human Perception and Performance* 36. 5: 1255.

Schaafsma, S. M., Pfaff, D. W., Spunt, R. P., & Adolphs, R., 2015. 'Deconstructing and reconstructing theory of mind'. *Trends in Cognitive Sciences* 19. 2: 65–72.

Schilbach, L., 2014. 'On the relationship of online and offline social cognition'. *Frontiers in Human Neuroscience* 8: 278.

Schneider, D., Nott, Z. E., & Dux, P. E., 2014. 'Task instructions and implicit theory of mind'. *Cognition* 133. 1: 43–47.

Schneider, D., Slaughter, V. P., & Dux, P. E., 2017. 'Current evidence for automatic Theory of Mind processing in adults'. *Cognition* 162: 27–31.

Schneider, D., Slaughter, V. P., Bayliss, A. P., & Dux, P. E., 2013. 'A temporally sustained implicit theory of mind deficit in autism spectrum disorders'. *Cognition* 129. 2: 410–417.

Schuwerk, T., Priewasser, B., Sodian, B., & Perner, J., 2018. 'The robustness and generalizability of findings on spontaneous false belief sensitivity: a replication attempt'. *Royal Society Open Science* 5. 5: 172273.

Senju, A., Southgate, V., Snape, C., Leonard, M., & Csibra, G., 2011. 'Do 18-month-olds really attribute mental states to others? A critical test'. *Psychological Science* 22. 7: 878–880.

Shamay-Tsoory, S. G., & Aharon-Peretz, J., 2007. 'Dissociable prefrontal networks for cognitive and affective theory of mind: A lesion study'. *Neuropsychologia* 45: 3054–3067.

Singh-Manoux, A., Kivimaki, M., Glymour, M. M., Elbaz, A., Berr, C., Ebmeier, K. P., ... & Dugravot, A., 2012. 'Timing of onset of cognitive decline: Results from Whitehall II prospective cohort study'. *BMJ* 344: d7622.

Southgate, V., & Vernetti, A., 2014. 'Belief-based action prediction in preverbal infants'. *Cognition* 130. 1: 1–10.

Southgate, V., Chevallier, C., & Csibra, G., 2010. 'Seventeen-month-olds appeal to false beliefs to interpret others referential communication'. *Developmental Science* 13. 6: 907–912.

Stack, J., & Romero-Rivas, C., 2020. 'Merit overrules theory of mind when young children share resources with others'. *PLoS One* 15. 1: 1–15.

Stone, V. E., Baron-Cohen, S., & Knight, R. T., 1998. 'Frontal lobe contributions to theory of mind'. *Journal of Cognitive Neuroscience* 10. 5: 640–656.

Strojny, P. M., Dużmańska-Misiarczyk, N., Lipp, N., & Strojny, A., 2020. 'Moderators of social facilitation effect in virtual reality: Co-presence and realism of virtual agents'. *Frontiers in Psychology* 11: 1252.

Sullivan, K., Zaitchik, D., & Tager-Flusberg, H., 1994. 'Preschoolers can attribute second-order beliefs'. *Developmental Psychology* 30. 3: 395.

Surtees, A., Apperly, I., & Samson, D., 2013. 'Similarities and differences in visual and spatial perspective-taking processes'. *Cognition* 129, 2: 426–438.

Vabalas, A., & Freeth, M., 2016. 'Brief report: Patterns of eye movements in face to face conversation are associated with autistic traits: Evidence from a student sample'. *Journal of Autism and Developmental Disorders* 46. 1: 305–314.

Van den Wildenberg, W. P., & van der Molen, M. W., 2004. 'Additive factors analysis of inhibitory processing in the stop-signal paradigm'. *Brain and Cognition* 56. 2: 253–266.

Wang, Z., & Su, Y., 2013. 'Age-related differences in the performance of theory of mind in older adults: A dissociation of cognitive and affective components'. *Psychology and Aging* 28. 1: 284–291.

Warnell, K. R., & Redcay, E., 2019. 'Minimal coherence among varied theory of mind measures in childhood and adulthood'. *Cognition* 191: 103997.

Wellman, H. M., & Bartsch, K., 1988. 'Young children's reasoning about beliefs'. *Cognition* 30. 3: 239–277.

Wellman, H. M., Cross, D., & Watson, J., 2001. 'Meta-analysis of theory-of-mind development: The truth about false belief'. *Child Development* 72. 3: 655–684.

Wesselmann, E. D., Bagg, D., Williams, K. D., 2009. '"I feel your pain": The effects of observing ostracism on the ostracism detection system'. *Journal of Experimental Social Psychology* 45: 1308–1311.

Wimmer, H., & Perner, J., 1983. 'Beliefs About beliefs—representation and constraining function of wrong beliefs in young children's understanding of deception'. *Cognition* 13. 1: 103–128.

Wu, S., & Keysar, B., 2007. 'The effect of culture on perspective taking'. *Psychological Science* 18. 7: 600–606.

Zanon, M., Novembre, G., Zangrando, N., Chittaro, L., & Silani, G., 2014. 'Brain activity and prosocial behaviour in a simulated life-threatening situation'. *NeuroImage* 98: 134–146.

Zelazo, P. D., Jacques, S., Burack, J. A., & Frye, D., 2002. 'The relation between theory of mind and rule use: Evidence from persons with autism-spectrum disorders'. *Infant and Child Development: An International Journal of Research and Practice* 11. 2: 171–195.

2
Social Interaction in Infancy

Tobias Schuwerk and Hannes Rakoczy

2.1 Introduction

The way we, adult humans, see and treat each other is very special. It is fundamentally different from our perception of, and interaction with, the rest of the natural world. Most fundamentally, we perceive each other[1] as subjects and not just as objects. There are several aspects to this peculiar conceptual framework of seeing each other as subjects (which comes under many names, including 'folk psychology' or 'Theory of Mind'): cognitive, emotional, moral, and many more. Here, we focus, from a developmental perspective, on what arguably are the most foundational conceptual elements of this framework: seeing individuals as rational intentional agents who have subjective perspectives on the world, who act for and are generally susceptible to reasons, and with whom one can thus enter into relationships of 'shared intentionality' in communication and cooperation.

In this chapter, we will describe milestones of the development of this conceptual framework (which, following established if unfortunate usage, we will mostly call 'Theory of Mind') in infancy (for a schematic overview, see Fig. 2.1). In Section 2.2, we will review evidence on the very early development, in the first weeks and months of life, of remarkable forms of social interaction and social perception that, though not yet manifestations of Theory of Mind themselves, may present important precursors. In Section 2.3, we will then describe the emergence of the first forms of Theory of Mind towards the end of the first year of life. At this stage, children begin to operate with a basic teleological stance: they understand that persons act in the pursuit of goals, and on the basis of perceptual access to facts. This fundamentally changes the way they interact with others, and opens up completely new avenues for communication and cooperation.

In Section 2.4, we address the question of when more refined and sophisticated, fully meta-representational forms of Theory of Mind emerge. In fully meta-representational Theory of Mind, one does not only ascribe access to values (goals) and facts to others, and explain their actions on that basis. Rather, one explicitly

---

[1] ... And, potentially (inter-individual and cross-cultural differences are huge in these respects) other animals and non-organic agents (robots, etc.) as well. For simplicity's sake, we will ignore these complications and largely focus on human interpersonal cognition and social interaction.

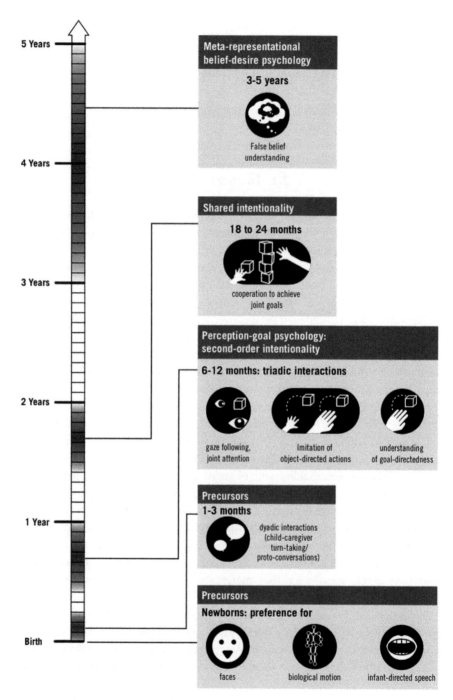

Fig. 2.1 Schematic overview of developmental milestones of social interaction in infancy

represents that and how others subjectively represent, potentially misrepresent, the world cognitively (beliefs) and conatively (desires)—which is why this framework also goes under the rubric 'belief–desire psychology'. Until recently, it was generally believed that children develop this more refined framework only much later, on the basis of linguistic and other experience. But new evidence from the past 15 years has suggested that even infants may be capable of full-blown meta-representation. In light of a serious replication crisis regarding these findings, however, it is currently rather unclear when, in fact, sophisticated, meta-representational Theory of Mind emerges. After reviewing the debates, the evidence, and the replication crisis, we conclude by summarizing the most important lessons, open questions, and future directions.

2.2 Precursors

2.2.1 Sensitivity to social information

From birth onwards, infants show a remarkable preference for social stimuli—that is, for any sensory information that is elicited by another individual (such as appearance, movement, sound, or smell). Faces carry rich information that is crucial for social interaction. Already newborns within their first hour after birth show a high sensitivity to faces.[2] When presented with a moving stimulus minutes after birth, they turn their eyes and head towards this stimulus. Yet, when the pattern displayed on these stimuli resembles key features that constitute a face (cf., Omer et al., 2019), newborns are most responsive to it (Goren et al., 1975; Johnson, 2005). They also have a preference for direct gaze (Farroni et al., 2002) and, within the next weeks, they begin to actively focus on key central regions, such as the eyes, when visually scanning faces (Haith et al.,1977). Furthermore, infants very efficiently detect faces in natural scenes. Those aged 3–12 months quickly detect and preferably look at faces embedded in visually complex settings (e.g. a person standing in a garden full of colourful flowers; Kelly et al., 2019).

Another feature that differentiates animate agents from the rest of the world is biological motion. When viewing dots moving on a screen, already very young infants prefer those displays in which the movement pattern of the dots resembles animate motion patterns (e.g. as if the dots were attached to the joints of a walking human) over the same display when it is presented upside down or over randomly moving dots (Bertenthal et al., 1984; Simion et al., 2008).

---

[2] Recent evidence suggests that even in the third trimester, fetuses show such a preference (Reid et al., 2017). Yet, a number of substantial methodological issues have been identified with this study (Scheel et al., 2018).

When adults talk to infants, they intuitively modify linguistic and prosodic features of their speech, a process presumably aiding early language acquisition. Infants, in turn, seem to be biased to preferentially attend to this form of speech. Cooper and Aslin (1990) documented a preference for such infant-directed speech already in newborns. A recent multi-lab replication study confirmed this effect in over 2,500 infants between 3 and 15 months of age (the ManyBabies Consortium, 2020).

2.2.2 Early forms of interaction

The above-reported examples demonstrate that, from birth on, infants orient towards social stimuli. When observing these actions in context with the caregiver's behaviour, it becomes evident that already within the first months of life early forms of interaction emerge. Caregivers elicit orienting reactions (and other actions infants are able to perform) and vice versa. Such reciprocal and contingent patterns of attention orienting, arm and leg movements, smiling and vocalization are termed 'child–caregiver turn-taking', or 'proto-conversations' (Bigelow, 1998; Brazelton et al.,1974; Trevarthen, 1979). Importantly, infants expect contingency in the behaviour of others. When the caregiver is instructed to suddenly remain unresponsive (e.g. stop smiling or cooing back at the infant), they react disturbed, sometimes try to reinitiate reciprocity but finally withdrawing from the caregiver ('still-face effect'; see Adamson & Frick, 2003).

A special form of early interaction is imitation, which presumably plays a key role in social learning (Piaget, 1952). Imitation of simple object-directed actions emerges at around 6–8 months of age (Barr et al., 1996). Whether newborns already imitate is a subject of ongoing discussion. For a long time, it has been assumed that shortly after birth infants imitate movements such as mouth opening or tongue protrusion (Meltzoff & Moore, 1977). However, a rigorous longitudinal replication study suggested that this conclusion is based on methodological artifacts like inadequate control conditions or analyses, or small outlier-biased samples (Oostenbroek et al., 2016; but see Meltzoff et al., 2018).

To conclude, infants seem to be tuned to orient towards the social world. More importantly, they already distinguish between animate agents and inanimate objects, and are more responsive towards animate agents (Legerstee, 1992). This provides an optimal basis for learning about others through experience. Moreover, from early on, infants interact with the social world through contingent turn-taking (for a review on potential underlying mechanisms, see Markova et al., 2019). These constitute essential pre-conditions towards an understanding of the mind (cf. Gergely & Watson, 1999; Jones & Klin, 2013).

2.3 The emergence of basic ('perception-goal') folk psychology

What we thus see in the first months of life are impressive forms of social sensitivity and interaction, and probably important precursors and foundations of more complex forms of social cognition. But, taken by themselves, they do not necessarily involve much social understanding (of others' mental life and subjective perspective) yet.

However, from the second half of the first year of life, we witness the emergence of a class of new phenomena that mark the first forms of true folk psychology. While infants engaged in dyadic interaction either with objects (in exploration and play) or with people (in proto-conversation) before, now begins triadic interaction: children interact with others in reference to (about) external objects—for example, in joint attention (e.g. the child follows and shares an adult's attention to an object) or imitation (the child reproduces another agent's intentional action on an external object) (Carpenter et al., 1998). According to the standard interpretation, this indicates the ontogenetically first and most basic form of second-order intentionality[3] (or folk psychology, or Theory of Mind): some grasp of others' intentional ('aboutness') relations to the world. Mature folk psychology operates with concepts for two classes of intentional states (termed 'propositional attitudes'): cognitive ones, paradigmatic beliefs, that aim at representing the world as it is; and conative ones, paradigmatic desires, that aim at representing the world as it subjectively ought to be. Fully fledged rational action explanation involves reference to pairs of intentional states of each type (e.g. 'He pressed the switch because he *wanted* to open the door and *thought* the switch was the door opener'). Mature folk psychology thus often comes under the name 'belief–desire psychology'.

The more basic folk psychology of infants does not necessarily involve a fully meta-representational appreciation of the subjectivity of beliefs (that represent things and states of affairs in certain subjective ways that may be accurate or inaccurate) and desires yet. But it does involve an understanding of basic cognitive states (in particular, perception) and basic conative states (in particular, goal-pursuit). It is thus often termed 'perception-goal' folk psychology (Wellman, 2011).

2.3.1 Understanding perception

A number of phenomena indicate that infants begin to understand something about perception towards the end of the first year of life (at the latest). At this time,

---

[3] Intentionality here refers, in the technical sense of the term as used in philosophy and cognitive science, to the aboutness of mental states that have semantic content, paradigmatic perception, belief, desire, intention, etc. (Brentano, 1874/1973; Searle, 1983).

they start following the gaze of others (Carpenter et al., 1998a). Gaze-following as such is widespread in the animal kingdom. Taken by itself, it is not necessarily indicative of any social-cognitive understanding, but could simply reflect low-level attention orienting mechanisms. Human gaze-following is special, though, from early on: infants do not just, in an orienting response, follow an onlooker's gaze (e.g. to a barrier) but actively try to find out what it is the other person is seeing or looking at (e.g. by crawling around barriers and looking for potential referents; Moll & Tomasello, 2004). Even more convincingly, infants only follow another agent's line of sight when they think that this agent can actually see (but not, for example, if she turns her head while wearing a blindfold; Brooks & Meltzoff, 2002).[4]

Numerous phenomena in infants' interaction and communication with others, as well as in their looking behaviour, suggest that they engage in what is often termed 'Level I perspective taking': understanding what others can and cannot see, or have and have not seen, even if that deviates from one's own perspective (Flavell et al.,1981). In many looking time and naturalistic interaction studies, children were confronted with situations in which another agent faced with several objects, all visible to the child, made ambiguous actions of referring to or reaching towards one of the objects. Crucially, the agent had visual access to only one of the objects, not to the other. In these studies, children during their second year expected that the agent would refer to or grasp only those objects that were perceptually available to them (e.g. Moll & Tomasello, 2006; Poulin-Dubois et al., 2007).

2.3.2 Understanding goal-directedness

Infants thus operate with a basic notion of perceptual perspectives on the world—arguably a precursor to fully fledged concepts of belief and other cognitive intentional states. Regarding conative intentional states, infants reveal a basic grasp of goal-directedness and intentional action. Corresponding evidence comes from studies on interaction, imitation, and looking time. Influential looking-time studies suggest that infants attribute goal-directedness and rational action to animated geometrical figures much like adults do in animations made popular by Heider and Simmel (1944).[5] In one study, an agent repeatedly jumped over an obstacle to reach a given goal. In the test phase, this agent then sometimes took the same detour on its way to the goal when the obstacle had been removed. Infants found the agent's apparent irrationality surprising and looked longer to the detour

---

[4] These early capacities for gaze-following have been found, in some studies, to be continuous with, and predictive of, later Theory of Mind (Brooks & Meltzoff, 2015; Kristen et al., 2011).
[5] An example of the original stimulus material that illustrates the phenomenon can be found at: https://www.youtube.com/watch?v=VTNmLt7QX8E

event than to an event in which the agent took the—novel but now rational—direct path (Gergely et al., 1995).

In their spontaneous interaction with others, infants also reveal sensitivity to goal-directedness and intentional action. For example, when another agent fails in pursuit of some goal (e.g. accidentally drops an object she needs that then falls out of her sight), children spontaneously offer instrumental help (e.g. pick up and hand over the object), but they do not do so in analogous situations in which the agent does not pursue the goal in question (e.g. when she voluntarily throws away the object; Warneken & Tomasello, 2006). Similarly, they distinguish between actions that fail, either because the agent was unable (wanted to but could not) or unwilling (did not even want to) to perform it successfully. For example, when an adult earnestly tries to give them some toys but repeatedly fails, they wait more patiently than when the adult teases them by almost handing them the object and then withdrawing it—even if the superficial movement characteristics of the two (unwilling versus unable) acts are closely matched (Behne et al., 2005).

Imitation, finally, presents a rich body of evidence for infants' understanding of goal-directed intentional action. Infants begin to imitate object-directed actions by others from around 9 months of age (Tomasello, 1999). Imitation, taken by itself—and in the wide sense of behavioural reproduction—remains highly ambiguous regarding the underlying social-cognitive capacities; it could reflect mere mimicry, emulation, or other superficial mechanisms. More specific and sophisticated forms of imitation, though, are less ambiguous. They indicate that infants do not just blindly reproduce superficial behaviour but understand and imitate intentional actions.

One case is differential imitation of the same superficial behaviour that is either marked as intentional action or as mere accidental behaviour. When children see an agent perform a behaviour (e.g. dropping an object into a box), they imitate when the agent marked it as intentional and goal-directed ('There!'), but not when she marked it as mere accident ('Oops!') (Carpenter et al., 1998). Imitative response to failed attempts is another case. When infants see an agent unsuccessfully trying to achieve a goal, they then do not imitate the failed means, but perform the action properly and successfully themselves—indicating that they understood what the agent was up to and not just how she superficially behaved (Meltzoff, 1995). Lastly, infants engage in what has been termed 'rational imitation'. They systematically imitate very exactly when they see the behavioural means an agent used as ends in themselves; and imitate creatively and efficiently when they think that the behavioural means used by the other agent were only means to an end, and they themselves have better means at hand to reach the same end. In a famous study on this phenomenon, infants saw an agent perform an instrumental action (switch on a light) with unusual means (pressing the switch with the head). In one condition, the agent had her hands free and thus could have used them (licensing the inference that using the head was an end in itself and not just a means to an end).

In the other condition, her hands were unavailable under a blanket (licensing the inference that the bizarre head-use was just a means to an end). In their imitation, infants used their hand to switch on the light in the hands-unavailable condition, but the head in the hands-free condition, indicating that their imitative responses were based on a rich rational interpretation of the agent's action in terms of means and ends (Gergely et al., 2002).

2.3.3 Shared intentionality

Infants thus operate with a rudimentary understanding of others as intentional agents (related to the world cognitively via perception and conatively via goal-directed intentional action). This constitutes the most basic form of individual intentionality of second order—that is, not only being an intentional agent oneself (first order), but understanding others and oneself as intentional agents (second order). Such simple individual second-order intentionality seems not to be restricted to humans, but also to be part of the cognitive repertoire of great apes, perhaps other non-human primates, and birds (Kaminski et al., 2008). Human infants, however, may be special in the following sense: from the time they develop perception-goal folk psychology, they do not just operate as individual intentional agents who understand others and themselves as such. Rather, they transcend individual intentionality (first and second order) and engage in shared or collective we-intentionality (Tomasello & Rakoczy, 2003).

Though it is a notoriously contested question in philosophy and psychology as to how best to analyse shared intentionality (e.g. Bratman, 1992; Searle, 1995), the basic phenomenon is intuitively clear: two people dancing tango together are not the sum of two individuals each dancing by themselves, not even when each understands about the other what she is doing individually. When A intends 'I tango' and B intends 'I tango', and A understands 'B intends to tango' and B understands 'A intends to tango', this may at most amount to dancing side by side but not to dancing together. What makes for a real duet is the shared intention, 'we dance together'.

Infants engage in such shared we-intentionality from the second year on. The clearest type of evidence comes from their cooperative actions with others, both instrumental and playful. Children from around 18 to 24 months coordinate with others in order to achieve joint goals, communicate appropriately, engage in division of labour and roles, and even indicate a sense of commitment (when we act together, we are committed to the pursuit of the joint goal, and to each other, in ways that go beyond mere individual goal pursuit; Warneken et al., 2006). From a comparative and evolutionary point of view, one possibility is that shared intentionality marks the ontogenetic beginnings of uniquely human social cognition. Whereas individual intentionality and basic forms of individual intentionality of second order are evolutionarily more ancient, and thus more widespread and developing in analogous ways in humans and other primates, the paths separate when it comes to shared intentionality, which only humans develop and which lays the ground for the subsequent development of culture, language, and all culturally and linguistically mediated forms of higher cognition (e.g. Tomasello, 2014).

2.4 The emergence of fully fledged belief–desire folk psychology

That basic forms of individual intentionality of second order (perception-goal psychology) and shared intentionality develop in infancy is a widely accepted consensus. When it comes to the question of when and how more sophisticated forms of Theory of Mind—in particular, meta-representational belief–desire folk psychology—develop, things get much more complicated (for an overview of the main complexities, see, e.g. Rakoczy, 2012).

2.4.1 Standard picture of Theory of Mind development

Until 15 years or so ago, the standard picture used to be the following: infants and toddlers operate with basic Theory of Mind that allows them to track what others have informational access to (perception) and what they are aiming at (goals). But this falls short in fundamental ways from the true and fully fledged meta-representational Theory of Mind that operates with propositional attitude concepts, such as belief and strong notions of subjectivity and perspective, and that develops later, from around age 4. One way to illustrate the fundamental difference is with recourse to different forms of perspective taking: infants and toddlers engage in so-called Level I perspective taking. Cognitively, they understand that different agents can perceive different things ('I see something that you cannot see', or vice versa). Conatively, they understand that different agents may have different aims or preferences ('You like broccoli, I like crackers', Repacholi & Gopnik, 1997). However, they are not yet capable of Level II perspective taking. That is, they cannot yet understand *how* agents represent situations in fine-grained propositional ways: that different agents—cognitively—can see one and the same state of affairs differently, and can thus possibly misrepresent reality (false beliefs), and that—conatively—people can have desires that are not only different but mutually incompatible (Perner & Roessler, 2012).

This sophisticated and fully fledged meta-representational Theory of Mind, according to the old standard picture, only develops in protracted ways on the basis of linguistic and other socio-cultural experiences, as well as domain-general cognitive processes such as executive function. Evidence comes from several sources: first of all, children begin to master all kinds of explicit verbal tasks that tap a meta-representational grasp of (mis-)representation from around age 4. Such tasks include the famous standard false-belief task in which children have to predict or explain how an agent will act on the basis of her mistaken belief about reality (Wimmer & Perner, 1983), appearance–reality tasks in which children have to contrast what an object is and what it visually appears to be (Flavell et al.,1983), and Level II perspective-taking tasks in which children have to distinguish how a given situation looks differently from different viewpoints (Flavell et al., 1981). Children do not only come to solve all these and conceptually related tasks around the same age, but performance is highly consistent and correlated across tasks, reinforcing the interpretation that they all tap the same underlying conceptual capacity (Perner & Roessler, 2012).

Regarding the role of executive function, many studies document that executive functions and meta-representational Theory of Mind (indicated in performance in false-belief and related tasks) are strongly correlated both synchronically and longitudinally, such that executive function at time 1 predicts Theory of Mind at time 2 but not vice versa (Carlson et al., 2004; Carlson & Moses, 2001; for a meta-analysis, see Devine & Hughes, 2014). With regard to the relation of language and Theory of Mind, the evidence is multifarious (for review, see, e.g. Astington & Baird, 2005; Milligan et al., 2007): first of all, general language proficiency and Theory of Mind are strongly correlated. More interestingly, and going beyond mere correlation, studies with deaf children speak more directly for a causal role of language in Theory of Mind development. Deaf children who acquire native sign language at home, and thus show normal linguistic development, also develop Theory of Mind in typical ways; deaf children of hearing parents, in contrast, acquire language in much delayed ways, and are equally delayed in their Theory of Mind (Peterson & Siegal, 1999). Additional converging evidence comes from speakers of Nicaraguan Sign Language. This relatively new sign language has undergone substantial linguistic complexification in the past few years, and speakers of the language who acquired it in its earlier (and thus grammatically less complex) stages are severely delayed in their Theory of Mind relative to speakers of later generations (with much more complex grammatical structure; Pyers & Senghas, 2009). Finally, experimental evidence from training studies corroborates this picture. It shows that specific experience with language, both pragmatic, semantic, and grammatical, boosts Theory of Mind development (e.g. Lohmann & Tomasello, 2003).

The standard theoretical interpretation of this developmental pattern used to be framed in terms of conceptual change. On the basis of language as a potential medium for conceptual thought, and on the basis of domain-general capacities such as working memory and executive function, new conceptual structures emerge, and children between 2 and 4 slowly progress from the more basic perception-goal folk psychology to the fully fledged meta-representational belief–desire folk psychology (e.g. Perner, 1991).

2.4.2 New empirical wave and early competence accounts

More recent theoretical accounts, however, question this standard interpretation, and new evidence challenges its empirical foundations. Nativist accounts have been the most elaborate opponents to the standard picture (e.g. Baillargeon et al., 2010; Carruthers, 2013; Leslie, 2005). According to nativism, meta-representational Theory of Mind, being largely innate, is in operation very early in ontogeny, in any case much earlier than assumed by the standard picture. The fact that children fail standard false-belief and related tasks until age 4 does not reveal any conceptual competence deficits (because there are no such deficits). What these failures indicate are merely performance limits: children fail these tasks not because they require meta-representational Theory of Mind, but because they have other extraneous task demands (verbal, inhibitory control, etc.) that make the tasks artificially difficult. Once such tasks demands are out of the way, children should well be able to bring to bear their precocious conceptual competence and pass Theory of Mind tasks. Another class of accounts, dual process theories, assume that humans operate with at least two kinds of processes of Theory of Mind reasoning: Type I processes develop early, operate in implicit and largely unconscious fashion, and embody some Theory of Mind propensity to represent mental states in basic ways that go beyond mere perception-goal psychology (even if not incorporating fully fledged belief–desire psychology yet). In contrast, Type II processes, basically corresponding to explicit Theory of Mind according to the standard picture, develop later, based on language and executive function, and operate in explicit and conscious ways (Apperly & Butterfill, 2009). Both nativist and dual process accounts share the assumption that there are precocious Theory of Mind capacities in place much earlier than assumed by the standard picture, and these should become visible in implicit tasks stripped of verbal and other performance factors.

A growing body of evidence from the past 15 years seems to empirically support this assumption. Studies with various types of non-verbal implicit tasks point to Theory of Mind capacities in children way before age 4, sometimes as young as 1 year of age (for review, see Baillargeon et al., 2010; Scott & Baillargeon, 2017). In *violation-of-expectation* (VoE) adaptations of standard false-belief tasks, infants have been found to look longer to events in which an agent acts inconsistently with her (true or false) beliefs than to those in which she acts belief-consistently (Onishi & Baillargeon, 2005). In *anticipatory looking* (AL) studies, children from 1 to 2 years have been found to look in anticipation to where an agent will go or act in accordance with her (true or false) belief (Southgate et al., 2007; Surian & Geraci, 2012). *Interaction-based* studies have suggested that children from 18 to 24 months of age, when spontaneously interacting and communicating with others, take into account what the other agents (truly or falsely) believe, and adapt their actions accordingly (Buttelmann et al., 2009; Knudsen & Liszkowski, 2012; Southgate et al., 2010).

2.4.3 Replication crisis

The standard picture that fully fledged meta-representational belief–desire folk psychology develops at around 4 years of age is underpinned by a solid and often replicated empirical basis. The most elaborate quantitative evaluation of this effect was provided by Wellman et al., (2001). In their meta-analysis of published false-belief tasks (by that time, spanning 178 studies and over 4,000 children), they found that, largely independent of task manipulations or country of origin, children become able to attribute false beliefs between 2½ and 5 years of age.

2.4.3.1 Replicability and validity of non-verbal implicit tasks

In contrast, the empirical basis supporting early competence accounts is much less solid. To date, there are about 30 published studies showing false-belief competency in children before their third birthday (Scott & Baillargeon, 2017). Further, these studies come from relatively few labs and often have small sample sizes (e.g. 10–25 infants per condition in the between-participants design of the most prominent studies by Buttelmann et al., 2009; Onishi & Baillargeon, 2005; Southgate et al., 2007). It is important to note that small sample sizes are also an issue of the previously published standard false-belief tasks and that this alone does not justify discarding findings from either task type. However, several recent studies point at three major issues with non-verbal implicit tasks that have not been observed in standard tasks.

First, positive evidence from each of the three non-verbal measures is now faced with several published failed replication attempts (e.g. VoE paradigms: Dörrenberg et al., 2018; Powell et al., 2018; Yott & Poulin-Dubois, 2016; AL paradigms: Burnside et al., 2018; Dörrenberg et al., 2018; Wiesmann et al., 2018; Kulke et al., 2018a; Schuwerk et al., 2018; Interaction-based paradigms: Crivello & Poulin-Dubois, 2018; Poulin-Dubois & Yott, 2018; Priewasser et al., 2018). Further, a survey revealed that additional unpublished non-replications existed (Kulke & Rakoczy, 2018). The replication attempts varied in how closely they adapted the original procedure (some used the original stimuli, some produced their own versions, many received advice from the original authors). The fact that all these studies, covering a broad spectrum from direct to conceptual replications (for a classification framework, see LeBel et al., 2018), failed to replicate the original findings speaks against the potential objection that those non-replications are attributable to poor implementation of the original procedures.

Second, measures of early false-belief competence seem to have poor construct validity. For example, the combination of results of the replication attempts of several tasks reported by Powell et al. (2018) suggests that performance in VoE paradigms might be driven by the infants' less sophisticated ability to track another's state of knowledge based on her perceptual access, rather than by false-belief understanding (for further alternative explanations, see Heyes, 2014; Perner &

Ruffman, 2005). Out of several attempts to replicate AL measures, a replication attempt of a paradigm employed by Low and Watts (2013) stood out because it was successful in a sample of adults (Kulke et al., 2018b). However, in a follow-up study, Kulke et al. showed that once potential confounds are removed from the stimulus material (an imbalance in the cueing of one of the two potential target locations), this paradigm also cannot be replicated (for a similar case, see Phillips et al., 2015). Additionally, the interaction-based paradigm by Buttelmann et al. (2009) is challenged by recent evidence supporting an alternative explanation of infants' task performance. The infants' performance in a control condition introduced by Priewasser et al. (2018) was incompatible with the interpretation that their helping behaviour is guided by the appreciation of the experimenter's false belief about the toy's location. Rather, it was in line with the non-mentalistic explanation that it is guided by the experimenter's likely goals in this particular situation (that the experimenter wants to find the toy in this hide-and-seek-like situation).

Third, non-verbal implicit tasks lack convergent validity. Several recent studies found minimal or no systematic correlations between the three most prominent task types (and even within different tasks of the same type) that are all supposed to tap the same underlying construct (Dörrenberg et al., 2018; Kulke et al., 2018a, 2018b; Poulin-Dubois & Yott, 2018; Powell et al., 2018; Yott & Poulin-Dubois, 2016). Thus, whereas findings from numerous variations of explicit false-belief tasks converge on the conclusion that explicit false-belief understanding develops at around 4 years of age (Wellman et al., 2001; see also Perner & Roesler, 2012), no such pattern emerges for early false-belief understanding (for a meta-analysis, see Barone et al., 2019).

In sum, recent studies question the theoretical claim of false-belief understanding in infancy. Positive findings are challenged by a growing body of non-replications. Further evidence suggests that in non-verbal implicit tasks, infants may track another person's state of knowledge, based on her perceptual access (distinguishing between information access knowledge and lack thereof), but that they don't consider this person's false belief. Lacking inter-task correlations suggest that the available task types do not measure one common phenomenon. Further, a recent meta-analysis by Barone and colleagues (2019) showed that a large variance of performance in these tasks remains unexplained. In other words, we do not entirely know yet what these tasks are measuring. Moreover, this meta-analysis identified a substantial publication bias in the literature currently available.

2.4.3.2 Interpretations of puzzling findings

So, what can be concluded from this complex and puzzling emerging picture? Is there a full-blown Theory of Mind in infancy? Two extreme positions frame the current debate (Baillargeon et al., 2018; Poulin-Dubois et al., 2018). On the one hand, one extreme position concludes 'yes, there is a Theory of Mind in infancy', as documented by the original studies. Unsuccessful replication attempts constitute false-negative findings. This claim often entails post-hoc explanations of why these replication attempts failed (Baillargeon et al., 2018). On the other hand, the opposite extreme position concludes 'no, there is no such thing as full-blown Theory of Mind in infancy', and the original findings might be false positives. The documented publication bias (Barone et al., 2019; Kulke & Rakoczy, 2018), as well as high exclusion rates based on flexible criteria (Schuwerk et al., 2018) and flexible parameter selections (e.g. Rubio-Fernández, 2019), may be seen as support for this interpretation.

Yet, neither of these extreme positions is conclusively justified at the moment. It is not convincing to draw strong conclusions about a full-blown, maybe inborn Theory of Mind in infancy based on relatively few studies, and to explain away non-replications with mostly methodological post-hoc arguments. At the same time, it is unjustified to discard the positive evidence and conclude that there is no Theory of Mind in infancy based on the recent failed replication attempts. In sum, the unsatisfying but, in light of the current empirical situation, most accurate answer to the question of whether infants already have a Theory of Mind is: 'We don't know yet' (Poulin-Dubois et al., 2018). Current theory building seems to be 'on hold' until the empirical situation is better understood.

2.4.3.3 Lessons learned and ways forward

The positive effect of this current situation is that it advances the field by changing its research culture. Against the background of the replication crisis in psychological science in general and its probable sources, particularly small sample sizes, publication bias, and questionable research practices (Button et al., 2013; John et al., 2012; Nosek et al., 2012; Open Science Collaboration, 2015), new ways to improve developmental psychological science are being explored. One such constructive response is the ManyBabies initiative (MB, https://manybabies.github.io; Frank et al., 2017), which tackles the above sources of poor replicability. This initiative aims at replicating influential experiments in developmental psychology through the cooperation of many labs, and thus, with large sample sizes, transparent methodological decisions throughout the project, and the publication of results irrespective of their outcome, it provides a framework for the promotion of reproducibility, best practices, and theory building in developmental research (Frank et al., 2017).

In the second project of this initiative, 'MB2: Theory of Mind in infancy', original authors and authors of replication attempts form a consortium to conduct multi-lab replication studies of the three most influential paradigms (VoE, AL, interaction-based). This project advances the field by bringing together researchers with very different theoretical positions, in the spirit of 'adversarial collaboration' (Mellers et al., 2001), to hold debates as objective and unbiased as possible. Controversies between original authors and authors of non-replication studies can get heated and bear the potential to stir up personal resentments. This leads to discussions that bind resources but do not advance the field. To be successful, researchers in the MB2 Consortium have to try to let passion and enthusiasm in what they do fuel challenging and confrontative but factual discussions. Additionally, by the implementation of general best practice recommendations combined with consensus on discipline- and paradigm-specific procedures, the ManyBabies initiative establishes new standards for methodological rigour (Frank et al., 2017; The ManyBabies Consortium, 2020; see also Rubio-Fernandez, 2018). In a first step, the MB2 Consortium developed new "best test" stimuli for a multi-lab conceptual replication attempt of AL paradigms. These stimuli will be used to test whether toddlers and adults track the epistemic state of an agent, specifically whether they differentiate between knowledge and ignorance. Evidence for this kind of epistemic state tracking can be considered as precondition to ask whether toddlers and adults also track true and false beliefs in this paradigm. Once this precondition is fulfilled, a worldwide call to participate in the attempt to replicate false-belief-congruent anticipatory looking will be made. To conclude, in this situation of contradicting empirical evidence, in which also meta-analyses have proven to be unhelpful (Barone et al., 2019; Van Elk et al., 2015), the MB2 project promises to shed light on the question of whether, and if so to what extent, infants already understand others' minds.

2.5 Summary

From birth on, infants are astonishingly well equipped to get in touch with the social world. Basic forms of social interaction shape the relationships between infants and their caregivers from early on and become continuously more sophisticated throughout the first year of life. By the second year, infants have acquired important developmental milestones of simple (perception-goal) folk psychology and shared intentionality. Around their fourth birthday, children develop a full-blown explicit meta-representational Theory of Mind, an essential foundation for successful social interaction. This standard picture of the development of social interaction has been questioned by research suggesting false-belief competence earlier in infancy. Yet, developments of recent years remind us to be careful in drawing strong conclusions on what infants can and cannot do on relatively thin empirical grounds. As in the case of neonatal imitation (and probably also fetal face preference, see Scheel et al., 2018), recent replication studies challenge the early competence view. Looking to the future, collaborative approaches implementing methodological rigour promise to generate solid knowledge on the development of social cognition and social interaction in infancy.

References

Adamson, L. B., & Frick, J. E., 2003. 'The still face: A history of a shared experimental paradigm'. *Infancy* 4. 4: 451–473.

Apperly, I. A., & Butterfill, S. A., 2009. 'Do humans have two systems to track beliefs and belief-like states?'. *Psychological Review* 116. 4: 953–970.

Astington, J. W., & Baird, J. A., 2005. 'Introduction: Why language matters'. In *Why Language Matters for Theory of Mind*, edited by J. W. Astington & J. A. Baird. Oxford University Press, pp. 3–25.

Baillargeon, R., Buttelmann, D., & Southgate, V., 2018. 'Invited commentary: Interpreting failed replications of early false-belief findings: Methodological and theoretical considerations'. *Cognitive Development* 46: 112–124.

Baillargeon, R., Scott, R. M., & He, Z., 2010. 'False-belief understanding in infants'. *Trends in Cognitive Sciences* 14. 3: 110–118.

Barone, P., Corradi, G., & Gomila, A., 2019. 'Infants' performance in spontaneous-response false belief tasks: A review and meta-analysis'. *Infant Behavior and Development* 57: 101350.

Barr, R., Dowden, A., & Hayne, H., 1996. 'Developmental changes in deferred imitation by 6- to 24-month-old infants'. *Infant Behavior and Development* 19. 2: 159–170.

Behne, T., Carpenter, M., Call, J., & Tomasello, M., 2005. 'Unwilling versus unable: Infants' understanding of intentional action'. *Developmental Psychology* 41. 2: 328–337.

Bertenthal, B. I., Proffitt, D. R., & Cutting, J. E., 1984. 'Infant sensitivity to figural coherence in biomechanical motions'. *Journal of Experimental Child Psychology* 37. 2: 213–230.

Bigelow, A. E., 1998. 'Infants' sensitivity to familiar imperfect contingencies in social interaction'. *Infant Behavior and Development* 21. 1: 149–162.

Bratman, M. E., 1992. 'Shared cooperative activity'. *The Philosophical Review* 101. 2: 327–341.

Brazelton, T. B., Koslowski, B., & Main, M., 1974. 'The origins of reciprocity: The early mother-infant interaction'. In *The Effect of the Infant on its Caregiver*, edited by M. Lewis & L. A. Rosenblum. Wiley, pp. 327–341.

Brentano, F. 1874/1973. *Psychologie vom Empirischen Standpunkt* [*Psychology from an Empirical Standpoint*]. Meiner.

Brooks, R., & Meltzoff, A., 2002. 'The importance of eyes: How infants interpret adult looking behavior'. *Developmental Psychology* 38: 958–966.

Brooks, R., & Meltzoff, A. N., 2015. 'Connecting the dots from infancy to childhood: A longitudinal study connecting gaze following, language, and explicit theory of mind'. *Journal of Experimental Child Psychology* 130: 67–78.

Burnside, K., Ruel, A., Azar, N., & Poulin-Dubois, D., 2018. 'Implicit false belief across the lifespan: Non-replication of an anticipatory looking task'. *Cognitive Development* 46: 4–11.

Buttelmann, D., Carpenter, M., & Tomasello, M., 2009. 'Eighteen-month-old infants show false belief understanding in an active helping paradigm'. *Cognition* 112. 2: 337–342.

Button, K. S., Ioannidis, J. P., Mokrysz, C., Nosek, B. A., Flint, J., Robinson, E. S., & Munafò, M. R., 2013. 'Power failure: Why small sample size undermines the reliability of neuroscience'. *Nature Reviews Neuroscience* 14. 5: 365.

Carlson, S. M., & Moses, L. J. 2001. 'Individual differences in inhibitory control and children's theory of mind'. *Child Development* 72. 4: 1032–1053.

Carlson, S. M., Mandell, D. J., & Williams, L., 2004. 'Executive function and Theory of Mind: Stability and prediction from ages 2 to 3'. *Developmental Psychology* 40. 6: 1105–1122.

REFERENCES

Carpenter, M., Akhtar, N., & Tomasello, M., 1998. 'Fourteen- through 18-month-old infants differentially imitate intentional and accidental actions'. *Infant Behavior & Development* 21. 2: 315–330.

Carpenter, M., Nagell, K., & Tomasello, M., 1998a. 'Social cognition, joint attention, and communicative competence from 9 to 15 months of age'. *Monographs of the Society for Research in Child Development* 63. 4: 176.

Carruthers, P., 2013. 'Mindreading in Infancy'. *Mind & Language* 28. 2: 141–172.

Cooper, R. P., & Aslin, R. N., 1990. 'Preference for infant-directed speech in the first month after birth'. *Child Development* 61. 5: 1584–1595.

Crivello, C., & Poulin-Dubois, D., 2018. 'Infants' false belief understanding: A non-replication of the helping task'. *Cognitive Development* 46: 51–57.

Devine, R. T., & Hughes, C., 2014. 'Relations between false belief understanding and executive function in early childhood: A meta-analysis'. *Child Development* 85. 5: 1777–1794.

Dörrenberg, S., Rakoczy, H., & Liszkowski, U., 2018. 'How (not) to measure infant Theory of Mind: Testing the replicability and validity of four non-verbal measures'. *Cognitive Development* 46: 12–30.

Farroni, T., Csibra, G., Simion, F., & Johnson, M. H., 2002. 'Eye contact detection in humans from birth'. *Proceedings of the National Academy of Sciences* 99. 14: 9602–9605.

Flavell, J. H., Flavell, E. R., & Green, F. L., 1983. 'Development of the appearance-reality distinction'. *Cognitive Psychology* 15: 95–120. Flavell, J. H., Everett, B. A., Croft, K., & Flavell, E. R., 1981. 'Young children's knowledge about visual perception: Further evidence for the Level 1–Level 2 distinction'. *Developmental Psychology* 17. 1: 99–103. Frank, M. C., Bergelson, E., Bergmann, C., Cristia, A., Floccia, C., Gervain, J., ... & Lew-Williams, C., 2017. 'A collaborative approach to infant research: Promoting reproducibility, best practices, and theory-building'. *Infancy* 22. 4: 421–435.

Gergely, G., & Watson, J. S., 1999. 'Early socio-emotional development: Contingency perception and the social-biofeedback model'. In *Early Social Cognition: Understanding Others in the First Months of Life*, edited by P. Rochate. Erlbaum, pp. 101–136.

Gergely, G., Bekkering, H., & Kiraly, I., 2002. 'Rational imitation in preverbal infants'. *Nature* 415. 6873: 755.

Gergely, G., Knadasdy, Z., Csibra, G., & Biro, S., 1995. 'Taking the intentional stance at 12 months of age'. *Cognition* 56. 2: 165–193.

Goren, C. C., Sarty, M., & Wu, P. Y., 1975. 'Visual following and pattern discrimination of face-like stimuli by newborn infants'. *Pediatrics* 56. 4: 544–549.

Haith, M. M., Bergman, T., & Moore, M. J., 1977. 'Eye contact and face scanning in early infancy'. *Science* 198. 4319: 853–855.

Heider, F., & Simmel, M., 1944. 'An experimental study of apparent behavior'. *The American Journal of Psychology* 57. 2: 243–259.

Heyes, C., 2014. 'False belief in infancy: A fresh look'. *Developmental Science* 17. 5: 647–659.

John, L. K., Loewenstein, G., & Prelec, D., 2012. 'Measuring the prevalence of questionable research practices with incentives for truth telling'. *Psychological Science* 23. 5: 524–532.

Johnson, M. H., 2005. 'Subcortical face processing'. *Nature Reviews Neuroscience* 6. 10: 766.

Jones, W., & Klin, A., 2013. 'Attention to eyes is present but in decline in 2–6-month-old infants later diagnosed with autism'. *Nature* 504. 7480: 427.

Kaminski, J., Call, J., & Tomasello, M., 2008. 'Chimpanzees know what others know, but not what they believe'. *Cognition* 109. 2: 224–234.

Kelly, D. J., Duarte, S., Meary, D., Bindemann, M., & Pascalis, O., 2019. 'Infants rapidly detect human faces in complex naturalistic visual scenes'. *Developmental Science* 22. 6: e12829.

Knudsen, B., & Liszkowski, U., 2012. '18-month-olds predict specific action mistakes through attribution of false belief, not ignorance, and intervene accordingly'. *Infancy* 17: 672–691.

Kristen, S., Sodian, B., Thoermer, C., & Perst, H., 2011. 'Infants' joint attention skills predict toddlers' emerging mental state language'. *Developmental Psychology* 47: 1207–1219.

Kulke, L., & Rakoczy, H., 2018. 'Implicit Theory of Mind—An overview of current replications and non-replications'. *Data in Brief* 16: 101–104.

Kulke, L., Reiß, M., Krist, H., & Rakoczy, H., 2018a. 'How robust are anticipatory looking measures of Theory of Mind? Replication attempts across the life span'. *Cognitive Development* 46: 97–111.

Kulke, L., von Duhn, B., Schneider, D., & Rakoczy, H., 2018b. 'Is implicit theory of mind a real and robust phenomenon? Results from a systematic replication study'. *Psychological Science* 29. 6: 888–900.

LeBel, E. P., McCarthy, R. J., Earp, B. D., Elson, M., & Vanpaemel, W., 2018. 'A unified framework to quantify the credibility of scientific findings'. *Advances in Methods and Practices in Psychological Science* 1. 3: 389–402.

Legerstee, M., 1992. 'A review of the animate-inanimate distinction in infancy: Implications for models of social and cognitive knowing'. *Early Development and Parenting* 1. 2: 59–67.

Leslie, A. M., 2005. 'Developmental parallels in understanding minds and bodies'. *Trends in Cognitive Science* 9. 10: 459–462.

Lohmann, H., & Tomasello, M., 2003. 'The role of language in the development of false belief understanding: A training study'. *Child Development* 74: 1130–1144.

Low, J., & Watts, J., 2013. 'Attributing false beliefs about object identity reveals a signature blind spot in humans' efficient mind-reading system'. *Psychological Science* 24. 3: 305–311.

Markova, G., Nguyen, T., & Höhl, S., 2019. 'Neurobehavioral interpersonal synchrony in early development: The role of interactional rhythms'. *Frontiers in Psychology* 10: 2078.

Mellers, B., Hertwig, R., & Kahneman, D., 2001. 'Do frequency representations eliminate conjunction effects? An exercise in adversarial collaboration'. *Psychological Science* 12. 4: 269–275.

Meltzoff, A. N., 1995. 'Understanding the intentions of others: Re-enactment of intended acts by 18-month-old children'. *Developmental Psychology* 31. 5: 838–850.

Meltzoff, A. N., & Moore, M. K., 1977. 'Imitation of facial and manual gestures by human neonates'. *Science* 198. 4312: 75–78.

Meltzoff, A. N., Murray, L., Simpson, E., Heimann, M., Nagy, E., Nadel, J., ... & Subiaul, F., 2018. 'Re-examination of Oostenbroek et al. (2016): Evidence for neonatal imitation of tongue protrusion'. *Developmental Science* 21. 4: e12609.

Milligan, K., Astington, J. W., & Dack, L. A., 2007. 'Language and theory of mind: Meta-analysis of the relation between language ability and false-belief understanding'. *Child Development* 78. 2: 622–646.

Moll, H., & Tomasello, M., 2004. '12- and 18-month-old infants follow gaze to spaces behind barriers'. *Developmental Science* 7. 1: F1–F9.

Moll, H., & Tomasello, M., 2006. 'Level I perspective-taking at 24 months of age'. *British Journal of Developmental Psychology* 24. 3: 603–613.

Nosek, B. A., Spies, J. R., & Motyl, M., 2012. 'Scientific utopia: II. Restructuring incentives and practices to promote truth over publishability'. *Perspectives on Psychological Science* 7. 6: 615–631.

Omer, Y., Sapir, R., Hatuka, Y., & Yovel, G., 2019. 'What is a face? Critical features for face detection'. *Perception* 4. 5: 437–446.

Onishi, K. H., & Baillargeon, R., 2005. 'Do 15-month-old infants understand false beliefs?'. *Science* 308. 5719: 255–258.
Oostenbroek, J., Suddendorf, T., Nielsen, M., Redshaw, J., Kennedy-Costantini, S., Davis, J., ... & Slaughter, V., 2016. 'Comprehensive longitudinal study challenges the existence of neonatal imitation in humans'. *Current Biology* 26. 10: 1334–1338.
Open Science Collaboration, 2015. 'Estimating the reproducibility of psychological science'. *Science* 349. 6251: aac4716.
Perner, J. 1991. *Understanding the Representational Mind*. MIT Press.
Perner, J., & Roessler, J., 2012. 'From infants' to children's appreciation of belief'. *Trends in Cognitive Sciences* 16. 10: 519–525.
Perner, J., & Ruffman, T., 2005. 'Infants' insight into the mind: How deep?'. *Science* 308. 5719: 214–216.
Peterson, C. C., & Siegal, M., 1999. 'Representing inner worlds: Theory of mind in autistic, deaf, and normal hearing children'. *Psychological Science* 10. 2: 126–129.
Phillips, J., Ong, D. C., Surtees, A. D., Xin, Y., Williams, S., Saxe, R., & Frank, M. C., 2015. 'A second look at automatic Theory of Mind: Reconsidering Kovács, Téglás, and Endress (2010)'. *Psychological Science* 26. 9: 1353–1367.
Piaget, J. 1952. *Play, Dreams and Imitation in Childhood*. W. W. Norton & Co.
Poulin-Dubois, D., & Yott, J., 2018. 'Probing the depth of infants' theory of mind: Disunity in performance across paradigms'. *Developmental Science* 21. 4: e12600.
Poulin-Dubois, D., Sodian, B., Metz, U., Tilden, J., & Schoeppner, B., 2007. 'Out of sight is not out of mind: Developmental changes in infants' understanding of visual perception during the second year'. *Journal of Cognition and Development* 8. 4: 401–425.
Poulin-Dubois, D., Rakoczy, H., Burnside, K., Crivello, C., Dörrenberg, S., Edwards, K., ... & Perner, J., 2018. 'Do infants understand false beliefs? We don't know yet–A commentary on Baillargeon, Buttelmann and Southgate's commentary'. *Cognitive Development* 48: 302–315.
Powell, L. J., Hobbs, K., Bardis, A., Carey, S., & Saxe, R., 2018. 'Replications of implicit theory of mind tasks with varying representational demands'. *Cognitive Development*, 46: 40–50.
Priewasser, B., Rafetseder, E., Gargitter, C., & Perner, J., 2018. 'Helping as an early indicator of a theory of mind: Mentalism or Teleology?'. *Cognitive Development* 46: 69–78.
Pyers, J. E., & Senghas, A., 2009. 'Language promotes false-belief understanding: Evidence from learners of a new sign language'. *Psychological Science* 20. 7: 805–812.
Rakoczy, H., 2012. 'Do infants have a theory of mind?'. *British Journal of Developmental Psychology* 30. 1: 59–74.
Reid, V. M., Dunn, K., Young, R. J., Amu, J., Donovan, T., & Reissland, N., 2017. 'The human fetus preferentially engages with face-like visual stimuli'. *Current Biology* 27. 13: 2052.
Repacholi, B. M., & Gopnik, A., 1997. 'Early reasoning about desires: Evidence from 14- and 18-month-olds'. *Developmental Psychology* 33. 1: 12–21.
Rubio-Fernández, P., 2018. 'What do failed (and successful) replications with the Duplo task show?'. *Cognitive Development*, 48, 316–320.
Rubio-Fernández, P., 2019. 'Publication standards in infancy research: Three ways to make Violation-of-Expectation studies more reliable'. *Infant Behavior and Development* 54: 177–188.
Scheel, A. M., Ritchie, S. J., Brown, N. J., & Jacques, S. L., 2018. 'Methodological problems in a study of fetal visual perception'. *Current Biology* 28. 10: R594–R596.
Schuwerk, T., Priewasser, B., Sodian, B., & Perner, J., 2018. 'The robustness and generalizability of findings on spontaneous false belief sensitivity: A replication attempt'. *Royal Society Open Science* 5. 5: 172273.

Scott, R. M., & Baillargeon, R., 2017. 'Early false-belief understanding'. *Trends in Cognitive Sciences* 21. 4: 237–249.
Searle, J. R. 1983. *Intentionality: An Essay in the Philosophy of Mind*. Cambridge University Press.
Searle, J. R. 1995. *The Construction of Social Reality*. Free Press.
Simion, F., Regolin, L., & Bulf, H., 2008. 'A predisposition for biological motion in the newborn baby'. *Proceedings of the National Academy of Sciences* 105. 2: 809–813.
Southgate, V., Chevallier, C., & Csibra, G., 2010. 'Seventeen-month-olds appeal to false beliefs to interpret others referential communication'. *Developmental Science* 13. 6: 907–912.
Southgate, V., Senju, A., & Csibra, G., 2007. 'Action anticipation through attribution of false belief by 2-year-olds'. *Psychological Science* 18. 7: 587–592.
Surian, L., & Geraci, A., 2012. 'Where will the triangle look for it? Attributing false beliefs to a geometric shape at 17 months'. *British Journal of Developmental Psychology* 30. 1: 30–44.
The ManyBabies Consortium, 2020. 'Quantifying sources of variability in infancy research using the infant-directed speech preference'. *Advances in Methods and Practices in Psychological Science (AMPPS)* 3. 1: 24–52.
Tomasello, M. 1999. *The Cultural Origins of Human Cognition*. Harvard University Press.
Tomasello, M. 2014. *A Natural History of Human Thinking*. Harvard University Press.
Tomasello, M., & Rakoczy, H., 2003. 'What makes human cognition unique? From individual to shared to collective intentionality'. *Mind and Language* 18. 2: 121–147.
Trevarthen, C., 1979. 'Communication and cooperation in early infancy. A description of primary intersubjectivity'. In *Before Speech: The Beginning of Human Communication*, edited by M. Bullowa. Cambridge University Press, pp. 530–571.
Van Elk, M., Matzke, D., Gronau, Q., Guang, M., Vandekerckhove, J., & Wagenmakers, E.-J., 2015. 'Meta-analyses are no substitute for registered replications: A skeptical perspective on religious priming'. *Frontiers in Psychology* 6: 1365.
Warneken, F., & Tomasello, M., 2006. 'Altruistic helping in human infants and young chimpanzees'. *Science* 311. 5765: 1301–1303.
Warneken, F., Chen, F., & Tomasello, M., 2006. 'Cooperative activities in young children and chimpanzees'. *Child Development* 77. 3: 640–663.
Wellman, H. M., 2011. 'Developing a theory of mind'. In *The Wiley-Blackwell Handbook of Childhood Cognitive Development*, edited by U. Goswami. Wiley-Blackwell, pp. 258–284.
Wellman, H. M., Cross, D., & Watson, J., 2001. 'Meta-analysis of theory-of-mind development: The truth about false belief'. *Child Development* 72. 3: 655–684.
Wiesmann, C. G., Friederici, A. D., Disla, D., Steinbeis, N., & Singer, T., 2018. 'Longitudinal evidence for 4-year-olds' but not 2- and 3-year-olds' false belief-related action anticipation'. *Cognitive Development* 46: 58–68.
Wimmer, H., & Perner, J., 1983. 'Beliefs about beliefs—Representation and constraining function of wrong beliefs in young children's understanding of deception'. *Cognition* 13. 1: 103–128.
Yott, J., & Poulin-Dubois, D., 2016. 'Are infants' theory-of-mind abilities well integrated? Implicit understanding of intentions, desires, and beliefs'. *Journal of Cognition and Development* 17. 5: 683–698.

3
Social Interaction in Early and Middle Childhood
The Role of Theory of Mind

Serena Lecce and Rory T. Devine

3.1 Introduction

Being able to navigate the social world successfully and to build and maintain positive social relationships is key to children's current and later adjustment (Lecce et al., 2017a; Davis et al., 2014; Hay et al., 2004; Ladd et al., 2008). From early to middle childhood, children's social lives change dramatically. In early childhood, social interactions tend to be supervised by adults and mainly happen within the family context. In middle childhood, children expand their social horizons to include peers and teachers (Del Giudice, 2014; Kramer & Kowal, 2005). From early to middle childhood, social interactions therefore become increasingly complex, less reliant on parents and caregivers, and more dependent on children's own social-cognitive skills.

In this chapter, we examine the cognitive basis of social interaction in early and middle childhood by focusing on the role of Theory of Mind ('ToM'). ToM refers to the ability to attribute mental states such as desires, thoughts, and emotions to others in order to explain, predict, and influence their behaviour (Premack & Woodruff, 1978). ToM reflects the ability to understand others' actions in terms of mental states, enabling children to take on the perspectives of others, and accordingly attune their behaviour. Extensive interest in ToM over the past four decades arguably reflects the assumption that ToM is required for many everyday social interactions. In this chapter, we examine critically the extent to which ToM is implicated in children's social interactions within and outside the family.

We use the term 'early childhood' to refer to the period between the ages of 2 and 5 years, which is sometimes referred to as the 'preschool years'. We use the term 'middle childhood' to refer to the developmental period between the ages of 6 and 12 years, which overlaps with the period of compulsory primary education in most 'Western' cultures (OECD, 2018). The majority of studies on ToM have focused on its emergence in early childhood (e.g. Wellman et al., 2001) but the past decade has seen an explosion of interest in ToM in middle childhood (e.g.

Hughes & Devine, 2015). Early and middle childhood are characterized by dramatic changes in children's ToM and their social horizons, and therefore provide an ideal developmental context for studying the links between ToM and children's social interactions (Hughes, 2016).

Children's social interactions have been studied since the early twentieth century using a wide array of methods including (1) direct observation of children's interactions with family members, teachers, and peers; (2) interviews and questionnaires completed by adults familiar with a target child; and (3) self- and peer-rated assessments (e.g. Brownell et al., 2015; Rubin et al., 2015). The breadth of methods reflects the view that children's ability to manage social interactions effectively (or 'social competence') involves both prosocial orientation (i.e. attempts to fulfil others' needs) and social initiative (i.e. attempts to fulfil one's own needs), and that social interactions occur across different contexts with diverse partners including family members, peers, and teachers (Huber et al., 2019; Raver & Zigler, 1997; Rydell et al.,1997). Diverse methods also reflect a dual focus on both social interaction behaviour (e.g. prosocial behaviours, social initiative) and the outcomes of individual differences in social interaction behaviour (e.g. friendship quality, peer status, and family relationship quality) (Rydell et al, 1997). We therefore adopt a broad definition of social interaction.

In the first section, we describe how ToM is measured, examine how ToM changes from preschool to the end of the primary school years, and discuss individual differences in ToM. In the second and third sections, we consider the links between individual differences in children's ToM and social interactions within the family (i.e. with parents and siblings) and outside the family (i.e. with peers and teachers). In the fourth and fifth sections, we address the theoretical and methodological implications of existing studies on ToM and social interactions, explain the 'Theory of Mind in Social Context' framework, and identify future directions for research in this field.

3.2 Theory of Mind in early and middle childhood: development and individual differences

For more than four decades, researchers have charted the development of children's understanding of others' minds (Wellman & Liu, 2004). In early childhood, the most widely used measure of children's ability to reason about others' minds is the 'false belief' task (Wimmer & Perner, 1983). In this task, children are required to predict or explain a character's behaviour by inferring the character's mistaken beliefs about the location of an object (moved in the character's absence; Wimmer & Perner, 1983), the unexpected contents of a standard container (e.g. pencils in a candy box; Perner et al.,1987), or the misleading identity of an object (e.g. a sponge that looks like a rock; Gopnik & Astington, 1988). Meta-analysis of 178 studies showed that children's performance on the false belief task improves between the ages of 2 and 5 years regardless of whether children attribute false beliefs to an agent about an object's location, appearance, or contents (Wellman et al, 2001). Complex versions of the false belief task have also been devised to measure children's ability to reason about a character's (false) beliefs about another character's beliefs (i.e. second-order false beliefs; Perner & Wimmer, 1985) and to predict emotions based on false beliefs (Harris et al.,1989). Researchers have also charted the early emergence of children's ability to reason about the difference between their own desires and others' desires, their own beliefs and others' beliefs, and their own knowledge and others' knowledge (Wellman & Liu, 2004). While sensitive to developmental differences in ToM, standard versions of these measures exhibit ceiling effects and cannot be used to study behavioural response differences in ToM beyond early childhood.

While researchers have yet to agree on a focal paradigm for studying the development of ToM in middle childhood, there has been a proliferation of innovative methods for measuring ToM beyond early childhood. Researchers have devised tasks using a variety of stimuli such as animations, audio clips, text vignettes, interactive computer tasks, and film clips to measure emotion understanding, perspective taking, intention attribution, and the ability to explain behaviour with reference to beliefs, knowledge, and desires (e.g. Banerjee et al., 2011; Baron-Cohen, et al.,1997; Castelli et al., 2000; Devine & Hughes, 2013; Dumontheil et al., 2010; Happé, 1994). Using these paradigms, researchers have expanded the developmental focus of work on ToM to include middle childhood (Banerjee et al, 2011; Devine & Hughes, 2013) and adolescence (Dumontheil et al, 2010). This work demonstrates that children's ability to make inferences about mental states in complex social situations, such as faux pas (Baron-Cohen et al., 1999), misunderstanding, double bluff, and irony (Devine & Hughes, 2016) becomes more flexible and accurate (Apperly, 2011; Bianco et al., 2016). Children also develop a more complex awareness of the links among multiple mental states (Lagattuta et al., 2016).

Beyond investigating age-related developmental differences in children's ToM, in the past two decades, researchers have documented striking variation in ToM between children of the same age. By administering batteries of standard and advanced ToM tasks to large samples of children (Dunn et al., 1991; Hughes & Devine, 2015), researchers have shown that, at any given age, some children excel at making inferences about mental states and others struggle in both early and middle childhood. These individual differences in ToM are hypothesized to reflect genuine lasting variation between children in their capacity to use their understanding of others' mental states, rather than temporary differences in the timing of development (Hughes & Devine, 2015). Supporting this view, individual differences in ToM exhibit short-term test-retest reliability (Devine & Hughes, 2016; Hughes et al., 2000) and rank-order stability across more prolonged intervals both in early (Astington & Jenkins, 1999) and middle (Caputi et al., 2012; Lecce et al., 2010; Peterson & Wellman, 2019) childhood, even over several years (Devine et al., 2016; Lecce et al., 2014). Individual differences in ToM cannot be attributed entirely to differences in other cognitive skills, such as executive function (i.e. the basic cognitive processes that underpin the ability to override entrenched habits, update information held in mind, and shift easily between tasks) or language ability, because variation in ToM in early childhood predicts individual differences in ToM in middle childhood over and above differences in these factors (Devine et al, 2016).

The enduring fascination with ToM reflects the assumption that it is crucial for everyday social interaction (Apperly, 2011; Dunn, 1995; Hughes, 2011; Ratcliffe, 2007). After all, if some children are better than others at reading others' thoughts, feelings, and desires, this might explain why some children are more socially competent than others. This assumption has its origins in autism research, which sought to explain social and communicative differences between children with autism and neurotypical children in terms of ToM 'deficits' (e.g. Baron-Cohen, 1995). This idea has been extended beyond individuals with autism to typically developing children (e.g. Dunn et al, 1991; Hughes & Leekham, 2004) and has given rise to what Apperly (2012) has called the 'social individual differences' perspective on ToM. Unlike theories concerning the social origins of children's ToM (e.g. Carpendale & Lewis, 2006) or the cognitive basis of ToM (e.g. Perner & Lang, 2000; Russell, 1996), which focus on explaining the acquisition of ToM in early childhood, the 'social individual differences' perspective focuses on how ToM is *used* and, therefore, on its outcomes. The social individual differences perspective has yet to provide the field with a formal account of how ToM influences social interaction. The absence of a clear theoretical account has meant that claims about the importance of ToM for children's social interactions are often unqualified, suggesting that ToM plays a part in most, if not all, aspects of everyday social life (Ratcliffe, 2007). In an effort to elaborate on the 'social individual differences' perspective, we now examine the available evidence on the relations between individual differences in ToM and social interaction in early and middle childhood. We consider the specificity of the links between individual differences in ToM, different aspects of social interaction behaviour, and the outcomes of social interaction, as well as the importance of context.

3.3 Theory of Mind and social interactions in the family

The majority of studies on ToM and social interaction have focused on elucidating how different facets of the family environment (e.g. parent–child interactions, family size) support the development of children's ToM (Devine & Hughes, 2018; Hughes & Leekam, 2004). In this section, we adopt a different perspective and examine whether and how children's ToM has an impact on social interaction in two key family relationships: parent–child and child–sibling relationships.

3.3.1 Parent–child interactions

Evidence for the effects of children's ToM on parent–child interactions is surprisingly scarce. This is remarkable given that numerous studies have shown modest but significant longitudinal links between parental mental-state talk (i.e. the quantity and quality of talk about thoughts, emotions, and desires) and children's ToM in early childhood (for meta-analysis: Devine & Hughes, 2018). Mental-state talk is hypothesized to be a dyadic phenomenon in which partners influence each other, and it is therefore plausible that children's ToM influences the way in which parents talk to their children (Dunn, 1996). For instance, parents may use more mental-state talk if they think their child is adept at understanding others' thoughts and feelings. Alternatively, parents may not feel the need to reference mental states explicitly if they think their child understands others' minds. Indirect support for child-driven effects on mental-state talk comes from studies indicating that mothers' mental-state talk changes depending on children's ToM development (e.g. Jenkins et al., 2003). Mothers not only tend to use more mental terms as children get older, but also refer to more complex categories of mental states (e.g. typically cognitions vs. desires), mirroring the increase in children's chances of understanding mental utterances (Adrián et al., 2007; Taumoepeau & Ruffman, 2008).

Direct support for the influence of children's ToM on parent–child interactions comes from longitudinal studies examining children's early ToM and parents' later mental-state talk. In one study, Ruffman et al. (2002) compared the strength of association between early parental mental-state talk at age 3 and later child ToM at age 4 with the association between early child ToM at age 3 and later parental mental-state talk at age 4. Challenging the view that children's ToM influences parent–child interactions, their analyses supported a unidirectional developmental association between early exposure to parental mental-state talk and later child ToM but not vice versa. Further examination of the links between individual differences in children's ToM and parents' later use of mental-state talk, using autoregressive cross-lagged or latent trajectory models, is needed to rule out child-driven effects on parent–child interactions (Devine & Hughes, 2018; Berry & Willoughby, 2017).

3.3.2 Sibling interactions

Moving beyond parent–child interactions, a considerable body of literature has sought to investigate the links between ToM and child–sibling interactions (Dunn,

2008; White & Hughes, 2017). The so-called 'sibling effect' suggests that children develop an understanding of others' minds through interactions with siblings (Peterson, 2000). Meta-analysis of 45 studies of children aged between 3 and 7 years suggests that there is a small but significant advantage in ToM for children with siblings, and for children with child-aged siblings in particular (Devine & Hughes, 2018). The evidence from middle childhood is sparse but indicates that having siblings is not associated with ToM performance (e.g. Miller, 2013).

Individual differences in ToM can in turn shape children's social interactions with siblings. For example, Hughes and Ensor (2005) showed that individual differences in young children's ToM was positively associated with parent-rated affection, comforting and concern, and helping and teaching between siblings, independently of children's age and language ability (Hughes & Ensor, 2005). Observational research has revealed two features of sibling interactions related to children's ToM development: cooperation and conflict. The sibling relationship is a fertile context for mentalizing (Hughes et al., 2007) and children who engage in frequent mental-state talk while playing at home with a sibling are more likely to participate in forms of coordinated (Hughes, 2011; Hughes et al., 2006) and joint pretend play in which they discuss roles and co-construct fantasy (Hughes, 2011; Hughes & Dunn, 1997; Howe et al., 1998).

Children's ToM is also important for another core dimension of child–sibling relationships: conflict (White and Hughes, 2017). Superior ToM performance in early childhood has been associated with low levels of observed conflict in child–sibling interactions (Cutting & Dunn, 2006). Foote and Holmes-Lonergan (2003) investigated the relations between the *type of argument* (i.e. other-oriented argument, self-oriented argument, and no use of argument) and mental-state talk during conflictual conversations between siblings. Children who scored higher on ToM tasks used a greater proportion of other-oriented strategies than children with lower ToM performance.

Studies examining the transition to siblinghood have illuminated the developmental importance of ToM for sibling interactions. Starting from the premise that there are strong individual differences in how children react to the arrival of a baby sibling (Volling, 2012), Song and Volling (2018) showed that ToM helps firstborn children adjust to this important life event and prevents the formation of conflictual sibling relationships. Their longitudinal research showed that the firstborn's ToM prior to the birth of a sibling positively predicted sibling engagement when the sibling was 4 months old (Song & Volling, 2018). Moreover, high levels of ToM among firstborn children when their sibling was 4 months old predicted lower levels of antagonistic sibling interactions when their sibling was 12 months old (Song et al., 2016). These results provide important insights into how ToM shapes children's social interactions with their siblings and, ultimately, the quality of sibling relationships.

The findings reported in this section suggest that, in addition to being shaped by early family social interactions (e.g. Devine & Hughes, 2018), individual differences in ToM in early childhood may underpin specific aspects of social interactions with family members. The majority of studies on ToM and social interaction in the family are informed by social constructivist accounts of mindreading (e.g. Carpendale & Lewis, 2006; Heyes & Frith, 2014), which focus on the social origins of ToM. This means that most studies have focused on how family social interactions give rise to the emergence of ToM in early childhood but not how ToM shapes family interactions. This section highlights the need for further study to investigate how ToM contributes to children's social interactions in the family in both early and middle childhood.

3.4 Theory of Mind and social interaction outside the family

The transition to formal education is accompanied by a widening of children's social horizons. In this section, we consider how ToM contributes to children's social interactions at school.

3.4.1 Social competence and prosocial behaviour

The first studies to investigate the impact of ToM on children's social interactions examined the relations between ToM and broadband measures of teacher-rated social competence. Several studies have documented weak-to-moderate associations between individual differences in ToM and teacher ratings of children's social competence, even when differences in age and language ability were controlled (e.g. Barreto et al., 2017; Lalonde & Chandler, 1995; Watson et al., 1999). In contrast, others have failed to show any unique association between ToM and teacher-rated social competence in early or middle childhood (e.g. Astington, 2003; Longobardi et al., 2016; Ronald et al., 2006). General measures of social competence, which encompass both intentional (i.e. behaviours requiring insight into others' minds) and conventional (i.e. the degree to which children follow the rules of acceptable social conduct) behaviours, may explain the inconsistent findings (Peterson et al., 2016). Reflecting this view, studies indicate that individual differences in ToM in early and middle childhood correlate moderately with teacher ratings of social interaction skills involved in forming and maintaining peer relations (e.g. convincing others, leading others, understanding the needs of others) even when age and language ability are considered (Peterson et al., 2007; Peterson et al., 2016). It is therefore imperative to focus on those social behaviours that require insights about others' minds.

The majority of studies examining the links between ToM and teacher-rated social competence have adopted cross-sectional designs. There are at least three ways to interpret associations between ToM and indicators of social competence. First, ToM might set the stage for the development of later social interaction behaviours. Second, positive social interactions with peers might provide a training ground for the development of insights about others' minds. Third, ToM and social competence may exhibit reciprocal developmental associations such that early ToM could give rise to positive social interactions, which in turn provide a fertile ground for the further development of ToM. Longitudinal designs, and more specifically cross-lagged designs, permit researchers to examine the developmental direction of detected associations between ToM and social interaction (Menard, 2002).

In one study, Razza and Blair (2009) tracked 68 children from preschool to kindergarten, and obtained measures of ToM and teacher-rated social competence (in addition to covariates such as language ability). There were moderate within-time correlations between ToM and social competence in preschool and in kindergarten. Longitudinal analyses revealed bidirectional associations between ToM and teacher-rated social competence (even when the effects of age, language ability, and prior scores were considered). In a second study, Devine et al, (2016) tracked 137 children from the first year of primary school (age 6) to the final year of primary school (age 10) obtaining measures of ToM and teacher-rated social competence. Longitudinal modelling revealed a unidirectional association between initial ToM and later social competence such that individual differences in ToM at age 6 uniquely predicted social competence at age 10 (above language ability and executive function) but not vice versa. These studies suggest that there is a unique developmental association between ToM and teacher-rated social competence in early and middle childhood but that the nature of this association might change in middle childhood.

Numerous studies have investigated the relations between children's ToM and prosocial behaviour—that is, voluntary behaviours that benefit others (Eisenberg et al., 2015). In a meta-analysis of 76 studies representing 6,432 children aged between 2 and 12, Imuta et al. (2016) examined the relations between ToM (measured using both affective understanding and cognitive understanding tasks) and prosocial behaviour (defined as helping, comforting, sharing, and cooperation). There was a modest association between ToM and prosocial behaviour ($r = .19$) suggesting that ToM contributes to, but does not entirely explain, prosocial behaviour. Interestingly, the relation between ToM and spontaneous prosocial behaviour (i.e. unprompted acts of helping, comforting, and cooperating) was greater than that between ToM and prompted prosocial behaviour (i.e. instances where children were requested to help, comfort, or cooperate). Moreover, the relations between ToM and helping, comforting and cooperating were stronger than the relation between ToM and sharing. ToM may therefore only be implicated when children are required to read another person's intent (e.g. attempting but failing to open a door) or detect another person's mistaken beliefs (e.g. picking up something someone has dropped without knowing) rather than carrying out behaviours to satisfy norms of good conduct. Caputi, Lecce, and colleagues examined the relations between ToM and prosocial behaviour in Italian children over the transition to primary school and found that individual differences in ToM at age 5 predicted prosocial behaviour at age 6 (Caputi et al, 2012). These findings point to a possible developmental relation between ToM and later prosocial behaviour, and highlight the need for future research to investigate this issue more deeply.

3.4.2 Peer status

How children are viewed by their peers is an important indicator of the success (or otherwise) of children's social interactions in early and middle childhood. Sociometric techniques, which involve asking children to rate their peers on various indicators of social behaviour or to nominate the peers they like most or least, have been used for almost a century by developmental researchers to gain insight into children's social interactions (Cillessen & Marks, 2017). The role of ToM in predicting children's peer status (i.e. the degree to which a child is liked or disliked by peers) has been investigated for nearly two decades. To investigate this hypothesis, Slaughter et al. (2015) conducted a meta-analysis integrating the results of 20 independent studies based on 2,096 children aged between 2 and 10 years, and reported a modest association between children's ToM and peer-rated popularity.

It is worth noting that the heterogeneity of the studies included in the meta-analysis meant that the effects of confounding variables (e.g. language ability), and direction of associations between peer status and ToM were not examined. However, several studies have shown unique concurrent associations between individual differences in ToM and peer status when controlling for language ability (e.g. Braza et al., 2009; Caputi et al, 2012). Stronger claims about the importance of the role of individual differences in ToM for children's peer status comes from longitudinal studies. Individual differences in ToM at age 5 predicted social competence at age 7, as indexed by peer acceptance and teacher ratings (questionnaire assessing social maturity and conduct problems) (Lecce et al, 2017b). Banerjee et al. (2011) followed two cohorts of British children over a period of two years and reported a bidirectional longitudinal association between ToM and children's peer status. These results suggest a developmental association between ToM and peer status in middle childhood. Further work is needed to determine whether the nature of the relations between ToM and peer acceptance changes across early and middle childhood.

3.4.3 Friendships

Children's ToM predicts both the quality of interactions between friends (i.e. pretend play and conflict-negotiation strategies; Maguire & Dunn, 1997; Dunn, 1999) and the ability to form and maintain close friendships. Peterson and Siegal (2002) showed that 4-year-old pre-schoolers with at least one reciprocated friend (i.e. when two friends both select each other as their friend when asked to identify their best friend) scored higher on ToM than their peers who had none, controlling for language ability and, crucially, for group peer status. More recently, Fink et al. (2015) showed that individual differences in ToM at age 5 predicted the likelihood of having a reciprocated friendship both at the start of school and longitudinally from age 5 to age 7.

Another important way children's ToM affects the quality of friendships is through variation in the content (i.e. mental versus non-mental) and the quality (i.e. connected versus unconnected) of conversational interactions between friends. Detailed observations of children's interactions with their friends show that children with superior ToM are more likely than their peers to engage in intimate and connected conversations about thoughts, feelings, and desires with their friends (e.g. Hughes & Dunn, 1998). While these studies have incorporated longitudinal elements, cross-lagged studies including measures of ToM and interactions with friends at two time points have yet to be undertaken. The developmental nature of the relations between ToM and the nature of friendship interactions remains unclear.

The evidence reported here sheds light on the nature of the associations between ToM and social interaction in early and middle childhood. It is clear that the ability to reason about others' minds is not *necessary* for all forms of social interaction (e.g. Astington, 2003). Our review shows that there are unique associations between ToM and certain specific forms of 'intentional' social interaction in the family (e.g. cooperation, conflict resolution with siblings) and at school (e.g. convincing peers, leading, and cooperating with peers) but not with other forms of social interaction, which arguably reflect the acquisition of social rules (e.g. compliance with social conventions). Future studies will benefit from adopting a fine-grained approach to understanding the relations between ToM and specific aspects of intentional social interaction. For example, authors have reported unique associations between individual differences in ToM and children's persuasiveness in social communication (Peterson et al., 2018) and in metaphor interpretation (Lecce et al., 2019). Taken together, the evidence reported in this chapter helps to refine claims about the relations between ToM and social interaction in early and middle childhood.

3.5 Theoretical implications

We began by introducing the 'social individual differences' perspective on ToM (Apperly, 2012). Rather than being a formal account of ToM, the social individual differences perspective refers to a widely held assumption within the literature that individual differences in ToM matter for children's social lives (e.g. Hughes, 2011). We now examine the theoretical implications of the evidence we have presented in this chapter, and propose a theoretical framework to guide future research on the relations between ToM and social interaction.

Earlier, we highlighted evidence that individual differences in ToM are genuine (i.e. not simply explained by other cognitive factors) and relatively stable over time (e.g. Hughes & Devine, 2015). The presence of unique associations between individual differences in ToM and a range of social interaction behaviours and social outcomes (even when factors such as language ability and executive function are considered) supports the view that individual differences in ToM are socially meaningful (e.g. Hughes, 2011). This is not to say that ToM allows only positive forms of social interactions. At this point, it is important to emphasize that ToM is a socially neutral tool that can be used in positive (e.g. cooperation, helping) or negative (e.g. lying, bullying) social interactions. Whether or not ToM is deployed for positive or negative outcomes reflects underlying social goals and motivations (Arsenio & Lemerise, 2001). If children wish to develop and maintain friendly interactions, their ability to reason about others' perspectives may be used for prosocial behaviour and attempts to achieve equitable resolutions. Alternatively, if children wish to dominate others, they may instead use their ToM to manipulate others and gain the upper hand. Moreover, children's propensity to use their understanding of others' minds at all may reflect differences in social motivation (i.e. the degree to which someone finds social interactions pleasurable and rewarding; Cragg & Chevalier, 2012). Children who have the ability to understand others' thoughts and feelings may not be motivated to use their insights about others' minds to engage in successful social interactions.

The ability to reason about others' minds is clearly not *sufficient* to engage in social interaction (Apperly, 2012; Astington, 2003). There is a profound difference between *having* and *using* an ability, and we cannot assume that children will always use their ToM in the same way across different social situations and with different social partners (Hughes, 2011). Individual differences in ToM task performance may reflect variation in ability, sensitivity, or motivation to use insights about others' minds (Hughes & Devine, 2015). Researchers should therefore adopt a more comprehensive view when looking at the social consequences of individual differences in ToM. We propose that researchers consider how children use their insights about others' minds in real-life contexts (e.g. Caputi et al, 2012).

The modest associations reported in this chapter may reflect the fact that key child characteristics moderate the associations between ToM and social outcomes. One obvious candidate is child gender. As children move from early to middle childhood, the social relationships of boys and girls tend to differentiate with the former being more dyadic and intimate (Geary et al., 2003; Maccoby, 2002), implying that social success for boys and girls relies on different skills. ToM performance in girls predicts high levels of cooperative interactions with caregivers and with peers but is associated with aggression towards peers in boys (Hughes et al., 2001; Walker, 2005). In middle childhood, the relations between ToM and peer acceptance, perceived loneliness, and social competence differs for boys and girls (Badenes et al., 2000; Banerjee et al, 2006; Devine & Hughes, 2013). Another potential moderator of the association between ToM and social interaction is age. Banerjee et al. (2011) reported that the effect of ToM on later peer relationships emerged after 10 years of age indicating that individual differences in ToM play a more prominent role for peer interaction once most children have mastered that skill. Furthermore, there is evidence of developmental continuity in the degree of association between ToM and teacher-rated social competence from early to middle childhood (e.g. Devine et al, 2016). In contrast, there is developmental discontinuity in the strength of the association between ToM and prosocial behaviour between early and middle childhood, with the associations between ToM and prosocial behaviour being stronger in middle childhood (Imuta et al., 2016). The moderating effects of child characteristics on the relations between ToM and social interaction require further investigation, and will clarify the role of ToM in specific social interactions.

Beyond investigating ToM in the context of specific social relationships (e.g. within the family, at school), researchers examining the relations between ToM and social interaction have paid only scant attention to the importance of context. The characteristics of social partners and the nature of the relationship with a specific partner must be considered. For example, studies indicate that children apply their understanding of mind in contrasting ways within different relationships. Preschoolers show a more advanced understanding of the causes of anger in mothers than in friends, and a more advanced understanding of the causes of sadness in friends than in mothers (Hughes & Dunn, 2002). In a similar way, children show better conflict negotiation with friends than with non-friends (Hartup et al., 1988) or with siblings (Dunn & Herrera, 1997). Furthermore, children are more inclined to consider the perspective of a friend than a sibling (Dunn et al., 1995) and of an in-group member than an out-group target (Gönültaş et al., 2020). Interestingly, the emotional quality of a relationship affects children's mindreading. For example, O'Connor and Hirsch (1999) found that adolescents refer more frequently to mental states when interviewed about teachers they liked than teachers they did not like. In a similar vein, Meins et al. (2014) posited that the proclivity to focus on mental states when describing others is a relational, rather than a trait-like, quality, which is affected by the intimacy of the particular relationship.

Greater understanding of the influence of social partners and, more generally, of social contextual features on whether or not children use their understanding of others' minds during social interactions is needed.

While there is compelling evidence for links between ToM and social outcomes, such as peer status, sibling relationship quality, or reciprocated friendships, the nature of this association remains unclear. The modest correlations between ToM and these distal social outcomes may reflect the fact that these associations are likely to be mediated by children's skilled use of specific social interaction behaviours. Supporting this hypothesis, Caputi et al. (2012) reported indirect associations between early ToM (age 5) and later peer acceptance (age 7), that were mediated by prosocial behaviour (age 6). More recently, Ronchi et al. (2019) tested a group of children (11.5 years at Time 1) three times over one year across the transition to secondary school. Results showed that ToM predicted lower levels of social anxiety over time and, in this way, higher levels of peer acceptance, as well as lower levels of peer rejection one year later. Together, these studies suggest that, in order to accrue positive social outcomes, ToM must be used for positive social interactions.

3.6 Theory of Mind in a social context

The findings reviewed in this chapter provide evidence that ToM is associated with specific social interaction behaviours and with important social outcomes in early and middle childhood. To elaborate on earlier assumptions about the importance of ToM for children's social lives, we propose a framework—the Theory of Mind in Social Context framework—to explain the relations between ToM and social interaction (see Fig. 3.1). The framework proposes underlying mechanisms and emphasizes the moderating role of contextual factors. It makes testable predictions and provides directions for future research.

The first set of predictions concern the relations between ToM and social interaction behaviours. We predict that individual differences in ToM will support a finite set of specific social interaction behaviours. ToM will be specifically implicated in the development of those behaviours needed to engage in social interactions that require understanding others' perspectives, thoughts, emotions, and desires, rather than social interactions based on following explicit rules or social conventions. It is unlikely that ToM will be sufficient for the emergence of these social interaction behaviours, and we acknowledge that other child characteristics (e.g. gender, age, motivation, language ability) and prior social experiences will shape these behaviours. We predict that specific child characteristics, such as gender and age, will moderate the association between ToM and social interaction. From a methodological point of view, the study of moderators highlights the need to recruit samples that are large enough to capture variation in task performance within a specific group (Devine, in press). More generally, researchers seeking to

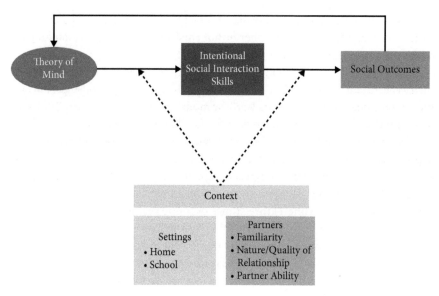

Fig. 3.1 Theory of Mind in a social context framework

elucidate the relations between ToM and social interactions should pay special attention to the nature of the tasks used to test both ToM and social behaviour. As far as ToM is concerned, although studies adopting batteries of ToM tasks indicate that performance across a range of different tasks can be explained by a single underlying latent factor (Devine & Hughes, 2013; Devine & Hughes, 2016; Devine et al., 2016; Lecce et al., 2017b), it is possible that there are associations between specific domains of mindreading (e.g. such as perspective taking, belief-emotion reasoning, false belief) and social interaction behaviours. Related to this point, future work will benefit from careful consideration of the measurement issues involved in capturing meaningful differences in social interaction behaviours. Rather than relying on peer or adult informants, structured observations of cooperation with unfamiliar peers, for example, can provide a window on individual differences in different facets of social interaction behaviour (Usher et al., 2015; Walker et al., 2015). Similarly, the moderating effects of social context on the relations between ToM and social interaction behaviours can be examined experimentally through carefully controlled exposure to peer social rejection in online games (e.g. Leary et al., 2006).

The second set of predictions concern the relations between ToM and social outcomes. It is unlikely that children's understanding of others' minds has a direct effect on social outcomes such as friendship quality, peer acceptance, or sibling relationship quality. We predict that ToM will have an indirect effect on specific social outcomes and that this effect will be mediated in part by individual differences in children's social interaction behaviours. Moreover, we also predict that there will be direct bidirectional developmental associations between social outcomes and ToM: social outcomes (but not social interaction behaviours) will set the stage for further refinement and ongoing development of ToM.

Testing developmental theories requires the adoption of developmental research designs, including longitudinal designs and intervention studies (Bryant, 1990). Longitudinal designs will shed light on the degree to which ToM is necessary for the development of social interaction skills and successful social outcomes. The field contains several examples of cross-lagged designs (e.g. Banerjee et al., 2011; Devine et al., 2016), which have illuminated the direction of associations between ToM and social competence. The adoption of multiple time points will permit researchers to investigate the degree to which *changes* in ToM are necessary for changes in social interaction using parallel process latent growth curve modelling (Berry & Willoughby, 2017).

Intervention studies will play a crucial role in determining whether change in ToM is sufficient to produce change in social interaction and social outcomes. Several short-term interventions have been developed to improve ToM in early and middle childhood (Hofmann et al., 2016; Lecce et al., 2014a) and could be leveraged to test the causal relations between ToM and specific dimensions of social interactions. Training studies also make it possible to compare the effect of different training conditions to test hypotheses regarding the associations between distinct aspects of ToM and specific social interaction behaviours. For example, it may be possible to compare the effect of different components of ToM such as understanding beliefs and understanding emotions, by designing a belief- and an emotion-based training condition to determine which one has the larger effect on children's social interactions.

The third set of predictions concern the moderating role of context. We predict that at least two contextual factors will moderate the association between ToM, social interaction, and social outcomes. First, the setting in which social interactions occur may reduce or amplify the need for children to deploy their understanding of others' minds. For example, expectations for social behaviour differ greatly at home and at school. Children may need to use their understanding of others' minds to behave competently in a classroom but not at home. If this is the case, then the correlations between social competence and ToM will be stronger in the classroom than in the home. Second, the relations between ToM and social interaction are likely to be influenced by children's social partners. The nature of the relationship (e.g. sibling versus friend), the degree of familiarity (e.g. how long a partner has been known), the social partner's ability (e.g. whether the social partner is an adult or a younger child) and group membership (e.g. whether the social partner is a member of the in- versus out-group) will determine the degree to which one needs to deploy ToM during social interactions.

Careful manipulation of ToM paradigms may provide insights into the effect of social context on the relations between ToM and social interaction. For example, modifications to the content of the Strange Stories task (Gönültaş et al., 2020; Perez-Zapata et al., 2016) and the Eyes task (Adams et al., 2010) can alter task performance depending on whether the target of the task is an in-group or out-group member. This strategy could be extended to study of the effects of the other partner characteristics on mindreading. Naturalistic observations of children interacting with different social partners are also needed to shed light on the moderating role of context on the relations between ToM and social interaction behaviour (e.g. Hughes et al., 2007). From a methodological point of view, the focus on the context and social partner will require the adoption of innovative statistical models to account for the reciprocal nature of human interactions. The actor-partner interaction model (APIM), for example, allows researchers to isolate the impact of each partner's characteristics (e.g. ToM) on their own and their partner's social behaviour (e.g. cooperation) (Kenny et al., 2006). Recent studies taking advantage of dyadic statistical approaches have demonstrated the importance of understanding the social context of children's interactions (Gibson et al., 2020). To date, however, few researchers in the area of ToM have adopted such a dyadic perspective. One notable exception is a recent study by Huyder et al. (2017) that examined children's social interaction in a cooperative task. Interestingly, the authors showed that young children's ToM was linked to fewer competitive behaviours not only in the children themselves but also in their partners. The authors argued that this partner effect may occur because younger children with better ToM act in a manner that demonstrates consideration for the other person, which in turn causes the partner to be less competitive than they would be otherwise.

3.7 Conclusions

Throughout this chapter, we have synthesized a fast-growing body of literature on the relations between individual differences in ToM and social interaction in early and middle childhood. Starting from the widely held assumption that ToM matters for children's social success (e.g. Hughes, 2011; Apperly, 2012), we have evaluated findings on children's social interactions within and outside the family. The evidence indicates that a) ToM is related to some, but not all, aspects of social interaction and social outcomes; b) the relation between ToM and social outcomes is likely to be mediated by intentional social interaction skills; c) and the link between ToM and social interaction is likely to be moderated by child factors and contextual variables. This review highlights the need to adopt a nuanced perspective on the role of ToM in children's social lives in early and middle childhood. We have proposed the Theory of Mind in Social Context framework to make novel and testable predictions about a) the processes through which ToM has an impact on social outcomes; and b) the circumstances in which an association between ToM and social interaction should be apparent. The integrative framework sets an agenda for future research by emphasizing (a) the mediating role of intentional social interaction behaviours in explaining the relations between ToM and social outcomes; and (b) the moderating role of partner-related variables (including familiarity, the nature and quality of the relationship, and the level of partner ToM ability) and of settings in strengthening or attenuating the relations between ToM and social interaction.

References

Adams, R. B., Jr., Rule, N., Franklin, R. G., Jr., Wang, E., Stevenson, M. T., Yoshikawa, S., . . . & Ambady, N., 2010. 'Cross-cultural reading the mind in the eyes: An fMRI investigation'. *Journal of Cognitive Neuroscience* 22: 97–108.

Adrián, J. E., Clemente, R. A., & Villanueva, L., 2007. 'Mothers' use of cognitive state verbs in picture-book reading and the development of children's understanding of mind: A longitudinal study'. *Child Development* 78. 4: 1052–1067.

Apperly, I. A. 2011. Mindreaders: the cognitive basis of theory of mind. Psychology Press.

Apperly, I. A., 2012. 'What is "theory of mind"? Concepts, cognitive processes and individual differences'. *Quarterly Journal of Experimental Psychology* 65. 5: 825–839.

Arsenio, W. F., & Lemerise, E. A., 2001. 'Varieties of childhood bullying: Values, emotion processes, and social competence'. *Social Development* 10. 1: 59–73.

Astington, J. W., 2003. 'Sometimes necessary, never sufficient: False-belief understanding and social competence'. In *Individual Differences in Theory of Mind*, edited by B. Repacholi & V. Slaughter. Psychology Press.

Astington, J. W., & Jenkins, J. M., 1999. 'A longitudinal study of the relation between language and theory-of-mind development'. *Developmental Psychology* 35. 5: 1311–1320.

Badenes, L. V., Clemente Estevan, R. A., & García Bacete, F. J., 2000. 'Theory of mind and peer rejection at school'. *Social Development* 9. 3: 271–283.

Banerjee, R., Watling, D., & Caputi, M., 2011. 'Peer relations and the understanding of faux pas: Longitudinal evidence for bidirectional associations'. *Child Development* 82. 6: 1887–1905.

Banerjee, R., Rieffe, C., Terwogt, M. M., Gerlein, A. M., & Voutsina, M., 2006. 'Popular and rejected children's reasoning regarding negative emotions in social situations: The role of gender'. *Social Development* 15. 3: 418–433.

Baron-Cohen, S. 1995. *Mindblindness: An Essay on Autism and Theory of Mind*. MIT press.

Baron-Cohen, S., Jolliffe, T., Mortimore, C., & Robertson, M., 1997. 'Another advanced test of theory of mind: Evidence from very high functioning adults with autism or asperger syndrome'. *Journal of Child Psychology and Psychiatry* 38. 7: 813–822.

Baron-Cohen, S., O'Riordan, M., Stone, V., Jones, R., & Plaisted, K., 1999. 'Recognition of faux pas by normally developing children and children with asperger syndrome or high-functioning autism'. *Journal of Autism and Developmental Disorders* 29. 5: 407–418.

Barreto, A., Dabney, W., Munos, R., Hunt, J. J., Schaul, T., van Hasselt, H. P., & Silver, D., 2017. 'Successor features for transfer in reinforcement learning'. In *Advances in Neural Information Processing Systems*, edited by I. Guyon et al. Neural Information Processing Systems Foundation, Inc.

Berry, D., & Willoughby, M. T., 2017. 'On the practical interpretability of cross-lagged panel models: Rethinking a developmental workhorse'. *Child Development* 88. 4: 1186–1206.

Bianco, F., Lecce, S., & Banerjee, R., 2016. 'Conversations about mental states and theory of mind development during middle childhood: A training study'. *Journal of Experimental Child Psychology* 149: 49–61.

Braza, F., Azurmendi, A., Munoz, J. M., Carreras, M. R., Braza, P., García, A., ... & Sánchez-Martín, J. R., 2009. 'Social cognitive predictors of peer acceptance at age 5 and the moderating effects of gender'. *British Journal of Developmental Psychology* 27. 3: 703–716.

Brownell, M. D., Nickel, N. C., Chateau, D., Martens, P. J., Taylor, C., Crockett, L., ... & Goh, C. Y. 2015. 'Long-term benefits of full-day kindergarten: A longitudinal population-based study'. *Early Child Development and Care* 185. 2: 291–316.

Bryant, P., 1990. 'Empirical evidence for causes in development'. In *Causes of Development: Interdisciplinary Perspectives*, edited by G. Butterworth & P. Bryant. Harvester Wheatstaff.

Caputi, M., Lecce, S., Pagnin, A., & Banerjee, R., 2012. 'Longitudinal effects of theory of mind on later peer relations: The role of prosocial behaviour'. *Developmental Psychology* 48. 1: 257–270.

Carpendale, J., & Lewis, C. 2006. *How Children Develop Social Understanding*. Blackwell Publishing.

Castelli, F., Happé, F., Frith, U., & Frith, C., 2000. 'Movement and mind: A functional imaging study of perception and interpretation of complex intentional movement patterns'. *NeuroImage* 12. 3: 314–325.

Cillessen, A. H. N., & Marks, P. E. L., 2017. 'Methodological choices in peer nomination research'. *New Directions for Child and Adolescent Development* 157: 21–44.

Cragg, L., & Chevalier, N., 2012. 'The processes underlying flexibility in childhood'. *Quarterly Journal of Experimental Psychology* 65. 2: 209–232.

Cutting, A. L., & Dunn, J., 2006. 'Conversations with siblings and with friends: Links between relationship quality and social understanding'. *British Journal of Developmental Psychology* 24. 1: 73–87.

Davis, P. E., Meins, E., & Fernyhough, C., 2014. 'Children with imaginary companions focus on mental characteristics when describing their real-life friends'. *Infant and Child Development* 23. 6: 622–633.

Del Giudice, M., 2014. 'Middle childhood: An evolutionary-developmental synthesis'. *Child Development Perspectives* 8. 4: 193–200.

Devine, R. T., 2021. 'Individual differences in theory of mind in middle childhood and adolescence'. In *Theory of Mind in Middle Childhood and Adolescence: Integrating Multiple Perspectives*, edited by S. Lecce & T. D. Devine. Psychology Press, pp. 55–76.

Devine, R. T., & Hughes, C., 2013. 'Silent films and strange stories: Theory of Mind, gender, and social experiences in middle childhood'. *Child Development* 84. 3: 989–1003.

Devine, R. T., & Hughes, C., 2016. 'Measuring theory of mind across middle childhood: Reliability and validity of the Silent Films and Strange Stories tasks'. *Journal of Experimental Child Psychology* 149: 23–40.

Devine, R. T., & Hughes, C., 2018. 'Family correlates of false belief understanding in early childhood: A meta-analysis'. *Child Development* 89. 3: 971–987.

Devine, R. T., White, N., Ensor, R., & Hughes, C., 2016. 'Theory of mind in middle childhood: Longitudinal associations with executive function and social competence'. *Developmental Psychology* 52. 5: 758–771.

Dumontheil, I., Apperly, I. A., & Blakemore, S. J., 2010. 'Online usage of theory of mind continues to develop in late adolescence'. *Developmental Science* 13. 2: 331–338.

Dunn, J., 1995. 'Children as psychologists: The later correlates of individual differences in understanding of emotions and other minds'. *Cognition and Emotion* 9. 2–3: 187–201.

Dunn, J., 1996. 'Family conversations and the development of social understanding'. In *Children, Research and Policy: Essays for Barbara Tizard*, edited by B. Bernstein & J. Brannen. Taylor & Francis.

Dunn, J., 1999. 'Siblings, friends, and the development of social understanding'. In *Relationships as Developmental Context: The Minnesota Symposia on Child Psychology*, edited by W. Collins & B. Laursen. Lawrence Erlbaum Associates, Inc.

Dunn, J., 2008. 'Relationships and children's discovery of the mind'. In *Social Life and Social Knowledge: Toward a Process Account of Development*, edited by U. Müller et al. Taylor & Francis Group/Lawrence Erlbaum Associates.

Dunn, J., & Herrera, C., 1997. 'Conflict resolution with friends, siblings, and mothers: A developmental perspective'. *Aggressive Behaviour* 23. 5: 343–357.

Dunn, J., Slomkowski, C., Donelan, N., & Herrera, C., 1995. 'Conflict, understanding, and relationships: Developments and differences in the preschool years'. *Early Education and Development* 6. 4: 303–316.

Dunn, J., Brown, J., Slomkowski, C., Tesla, C., & Youngblade, L., 1991. 'Young children's understanding of other people's feelings and beliefs: Individual differences and their antecedents'. *Child Development* 62. 6: 1352–1366.Eisenberg, N., Spinrad, T. L., & Knafo-Noam, A., 2015. 'Prosocial development'. In *Handbook of Child Psychology and Developmental Science: Socioemotional Processes*, edited by M. E. Lamb & R. M. Lerner. John Wiley & Sons Inc.

Fink, E., Begeer, S., Peterson, C. C., & Slaughter, V., 2015. 'Friends, friendlessness, and the social consequences of gaining a theory of mind'. *British Journal of Developmental Psychology* 33. 1: 27–30.

Foote, R. C., & Holmes-Lonergan, H., 2003. 'Sibling conflict and theory of mind'. *British Journal of Developmental Psychology* 21. 1: 45–58.

Geary, D. C., Byrd-Craven, J., Hoard, M. K., Vigil, J., & Numtee, C., 2003. 'Evolution and development of boys' social behaviour'. *Developmental Review* 23. 4: 444–470.

Gibson, J. L., Fink, E., Torres, P. E., Browne, W. V., & Mareva, S., 2020. 'Making sense of social pretense: The effect of the dyad, sex, and language ability in a large observational study of children's behaviors in a social pretend play context'. *Social Development* 29. 2: 526–543.

Gönültaş, S., Selçuk, B., Slaughter, V., Hunter, J. A., & Ruffman, T., 2020. 'The capricious nature of theory of mind: Does mental state understanding depend on the characteristics of the target?'. *Child Development* 91. 2: 280–298.

Gopnik, A., & Astington, J., 1988. 'Children's understanding of representational change and its relation to the understanding of false belief and the appearance-reality distinction'. *Child Development* 59. 1: 26–37.

Happé, F., 1994. 'An advanced test of theory-of-mind: Understanding of story characters' thoughts and feelings by able autistic, mentally handicapped and normal children and adults'. *Journal of Autism and Developmental Disorders* 24. 2: 129–154.

Harris, P. L., Johnson, C., Hutton, D., Andrews, G., & Cooke, T., 1989. 'Young children's theory of mind and emotion'. *Cognition and Emotion* 3. 4: 379–400.

Hartup, W. W., Laursen, B., Stewart, M. I., & Eastenson, A., 1988. 'Conflict and the friendship relations of young children'. *Child Development* 59. 6: 1590–1600.

Hay, D. F., Payne, A., & Chadwick, A., 2004. 'Peer relations in childhood'. *Journal of Child Psychology and Psychiatry* 45. 1: 84–108.

Heyes, C. M., & Frith, C. D., 2014. 'The cultural evolution of mind reading'. *Science* 344. 6190: 1357.

Hofmann, S. G., Doan, S. N., Sprung, M., Wilson, A., Ebesutani, C., Andrews, L. A., ... & Harris, P. L., 2016. 'Training children's theory-of-mind: A meta-analysis of controlled studies'. *Cognition* 150: 200–212.

Howe, N., Petrakos, H., & Rinaldi, C. M., 1998. '"All the sheeps are dead. He murdered them": Sibling pretense, negotiation, internal state language, and relationship quality'. *Child Development* 69. 1: 182–191.

Huber, L., Plötner, M., & Schmitz, J., 2019. 'Social competence and psychopathology in early childhood: A systematic review'. *European Child and Adolescent Psychiatry* 28. 4: 443–459.

Hughes, C. 2011. *Social Understanding and Social Lives. From Toddlerhood through to the Transition to School*. Psychology Press.

Hughes, C., 2016. 'Theory of mind grows up: Reflections on new research on theory of mind in middle childhood and adolescence'. *Journal of Experimental Child Psychology* 149: 1–5.Hughes, C., & Devine, R. T., 2015. 'Individual differences in Theory of Mind from pre-school to adolescence: Achievements and directions'. *Child Development Perspectives* 9. 3: 149–153.

Hughes, C., & Dunn, J., 1997. 'Pretend you didn't know': Preschoolers' talk about mental states in pretend play'. *Cognitive Development* 12. 4: 477–499.

Hughes, C., & Dunn, J., 1998. 'Understanding mind and emotion: Longitudinal associations with mental-state talk between young friends'. *Developmental Psychology* 34. 5: 1026–1037.

Hughes, C., & Dunn, J., 2002. '"When I say a naughty word". A longitudinal study of young children's accounts of anger and sadness in themselves and close others'. *British Journal of Developmental Psychology* 20. 4: 515–535.

Hughes, C., & Ensor, R., 2005. 'Executive Function and Theory of Mind in 2 year olds: A family affair?'. *Developmental Neuropsychology* 28. 2: 645–668.

Hughes, C., & Leekam, S., 2004. 'What are the links between theory of mind and social relations? Review, reflections and new directions for studies of typical and atypical development'. *Social Development* 13. 4: 590–619.

Hughes, C., Deater-Deckard, K., & Cutting, A. L., 2001. 'Speak roughly to your little boy'? Sex differences in the relations between parenting and preschoolers' understanding of mind'. *Social Development* 8. 2: 143–160.

Hughes, C., Lecce, S., & Wilson, C., 2007. '"Do you know what I want?" Preschoolers' talk about desires, thoughts and feelings in their conversations with sibs and friends'. *Cognition and Emotion* 21. 2: 330–350.

Hughes, C., Fujisawa, K., Ensor, R., Lecce, S., & Marfleet, R., 2006. 'Cooperation and conversations about the mind: A study of individual differences in two-year-olds and their siblings'. *British Journal of Developmental Psychology* 24. 1: 53–72.

Hughes, C., Adlam, A., Happé, F., Jackson, J., Taylor, A., & Caspi, A., 2000. 'Good test-retest reliability for standard and advanced false-belief tasks across a wide range of abilities'. *Journal of Child Psychology and Psychiatry* 41. 4: 483–490.

Huyder, V., Nilsen, E. S., & Bacso, S. A., 2017. 'The relationship between children's executive functioning, theory of mind, and verbal skills with their own and others' behaviour in a cooperative context: Changes in relations from early to middle school-age'. *Infant and Child Development* 26. 6: e2027.

Imuta, K., Henry, J. D., Slaughter, V., Selcuk, B., & Ruffman, T., 2016. 'Theory of mind and prosocial behaviour in childhood: A meta-analytic review'. *Developmental Psychology* 52. 8: 1192–1205.

Jenkins, J. M., Turrell, S. L., Kogushi, Y., Lollis, S., & Ross, H. S., 2003. 'A longitudinal investigation of the dynamics of mental state talk in families'. *Child Development* 74. 3: 905–920.

Kenny, D. A., Kashy, D. A., & Cook, W. L. 2006. *Dyadic Data Analysis*. Guilford Press.

Kramer, L., & Kowal, A. K., 2005. 'Sibling relationship quality from birth to adolescence: the enduring contributions of friends'. *Journal of Family Psychology* 19. 4: 503–511.

Ladd, G. W., Herald-Brown, S. L., & Reiser, M., 2008. 'Does chronic classroom peer rejection predict the development of childrens classroom participation during the grade school years?'. *Child Development* 79. 4: 1001–1015.

Lagattuta, K. H., Elrod, N. M., & Kramer, H. J., 2016. 'How do thoughts, emotions, and decisions align? A new way to examine theory of mind during middle childhood and beyond'. *Journal of Experimental Child Psychology* 149: 116–133.

Lalonde, C. E., & Chandler, M. J., 1995. 'False belief understanding goes to school: On the social-emotional consequences of coming early or late to a first theory of mind'. *Cognition and Emotion* 9. 2–3: 167–185.

Leary, M. R., Twenge, J. M., & Quinlivan, E., 2006. 'Interpersonal rejection as a determinant of anger and aggression'. *Personality and Social Psychology Review* 10. 2: 111–132.

Lecce, S., Caputi, M., & Pagnin, A., 2014. 'Long-term effect of theory of mind on school achievement: The role of sensitivity to criticism'. *European Journal of Developmental Psychology* 11. 3: 305–318.

Lecce, S., Bianco, F., Devine, R., & Hughes, C., 2017b. 'Relations between ToM and EF in middle childhood: A short-term longitudinal study'. *Journal of Experimental Child Psychology*, 163: 69–86.

Lecce, S., Caputi, M., Pagnin, A., & Banerjee, R., 2017a. 'Theory of mind and school achievement: The mediating role of social competence'. *Cognitive Development* 44: 85–97.

Lecce, S., Bianco, F., Devine, R. T., Hughes, C., & Banerjee, R., 2014a. 'Promoting theory of mind during middle childhood: A training program'. *Journal of Experimental Child Psychology* 126: 52–67.Lecce, S., Ronchi, L., Del Sette, P., Bischetti, L., & Bambini, V., 2019. 'Interpreting physical and mental metaphors: Is theory of mind associated with pragmatics in middle childhood?' *Journal of Child Language* 46. 2: 393–407.

Lecce, S., Zocchi, S., Pagnin, A., Palladino, P., & Taumoepeau, M., 2010. 'Reading minds: The relation between children's mental state knowledge and their metaknowledge about reading'. *Child Development* 81. 6: 1876–1893.

Longobardi, E., Spataro, P., Frigerio, A., & Rescorla, L., 2016. 'Gender differences in the relationship between language and social competence in preschool children'. *Infant Behaviour & Development* 43: 1–4.

Maccoby, E. E., 2002. 'Gender and group process: A developmental perspective'. *Current Directions in Psychological Science* 11. 2: 54–58.

Maguire, M. C., & Dunn, J., 1997. 'Friendships in early childhood, and social understanding'. *International Journal of Behavioural Development* 21. 4: 669–686.

Meins, E., Fernyhough, C., & Harris-Waller, J., 2014. 'Is mind-mindedness trait-like or a quality of close relationships? Evidence from descriptions of significant others, famous people, and works of art'. *Cognition* 130. 3: 417–427.

Menard, S. 2002. *Longitudinal Research*. Sage.

Miller, S. A. 2013. *Theory of Mind: Beyond the Preschool Years*. Psychology Press.

O' Connor, T. G., & Hirsch, N., 1999. 'Intra-individual differences and relationship-specificity of mentalising in early adolescence'. *Social Development* 8. 2: 256–274.

OECD (Organisation for Economic Co-operation and Development), 2018. *Education at a Glance 2018: OECD Indicators*. OECD Publishing.

Perez-Zapata, D., Slaughter, V., & Henry, J., 2016. 'Cultural effects on mindreading'. *Cognition* 146: 410–414.

Perner, J., & Lang, B., 2000. 'Theory of mind and executive function: Is there a developmental relationship?' In *Understanding Other Minds: Perspectives from Developmental Cognitive Neuroscience*, edited by S. Baron-Cohen et al. Oxford University Press.

Perner, J., & Wimmer, H., 1985. 'John thinks that Mary thinks that ...' Attribution of second-order beliefs by 5- to 10-year-old children'. *Journal of Experimental Child Psychology* 39. 3: 437–471.

Perner, J., Leekam, S. R., & Wimmer, H., 1987. 'Three year-olds' difficulty with false belief: The case for a conceptual deficit'. *British Journal of Developmental Psychology* 5. 2: 125–137.

Peterson, C. C., 2000. 'Influence of siblings' perspectives on theory of mind'. *Cognitive Development* 15. 4: 435–455.

Peterson, C. C., & Siegal, M., 2002. 'Mindreading and moral awareness in popular and rejected preschoolers'. *British Journal of Developmental Psychology* 20. 2: 205–224.

Peterson, C. C., & Wellman, H. M., 2019. 'Longitudinal theory of mind (ToM) development from preschool to adolescence with and without tom delay'. *Child Development* 90. 6: 1917–1934.

Peterson, C. C., Slaughter, V. P., & Paynter, J., 2007. 'Social maturity and theory of mind in typically developing children and those on the autism spectrum'. *Journal of Child Psychology and Psychiatry* 48. 12: 1243–1250.

Peterson, C. C., Slaughter, V., & Wellman, H., M. 2018. 'Nimble negotiators: How theory of mind (ToM) interconnects with persuasion skills in children with and without ToM delay'. *Developmental Psychology* 54. 3: 494–509.Peterson, C., Slaughter, V., Moore, C., & Wellman, H. M., 2016. 'Peer social skills and theory of mind in children with autism, deafness, or typical development'. *Developmental Psychology* 52. 1: 46–57.

Premack, D., & Woodruff, G., 1978. 'Does the chimpanzee have a theory of mind?'. *Behavioural and Brain Sciences* 1. 4: 515–526.

Ratcliffe, M., 2007. 'From folk psychology to commonsense'. In *Folk Psychology Re-Assessed*, edited by D. D. Hutto & M. Ratcliff. Springer.

Raver, C. C., & Zigler, E. F., 1997. 'Social competence: An untapped dimension of head start's success'. In *Review of Child Development Research*, edited by L. W. Hoffman & M. Hoffman. University of Chicago Press.

Razza, R. A., & Blair, C., 2009. 'Associations among false-belief understanding, executive function, and social competence: A longitudinal analysis.' *Journal of Applied Developmental Psychology* 30. 3: 332–343.

Ronald, A., Viding, E., Happé, F., & Plomin, R., 2006. 'Individual differences in theory of mind ability in middle childhood and links with verbal ability and autistic traits: A twin study'. *Social Neuroscience* 1. 3–4: 412–425.

Ronchi, L., Banerjee, R., & Lecce, S., 2019. 'ToM and peer relationships: the role of social anxiety'. *Social Development* 29. 2: 478–493.

Rubin, K. H., Bukowski, W. M., & Bowker, J. C., 2015. 'Children in peer groups'. In *Handbook of Child Psychology and Developmental Science, Ecological Settings and Processes*, edited by R. M. Lerner et al. John Wiley & Sons.

Ruffman, T., Slade, L., & Crowe, E., 2002. 'The relation between children's and mothers' mental state language and theory-of-mind understanding'. *Child Development* 73. 3: 734–751.

Russell, J. 1996. *Agency: Its Role in Mental Development*. Lawrence Erlbaum Associates, Ltd.

Rydell, A., Hagekull, B., & Bohlin, G., 1997. 'Measurement of two social competence aspects in middle childhood'. *Developmental Psychology* 33. 5: 824–833.

Slaughter, V., Imuta, K., Peterson, C. C., & Henry, J. D., 2015. 'Meta-analysis of theory of mind and peer popularity in the preschool and early school years'. *Child Development* 86. 4: 1159–1174.

Song, J. H., & Volling, B. L., 2018. 'Theory-of-Mind development and early sibling relationships after the birth of a sibling: Parental discipline matters'. *Infant and Child Development* 27. 1: e2053.

Song, J. H., Volling, B. L., Lane, J. D., & Wellman, H. M., 2016. 'Aggression, sibling antagonism, and theory of mind during the first year of siblinghood: A developmental cascade model'. *Child Development* 87. 4: 1250–1263.

Taumoepeau, M., & Ruffman, T., 2008. 'Stepping stones to others' minds: Maternal Talk relates to child mental state language and emotion understanding at 15, 24, and 33 months'. *Child Development* 79. 2: 284–302.

Usher, L. V., Burrows, C. A., Schwartz, C. B., & Henderson, H. A., 2015. 'Social competence with an unfamiliar peer in children and adolescents with high functioning autism: Measurement and individual differences'. *Research in Autism Spectrum Disorders*, 17: 25–39.

Volling, B. L., 2012. 'Family transitions following the birth of a sibling: An empirical review of changes in the firstborn's adjustment'. *Psychological Bulletin* 138. 3: 497–528.

Walker, O. L., Degnan, K. A., Fox, N. A., & Henderson, H. A., 2015. 'Early social fear in relation to play with an unfamiliar peer: actor and partner effects'. *Developmental Psychology*, 51: 1588–1596.

Walker, S., 2005. 'Gender differences in the relationship between young children's peer-related social competence and individual differences in Theory of Mind'. *Journal of Genetic Psychology* 166. 3: 297–312.

Watson, A. C., Nixon, C. L., Wilson, A., and Capage, L., 1999. 'Social interaction skills and theory of mind in young children'. *Developmental Psychology* 35. 2: 386–391.

Wellman, H. M., & Liu, D., 2004. 'Scaling of theory-of-mind tasks'. *Child Development* 75. 2: 523–541.

Wellman, H. M., Cross, D., & Watson, J., 2001. 'Meta-analysis of theory-of-mind development: The truth about false belief'. *Child Development* 72. 3: 655–684.

White, N., & Hughes, C. 2017. *Why Siblings Matter: The Role of Brother and Sister Relationships in Development and Wellbeing*. Psychology Press.

Wimmer, H., & Perner, J., 1983. 'Beliefs about beliefs: Representation and constraining function of wrong beliefs in young children's understanding of deception'. *Cognition* 13. 1: 103–128.

4
Development of Social Cognition in Adolescence and the Importance of Mating

Sarah Donaldson and Kathryn Mills

4.1 Introduction

Adolescence is a time of intense changes in biology, cognition, behaviour, and social contexts (Burke et al., 2017). A primary function of adolescence is to master the social complexities of humans, a main tenant of which includes navigating romantic relationship dynamics. Despite the clear necessity for acquiring the skills to successfully mate during this time of reproductive development, current developmental cognitive literature lacks a framework for understanding how social cognitive development benefits mating psychology during adolescence.

Beginning with puberty, vast biological changes occur that are critical for the development of social, emotional, and cognitive maturation as it relates to romantic and sexual experiences. This chapter will highlight aspects of social cognitive development in adolescence, including underlying neurological changes, in which a mating-focused perspective could improve our understanding of the interrelated dynamics of this period of life. Indeed, the formation of romantic relationships and new sexual experiences comprise a large part of the adolescent experience, and underlying cognitive processes, such as sexual attraction/arousal, interpretation of others' intentions or emotions, sensitivity to social feedback, and various aspects of executive functioning, likely develop concurrently that both influence and are influenced by this new social context. These various cognitive processes involved in navigating mating interactions are referred to as 'mating intelligence' (Geher et al., 2008) and have been extensively investigated in adults, yet the developmental trajectory of these processes is lacking. To achieve full *reproductive competence*, adolescents must be able to identify potential mates, practise engaging in romantic relationship experiences (including sexual experiences), and develop coping mechanisms for relationship dissolutions. While there have been many investigations focused on the risks associated with sexual activity in adolescence (Ewing et al., 2015; Victor & Hariri, 2016), few have identified the normative, healthy behaviours and cognitive mechanisms related to dating and sex that are necessary for psychological adjustment and well-being into adulthood (Suleiman et al., 2017).

4.1.1 Defining adolescence

Adolescence is often understood as the period of time between childhood and adulthood, when youths experience a vast expansion in the complexities of their social environment and undergo significant development in underlying cognitive processes. This period begins with the biological initiation of puberty, which in some can begin as early as 7–10 years old, yet the ending of adolescence varies by different organizational definitions. For example, the World Health Organization defines an 'adolescent' as anyone between the ages of 10 and 19 years old, while the term 'young person' is used for anyone between 10 and 24 years old (www.who.int). Alternatively, the American Academy of Pediatrics (AAP) uses a more inclusive definition of the adolescent age range as being between 10 and 21 years old, and this is the definition of adolescence used throughout this chapter. We also use AAP's breakdown of age periods, with early adolescence ranging from 10 to 13 years old (when pubertal changes develop), middle adolescence including anyone 14–17 years old (during which many teens report interest in sexual and romantic relationships), and late adolescence as anyone between 18 and 21 years old (www.healthychildren.org). The end of adolescence is somewhat ambiguous and can be marked by substantially different processes across cultures (Schlegel & Barry III, 1991). However, a common hallmark involves the transition away from parental dependency to more adult-typical roles and responsibilities, including a socially recognized union of a romantic, intimate partnership (i.e. marriage) where one begins to live with one or more long-term partners (Ember et al., 2017). Thus, understanding social cognitive processes related to mating is essential to understanding adolescent development, and can lead to translational opportunities that support this age group throughout this intense period of reproductive growth. This chapter will cover social cognitive development across adolescence, with a special focus on how these cognitive processes facilitate maturation in the realm of intimate relationships.

4.2 Adolescent social cognition

Investigating social cognitive development in adolescence means exploring the mental processes required to navigate an increasingly complex social environment. With the advancement of neuroimaging methods, there has been much growth in the understanding of general adolescent social cognition. However, there is very little research identifying how the maturation of social cognitive processes relates to reproductive competence (i.e. mating intelligence). For example, while prior research has found evidence for neurological and cognitive development in perspective-taking processes during adolescence (Dumontheil et al., 2010; Garcia & Scherf, 2015; Sebastian et al., 2012), there is a gap in our understanding of how these advancements facilitate romantic interactions among youth. In the following sections, we will first discuss changes in the adolescent social environment. Then, we will describe how underlying hormonal and neurological changes during puberty influence the development of adolescent social cognition in order to support more nuanced social interactions, particularly in the realm of dating. Then, we will focus discussion on cognitive processes related to social a) perception, b) information processing, and c) regulation. Throughout, we will emphasize how incorporating a mating perspective to these processes may reveal a fuller picture of adolescent social cognitive development.

4.2.1 Social changes

From an evolutionary perspective, it is important to consider the social environment in which our human ancestors evolved. Hunter-gatherer societies provide a relatively close approximation of early human culture (Ember et al., 2014) because it has been argued that, for the vast majority of primate evolution, humans and other great apes existed in small cooperative groups, subsisting on hunted animals and foraged wild plants (Fitzhugh, 2003). Although current human cultures differ substantially from evolutionary environments, the slower timescale of evolution by natural selection indicates that cognitive, emotional, and behavioural adaptations that address evolutionary survival pressures are still with us today (i.e. mismatch hypotheses; Li et al., 2018). Thus, modern societies can both reflect and influence evolved psychological adaptations relevant to survival and reproduction. Similar to past environments, in modern hunter-gatherer societies, young males focus their peer interactions on physical competitions, while young females are encouraged to focus on enhancing attractiveness in order to signal reproductive capacity (Ember et al., 2017; Schlegel & Barry III, 1991). Such intrasexual physical competition and displays of sexual receptivity are core aspects of sexual selection (the ability to attract and engage in reproduction opportunities across primate species; for review, see Puts, 2016), thus interactions with members of the same- and opposite-sex likely take on new meaning during this developmental window. Not only do these physical displays influence attraction between peers (Little, 2015), but they also serve as indicators of status and sexual maturation to the group as a whole, likely influencing societal and parental decisions regarding mating partnerships.

Globally, adolescents begin to take on more roles and responsibilities and enter more complex social environments compared with younger children. In developing countries, adolescents typically take on more adult-like responsibilities modelled by older, same-gender family members, but leisure time is spent primarily among peers, distinctly apart from adults. In industrialized societies, it is common for children to transition to new schools, grouped with same-age peers, and encounter new status hierarchies where many are initially relegated to lower standing (Eder, 1985; Eder & Kinney, 1995). Even those who may have gained popularity in primary school must navigate new social standings when entering a different school with older, more experienced youth (Ojanen & Nostrand, 2014). As mentalizing structures continue to mature from childhood through adolescence (4.2.3.2. Mentalizing, pp. 79–80), it is likely that secondary-schoolers continue to develop increasingly nuanced conceptualizations of self, including an understanding of how peers view or accept them (e.g. Burrow & Rainone, 2017). This likely facilitates the exploration of more independent social identities available within this expanded social network. However, empirical evidence for this is lacking.

Indeed, adolescents are particularly sensitive to social feedback (Platt et al., 2013; Silvers et al., 2017, 2012). This sensitivity might facilitate a preoccupation with status (i.e. popularity), which is evident among adolescents (van den Berg et al., 2019; van den Broek et al., 2016). For example, the social reorientation hypothesis proposed by Nelson and colleagues (2005) states that adolescent social development is characterized by a marked increase in interest and time spent with peers as they establish individual identities. While the salience of peer evaluation likely represents a continuation of processes initiated during childhood, there is evidence of increased neural activation in brain regions supporting a social reorientation, with some changes related to pubertal development (medial prefrontal cortex; Pfeifer et al., 2013) and some related to age (temporoparietal junction; Blakemore and Robbins, 2012). Moreover, different types of social feedback differentially affect social cognitive networks, with social rejection increasing connectivity between the anterior cingulate cortex (ACC) and the insula (McIver et al, 2019), while social inclusion is related to decreased functional connectivity between the ventral ACC and the medial prefrontal cortex (mPFC) (Bolling et al., 2011). Social rejection and acceptance give adolescents valuable feedback in understanding their own social status within a particular context (e.g. high school, sports teams, youth clubs) and may provide motivation to achieve social approval, or to avoid social rejection. Thus, advancing and maintaining social status (i.e. popularity) among peers should represent a primary motive as adolescents enter the new social environments of secondary school (Mansfield & Wosnitza, 2010), particularly given its association with increased access to resources and mating opportunities among many primate species, including macaques (Rodriguez-Llanes et al., 2009) and humans (Bercovitch, 1991; Hopcroft, 2006).

One of the most notable differences in social dynamics between primary school-aged groups and secondary school-aged groups is the formation of romantic relationships that are more intimate and contain a sexualized component. For example, there is cross-cultural evidence that first sexual experiences and romantic relationships occur during the teenage years. In Western societies, the average age of first intercourse is around 17 years, however other sexual (non-intercourse) behaviours begin earlier (CDC, 2017). In non-Western cultures, the average age of first sexual intercourse is estimated to be between 18 and 19 years (Bearinger et al., 2007). Age of first sexual behaviours other than intercourse in developing countries has yet to be investigated, but is assumed to occur prior to intercourse (Bellizzi et al., 2019; Patton et al., 2012). It is not surprising that interest and engagement in dating and sexual activity blossom at the same time that youths experience biological changes that signal sexual receptivity (i.e. secondary sex characteristics). However, research linking pubertal development with the emergence of social cognitive processes that support sexual attraction and romantic relationship initiation is only just beginning (Cornwell et al., 2006; Harden et al., 2018; Suleiman et al., 2017). Exactly how adolescent social cognition supports mating interactions over adolescent development is essential to understanding how youths navigate this new social context.

4.2.2 Pubertal hormones, brain development, and social cognition

4.2.2.1 Puberty and hormones

While adolescents encounter new and increasingly complex social situations, underlying biological functions and supporting social-cognitive structures show concurrent development. Puberty can be considered as a coordinated suite of rapid, physical, and cognitive changes transitioning children into reproductively capable adolescents (Ellis et al., 2012), and is driven by secretions of adrenal androgens and gonadal steroids, beginning in late childhood/early adolescence, around ages 7–10 years old (Sisk & Foster, 2004; Sisk & Zehr, 2005). Adrenarche refers to the release of androgens (DHEA, DHEA-S) from the matured adrenal gland and gonadarche refers to hormonal secretions from the hypothalamus that stimulate production of reproductive hormones (e.g. oestradiol, testosterone, progesterone) as part of the hypothalamic-pituitary-gonadal (HPG) axis (Peper et al., 2010). Once adrenarche and gonadarche are initiated, puberty is marked by sharp increases in testosterone in both sexes, although the developmental shift is stronger in males compared with females (Booth et al., 2006; Braams et al., 2015). While males show a steady increase in testosterone across adolescence, peaking in early adulthood, female testosterone shows more cyclic patterns, coupled with hormonal changes across the menstrual cycle (Judd & Yen, 1973).

The rise in testosterone during puberty influences neural structures associated with general and social cognitive processes, such as sensation seeking (Campbell et al., 2010; Harden et al., 2018), reward sensitivity (Braams et al., 2015; Dreher et al., 2016; Lombardo et al., 2012; Spielberg et al., 2014), social aggression (Dreher et al., 2016; Rowe et al., 2004), and social information processing (Cservenka et al., 2015; Nelson et al., 2016). Through neural organization, pubertal hormone secretions help activate a set of new drives and perceptual processes associated with sexual reproduction (Ellis et al., 2012; Schulz & Sisk, 2016). Testosterone levels influence social information processing systems in youth, such as interpreting facial emotions (Cservenka et al., 2015; Nelson et al., 2016) and perceiving gender cues (Johnston et al., 2003). Subcortical brain structures that are influenced in-utero by testosterone are later affected by the same hormone in early adolescence to be more responsive to positively, compared with negatively, valenced facial cues (Lombardo et al., 2012). Reproductive hormone mechanisms also modulate identification and attraction towards mating-relevant facial cues, such as jaw size, brow projection and height, eye size, and other facial proportions that correlate with estimates of facial masculinity or femininity (Roney et al., 2011). Therefore, linking social cognitive shifts and perception of specific mating cues in the face and body would be an important next step in revealing how pubertal hormones attune cognitive systems towards mating and reproduction (Suleiman et al., 2017).

Testosterone also increases sensitivity to social engagement cues by enhancing attention to social threat (Wirth & Schultheiss, 2007), motivation to act (Bos et al., 2012), and sensitivity to social rewards (van Honk et al., 2004), all of which play vital roles in status maintenance and intrasexual competition for mates, supporting evolutionary models that proclaim testosterone's role in mediating status-seeking and mate-seeking motivations in adults (Eisenegger et al., 2011; Ellis et al., 2012; Mazur & Booth, 1998; Wingfield et al., 1990). The biosocial model of status (Mazur & Booth, 1998) claims that testosterone reactivity in adults motivates competitive and risky decisions that serve to increase status and, ultimately, greater reproductive opportunities (for review, see Apicella & Dreber, 2015). Testosterone levels are also related to increases in reward sensitivity and risk taking observed during adolescence (Braams et al., 2015). In a longitudinal study of participants aged 8–27 years old, changes in testosterone levels were positively associated with reward sensitivity, as reflected in both self-report accounts and activity in the nucleus accumbens (NAcc) (Braams et al., 2015). Further, this study found that NAcc sensitivity followed a quadratic pattern (peaking in adolescence), as did risk taking, providing evidence for a link between pubertal hormones, reward sensitivity, and risk taking (Braams et al., 2015). Given the high concentration of testosterone (and other androgen) receptors in the NAcc (Lu et al., 1998), it is likely that changing hormone levels during puberty influence neurological changes in the NAcc, mediating the link between the NAcc and risk taking behaviours. Other neuroimaging studies have shown a link between oestrogen and risk taking in girls, particularly aggressive risk taking, in the middle window of their menstrual cycle (Vermeersch et al., 2008).

Notably, risk taking behaviour in laboratory tasks has been found to increase in adolescence particularly when peers are ostensibly watching, indicating a distinct social influence on these cognitive processes (Gardner & Steinberg, 2005; Peake et al., 2013). It could be that the presence of peers motivates status concerns leading to increased risky decisions (in order to gain or maintain popularity), yet this link has not been empirically investigated. Given hormonal influences on physical, neurological, and cognitive development related to reward sensitivity and risk taking, it is likely that natural selection has favoured motivations, behaviours, and cognitions that appear at the same time as reproductive capability (e.g. puberty and adolescence). For example, perhaps adolescents who were willing to take risks in order to increase their status among peers were likely to have early and more frequent copulatory encounters (and therefore higher reproductive success) compared with those who did not. An understanding of how risk taking and supporting neurological structures relate to status motivation in adolescents would give valuable insight into the normative mating experiences during adolescence.

While hormone fluctuations likely interact with social cognitive processes to guide status-maintenance and mating behaviours, specific hormone relationships with mating cognition is understudied. For example, the link between testosterone and reproductive behaviours is well established in non-human animal models (Romeo et al., 2003; Rupp & Wallen, 2007). However, evidence in adults and youth is mixed, with some studies finding a positive association (Braams et al., 2014; Buster et al., 2005; Halpern et al., 1997; 1998) and others finding a negative association (Burnham, 2007; Gray et al., 2004) or no relationship (Halpern et al., 1997, 1998; Roney & Simmons, 2013). Reproductive behaviour is presumably mediated by several processes, including attraction and sexual desire, which are also influenced by pubertal hormones. In terms of sexual motivations, researchers have found that, rather than testosterone, oestradiol and progesterone are linked with sexual desire and behaviour in females. However, the direction of the association differed by hormone. While oestradiol correlated with an increase in sexual desire, progesterone associated with declines in sexual motivation (Rupp & Wallen, 2007). Social neuro-endocrinology work would benefit from advancements in understanding the developmental trajectory of the link between reproductive hormones (i.e. oestrogen, progesterone, and testosterone) and social cognition that facilitates mating behaviours, such as arousal, sexual attraction, and desire.

4.2.2.2 The social brain

There is much research devoted to understanding how puberty and pubertal hormones relate to underlying neurological development in brain structures that support social cognition related to decision making, sensation seeking, risk taking, reward, and mood control (Vijayakumar et al., 2018). A particularly important aspect of social living is interpreting and understanding the thoughts, beliefs, perspectives, and intentions of others, a collection of social-cognitive processes known as 'mentalizing' (Blakemore & Mills, 2014). Modern neuroimaging research has revealed brain networks associated with mentalizing processes that show substantial structural and functional growth during adolescence. This network, often referred to as 'the social brain' (Blakemore, 2008; Blakemore & Mills, 2014) includes the (mPFC), the temporoparietal junction (TPJ), the posterior superior temporal sulcus (pSTS) and the anterior temporal cortex (ATC; Frith & Frith, 2010; Mills, et al., 2014). The mPFC is recruited more by adolescents, compared with adults, during social cognitive tasks, and is implicated in identifying the mental states and intentions of others (Blakemore, 2008). TPJ activation is evident when youths and adults attempt to infer mental states of others, rather than simply receiving information about another individual. In close anatomical proximity to the TPJ, the pSTS is activated when processing social information conveyed through gestures, eye gaze, and other body movements (Puce & Perrett, 2003). The ATC has been shown to underlie the interpretation of social narratives and processing of social scripts (Olson et al., 2013). While many of these structures and cognitions are evident in childhood, it is proposed that the specialization of these anatomically distinct regions influence the mastery of increasingly complex social interactions during adolescence (Blakemore & Mills, 2014). In the following sections, we will demonstrate how the development of the social brain can both influence, and be influenced by, the development of social cognition across adolescence, with particular focus on how these underlying mechanisms may support the development of mating cognition.

4.2.3 Specific advancements in adolescent social cognition

4.2.3.1 Face perception

While obtaining information from faces is an ability that matures throughout infancy and childhood, adolescents begin to use the face to process more complex social cues, which likely include judgements of attraction (Saxton et al., 2009), social status, and inference of intention and emotion (Maner et al., 2007). Accordingly, the neural systems underlying facial processing have been found to change across adolescence (Monk et al., 2003; Pfeifer et al., 2011; Yurgelun-Todd & Killgore, 2006). Advancements in neuroimaging and electrophysiological measurements have allowed researchers to examine the neurological underpinnings of person-perception, particularly in the pSTS. Activation patterns in this area have been found to relate to interpreting complex social gestures (Pelphrey et al., 2004; Puce & Perrett, 2003). Cohen Kadosh and colleagues (2011; 2013) sought to identify functional connectivity of the face-processing network in the brain across development, comparing children, adolescents, and young adults as they detected various facial cues while in a functional magnetic resonance imaging (fMRI) scanner. Participants were instructed to detect eye-gaze direction, facial identity, and emotional expression in a series of facial images. Researchers found that, while a core face-processing network was activated for all three age groups, modulation of this network connectivity according to face-processing task showed age-related growth. For adults, detecting facial identity was related to increased connectivity between the inferior occipital gyrus (IOG) and the fusiform gyrus, while detecting an emotional expression modulated connectivity between the IOG and superior temporal sulcus (STS). No such modulation was identified for children aged 7–11 years old (Cohen Kadosh et al., 2011), implying that specialization of this network must develop over adolescence. Follow-up work found that changes in this face-processing network connectivity were related to continued structural development of underlying brain structures, which may relate to more advanced cognitive strategies used in perceiving information from the face (Cohen Kadosh et al., 2013; Kilford et al., 2016).

Missing from adolescent person-perception literature is identifying ways in which neural facial processing networks become specialized for specific mating cues. Given the body's biological transformation towards reproduction, it is likely that concurrent neurological and cognitive processes also shift towards the detection of mating cues from facial features. In the field of evolutionary psychology, researchers have identified facial cues linked with reproductive fitness (Cornwell et al., 2006; for review, see Little, 2015) and have demonstrated that adults are more attracted to facial aspects that signal health and reproductive capacity (reviewed in Little, 2015). Therefore, it is proposed that natural selection has favoured cognitive strategies that direct attention towards reproductively fit individuals, capable of conceiving and caring for children. For example, naturally cycling females (those who have natural menstrual cycles with no hormonal birth control) report increased attraction to men with highly masculine faces, particularly during her window of ovulation (the 2–3 day period when women are most likely to conceive; Barrett & Marshall, 1969; Dixson et al., 2018; Little & Jones, 2012). Facial masculinity has a direct positive association with testosterone in men, and indicates high immunocompetence (Furman et al., 2014; Penton-Voak & Chen, 2004; Rhodes et al., 2003). Indeed, there is some evidence to suggest that ovulating women have a specialized ability to detect fitness cues in men's faces (Durante et al., 2012; Jones et al., 2019; Peters et al., 2009).

Taken together, this points to a putative shift in motivational systems during the ovulatory window when females are more interested in obtaining good genes for offspring, while favouring less masculine faces and more long-term mating strategies during other parts of the menstrual cycle (for review, see Jones et al., 2019). Additionally, adult heterosexual males (Roberts et al., 2004) and females (Lobmaier et al., 2016) are able to detect ovulation cues in the faces of females, finding that facial images of ovulating females are more attractive compared with the same female when she is not ovulating. It is likely that detecting ovulation cues from the face helps motivate and direct attention towards females who are especially likely to conceive. These proposed evolutionary adaptations have yet to be explored from a developmental perspective, which would provide essential information on how face-perception becomes attuned to mating cues as part of the body's biological shift towards reproduction (i.e. puberty). This evolutionary psychological theory around face perception requires further evidence from developmental investigations identifying how these neural structures and associated facial preferences begin to incorporate mating cues over adolescence.

4.2.3.2 Mentalizing

A fundamental aspect of social cognition involves the ability to detect, interpret, and understand the intentions, thoughts, and feelings of others, collectively known as 'mentalizing'. This ability requires the integration of a wide range of advanced perceptual, social cognitive, and affective skills, such as perspective-taking, emotion attribution, and interpreting the intentions of others, which develop from infancy and throughout childhood (Blakemore & Mills, 2014; Garcia & Scherf, 2015). The ability to reason about another individual's mental state is crucial to the development and maintenance of pair bonds, which facilitate biparental care, coordinating behaviours, and resource investments geared towards rearing young (Wlodarski & Dunbar, 2014). Ascertaining the beliefs and intentions of a potential or bonded romantic partner (referred to as 'cross-sex mind reading'; Geher & Kaufman, 2011) ensures directed reproductive behaviours (e.g. focusing efforts on someone who likely reciprocates your feelings, or who shares your desire for an exclusive romantic relationship) and better cooperation (e.g. perceiving another's needs or intentions) with a partner during child-rearing. This points to unique cognitive processes within a mating context, including cross-sex mind reading, flexible mating strategies (weighing risks and benefits of enacting short-term versus long-term mating strategies), being able to read cues that reliably indicate fitness or infidelity, and identifying and out-competing intrasexual rivals, that directly aid in romantic relationship formation and maintenance (Geher et al., 2008). However, it has yet to be examined whether the continued development of mentalizing during adolescence incorporates mating-focused social cues along with concurrent biological shifts towards reproductive competence.

As mentioned earlier (4.2.2.2. The Social Brain, p. 76), key regions responsible for attributing mental states to others involve many parts of the social brain, including the TPJ, pSTS, ATC, and the dorsal medial prefrontal cortex (dmPFC). Notably, many researchers have found a decrease in dmPFC activation between adolescence and adulthood (reviewed in Blakemore, 2008). Tasks used to investigate mentalizing in adolescents include identifying preferences and attitudes of oneself versus a hypothetical 'other' (Burrows et al., 2016), and understanding others' intentions (Blakemore et al., 2007) and emotional states (Gunther Moor et al., 2012; Overgaauw et al., 2015), as well as understanding irony (Wang et al., 2006). A common paradigm for studying mentalizing is the

Reading the Mind in the Eyes task (RMET; Baron-Cohen et al., 2001), where participants view cropped facial photos showing just the eyes and are asked to interpret the mental and emotional state of the person in the photo. Gunther Moor et al. (2012) compared neural activity in social brain networks during this task between early, mid, and late adolescents. These researchers found that all ages recruited the pSTS during the mentalizing task (compared with a control condition where participants estimated age and gender of photographed subjects). However, only the youngest group of participants showed additional engagement of the dmPFC (Gunther Moor et al., 2012). Follow-up work demonstrated the same pattern in a longitudinal analysis—namely, that the dmPFC follows a quadratic growth pattern such that it is heavily recruited in early and late adolescents during the RMET, but not so much during mid-adolescence (Overgaauw et al., 2015). The modulated activation of the dmPFC likely reflects an increase in cognitive control strategies engaged during social situations for adolescents compared with adults (Dumontheil et al., 2012; Kilford et al., 2016; Mills et al., 2014).

Reasoning about another's emotions and intentions in tasks such as the RMET is particularly useful in targeting potential romantic partners (e.g. identifying those who are attracted to you) and maintaining romantic relationships (e.g. understanding needs, wants, and desires of a romantic partner). Specifically, compared with children, adolescents encounter a completely new set of mentalizing demands when it comes to mating, such as (1) recognizing that others may view them in a sexualized way, and (2) determining whether romantic feelings are reciprocated. These new mentalizing requirements add an additional layer of processing when interpreting others' desires or feelings, and could therefore influence demands on the cognitive control system. Wlodarski and Dunbar (2014) investigated whether a romantic versus a neutral prime influenced performance on the RMET for adults in current romantic relationships. Results showed that participants were significantly better at interpreting the emotional states of others after a love prime compared with a neutral prime. A good next step would be to use facial images of neutral versus potential romantic partners in the RMET with adolescents to determine whether this mating context influences recruitment of pSTS and mPFC structures, which may reveal a particular mating-focused specialization within mentalizing processes.

A crucial aspect of mentalizing is the ability to take another person's perspective while inhibiting one's own, a process that requires effortful cognitive control. While perspective taking shows substantial development in childhood, there is evidence that the propensity to take another's perspective continues to develop throughout adolescence as well (Dumontheil et al., 2010). However, perspective-taking performance has been found to decrease under cognitive load, suggesting that general cognitive resources are required to successfully inhibit one's own perspective to take another's (Mills et al., 2015). Further, individual differences in inhibitory control can partly account for errors in perspective taking above age differences (Symeonidou et al., 2016).

Neuroimaging work examining perspective taking in adults and adolescents found that adults recruited more fronto-parietal cognitive control regions than adolescents when inhibiting one's own perspective (Dumontheil et al., 2012). Further, adolescents recruit the social brain when engaging in both cognitive mentalizing (understanding thoughts, perspectives, and intentions of others) and affective mentalizing (recognizing and interpreting other's affective states) (Sebastian et al., 2012). Increased perspective-taking has also been linked to the left TPJ and dorsolateral PFC during economic interactions involving trust and reciprocity (Fett et al., 2014; van den Bos et al., 2011), indicating an interaction of social cognition and cognitive control systems during adolescence.

Within a mating context, cross-sex mind reading involves not only assessing whether the desired 'other' is interested in you, but also estimating what they want and desire in a potential partnership. In a study conducted by De Backer et al. (2007), 481 participants (65% female) stated their current desire for either a short-term or long-term sexual relationship and wrote a 'personal ad' to look for a potential mate. They then selected their preferred potential mating partner from a set of personal ads written by other participants. To engage in cross-sex mind reading, participants were then asked to estimate which personal ads the opposite sex might pick. A significant interaction was found between sex and mating strategy such that males were more accurate at assessing female long-term mating desires (selecting more long-term-focused ads when cross-sex mind reading for females) and females were more accurate in guessing the short-term mating desires of men (selecting more short-term focused ads when cross-sex mind reading for males). From an evolutionary context, accuracy in this realm is essential for reproductive fitness, given the sex-differentiated risks associated with errors. According to error management theory (Haselton & Buss, 2000) men tend to *overestimate* a woman's preferences for short-term encounters because of the high cost of passing up a conception opportunity (lowering their overall reproductive fitness) while women tend to *underestimate* a man's willingness to engage in a long-term relationship, because the costs of being wrong are extremely high. If a woman's assumption about a man's long-term mating intentions is incorrect (believing a partner is interested in a long-term, committed relationship when he is not), women must then spend extensive time and energy resources towards child-rearing with little help. Thus, perspective-taking within a mating context is an essential skill that must be developed post-puberty, because detecting the mating intentions of another individual has vast implications for intimate relationship formation. Given that these mating-focused perspective-taking abilities were explored primarily with heterosexual adults, future work should seek to identify how perspective-taking abilities become specialized for mating-relevant inferences during adolescence, particularly when adolescents begin to explore sexual orientation and identity.

4.2.3.3 Executive functioning and emotional regulation

Executive functioning includes several skills such as sustained attention, motivation, planning and prioritization, goal-directed persistence, response inhibition, and emotional regulation (Dawson & Guare, 2018). Executive functioning and affective/motivational systems can interact in two key ways. First, bottom-up processes can cause the modification or disruption of executive control strategies with interference by intense emotional responses. Second, top-down processes refer to ways in which cognitive control systems exert influence over affective responses, such as re-structuring interpretations of emotional events (Dawson & Guare, 2018; Kilford et al., 2016).

Research investigating the relationship between affective processes and cognitive control often assess inhibitory control (i.e. the ability to focus attention on particular stimuli while ignoring competing emotional information). In these studies, participants must suppress goal-irrelevant stimuli while given emotional contexts or distractions. This ability to suppress affective responses to social stimuli appears to develop over the course of adolescence (for review, see Kilford et al., 2016). While processing feelings and emotions, there is evidence for increased functional connectivity between vmPFC and both the amygdala and ventral striatum in youth (Herting et al., 2015; Pfeifer et al., 2011; Somerville et al., 2013; Spielberg et al., 2014; van den Bos et al., 2012). The vmPFC, and its connectivity to the amygdala, is central in affect regulation systems, in habituation of affective stimuli, and in the formation/pursuit of socially relevant goals (Pessoa, 2009). Youths show decreased activation in the vmPFC in response to emotional stimuli (Barbalat et al., 2013; Hare et al., 2009; Kilford et al., 2016), suggesting that adolescents show decreased activity in frontal regulatory regions and increased connectivity with the emotionally sensitive amygdala. Researchers have described this imbalance in terms of Dual-Systems (or the Imbalance) Model, proposing that the under-developed cognitive control system, along with the highly developed affective and emotional system, leads to increased risk taking in adolescence (Steinberg, 2010; Casey et al., 2008). According to this perspective, youth are overly influenced by rewards, and unable to regulate reward-motivation towards more safe choices because of the relatively protracted development of frontal lobe areas. Indeed, motivational/reward pathways are more sensitive in affective contexts during adolescence, which may underlie the increase in risky choices in this age group compared with adults (Blakemore & Robbins, 2012; Burnett et al., 2010). However, given the extreme variability in fMRI studies investigating cognitive control and affective/motivational processes, the evidence in support of the Dual-Systems Model is more nuanced (Kilford et al., 2016).

More recently, social cognitive work has investigated the Dual-Systems Model as it relates to social context. PFC recruitment is more flexible during adolescence, and is particularly sensitive to social and affective stimuli (Casey, 2015; Pfeifer & Allen, 2016; van den Bos & Eppinger, 2016). For example, the presence of peers is a social context that influences brain regions in the motivational/affective processing system, such that adolescents take more risks with peers present (Chein et al., 2011; Smith et al., 2014, 2015). Adults showed greater activity in lateral PFC during decisions, regardless of social context, while adolescents show increased use of ventral striatum and lateral orbitofrontal cortex when making decisions when peers are present versus when alone (Chein et al., 2011). Similar responses are seen in adolescence when playing another laboratory task assessing risk taking (McCormick & Telzer, 2016). Responses that vary according to social context might allow for more creative and adaptive responses that help navigate new, complex, and rapidly changing social contexts adolescents encounter (Kilford et al., 2016). Indeed, different behavioural responses can be adaptive or maladaptive depending on the particular social situation, wherein a seemingly 'risky' choice actually yields better overall adaptive value for the individual.

According to evolutionary literature, behaviours often associated with inhibitory control capacities are related to trade-offs one makes between 'fast' or 'slow' life history strategies (Wenner et al., 2013). Life history theory relates a suite of behaviours and biological milestones to the environmental context such that certain strategies are more useful in particular environments. In unstable, unpredictable, impoverished environments, a faster life history strategy would be beneficial, including traits such as early menarche, earlier age of first sexual encounter, earlier age at first birth, and having multiple births across the lifespan. This is because one's life expectancy is pretty low in these relatively dangerous environments so procreating early and often leads to higher overall reproductive success. Alternatively, later menarche, longer sexual abstinence, and investing heavily in only few children is most beneficial in stable, predictable, and resource-rich environments (Kaplan & Gangestad, 2005). These traits and behaviours are mediated by executive functions that motivate and organize behaviours within particular contexts. In more unpredictable environments, actions focused on short-term gains are increasingly adaptive, whereas actions biased towards long-term benefits are advantageous within stable, resource-rich environments (Wenner et al., 2013).

Therefore, viewing adolescent risk taking with this evolutionary lens could partially explain variance in the neural correlates of risky behaviour in regards to sexual activity and romantic relationship formation. Adolescents who experience early sexual development, or who make risky sexual choices such as not using protection or having multiple sex partners, or who enjoy more casual romantic relationships, could be making the most adaptive decisions for their genetic background and environment. A more holistic approach incorporating both proximate and ultimate influences on mating behaviours in adolescence will give a clearer picture on how youth navigate new and more complex social situations.

A likely motivator of potentially risky choices involves one's emotional state, or 'affect'. Social affect refers to the interaction between emotions and behaviour when communicating with others (Kilford et al., 2016), and social affective interpretations increase in salience during adolescent development (Rubia et al., 2006; Silvers et al., 2012; Somerville et al., 2013). This social affect becomes highly sensitive during adolescence, resulting in strong emotional responses to social feedback and social situations. In particular, negative feedback or social rejection from peers typically results in more distress and anxiety in youth compared with adults and children, and this effect is strongest in early adolescence (Burke et al., 2017; Kilford et al., 2016; Platt et al., 2013). Older adolescents and adults are better able to regulate emotional responses to social rejection and show heightened responses in the right ventrolateral PFC (vlPFC; Silvers et al., 2017, 2012). Studies using a simulated computer game (Cyberball) in which the participant experiences rejection from peers who do not throw the ball to them have furthered this finding. Specifically, compared with adults and children, adolescents show reduced activation of right vlPFC, indicating a positive association between right vlPFC activation and emotional regulation in response to rejection in Cyberball (Bolling et al., 2016; Cheng et al., 2019; Vijayakumar et al., 2017). Additionally, functional connectivity between right vlPFC and ventral ACC increases with age during adolescence, but only when participants feel excluded (Bolling et al., 2011, 2016; Vijayakumar et al., 2017). One such emotional regulation strategy includes emotional re-appraisal, or the ability to change one's thoughts and feelings about an emotional event (Jazaieri et al., 2014; Xie et al., 2016), a process which requires the integration of cognitive control processes and perspective-taking (McRae et al., 2012; Vijayakumar et al., 2017). While this research looks at rejection from a peer group during a simulated game, it has yet to be investigated whether neural responses to social rejection differ between peers and a potential romantic partner. More evidence is needed to determine at what age mating motivations begin to become salient, the developmental trajectory of mating motivations, and cognitive control strategies used to mitigate emotional reactions to success or failure in this realm. For example, how does rejection from a potential mate influence one's identity or self-esteem, and can emotional reappraisal help adolescents decrease negative feelings when such events occur?

In adults, 'love' as an affective state has been investigated from a neurological and cognitive perspective. However, the developmental trajectory of these neural underpinnings have yet to be explored. Passionate or romantic love is defined as a 'state of intense longing for union with another' (Acevedo et al., 2012). Recent fMRI research on individuals who claim to be 'deeply in love' have revealed unique patterns of brain activation when viewing images of the romantic partner versus images of acquaintances. Specifically, images of the romantic partner correlated with increased activation in the brain's reward system, such as caudate nucleus and putamen, as well as regions related to reward processing, emotion regulation, and sensory integration, including the insula, ACC, and the subcortical ventral tegmental area (VTA). Follow-up work asked participants to rate the intensity of their romantic feelings towards their partner, and found a dose–response relationship between self-reported intensity and activations in these regions. Similarly, implicit romantic love primes activated regions associated with representations of others and the self—namely, the fusiform and angular gyri (Ortigue et al., 2010).

Neuroimaging work has also found differing neural activation patterns between initial romantic pairing and established romantic relationships. Symptoms associated with early-stage love include craving for union, focused attention, increased energy when with the partner, sexual attraction, and thinking about the partner when apart (Acevedo et al., 2012). Regions implicated in early-stage romantic love include the right VTA and the caudate nucleus, which are important in motivation, reinforcement learning, and decision making (Acevedo & Aron, 2014; Aron et al., 2005; Beauregard et al., 2009; Carter et al., 2009; Cooper et al., 2014). Importantly, the VTA also plays a role in neural networks underlying motivational and reward systems implicated in behaviours necessary for survival (Carter et al., 2009). For example, similar regions are activated in response to food (Hare et al., 2009) and monetary gains, as well as highly motivational stimuli (Carter et al., 2009; Knutson & Greer, 2008). This is consistent with romantic love as a 'desire for union with another', which must influence reproductive motivations. Furthermore, the dorsal striatum is activated during romantic relationship initiation, which is also associated with goal-directed behaviour necessary to attain rewarding stimuli (Knutson & Greer, 2008). Together, these activation patterns within romantic relationships suggest underlying motivational mechanisms for seeking and maintaining romantic pair-bonds (Acevedo & Aron, 2014). Thus, investigating neural activity in adolescents who are interested in romantic relationships would strengthen the argument for adolescence representing an infection point in the development of mating-specific social cognition.

4.2.3.4 Implications for mental health
Understanding the development of social cognitive development in the context of mating can inform potential translational opportunities for adolescents with depression, an illness characterized by low self-esteem, worthlessness, and negative rumination (Manani & Sharma, 2013). Depression symptoms typically increase during adolescence, and are related to high levels of interpersonal stress (Davey et al., 2008) and decreased quality in peer relationships (Mendle et al., 2012). Uniting both social-cognitive and evolutionary-based frameworks, specific interventions may be formed to help adolescents navigate mating interactions that might otherwise lead to poorer self-evaluations. Given that adolescents experience almost constant fluctuations in social dynamics (e.g. many short-term romantic relationships, changing friend groups) and are especially sensitive to social rejection from peers during this time (Burke et al., 2017; Kilford et al., 2016), it is likely that rejection from a potential romantic interest can have a severe impact on an adolescent's self-esteem and feelings of worthiness. Further, several underlying neural structures involved with self-referential processing (i.e. mPFC, ACC,

precuneus) are still developing as the 'social brain network' matures across adolescence. Therefore, peer rejection (particularly from a potential love interest) or the dissolution of a romantic relationship may influence the development of these structures, or perhaps negative reflections about the self within these situations result from processing deficits in these areas. Moving forward, researchers should identify how the mating context may influence the development of psychopathology in adolescence, and design interventions targeted for healthy development, maintenance, and dissolution of romantic relationships as part of a normative developmental process.

4.3 Conclusion

As Suleiman et al. (2017) succinctly stated, 'while existing neurodevelopmental models have integrated our current understanding of adolescent brain development... there has been surprisingly little focus on the importance of adolescence as a sensitive period for romantic and sexual development (p. 209)'. Given the importance of reproduction and pair-bonding from an evolutionary perspective, the period of adolescence may serve to foster the development of social cognition within a mating context at the same time as biological changes ready the body for copulation and conception. Hormonal and neurological changes at puberty form dynamic interactions with new and increasingly more complex social environments in the adolescent experience, allowing for more nuanced social cognitive strategies across development. This is evidenced by findings that many social cognitive processes that mature during adolescence share underlying mechanisms with mating-focused behaviours and cognition; however, integrating these fields of research is only just beginning. It will be important for future investigators to identify how adolescent social cognition supports romantic and sexual development during this time, and how mating cognition and experiences in adolescence represent normative developmental milestones necessary for health and well-being into adulthood.

References

Acevedo, B. P., & Aron, A. P., 2014. 'Romantic love, pair-bonding, and the dopaminergic reward system'. In *Mechanisms of Social Connection: From Brain to Group*, edited by M. Mikulincer & P. R. Shaver. American Psychological Association.

Acevedo, B. P., Aron, A., Fisher, H. E., & Brown, L. L., 2012. 'Neural correlates of long-term intense romantic love'. *Social Cognitive and Affective Neuroscience* 7. 2: 145–159.

Apicella, C. L., & Dreber, A., 2015. 'Sex differences in competitiveness: Hunter-gatherer women and girls compete less in gender-neutral and male-centric tasks'. *Adaptive Human Behavior and Physiology* 1. 3: 247–269.

Aron, A., Fisher, H., Mashek, D. J., Strong, G., Li, H., & Brown, L. L., 2005. 'Reward, motivation, and emotion systems associated with early-stage intense romantic love'. *Journal of Neurophysiology* 94. 1: 327–337.

Barbalat, G., Bazargani, N., & Blakemore, S.-J., 2013. 'The influence of prior expectations on emotional face perception in adolescence'. *Cerebral Cortex* 23. 7: 1542–1551.

Baron-Cohen, S., Wheelwright, S., Hill, J., Raste, Y., & Plumb, I., 2001. 'The 'Reading the mind in the eyes' test revised version: A study with normal adults, and adults with asperger syndrome or high-functioning autism'. *Journal of Child Psychology and Psychiatry, and Allied Disciplines* 42. 2: 241–251.

Barrett, J. C., & Marshall, J., 1969. 'The risk of conception on different days of the menstrual cycle'. *Population Studies* 23. 3: 455–461.

Bearinger, L. H., Sieving, R. E., Ferguson, J., & Sharma, V., 2007. 'Global perspectives on the sexual and reproductive health of adolescents: Patterns, prevention, and potential'. *Lancet* 369. 9568: 1220–1231.

Beauregard, M., Courtemanche, J., Paquette, V., & St-Pierre, É. L., 2009. 'The neural basis of unconditional love'. *Psychiatry Research: Neuroimaging* 172. 2: 93–98.

Bercovitch, F. B., 1991. Social stratification, social strategies, and reproductive success in primates. *Ethology and Sociobiology*, 12. 4: 315–333.

Bellizzi, S., Ali, M. M., & Cleland, J., 2019. 'Long-term trends in reproductive behavior among young women in four countries, 1995–2009'. *Journal of Adolescent Health* 64. 2: 201–210.

Blakemore, S.-J., 2008. 'The social brain in adolescence'. *Nature Reviews Neuroscience* 9. 4: 267–277.

Blakemore, S.-J., & Mills, K. L., 2014. 'Is adolescence a sensitive period for sociocultural processing?'. *Annual Review of Psychology* 65. 1: 187–207.

Blakemore, S.-J., & Robbins, T. W., 2012. 'Decision-making in the adolescent brain'. *Nature Neuroscience* 15. 9: 1184–1191.

Blakemore, S.-J., den Ouden, H., Choudhury, S., & Frith, C., 2007. 'Adolescent development of the neural circuitry for thinking about intentions'. *Social Cognitive and Affective Neuroscience* 2. 2: 130–139.Bolling, D. Z., Pelphrey, K. A., & Wyk, B. C. V., 2016. 'Unlike adults, children and adolescents show predominantly increased neural activation to social exclusion by members of the opposite gender'. *Social Neuroscience* 11. 5: 475–486.

Bolling, D. Z., Pitskel, N. B., Deen, B., Crowley, M. J., Mayes, L. C., & Pelphrey, K. A., 2011. 'Development of neural systems for processing social exclusion from childhood to adolescence'. *Developmental Science* 14. 6: 1431–1444.

Booth, A., Granger, D. A., Mazur, A., & Kivlighan, K. T., 2006. 'Testosterone and social behavior'. *Social Forces* 85. 1: 167–191.

Bos, P. A., Panksepp, J., Bluthé, R.-M., & van Honk, J., 2012. 'Acute effects of steroid hormones and neuropeptides on human social-emotional behavior: A review of single administration studies'. *Frontiers in Neuroendocrinology* 33. 1: 17–35.

Braams, B. R., Duijvenvoorde, A. C. K., van Peper, J. S., & Crone, E. A., 2015. 'Longitudinal changes in adolescent risk-taking: A comprehensive study of neural responses to rewards, pubertal development, and risk-taking behavior'. *Journal of Neuroscience* 35. 18: 7226–7238.

Braams, B. R., van Leijenhorst, L., & Crone, E. A., 2014. 'Risks, rewards, and the developing brain in childhood and adolescence'. In *The Neuroscience of Risky Decision Making*, edited by V. F. Reyna & V. Zayas. American Psychological Association.

Burke, A. R., McCormick, C. M., Pellis, S. M., & Lukkes, J. L., 2017. 'Impact of adolescent social experiences on behavior and neural circuits implicated in mental illnesses'. *Neuroscience & Biobehavioral Reviews* 76: 280–300.

Burnett, S., Bault, N., Coricelli, G., & Blakemore, S.-J., 2010. 'Adolescents' heightened risk-seeking in a probabilistic gambling task'. *Cognitive Development* 25. 2: 183–196.

Burnham, T. C., 2007. 'High-testosterone men reject low ultimatum game offers'. *Proceedings of the Royal Society B: Biological Sciences* 274. 1623: 2327–2330.

Burrow, A. L., & Rainone, N., 2017. How many likes did I get?: Purpose moderates links between positive social media feedback and self-esteem. *Journal of Experimental Social Psychology* 69: 232–236.

Burrows, C. A., Laird, A. R., & Uddin, L. Q., 2016. 'Functional connectivity of brain regions for self- and other-evaluation in children, adolescents and adults with autism'. *Developmental Science* 19. 4: 564–580.

Buster, J. E., Kingsberg, S. A., Aguirre, O., Brown, C., Breaux, J. G., Buch, A., Rodenberg, C. A., Wekselman, K. & Casson, P., 2005. 'testosterone patch for low sexual desire in surgically menopausal women: A randomized trial'. *Obstetrics & Gynecology* 105. 5: 944.

Campbell, B. C., Dreber, A., Apicella, C. L., Eisenberg, D. T. A., Gray, P. B., Little, A. C., ... & Lum, J. K., 2010. 'Testosterone exposure, dopaminergic reward, and sensation-seeking in young men'. *Physiology & Behavior* 99. 4: 451–456.

Carter, R. M., Macinnes, J. J., Huettel, S. A., & Adcock, R. A., 2009. 'Activation in the VTA and nucleus accumbens increases in anticipation of both gains and losses'. *Frontiers in Behavioral Neuroscience* 3: 21.

Casey, B. J., 2015. 'Beyond simple models of self-control to circuit-based accounts of adolescent behavior'. *Annual Review of Psychology* 66. 1: 295–319.

Casey, B. J., Getz, S., & Galvan, A., 2008. The adolescent brain. *Developmental review* 28. 1: 62–77.

Centers for Disease Control and Prevention (CDC). 2017, June 22. *Over Half of U.S. Teens Have Had Sexual Intercourse by Age 18, New Report Shows*. https://www.cdc.gov/nchs/pressroom/nchs_press_releases/2017/201706_NSFG.htm

Chein, J., Albert, D., O'Brien, L., Uckert, K., & Steinberg, L., 2011. 'Peers increase adolescent risk taking by enhancing activity in the brain's reward circuitry: Peer influence on risk taking'. *Developmental Science* 14. 2: F1–F10.

Cheng, T. W., Vijayakumar, N., Flournoy, J. C., Macks, Z. O., de Peake, S. J., Flannery, J. E., ... & Pfeifer, J. H., 2019. 'Feeling left out or just surprised? Neural correlates of social exclusion and over-inclusion in adolescence'. *BioRxiv* 524934.

Cohen Kadosh, K., Cohen Kadosh, R., Dick, F., & Johnson, M. H., 2011. 'Developmental changes in effective connectivity in the emerging core face network'. *Cerebral Cortex* 21. 6: 1389–1394.

Cohen Kadosh, K., Johnson, M. H., Dick, F., Cohen Kadosh, R., & Blakemore, S.-J., 2013. 'Effects of age, task performance, and structural brain development on face processing.' *Cerebral Cortex* 23. 7: 1630–1642.

Cooper, J. C., Dunne, S., Furey, T., & O'Doherty, J. P., 2014. 'The role of the posterior temporal and medial prefrontal cortices in mediating learning from romantic interest and rejection'. *Cerebral Cortex* 24. 9: 2502–2511.

Cornwell, R. E., Law Smith, M. J., Boothroyd, L. G., Moore, F. R., Davis, H. P., Stirrat, M., ... & Perrett, D. I., 2006. 'Reproductive strategy, sexual development and attraction to facial characteristics'. *Philosophical Transactions of the Royal Society B: Biological Sciences* 361. 1476: 2143–2154.

Cservenka, A., Stroup, M. L., Etkin, A., & Nagel, B. J., 2015. 'The effects of age, sex, and hormones on emotional conflict-related brain response during adolescence'. *Brain and Cognition* 99: 135–150.

Davey, C. G., Yücel, M., & Allen, N. B., 2008. The emergence of depression in adolescence: Development of the prefrontal cortex and the representation of reward. *Neuroscience & Biobehavioral Reviews*, 32. 1: 1–19.

Dawson, P., & Guare, R. 2018. *Executive Skills in Children and Adolescents: A Practical Guide to Assessment and Intervention*, Guilford Press.

De Backer, C., Farinpour, L., & Braeckman, J. 2007. Mating intelligence in personal ads: do people care about mental traits, and do self-advertised traits match opposite-sex preferences? Mating intelligence: theoretical, experimental, and differential perspectives (pp. 77–102). Lawrence Erlbaum Associates.

Dixson, B. J. W., Blake, K. R., Denson, T. F., Gooda-Vossos, A., O'Dean, S. M., Sulikowski, D., . . . & Brooks, R. C., 2018. 'The role of mating context and fecundability in women's preferences for men's facial masculinity and beardedness'. *Psychoneuroendocrinology* 93: 90–102.

Dreher, J.-C., Dunne, S., Pazderska, A., Frodl, T., Nolan, J. J., & O'Doherty, J. P., 2016. 'Testosterone causes both prosocial and antisocial status-enhancing behaviors in human males'. *Proceedings of the National Academy of Sciences of the United States of America* 113. 41: 11633–11638.

Dumontheil, I., Hillebrandt, H., Apperly, I. A., & Blakemore, S.-J., 2012. 'Developmental differences in the control of action selection by social information'. *Journal of Cognitive Neuroscience* 24. 10: 2080–2095.

Dumontheil, I., Küster, O., Apperly, I. A., & Blakemore, S.-J., 2010. 'Taking perspective into account in a communicative task'. *NeuroImage* 52. 4: 1574–1583.

Durante, K. M., Griskevicius, V., Simpson, J. A., Cantú, S. M., & Li, N. P., 2012. 'Ovulation leads women to perceive sexy cads as good dads'. *Journal of Personality and Social Psychology* 103. 2: 292–305.

Eder, D., 1985. The cycle of popularity: Interpersonal relations among female adolescents. *Sociology of Education* 58. 3: 154–165.

Eder, D., & Kinney, D. A., 1995. The effect of middle school extra curricular activities on adolescents' popularity and peer status. *Youth & Society* 26. 3: 298–324.

Eisenegger, C., Haushofer, J., & Fehr, E., 2011. 'The role of testosterone in social interaction'. *Trends in Cognitive Sciences* 15. 6: 263–271.

Ellis, B. J., Del Giudice, M., Dishion, T. J., Figueredo, A. J., Gray, P., Griskevicius, V., . . . & Wilson, D. S., 2012. 'The evolutionary basis of risky adolescent behavior: Implications for science, policy, and practice'. *Developmental Psychology* 48. 3: 598–623.

Ember, C. R., Ember, M., & Peregrine, P. N., 2014. *Human Culture: Highlights of Cultural Anthropology*. Pearson.

Ember, C. R., Pitek, E., & Ringen, E. J., 2017. 'Adolescence'. In *Explaining Human Culture*, edited by C. R. Ember, Human Relations Area Files. https://hraf.yale.edu/teach-ehraf/adolescence/

Ewing, S. W. F., Houck, J. M., & Bryan, A. D., 2015. 'Neural activation during response inhibition is associated with adolescents' frequency of risky sex and substance use'. *Addictive Behaviors* 44: 80–87.

Fett, A.-K. J., Shergill, S. S., Gromann, P. M., Dumontheil, I., Blakemore, S.-J., Yakub, F., & Krabbendam, L., 2014. 'Trust and social reciprocity in adolescence—A matter of perspective-taking'. *Journal of Adolescence* 37. 2: 175–184.

Fitzhugh, B., 2003. 'The evolution of complex hunter-gatherers'. In *The Evolution of Complex Hunter-Gatherers*, pp. 1–10. Springer.

Frith, U., & Frith, C., 2010. 'The social brain: Allowing humans to boldly go where no other species has been'. *Philosophical Transactions of the Royal Society B: Biological Sciences* 365. 1537: 165–176.

Furman, D., Hejblum, B. P., Simon, N., Jojic, V., Dekker, C. L., Thiébaut, R., . . . & Davis, M. M., 2014. 'Systems analysis of sex differences reveals an immunosuppressive role for testosterone in the response to influenza vaccination'. *Proceedings of the National Academy of Sciences* 111. 2: 869–874.

Garcia, N. V., & Scherf, K. S., 2015. 'Emerging sensitivity to socially complex expressions: a unique role for adolescence?' *Child Development Perspectives* 9. 2: 84–90.

Gardner, M., & Steinberg, L., 2005. 'Peer influence on risk taking, risk preference, and risky decision making in adolescence and adulthood: An experimental study'. *Developmental Psychology* 41. 4: 625.

Geher, G., & Kaufman, S.B., 2011. 'Mating intelligence'. In *The Cambridge Handbook of Intelligence*, pp. 603–620. Cambridge University Press.

Geher, G., Miller, G., & Murphy, J., 2008. 'Mating intelligence: Toward an evolutionarily informed construct'. In *Mating Intelligence: Sex, Relationships, and the Mind's Reproductive System*, edited by G. Geher, G. Miller. Psychology Press, pp. 3–34.

Gray, P. B., Chapman, J. F., Burnham, T. C., McIntyre, M. H., Lipson, S. F., & Ellison, P. T., 2004. 'Human male pair bonding and testosterone'. *Human Nature* 15. 2: 119–131.

Gunther Moor, B., Op de Macks, Z. A., Güroğlu, B., Rombouts, S. A. R. B., Van der Molen, M. W., & Crone, E. A., 2012. 'Neurodevelopmental changes of reading the mind in the eyes'. *Social Cognitive and Affective Neuroscience* 7. 1: 44–52.

Halpern, C. T., Udry, J. R., & Suchindran, C., 1997. 'Testosterone predicts initiation of coitus in adolescent females'. *Psychosomatic Medicine* 59. 2: 161.

Halpern, C. T., Udry, R., & Suchindran, C., 1998. 'Monthly measures of salivary testosterone predict sexual activity in adolescent males'. *Archives of Sexual Behavior* 27. 5: 445–465.

Harden, K. P., Mann, F. D., Grotzinger, A. D., Patterson, M. W., Steinberg, L., Tackett, J. L., & Tucker-Drob, E. M., 2018. 'Developmental differences in reward sensitivity and sensation seeking in adolescence: Testing sex-specific associations with gonadal hormones and pubertal development'. *Journal of Personality and Social Psychology* 115. 1: 161–178.

Hare, T. A., Camerer, C. F., & Rangel, A., 2009. 'Self-control in decision-making involves modulation of the vmPFC valuation system'. *Science* 324. 5927: 646–648.

Haselton, M.G., & Buss, D.M., 2000. Error management theory: A new perspective on biases in cross-sex mind reading. *Journal of Personality and Social Psychology* 78. 1: 81–91.

Herting, M. M., Gautam, P., Spielberg, J. M., Dahl, R. E., & Sowell, E. R., 2015. 'A longitudinal study: Changes in cortical thickness and surface area during pubertal maturation'. *PLoS One* 10. 3: e0119774.

Hopcroft, R. L., 2006. Sex, status, and reproductive success in the contemporary United States. *Evolution and Human Behavior* 27. 2: 104–120.

Jazaieri, H., Morrison, A. S., Goldin, P. R., & Gross, J. J., 2014. 'The role of emotion and emotion regulation in social anxiety disorder'. *Current Psychiatry Reports* 17. 1: 531.

Johnston, L., Arden, K., Macrae, C. N., & Grace, R. C., 2003. 'The need for speed: The menstrual cycle and person construal'. *Social Cognition* 21. 2: 89–100.

Jones, B. C., Hahn, A. C., & De Bruine, L. M., 2019. 'Ovulation, sex hormones, and women's mating psychology'. *Trends in Cognitive Sciences* 23. 1: 51–62.

Judd, H. L., & Yen, S. S., 1973. 'Serum androstenedione and testosterone levels during the menstrual cycle'. *Journal of Clinical Endocrinology and Metabolism* 36. 3: 475–481.

Kaplan, H. S., & Gangestad, S. W., 2005. 'Life history theory and evolutionary psychology'. In *Handbook of Evolutionary Psychology*, edited by D. M. Buss, pp. 68–95. John Wiley & Sons.

Kilford, E. J., Garrett, E., & Blakemore, S.-J., 2016. 'The development of social cognition in adolescence: An integrated perspective'. *Neuroscience & Biobehavioral Reviews* 70: 106–120.

Knutson, B., & Greer, S. M., 2008. 'Anticipatory affect: Neural correlates and consequences for choice'. *Philosophical Transactions of the Royal Society B: Biological Sciences* 363. 1511: 3771–3786.

Li, N.P., van Vugt, M., & Colarelli, S.M., 2018. The evolutionary mismatch hypothesis: Implications for psychological science. *Current Directions in Psychological Science*, 27. 1: 38–44.

Little, A. C., 2015. 'Attraction and human mating'. In *Evolutionary Perspectives on Social Psychology*, edited by V. Zeigler-Hill et al., Springer International Publishing.

Little, A. C., & Jones, B. C., 2012. 'Variation in facial masculinity and symmetry preferences across the menstrual cycle is moderated by relationship context'. *Psychoneuroendocrinology* 37. 7: 999–1008.

Lobmaier, J. S., Bobst, C., & Probst, F., 2016. 'Can women detect cues to ovulation in other women's faces?' *Biology Letters* 12. 1: 20150638.

Lombardo, M. V., Ashwin, E., Auyeung, B., Chakrabarti, B., Lai, M.-C., Taylor, K., … & Baron-Cohen, S., 2012. 'Fetal programming effects of testosterone on the reward system and behavioral approach tendencies in humans'. *Biological Psychiatry* 72. 10: 839–847.

Lu, S., McKenna, S. E., Cologer-Clifford, A., Nau, E. A., & Simon, N. G., 1998. 'Androgen receptor in mouse brain: sex differences and similarities in autoregulation'. *Endocrinology* 139. 4: 1594–1601.

Manani, P., & Sharma, S. 2013. Self esteem and suicidal ideation: a correlational study. *MIER Journal of Educational Studies Trends & Practices* 75–83.

Maner, J. K., Gailliot, M. T., & DeWall, C. N. 2007. Adaptive attentional attunement: Evidence for mating-related perceptual bias. *Evolution and Human Behavior* 28(1): 28–36.

Mansfield, C. F., & Wosnitza, M., 2010. 'Motivation goals during adolescence: A cross-sectional perspective'. *Issues in Educational Research* 20. 2: 149–165.

Mazur, A., & Booth, A., 1998. 'Testosterone and dominance in men'. *Behavioral and Brain Sciences* 21. 3: 353–363.

McCormick, E. M., & Telzer, E. H., 2016. 'Adaptive adolescent flexibility: Neurodevelopment of Decision-making and learning in a risky context'. *Journal of Cognitive Neuroscience* 29. 3: 413–423.

McIver, T. A., Bosma, R. L., Goegan, S., Sandre, A., Klassen, J., Chiarella, J., … & Craig, W., 2019. Functional connectivity across social inclusion and exclusion is related to peer victimization and depressive symptoms in young adults. *Journal of Affective Disorders* 253: 366–375.

McRae, K., Gross, J. J., Weber, J., Robertson, E. R., Sokol-Hessner, P., Ray, R. D., … & Ochsner, K. N., 2012. 'The development of emotion regulation: An fMRI study of cognitive reappraisal in children, adolescents and young adults'. *Social Cognitive and Affective Neuroscience* 7. 1: 11–22.

Mendle, J., Harden, K. P., Brooks-Gunn, J., & Graber, J. A., 2012. Peer relationships and depressive symptomatology in boys at puberty. *Developmental Psychology* 48. 2: 429–435.

Mills, K. L., Dumontheil, I., Speekenbrink, M., & Blakemore, S. J., 2015. Multitasking during social interactions in adolescence and early adulthood. *Royal Society Open Science* 2. 11: 150117.

Mills, K. L., Lalonde, F., Clasen, L. S., Giedd, J. N., & Blakemore, S.-J., 2014. 'Developmental changes in the structure of the social brain in late childhood and adolescence'. *Social Cognitive and Affective Neuroscience* 9. 1: 123–131.

Monk, C. S., McClure, E. B., Nelson, E. E., Zarahn, E., Bilder, R. M., Leibenluft, E., … & Pine, D. S., 2003. 'Adolescent immaturity in attention-related brain engagement to emotional facial expressions'. *NeuroImage* 20. 1: 420–428.

Nelson, E. E., Jarcho, J. M., & Guyer, A. E., 2016. 'Social re-orientation and brain development: An expanded and updated view'. *Developmental Cognitive Neuroscience* 17: 118–127.

Nelson, E. E., Leibenluft, E., McClure, E. B., & Pine, D. S., 2005. 'The social re-orientation of adolescence: A neuroscience perspective on the process and its relation to psychopathology'. *Psychological Medicine* 35. 2: 163–174.

Ojanen, T., & Nostrand, F. V., 2014. Social goals, aggression, peer preference, and popularity: Longitudinal links during middle school. *Developmental Psychology* 50. 8: 2134–2143.

Olson, I. R., McCoy, D., Klobusicky, E., & Ross, L. A., 2013. 'Social cognition and the anterior temporal lobes: A review and theoretical framework'. *Social Cognitive and Affective Neuroscience* 8. 2: 123–133.

Ortigue, S., Bianchi-Demicheli, F., Patel, N., Frum, C., & Lewis, J. W., 2010. 'Neuroimaging of love: FMRI meta-analysis evidence toward new perspectives in sexual medicine'. *Journal of Sexual Medicine* 7. 11: 3541–3552.

Overgaauw, S., van Duijvenvoorde, A. C. K., Gunther Moor, B., & Crone, E. A., 2015. 'A longitudinal analysis of neural regions involved in reading the mind in the eyes'. *Social Cognitive and Affective Neuroscience* 10. 5: 619–627.

Patton, G. C., Coffey, C., Cappa, C., Currie, D., Riley, L., Gore, F., … & Ferguson, J., 2012. 'Health of the world's adolescents: A synthesis of internationally comparable data'. *Lancet* 379. 9826: 1665–1675.

Peake, S. J., Dishion, T. J., Stormshak, E. A., Moore, W. E., & Pfeifer, J. H., 2013. 'Risk-taking and social exclusion in adolescence: Neural mechanisms underlying peer influences on decision-making'. *NeuroImage* 82: 23–34.

Pelphrey, K. A., Morris, J. P., & McCarthy, G., 2004. 'Grasping the intentions of others: The perceived intentionality of an action influences activity in the superior temporal sulcus during social perception'. *Journal of Cognitive Neuroscience* 16. 10: 1706–1716.

Penton-Voak, I. S., & Chen, J. Y., 2004. 'High salivary testosterone is linked to masculine male facial appearance in humans'. *Evolution and Human Behavior* 25. 4: 229–241.

Peper, J. S., Brouwer, R. M., van Leeuwen, M., Schnack, H. G., Boomsma, D. I., Kahn, R. S., & Hulshoff Pol, H. E., 2010. 'HPG-axis hormones during puberty: A study on the association with hypothalamic and pituitary volumes'. *Psychoneuroendocrinology* 35. 1: 133–140.

Pessoa, L., 2009. 'How do emotion and motivation direct executive control?'. *Trends in cognitive sciences*, 13. 4: 160–166.

Peters, M., Simmons, L. W., & Rhodes, G., 2009. 'Preferences across the menstrual cycle for masculinity and symmetry in photographs of male faces and bodies'. *PLoS One* 4. 1: e4138.

Pfeifer, J. H., & Allen, N. B., 2016. 'The audacity of specificity: Moving adolescent developmental neuroscience towards more powerful scientific paradigms and translatable models'. *Developmental Cognitive Neuroscience* 17: 131–137.

Pfeifer, J. H., Masten, C. L., Moore III, W. E., Oswald, T. M., Mazziotta, J. C., Iacoboni, M., & Dapretto, M., 2011. 'Entering adolescence: Resistance to peer influence, risky behavior, and neural changes in emotion reactivity'. *Neuron* 69. 5: 1029–1036.

Pfeifer, J. H., Kahn, L. E., Merchant, J. S., Peake, S. J., Veroude, K., Masten, C. L., … & Dapretto, M., 2013. Longitudinal change in the neural bases of adolescent social self-evaluations: Effects of age and pubertal development. *Journal of Neuroscience* 33. 17: 7415–7419.

Platt, B., Kadosh, K. C., & Lau, J. Y. F., 2013. 'The role of peer rejection in adolescent depression'. *Depression and Anxiety* 30. 9: 809–821.

Puce, A., & Perrett, D., 2003. 'Electrophysiology and brain imaging of biological motion'. *Philosophical Transactions of the Royal Society of London. Series B, Biological Sciences* 358. 1431: 435–445.

Puts, D., 2016. Human sexual selection. *Current Opinion in Psychology* 7: 28–32.

Rhodes, G., Chan, J., Zebrowitz, L. A., & Simmons, L. W., 2003. 'Does sexual dimorphism in human faces signal health?'. *Proceedings of the Royal Society of London. Series B: Biological Sciences* 270. 1: S93–S95.

Roberts, S. C., Havlicek, J., Flegr, J., Hruskova, M., Little, A. C., Jones, B. C., … & Petrie, M., 2004. 'Female facial attractiveness increases during the fertile phase of the menstrual cycle'. *Proceedings of the Royal Society of London. Series B: Biological Sciences* 271. 5: S270–S272.

Rodriguez-Llanes, J.M., Verbeke, G., & Finlayson, C., 2009. 'Reproductive benefits of high social status in male macaques (Macaca)'. *Animal Behaviour* 78. 3: 643–649.

Romeo, R. D., Schulz, K. M., Nelson, A. L., Menard, T. A., & Sisk, C. L., 2003. 'Testosterone, puberty, and the pattern of male aggression in Syrian hamsters'. *Developmental Psychobiology* 43. 2: 102–108.

Roney, J. R., & Simmons, Z. L., 2013. 'Hormonal predictors of sexual motivation in natural menstrual cycles'. *Hormones and Behavior* 63. 4: 636–645.

Roney, J. R., Simmons, Z. L., & Gray, P. B., 2011. 'Changes in estradiol predict within-women shifts in attraction to facial cues of men's testosterone'. *Psychoneuroendocrinology* 36. 5: 742–749.

Rowe, R., Maughan, B., Worthman, C. M., Costello, E. J., & Angold, A., 2004. 'Testosterone, antisocial behavior, and social dominance in boys: Pubertal development and biosocial interaction'. *Biological Psychiatry* 55. 5: 546–552.

Rubia, K., Smith, A. B., Woolley, J., Nosarti, C., Heyman, I., Taylor, E., & Brammer, M., 2006. 'Progressive increase of frontostriatal brain activation from childhood to adulthood during event-related tasks of cognitive control'. *Human Brain Mapping* 27. 12: 973–993.

Rupp, H. A., & Wallen, K., 2007. 'Relationship between testosterone and interest in sexual stimuli: The effect of experience'. *Hormones and Behavior* 52. 5: 581–589.

Saxton, T. K., DeBruine, L., Jones, B., Little, A., Roberts, S., 2009. 'Face and voice attractiveness judgements change during adolescence'. *Evolution and Human Behavior* 30: 398–408.

Schlegel, A., & Barry III, H., 1991. *Adolescence: An Anthropological Inquiry*. Free Press.

Schulz, K. M., & Sisk, C. L., 2016. 'The organizing actions of adolescent gonadal steroid hormones on brain and behavioral development'. *Neuroscience & Biobehavioral Reviews* 70: 148–158.

Sebastian, C. L., Fontaine, N. M. G., Bird, G., Blakemore, S.-J., De Brito, S. A., McCrory, E. J. P., & Viding, E., 2012. 'Neural processing associated with cognitive and affective Theory of Mind in adolescents and adults'. *Social Cognitive and Affective Neuroscience* 7. 1: 53–63.

Silvers, J. A., McRae, K., Gabrieli, J. D. E., Gross, J. J., Remy, K. A., & Ochsner, K. N., 2012. 'Age-related differences in emotional reactivity, regulation, and rejection sensitivity in adolescence'. *Emotion* 12. 6: 1235.

Silvers, J. A., Insel, C., Powers, A., Franz, P., Helion, C., Martin, R. E., … & Ochsner, K. N., 2017. 'VlPFC–vmPFC–amygdala interactions underlie age-related differences in cognitive regulation of emotion'. *Cerebral Cortex* 27. 7: 3502–3514.Sisk, C. L., & Foster, D. L., 2004. 'The neural basis of puberty and adolescence'. *Nature Neuroscience* 7. 10: 1040–1047.

Sisk, C. L., & Zehr, J. L., 2005. 'Pubertal hormones organize the adolescent brain and behavior'. *Frontiers in Neuroendocrinology* 26. 3: 163–174.

Smith, A. R., Chein, J., & Steinberg, L., 2014. 'Peers increase adolescent risk taking even when the probabilities of negative outcomes are known'. *Developmental Psychology* 50. 5: 1564.

Smith, A. R., Steinberg, L., Strang, N., & Chein, J., 2015. 'Age differences in the impact of peers on adolescents' and adults' neural response to reward'. *Developmental Cognitive Neuroscience* 11: 75–82.

Somerville, L. H., Jones, R. M., Ruberry, E. J., Dyke, J. P., Glover, G., & Casey, B. J., 2013. 'The medial prefrontal cortex and the emergence of self-conscious emotion in adolescence'. *Psychological Science* 24. 8: 1554–1562.

Spielberg, J. M., Olino, T. M., Forbes, E. E., & Dahl, R. E., 2014. 'Exciting fear in adolescence: Does pubertal development alter threat processing?' *Developmental Cognitive Neuroscience* 8: 86–95.

Steinberg, L., 2010. 'A dual systems model of adolescent risk-taking'. *Journal of the International Society for Developmental Psychobiology* 52. 3: 216–224.

Suleiman, A. B., Galván, A., Harden, K. P., & Dahl, R. E., 2017. 'Becoming a sexual being: The 'elephant in the room' of adolescent brain development'. *Developmental Cognitive Neuroscience* 25: 209–220.

Symeonidou, I., Dumontheil, I., Chow, W.-Y., & Breheny, R., 2016. 'Development of online use of theory of mind during adolescence: An eye-tracking study'. *Journal of Experimental Child Psychology* 149: 81–97.

van den Berg, Y. H. M., Burk, W. J., & Cillessen, A. H. N., 2019. 'The functions of aggression in gaining, maintaining, and losing popularity during adolescence: A multiple-cohort design'. *Developmental Psychology* 55. 10: 2159.

van den Bos, W., & Eppinger, B., 2016. 'Developing developmental cognitive neuroscience: From agenda setting to hypothesis testing'. *Developmental Cognitive Neuroscience* 17: 138–144.

van den Bos, W., Cohen, M. X., Kahnt, T., & Crone, E. A., 2012. 'Striatum-medial prefrontal cortex connectivity predicts developmental changes in reinforcement learning'. Cerebral Cortex 22. 6: 1247–1255.

van den Bos, W., van Dijk, E., Westenberg, M., Rombouts, S. A. R. B., & Crone, E. A., 2011. 'Changing brains, changing perspectives: The neurocognitive development of reciprocity'. *Psychological Science* 22. 1: 60–70.

van den Broek, N., Deutz, M. H. F., Schoneveld, E. A., Burk, W. J., & Cillessen, A. H. N., 2016. 'Behavioral correlates of prioritizing popularity in adolescence'. *Journal of Youth and Adolescence* 45. 12: 2444–2454.

van Honk, J., Schutter, D. J. L. G., Hermans, E. J., Putman, P., Tuiten, A., & Koppeschaar, H., 2004. 'Testosterone shifts the balance between sensitivity for punishment and reward in healthy young women'. *Psychoneuroendocrinology* 29. 7: 937–943.

Vermeersch, H., T'Sjoen, G., Kaufman, J.-M., & Vincke, J., 2008. 'Estradiol, testosterone, differential association and aggressive and non-aggressive risk-taking in adolescent girls'. *Psychoneuroendocrinology* 33. 7: 897–908.

Victor, E. C., & Hariri, A. R., 2016. 'A neuroscience perspective on sexual risk behavior in adolescence and emerging adulthood'. *Development and Psychopathology* 28. 2: 471–487.

Vijayakumar, N., Cheng, T. W., & Pfeifer, J. H., 2017. 'Neural correlates of social exclusion across ages: A coordinate-based meta-analysis of functional MRI studies'. *NeuroImage* 153: 359–368.

Vijayakumar, N., Op de Macks, Z., Shirtcliff, E. A., & Pfeifer, J. H., 2018. 'Puberty and the human brain: Insights into adolescent development'. *Neuroscience & Biobehavioral Reviews* 92: 417–436.

Wang, A. T., Lee, S. S., Sigman, M., & Dapretto, M., 2006. 'Neural basis of irony comprehension in children with autism: The role of prosody and context'. *Brain: A Journal of Neurology* 129. 4: 932–943.

Wenner, C. J., Bianchi, J., Figueredo, A. J., Rushton, J. P., & Jacobs, W. J., 2013. Life history theory and social deviance: The mediating role of executive function. *Intelligence* 41. 2: 102–113.

Wingfield, J. C., Hegner, R. E., Dufty, Alfred M., & Ball, G. F., 1990. 'The 'Challenge Hypothesis': Theoretical implications for patterns of testosterone secretion, mating systems, and breeding strategies'. *American Naturalist* 136. 6: 829–846.

Wirth, M. M., & Schultheiss, O. C., 2007. 'Basal testosterone moderates responses to anger faces in humans'. *Physiology & Behavior* 90. 2–3: 496–505.

Wlodarski, R., & Dunbar, R. I. M., 2014. 'The effects of romantic love on mentalising abilities'. *Review of General Psychology* 18. 4: 313–321.

Xie, X., Mulej Bratec, S., Schmid, G., Meng, C., Doll, A., Wohlschläger, A., … & Sorg, C., 2016. 'How do you make me feel better? Social cognitive emotion regulation and the default mode network'. *NeuroImage* 134: 270–280.

Yurgelun-Todd, D. A., & Killgore, W. D. S., 2006. 'Fear-related activity in the prefrontal cortex increases with age during adolescence: A preliminary fMRI study'. *Neuroscience Letters* 406. 3: 194–199.

5
Mindreading in Adults
Cognitive Basis, Motivation, and Individual Differences

Ian A. Apperly and J. Jessica Wang

5.1 Introduction

Research on mindreading in adults has come a long way in the past 15 years. Whereas mindreading was once considered a topic of relevance only in early childhood, it has become increasingly clear that this approach, however interesting, was rather myopic. In particular, studying how infants and children first come to think about other minds falls far short of providing an account of how older children and adults mindread successfully, or how this success varies between contexts and between individuals. The expansion of interest in research on adults has led to the development of many new paradigms, and to an increased interest in the factors that influence performance, not just the ability in principle to succeed under optimal conditions. There is also a proliferation of terminology, which may or may not correspond to differences in theories or concepts. We take the term 'mindreading' to be synonymous with 'Theory of Mind' (ToM) and 'mentalizing', which are in common usage. 'Perspective taking' and 'empathizing' are used in a variety of ways by different authors in different research traditions, with varying degrees of precision and theoretical commitment. We do not aim to assimilate all these approaches or settle any conflicts here. Instead, we try to see the wood that is emerging from the rapid growth of trees by relating tasks to a cognitive model of component processes in mindreading. This approach highlights similarities or differences between tasks (such as whether or not a mental state must be inferred), and leaves open some potentially important questions—for example, about similarities and differences between inferences about beliefs *versus* inferences about visual perspectives. This will surely turn out to be wrong in a variety of ways, but we hope that even the mistakes may be a useful guide for future work.

We begin by describing a cognitive model of mindreading that attempts to make sense of a range of experimental results, and provides a framework for ongoing work. We discuss some of the challenges that arise when we switch from asking questions about the universal components of mindreading to questions about individual differences in performance. This leads into a discussion of motivation, which has tended to be overlooked as an influence on mindreading performance, but which may provide critical sources of variation between individuals.

5.2 A cognitive model of mindreading

Most mindreading tasks—even the simplest ones used with children—combine and confound multiple processing steps involved in inferring what someone else might think or feel, in storing this information, and in using it to explain, predict, or justify behaviour. This poses a serious challenge for researchers because, if we want to know how memory and cognitive control processes contribute to mindreading, how different brain regions might support mindreading, or how and why people might vary in their mindreading abilities, then we really need a cognitive model and suitable tasks that allow component processes to be studied independently. Here, we summarize such a model from Apperly (2010), and the evidence that supports the distinctions it draws. Relevant tasks are described briefly here, just to illustrate their emphasis on different processes. In later sections, we employ the model to interpret the emerging literature on individual differences in mindreading in adult participants, and these sections also do more justice to the broader findings with these and other tasks.

The model is pitched at Marr's 'computational' level of description (Marr, 1982), and so aims to capture intuitively plausible components of 'what the system needs to do' during mindreading. Such models are agnostic about the functional and neural implementation of the processes they describe, but can provide a useful way of thinking about the demands of particular tasks, and how they relate to functional and neural processes.

The horizontal dimension of Fig. 5.1 distinguishes *inference*, *storage*, and *use* of mindreading information. A combination of laboratory tasks helps isolate these distinctive stages, their behavioural effects, and neural correlates. Just as people sometimes tell us what they think or feel, laboratory tasks can obviate the need for inferring new mental states by directly telling participants what a character believes or wants. One such task targets the *storage* of mindreading information, because participants simply reported back information they had been told about a character's belief, with no need to use that information to explain or predict behaviour (Apperly et al., 2008). Participants read two briefly presented sentences describing a character's belief and reality (e.g. 'He thinks the object on the table is blue'/'Really, the object on the table is yellow'), which were followed by a picture that probed for the information in one of the two sentences. In this task, 'egocentric' effects were evident in slower responses to both belief and reality probes when the character's belief was false rather than true or neutral. An extension of this task required participants to *store* and *use* mindreading information to predict a character's behaviour based on their desire to avoid or obtain a target object and

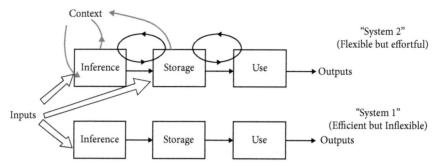

Fig. 5.1 A cognitive model of mindreading (simplified from Apperly, 2010)
The model distinguishes processes involved in inference, storage, and use of information about others' mental states. 'System 2' makes flexible, context-sensitive mindreading inferences by drawing richly upon background knowledge in processes represented by great arrows. Oval arrows indicate that System 2 mindreading will often involve repeated cycles of reasoning. 'System 1' processes manage to be more cognitively efficient by limiting their interaction with background information and limiting their processing over inputs. For clarity, only a single System 1 process is depicted, but there are likely to be multiple processes—for example, to enable mindreading of belief-like states, goals, and emotions.

Adapted with permission from Apperly, I.A. 2010. *Mindreaders: The Cognitive Basis of" Theory of Mind"*. Psychology Press.

their true or false belief about its location (e.g. Apperly et al., 2011). Response times were slower when the character's belief was false and their desire was negative. The effects of belief and desire were associated with variation in neural activity in the bilateral temporo-parietal junction, but not the medial prefrontal cortex (mPFC; Hartwright et al., 2012): a surprising result because each of these brain regions is implicated in the great majority of neuroimaging studies of mindreading. Activity in the mPFC *was* observed in a follow-up study in which mindreading inferences were introduced to the task (Hartwright et al., 2014), suggesting that the different functions in Fig. 5.1 are supported by different neural correlates—patterns that are obscured when mindreading tasks confound these functions. Finally, the widely used 'director task' (Keysar et al., 2000, 2003) minimizes demands on inference and storage (at least in cases where the director's discrepant perspective is always visually apparent), and focuses primarily on the need for participants to *use* the director's perspective to interpret their instructions. 'Egocentric' biases are observed in a high frequency of eye movements and errors whereby participants struggle or fail to integrate the director's perspective with their interpretation of their instruction, but such biases may not be apparent in earlier processing (Barr, 2008).

The vertical dimension in Fig. 5.1 distinguishes between 'System 1' and 'System 2' processes (e.g. Evans & Stanovich, 2013). System 2 processes enable mindreading that is highly flexible but relatively demanding of scarce resources for memory and cognitive control (e.g. Apperly & Butterfill, 2009; Low et al., 2016). Flexibility is essential, because there is no principled limit on the thoughts, intentions, knowledge, or feelings we can ascribe to others, provided they are mental states we could entertain for ourselves (e.g. Apperly, 2010). The claim that System 2 mindreading is demanding is supported by evidence that mindreading is not automatic (Apperly et al., 2006; Back & Apperly, 2010), that it can be disrupted by concurrent performance of an effortful task (Bull et al., 2008) and that individual differences in mindreading, memory, and cognitive control are often correlated (e.g. Bradford et al., 2015; German & Hehman, 2006; Mckinnon & Moscovich, 2007; Qureshi et al., 2020). System 1 is more efficient than System 2, but at the expense of being less flexible. Increased efficiency is indicated by evidence that some (but not all) mindreading is relatively automatic, and relatively independent of cognitive control processes (e.g. Kovács et al., 2010; Qureshi et al., 2010; Samson et al., 2010; van der Wel et al., 2014). There is evidence to suggest that these effects are only apparent for relatively simple problems (such as inferring what someone sees; Samson et al., 2010) and not for more complex problems (such as inferring precisely how they see it from their perspective; Surtees et al., 2016) suggesting limited flexibility in System 1 processes, consistent with the characteristics of System 1 processes in other domains such as number cognition or logical reasoning (Evans & Stanovich, 2013).

Figure 5.1 foregrounds the fact that mindreading requires inference, storage, and use of the mental states of 'others', but of course the mindreader also has their own 'self' perspective. The self perspective is both the essential background against which other people's mental states are represented and also a potent source of competition for attention and responses. Most obviously, the 'egocentric' effects described above (Apperly et al., 2011; Barr, 2008) arise because of interference or competition from one's own perspective when the target for mindreading has mental states that differ (even for very simple differences, such as when an object is known to self but not to the other). Importantly, an analogous 'altercentric' interference effect can arise for the mindreader who, once they represent the contrasting perspective of the other, then finds it more difficult to make a judgement according to their own perspective (Apperly et al., 2008; Back & Apperly, 2010; Kovács et al., 2010; Samson et al., 2010; Van der Wel et al., 2014; Wang et al., 2019). It is debated whether some paradigms give the misleading appearance of altercentric effects, which may instead be due to automatic cueing of visual attention (e.g. Cole et al., 2017; Heyes, 2014, for opposing views). However, altercentric interference also arises in a range of paradigms that do not include such cues (e.g. Apperly et al., 2008), or where the slow time course or nature of the stimuli makes such cueing implausible as an explanation for the effect (Back & Apperly, 2010; Surtees et al. 2016). Therefore, the phenomenon of altercentric interference is well evidenced, even if care must be taken with interpreting specific instances.

Resisting egocentric and altercentric interference is correlated with brain activity in the right inferior frontal gyrus (IFG), a brain region commonly associated with resolving competition between conflicting responses (Hartwright et al., 2012; McCleery et al., 2011; Wagner et al., 2001). Temporary disruption or permanent lesions to IFG result in increased egocentrism (Hartwright et al., 2016; Samson et al., 2005, 2015). Importantly, these effects are apparent when there is conflict between self and other perspectives (as in false belief tasks), but not for equally demanding mindreading conditions that involve predicting that an agent will avoid an object they do not like rather than seek an object that they do like (Hartwright et al., 2016), or non-mindreading conditions involving mismatches between stimulus and response (Samson et al., 2015). There are, of course, many factors that influence performance on a given mindreading task, and these are of little theoretical interest when they are specific to a particular task. In contrast to this, the need to resolve interference between perspectives is a demand that arises in many tasks, and appears to recruit distinctive cognitive control processes with reliable neural correlates.

In summary, while it is very far from being exhaustive, this model offers a systematic way of thinking about the cognitive demands of mindreading, how they can be decomposed and investigated in different mindreading tasks, and how they are supported by different brain processes.

5.3 Individual differences

Everyday intuition suggests that some people are more socially able than others, that some people are better mindreaders than others, and perhaps that these two abilities are related. However, turning these intuitions into meaningful hypotheses poses significant challenges, both in terms of conceptualizing how mindreading might vary, and in measuring such variation robustly. Inspiration for how to address these challenges might be drawn from the analogous case of understanding the structure and predictive significance of individual differences in executive function (e.g. Friedman & Miyake, 2017).

5.3.1 Conceptualization

Theories about the development of mindreading typically emphasize the acquisition of core concepts of desire, knowledge, belief, etc. (e.g. Wellman, 2014), though even in development it is far from clear that commonly observed individual differences in mindreading arise from variation in concepts (Apperly, 2012). Even more clearly, thinking in terms of mindreading concepts does not help us understand variability of mindreading in typical adults, because there is no variance in the possession of such concepts beyond late childhood. Instead, we might expect adults to vary in the speed and efficiency of their mindreading, and (as we shall come to later) in their motivation or propensity for mindreading. The model and findings above help organize these questions. First, System 2 processes, which are relatively effortful, are likely to leave more room for individual differences than System 1 processes, which are relatively automatic. Second, because memory and executive function are deeply implicated in System 2 processes, it seems likely that variation in these abilities contributes to variation in System 2 mindreading. Third, mindreading involves multiple component processes (e.g. inference, storage, and use) that may vary in their demands on memory and cognitive control, and also in the degree to which they generate individual differences. One ultimate goal should be to understand precisely which processes act as limiting steps, such that they generate individual differences in performance. Another should be to relate such differences to real social outcomes.

5.3.2 Measurement challenges: one

Because adults perform at ceiling on tests for mindreading concepts developed for use with children, one move in the literature has been to devise 'advanced' tasks that generate variance by being more subtle or complicated (e.g. Baron-Cohen et al., 2001; Castelli et al., 2000; Dziobek et al., 2006). For instance, the 'Reading the Mind in the Eyes' task (Baron-Cohen, 1997) shows participants the eye region of faces and requires them to match subtle facial expressions to verbal descriptions. Castelli et al.'s (2000) 'animated triangles' task requires participants to supply short verbal descriptions for the behaviour of geometric figures that appear to be enacting social scenarios. The Movie Assessment of Social Cognition (Dziobek et al., 2006) prompts participants for verbal interpretations of the relatively complex thoughts and feelings of four characters in a realistic movie of social interactions. These tasks consistently generate individual differences in performance, and demonstrate criterion validity by correlating with sub-clinical social characteristics associated with autism and psychosis (Baron-Cohen et al., 2001; Abell et al., 2000; Dziobek et al., 2006). However, the complexity of these tasks, while successful in generating variance in performance, serves to obscure the underlying cognitive processes. It is not possible to tell whether participants experience difficulty with inferring or storing mental states, or with using them to frame a judgement or explanation. Additionally, it is difficult or impossible to be sure whether difficulty is driven by the 'social' complexity of the task, by 'non-social' complexity (such as the general demands to make judgements or explanations of equivalent complexity), or by other incidental features (such as the need to sustain attention over the course of the task). Therefore, while these tasks are surely useful, they do little to help us understand the cognitive basis of mindreading abilities or how different component processes contribute to individual differences in mindreading. The rest of this discussion will concern tasks that do afford this more mechanistic approach.

5.3.2.1 Mindreading tasks sometimes correlate with other cognitive and social tasks

German and Hehman (2006) had participants read short vignettes, for which comprehension required inferences about a character's beliefs and desires, storage of this information, and use of this information to predict their behaviour in response to a test question. German and Hehman found that the speed and accuracy of adults' responses were correlated with working memory capacity, processing speed, and inhibitory control. The director task requires participants to move items around a grid in response to the directions of a speaker/director whose visual perspective means they can only see some of the items. On critical trials, a correct interpretation of their messages requires participants to ignore a referent that is the best fit for the message from their own perspective and select the reference that is the best fit from the director's perspective. Correlations have been observed between egocentric effects on this task, and its variants and performance on tests of inhibitory control (Brown-Schmidt, 2009; Qureshi et al., 2020), and working memory capacity (Lin et al., 2010). However, other studies have failed to observe similar effects (Brown-Schmidt, 2012; Cane et al., 2017; Ryskin et al., 2014).

A small number of studies have examined the criterion validity of these laboratory tasks. Abu-Akel et al. (2015) found that egocentric errors on the director task were predicted by questionnaire-based assessments of participants' sub-clinical characteristics associated with autism and psychosis, as well as the interaction of these characteristics. On similar tasks, Nilsen and Duong (2013) found more errors among participants with more depressive symptoms (though see Ferguson & Cane, 2017, for conflicting findings), and Converse et al. (2008) found fewer errors in participants induced to have a low/negative mood compared with a high/positive mood. Bukowski and Samson (2017) used a simple visual perspective-taking task in which participants judged how many dots could be seen on the walls of a cartoon room either from the perspective of an avatar standing in the room or from participants' own 'self' perspective. Bukowski and Samson pooled data over judgements for self and avatar, and created an index of 'self-other interference' by comparing speed and accuracy of responses for trials on which self and other perspectives were consistent versus inconsistent. These authors found that participants who showed the lowest interference between self and other perspectives also gave higher assessments of their own perspective-taking abilities on the perspective-taking sub-scale of the Interpersonal Reactivity Index (Davis, 1980). Together, these studies provide some evidence that variance in performance on mindreading tasks is not merely 'measurement error' or random variation, but may be systematically related to individual variability in other cognitive processes, and traits related to social ability. However, it is notable that these investigations are relatively few and the findings are far from consistent.

5.3.2.2 Mindreading tasks do not always correlate with each other

Strikingly, a number of recent studies have failed to find correlations between the performance of adults tested on more than one mindreading task. Warnell and Redcay (2019) employed four very diverse tasks that assessed the use of mental state terms in descriptions of silent film clips (Rice & Redcay, 2015), Reading the Mind in the Eyes (Baron-Cohen et al., 2001), reasoning about recursive mental states (Stiller & Dunbar, 2007), deductive reasoning about beliefs and desires (Apperly et al., 2011), and pragmatic language comprehension (Koster-Hale et al., 2012, unpublished). No correlation coefficient greater than 0.125 was observed and all were non-significant. Ryskin et al. (2014) examined the relationship between participants' successful avoidance of egocentric eye fixations during a comprehension task and their non-egocentric use of adjectives to clarify their message to an ignorant listener in a speech production task. No correlation was observed, which could not be wholly attributed to poor internal reliability of the comprehension task data. Of course, this could be because one or other of these measures was not truly indexing egocentrism, or because egocentrism can arise in different ways in different tasks (see below). Qureshi et al. (2020) found no correlation between adults' egocentric errors on a version of the director task and egocentric bias (or self-other interference) in response times on a simple visual perspective-taking task, despite each showing good internal reliabilities and distinctive (though modest) correlations with tests of inhibitory control. Wang et al. (2019) also found no correlation between these mindreading tasks in a sample of British and Taiwanese participants. In the following sections, we consider what might account for the limited evidence of correlations in these studies.

5.3.3 Measurement challenges: two

These findings are rather sobering, but our view is that they should prompt researchers to think harder about the distinct challenges involved in measurement of individual differences. (To be clear, we include ourselves among those who would benefit from thinking harder! See Qureshi et al., 2020, for related discussion.)

5.3.3.1 Good laboratory tasks are not always good measures: a lesson from research on executive function

While the literature on individual differences in executive function has successfully revealed distinctive patterns of covariance among tasks, and distinctive relationships with intelligence (e.g. Friedman & Miyake, 2017, for a recent review), it has been noted that the correlations among laboratory executive tasks are often low, and laboratory tasks may not correlate at all with self-assessed traits for the same abilities, or supposedly related real-world outcomes (such as dieting, smoking, or gambling; e.g. Eisenberg et al., 2019). One possibility is that laboratory tasks are measuring abilities of limited real-world relevance. Alternatively, Hedge et al. (2018) point out that such outcomes might follow naturally from the fact that laboratory tasks (such as classic executive function tasks, and almost all the mindreading tasks described above) are typically optimized to detect differences between different experimental conditions. In doing so, we tend to test participants on multiple trials that are similar or even identical within the level of an experimental factor, which of course minimizes individual differences in performance between participants. What is needed is a different approach that varies the level of difficulty of a particular process in systematic and theoretically informative ways. For example, to test the storage of mindreading information, we need a task within which we can independently vary the 'load' on storage, perhaps by systematically varying the number of people whose mental states need to be tracked and/or the number of mental states for each person. Such an approach greatly increases the chances of detecting differences between high- and low-performing individuals.

5.3.3.2 Some mindreading processes may be necessary but not limiting for healthy adults

Varying the 'load' on a particular process may sometimes be a productive way of generating valid individual differences in performance. However, this is unlikely always to be the case, (1) because serial processing often results in only one limiting 'bottleneck', and (2) because some component processes may not pose a significant challenge for healthy adults within any realistic range of load. For example, converging evidence from dual-tasking studies, neuropsychology, neuroimaging, and neural stimulation suggests that inhibitory control processes associated with the right IFG are necessary for controlling interference between self and other perspectives (see above). However, the need to control interference between perspectives only arises once participants begin trying to infer or store mindreading information. As we shall discuss below, there are grounds for thinking that people vary in their motivation or propensity for mindreading in the first place, which could effectively overshadow effects due to variation in inhibitory control, which only contribute to individual differences once mindreading has been initiated. Additionally, even when mindreading is initiated and inhibitory control is necessary, this does not mean that the need for inhibitory control stretches the capacity of healthy adults to meet this demand. This may be especially true for laboratory tasks, but it may also be true that mindreading 'in the wild' of everyday life does not normally place demands on inhibitory control that any healthy adult struggles to meet. If this were so, then individual differences in inhibitory control would not predict individual differences in mindreading, and neither would predict individual differences in real-life social ability. All this could be true, despite real-life social ability being functionally dependent upon the successful deployment of inhibitory control during mindreading. Reality may be less extreme than these illustrations but, nevertheless, it is important to recognize that individual differences in mindreading are only likely to arise from a sub-set of the processes that are necessary.

5.3.4 Mindreading apples and oranges

The earlier section on the cognitive basis of mindreading made the case that, far from being a monolithic, 'black box' function, mindreading has multiple component processes giving rise to distinctive behavioural effects and neural correlates. It follows that, when we turn to consider individual differences in performance, no single task or measure is likely to capture all sources of variability in mindreading. Nor will it necessarily be the case that (say) someone who shows a high propensity for spontaneous mindreading inferences (without explicit task instruction) also shows a high capacity for storing complex mental states of multiple individuals, or for resisting interference between self and other perspectives.

Importantly, the same principle applies even within narrower classes of phenomena, such as self-other interference effects. As described above, egocentric interference effects are very commonly observed when mindreading tasks involve conflict between the perspective of self and other, and it would be parsimonious to suppose that these reflected the same underlying processes. This was part of the motivation for Qureshi et al. (2020) looking for a relationship between egocentric errors on the director task and self-other interference on a simple visual perspective-taking task. However, while such relationships are surely possible, they are very far from inevitable—self-other interference effects may arise in different ways on different tasks, because they tap different stages of processing. For example, both the director task and the visual perspective-taking task used by Qureshi et al. (2020) involve processing what another person can see (so-called 'Level-1 visual perspective taking'). On the simple visual perspective-taking task, there is evidence that calculation of self and other perspectives involves processes that dissociate from selection of the correct perspective for responding on a given trial (Qureshi et al., 2010). Evidence from event-related potentials (ERPs) suggests that participants first calculate and then select the appropriate perspective, and it is the latter selection process that is associated with brain activity in the right IFG, and which influences speed and accuracy of responses.

In contrast, in the director task, there is evidence that egocentric errors arise when participants, who have already processed the director's visual perspective, fail to integrate this perspective with their instruction to move objects around a grid (Barr, 2008). Different functional origins for the interference effects on the tasks used by Qureshi et al. (2020) would help explain why these effects were not correlated. More importantly, this case points to a more general lesson that 'egocentrism' and other self-other interference effects are not one phenomenon, but many. They may be better regarded as a family of phenomena, with an abstract similarity and common origin in the functional requirement of representing conflicting perspectives. Whether or not there will be correlations between individual differences in such interference effects will depend on how errors, response time differences, or other behavioural indices actually arise in the mindreading process tapped by a particular task.

5.4 Motivation

The discussions in previous sections come together when considering the roles of motivation in mindreading. Evidence that mindreading is frequently dependent on scarce cognitive resources creates a potential role for motivation in determining whether or not these resources will be prioritized for mindreading over other activity. We will review evidence that suggests situational motivators (henceforth *situational incentives*), such as monetary reward, may influence the likelihood of mindreading. We will also examine evidence for significant variation in individuals' social motivation, empathy, mind-mindedness, and sub-clinical autistic and psychotic characteristics (henceforth *mindreading propensity*), which raises the possibility that these traits may contribute to individual differences in mindreading and social ability. This discussion will motivate a distinction between the willingness and capacity to engage in effortful mindreading *versus* the propensity to even think of it in the first place.

5.4.1 Mindreading needs situational incentives

A number of situational incentives for mindreading have been studied and shown to have varied degrees of effectiveness on mindreading. Social relationships and social hierarchy can be effective incentives for both human and non-human primates. A classic study of chimpanzees' visual perspective taking utilized the hierarchical nature of the relationship between participating chimpanzees to set up an optimal condition in which to observe perspective taking in chimpanzees (Hare et al., 2001). It was shown that a subordinate chimpanzee was incentivized to account for a dominant chimpanzee's visual perspective in order to maximize its chances of winning food. In contrast, a dominant chimpanzee would not have had the same incentives when faced with food competition against a subordinate chimpanzee. Evidence from humans also suggest that social relationship can be an effective mindreading incentive. Savitsky and colleagues (2011) showed that, in a variation of the director task, young adults performed worse when they were required to use the perspective of a friend or romantic partner rather than a stranger. This is plausibly due to the participants being overly confident about their ability to communicate with a close-other. Interestingly, Zhang et al. (2018) found what appeared to be the reverse pattern. Their elderly adult participants who were tested on a set of ToM tests by a family relative performed better on a faux pas judgement task than those whose tests were administered by a stranger. The authors suggest that, because older adults have limited cognitive resources available to them, these resources are only expended when necessary (also see the selective engagement hypothesis by Hess, 2006; 2014). These studies highlight the incentives carried by social relationships and social hierarchy in both human and non-human primates, and the fact that the relative importance of these incentives may vary across the lifespan.

On the other hand, while monetary reward is a commonly used incentive in behavioural economics studies, it does not appear to have a straightforward effect on mindreading. Cane et al. (2017) employed a variation of the director task whereby participants were given a limited window to use a director's perspective and resolve reference early. When no monetary incentive was offered, participants did not take the opportunity to use the director's perspective early. When monetary incentive was offered to reward fast and accurate responses, earlier perspective use was only seen under a low, but not high, concurrent cognitive load. Lane and Liersch (2012) employed a spoken communication task in which participants were asked to withhold a piece of secret information from a communicative partner, who could capitalize on the secret information to the participants' detriment. Strikingly, when participants were offered monetary reward to withhold the secret, they were more likely to reveal the secret compared with when they offered non-monetary course credit. These findings clearly indicated that financial incentives cannot buy good mindreading.

A recent study of our own suggests that non-monetary incentives could be provided through a simple manipulation of the overt instructions (Wang et al., 2020). Using a standard computer-based director task, we found that a clear introductory example setting out the ways in which a director's perspective needs to be used was highly effective in reducing egocentric errors. The novel instruction not only improved the overall accuracy, but also resulted in fewer errors prior to the first correct response, and a lower (but still notable) error rate after the first correct response. This pattern would not be observed if the novel instruction had simply enabled more participants to understand what the task required. Instead, our results suggested that the novel instruction motivated participants to try harder at integrating the director's perspective to interpret their instructions even if it was effortful. In a second experiment, we orthogonally manipulated the incentives to inhibit one's own perspective *versus* the incentives to use others' perspectives. We found that the latter manipulation benefitted performance the most, indicating that the ways in which others' perspectives need to be used is most likely overlooked by participants in the absence of additional incentives.

Perhaps somewhat contrary to our intuition about motivation, monetary incentives appeared to be the least effective of the situational incentives reviewed here. Social relationships clearly moderate mindreading in both human and non-human primates. The hierarchy and varied degrees of closeness embedded in human social relationships offer an opportunity to model the real-life dynamics between individuals, and their incentives to read each other's minds. Social relationships not only provide situational incentives: they may also be interacting factors with age, as one's social role and access to cognitive resources change across the lifespan (e.g. Hess, 2014). Finally, incentives delivered via task instructions could offer a productive way to understand the dynamics between multiple incentives. It is clear that mindreading is not a fixed capacity for an individual that is deployed whenever it might be necessary: instead, the extent to which individuals expend effort to mindread is very much dependent on the situational incentives.

5.4.2 Mindreading propensity

Individual differences in mindreading are likely underpinned by the necessary competence and capacity, situational incentives, *and* the varied propensities to think about others' minds. This section reviews examples of such variability, which can be seen in domains of empathy, mind-mindedness, and sub-clinical autistic and psychotic characteristics.

Empathy, as measured by self-reported tendency to have concerns for others, has been shown to relate to the degrees to which individuals spontaneously keep track of others' mental states when it is unnecessary to do so (Ferguson et al., 2015; Meert et al., 2017; Nielsen et al., 2015). All three studies employed tasks where participants were not explicitly required to keep track of others' beliefs or visual perspectives but needed instead to infer this information spontaneously. The degrees to which participants spontaneously tracked others' mental states were captured as the aforementioned 'altercentric' intrusions, on trials where participants made judgements about their own visual perspectives and beliefs (Meert et al., 2017; Nielsen et al., 2015), or alternatively, as an ERP signal (N400), which closely follows the detection of semantic inconsistencies between a protagonist's belief and statements about their belief (Ferguson et al., 2015). These sensitive measures of ERP and response times revealed additional processing of others' beliefs, which were unlikely to be carried out deliberately. It is not possible to infer the causal relationship between empathetic concerns and spontaneous belief tracking based on such correlations. However, it is plausible that the propensity to have concerns about others accounts for at least some variability in mindreading.

Mind-mindedness refers to the extent to which parents use mental state language rather than physical or behavioural appearance to describe their infants. Meins and colleagues (1998) found that parental mind-mindedness at their child's third year of life is predictive of the child's ToM task performance at 4–5 years of age. Meins and colleagues have argued that mind-mindedness only affects an individual's propensity for mindreading in close personal relationships (e.g. Meins et al., 2014), but other work suggests that adults show meaningful individual differences in the rate at which they focus on mental states when asked to explain or interpret stories (e.g. Dodell-Feder et al., 2013), simple animations (Castelli et al., 2000), and movies (Dziobek et al., 2006). Critically, more mindreading does not necessarily lead to positive social outcomes. Studies employing these tasks suggest that it is possible to engage in excessive attribution of mental states, leading to misinterpretation and misjudgement of social scenarios. This tendency for 'overmentalizing' is higher in patients with schizophrenia (e.g. Montag et al., 2011) and Tourette syndrome (Eddy & Cavanna, 2015). Altogether, these studies suggest that the motivation and propensity to focus on mental states is a source of variation between individuals. However, such motivation does not guarantee positive social outcomes.

Finally, as previously mentioned, sub-clinical autistic and psychotic characteristics and their interaction have been shown to correspond to rates of egocentric errors in the director task (Abu-Akel et al., 2015). This is of considerable interest because it highlights a new dimension with which mindreading abilities vary within the sub-clinical population. Furthermore, it provides a bridge between the clinical and sub-clinical domains. The tradition of contrasting clinical versus sub-clinical groups may have led us to overlook the variability within these populations. In light of the current consideration about mindreading propensity, we turn to the literature on social cognitive deficits in autism spectrum disorder (ASD).

The social motivation theory (Chevallier et al., 2012) postulates that typically developed individuals readily orient to social information and are rewarded intrinsically by these social experiences, leading to the development of expertise in social information. In contrast, individuals with ASD lack the initial desire for social interaction or to orient to social information. Therefore, individuals with ASD are thought more likely to develop expertise in non-social information. In contrast, the Mindblindness framework (Baron-Cohen, 1997) reverses this causal story, suggesting that individuals with ASD have an initial deficit in the understanding of social signals, which leads to diminished interest and motivation in social information. While we are in no position to adjudicate on the theoretical debate, the fact that both theoretical frameworks emphasize the role of motivation highlights the necessity to include motivational factors into models of individual differences. Furthermore, we could take lessons on task design and selection from the clinical social cognition literature. Most mindreading tasks in the sub-clinical domain explicitly prompt mindreading and require judgements of simple mindreading problems under strong contextual constraints. These properties may leave little or no room for motivation to have effects. Additionally, 'advanced' mindreading tasks for typically developed adults are prone to be laden with cognitive demands that are not specifically related to mindreading. While these demands may realistically reflect the greater complexity of some instances of real-life mindreading, variability in performance on such tasks may tell us more about individuals' general processing capacities than their mindreading abilities per se.

5.4.3 Mindreading propensity meets situational incentives

It seems reasonable to expect mindreading propensity to interact with situational incentives. While we are not aware of any direct investigation of such an interaction, an example of the meeting between mindreading propensity and mindreading incentives comes from recent development in the cross-cultural domain. For background: an influential cross-cultural framework by Markus and Kitayama (1991) postulates that the ways in which the self is conceptualized is shaped by the cultural framework one operates within. Individuals from Western cultures are likely to construe the self as independent of others, whereas individuals from East Asian cultures are likely to construe a self-concept that is interdependent and inclusive of important others. Markus and Wurf (1987) argued that an independent self-construal would motivate self-serving actions, while Markus and Kitayama (1991) suggest that an interdependent self-construal would motivate social actions as a replacement for self-focused motives. Following this line of reasoning, Wu and Keysar (2007; see Wu et al., 2013 for further analysis of the original data) tested a group of American home students and a group of newly arrived Chinese international students at an American university. They found that both groups of students showed similar levels of initial egocentrism on the aforementioned director task. However, the Chinese students were quicker to correct themselves, and attended to the director's perspective rather than their own. It is possible that culturally shaped self-construal propels the mindreading system to attend others' perspectives at different speeds. Interestingly, two recent studies that have tested each cultural group in their native environments both pointed towards similarities across independent and interdependent cultures (Bradford et al., 2018; Wang et al., 2019). Our own findings suggest that there were no observable differences between British and Taiwanese participants in the behavioural responses and eye movement records in perspective-calculation (Level-1 visual perspective-taking task; Samson et al., 2010) or perspective-use (director task; Apperly et al., 2010). It seems reasonable to speculate that the asymmetry in the students' status in the Wu and Keysar study (2007) may have led to different incentives. It is possible that the way in which the Chinese students were specifically recruited for their recent arrival in the U.S. and their cultural identity gave them some incentives to work harder at the task, whereas the home students did not have such incentives. Of course, this is an empirical question that requires verification. Additionally, given the body of evidence behind contrasting processing styles between independent and interdependent cultures (see Nisbett & Miyamoto, 2005, for a brief review), it is quite possible that what cross-cultural studies capture is the interaction between mindreading propensity, as shaped by culture, along with situational incentives. Furthermore, differences in self-focused *versus* other-focused processing has been observed within a Western culture (Bukowski & Samson, 2017). These studies suggest that mindreading propensity is a likely dimension on which mindreading varies between individuals and cultures, and that the intrinsic propensity to mindread should be taken into account alongside situational incentives.

5.5 Closing remarks and remaining questions

In summary, motivation to mindread clearly does not guarantee successful mindreading. However, mindreading is still influenced by individuals' propensity to mindread and a number of situational factors they may encounter. There are a number of remaining questions to be addressed. For instance, referring back to the cognitive model summarized above (Apperly, 2010), currently it is not clear whether motivation affects all stages of mindreading and whether it can influence mindreading processes associated with both systems. We have seen associations between efficient belief tracking and empathy. However, we simply do not know whether situational incentives for mindreading could affect efficient mindreading. One might predict that automatic processes, such as Level-1 visual perspective calculation, will be relatively immune from external manipulation. Though, if anything was going to affect such processing, it might be between-participant variation in propensity to attend to social stimuli. Furthermore, the operationalization of motivation has mostly been simplified to reward versus no-reward conditions. The Wang et al. (2019) study was one of the first to introduce orthogonal manipulation of incentives for different aspects of mindreading: in this case, inhibiting one's own perspective and using the other's perspective to constrain reference. This type of design would shed light on the potential interactions between a number of incentivizing factors. Finally, drawing together the different themes of this chapter, it is clear that a competent mindreader needs to have the cognitive flexibility and the motivation to mindread at socially appropriate and relevant times. While we suspect that all these factors may contribute to individual differences in mindreading, we suspect that there will be predictable circumstances in which some are more important than others, and this will be critical for understanding the success (and occasional conspicuous failure) of mindreading to enable successful social interactions.

References

Abell, F., Happe, F., & Frith, U., 2000. 'Do triangles play tricks? Attribution of mental states to animated shapes in normal and abnormal development'. *Cognitive Development* 15. 1: 1–16.

Abu-Akel, A. M., Wood, S. J., Hansen, P. C., & Apperly, I. A., 2015. 'Perspective-taking abilities in the balance between autism tendencies and psychosis proneness'. *Proceedings of the Royal Society B: Biological Sciences* 282. 1808: 20150563.

Apperly, I. A. 2010. *Mindreaders: The Cognitive Basis of 'Theory of Mind'*. Psychology Press.

Apperly, I. A., 2012. 'What is "theory of mind"? Concepts, cognitive processes and individual differences'. *Quarterly Journal of Experimental Psychology* 65. 5: 825–839.

Apperly, I. A., & Butterfill, S. A., 2009. 'Do humans have two systems to track beliefs and belief-like states?'. *Psychological Review* 116. 4: 953–970.

Apperly, I. A., Back, E., Samson, D., & France, L., 2008. 'The cost of thinking about false beliefs: Evidence from adult performance on a non-inferential theory of mind task'. *Cognition* 106: 1093–1108.

Apperly, I. A., Riggs, K. J., Simpson, A., Chiavarino, C., & Samson, D., 2006. 'Is belief reasoning automatic?'. *Psychological Science* 17. 10: 841–844.

Apperly, I. A., Warren, F., Andrews, B. J., Grant, J., & Todd, S., 2011.'Error patterns in the belief-desire reasoning of 3- to 5-year-olds recur in reaction times from 6 years to adulthood: Evidence for developmental continuity in theory of mind'. *Child Development* 82. 5: 1691–703.

Apperly, I. A., Carroll, D. J., Samson, D., Humphreys, G. W., Qureshi, A., & Moffitt, G., 2010. 'Why are there limits on theory of mind use? Evidence from adults' ability to follow instructions from an ignorant speaker'. *Quarterly Journal of Experimental Psychology* 63. 6: 1201–1217.

Back, E., & Apperly, I. A., 2010. 'Two sources of evidence on the non-automaticity of true and false belief ascription'. *Cognition* 115. 1: 54–70.

Baron-Cohen, S. 1997. *Mindblindness: An Essay on Autism and Theory of Mind*. MIT Press.

Baron-Cohen, S., Wheelwright, S., Hill, J., Raste, Y., & Plumb, I., 2001. 'The "Reading the Mind in the Eyes" Test revised version: a study with normal adults, and adults with Asperger syndrome or high-functioning autism'. *The Journal of Child Psychology and Psychiatry and Allied Disciplines* 42. 2: 241–251.

Barr, D. J., 2008. 'Pragmatic expectations and linguistic evidence: Listeners anticipate but do not integrate common ground'. *Cognition* 109. 1: 18–40.

Bradford, E. E., Jentzsch, I., Gomez, J. C., Chen, Y., Zhang, D., & Su, Y., 2018. 'Cross-cultural differences in adult theory of mind abilities: a comparison of native-English speakers and native-Chinese speakers on the self/other differentiation task'. *Quarterly Journal of Experimental Psychology* 71. 12: 2665–2676.

Bradford, E. E. F., Jentzsch, I., & Gomez, J-C., 2015. 'From self to social cognition: Theory of Mind mechanisms and their relation to Executive Functioning'. *Cognition* 138: 21–34.

Brown-Schmidt, S., 2009. 'The role of executive function in perspective taking during on-line language comprehension'. *Psychonomic Bulletin & Review* 16: 893–900.

Brown-Schmidt, S., 2012. 'Beyond common and privileged: gradient representations of common ground in real-time language use'. *Language and Cognitive Processes* 27. 1: 62–89.

Bukowski, H., & Samson, D., 2017. 'New insights into the inter-individual variability in perspective taking'. *Vision* 1. 1: 8.

Bull, R., Phillips, L. H., & Conway, C. A., 2008. 'The role of control functions in mentalizing: Dual-task studies of Theory of Mind and executive function'. *Cognition* 107: 663–672.

Cane, J. E., Ferguson, H. J., & Apperly, I. A., 2017. 'Using perspective to resolve reference: The impact of cognitive load and motivation'. *Journal of Experimental Psychology: Learning, Memory, and Cognition* 43. 4: 591–610.

Castelli, F., Happé, F., Frith, U., & Frith, C., 2000. 'Movement and mind: A functional imaging study of perception and interpretation of complex intentional movement patterns'. *NeuroImage* 12. 3: 314–325.

Chevallier, C., Kohls, G., Troiani, V., Brodkin, E. S., & Schultz, R. T., 2012. 'The social motivation theory of autism'. *Trends in Cognitive Sciences* 16. 4: 231–239.

Cole, G. G., Atkinson, M. A., D'Souza, A. D., & Smith, D. T., 2017. 'Spontaneous perspective taking in humans?'. *Vision* 1. 2: 17.

Converse, B. A., Lin, S., Keysar, B., & Epley, N., 2008. 'In the mood to get over yourself: Mood affects theory-of-mind use'. *Emotion* 8. 5: 725.

Davis, M. H., 1980. 'A multidimensional approach to individual differences in empathy'. *JSAS Catalog of Selected Documents in Psychology* 10: 85.

Dodell-Feder, D., Lincoln, S. H., Coulson, J. P., & Hooker, C. I., 2013. 'Using fiction to assess mental state understanding: a new task for assessing theory of mind in adults'. *PLoS One* 8. 11: e81279.

Dziobek, I., Fleck, S., Kalbe, E., Rogers, K., Hassenstab, J., Brand, M., ... & Convit, A., 2006. 'Introducing MASC: A movie for the assessment of social cognition'. *Journal of Autism and Developmental Disorders* 36. 5: 623–636.

Eddy, C. M., & Cavanna, A. E., 2015. 'Triangles, tricks and tics: Hyper-mentalizing in response to animated shapes in Tourette syndrome'. *Cortex* 71: 68–75.

Eisenberg, I. W., Bissett, P. G., Enkavi, A. Z., Li, J., MacKinnon, D. P., Marsch, L. A., & Poldrack, R. A., 2019. 'Uncovering the structure of self-regulation through data-driven ontology discovery'. *Nature Communications* 10. 1: 2319.

Evans, J. S. B., & Stanovich, K. E., 2013. 'Dual-process theories of higher cognition: Advancing the debate'. *Perspectives on Psychological Science* 8. 3: 223–241.

Ferguson, H. J., & Cane, J., 2017. 'Tracking the impact of depression in a perspective-taking task'. *Scientific Reports* 7. 1: 14821.

Ferguson, H. J., Cane, J. E., Douchkov, M., & Wright, D., 2015. 'Empathy predicts false belief reasoning ability: evidence from the N400'. *Social Cognitive and Affective Neuroscience* 10. 6: 848–855.

Friedman, N. P., & Miyake, A., 2017. 'Unity and diversity of executive functions: Individual differences as a window on cognitive structure'. *Cortex* 86: 186–204.

German, T. P., & Hehman, J. A., 2006. 'Representational and executive selection resources in "theory of mind": Evidence from compromised belief-desire reasoning in old age'. *Cognition* 101. 1: 129–152.

Hare, B., Call, J., & Tomasello, M., 2001. 'Do chimpanzees know what conspecifics know?'. *Animal Behaviour* 61. 1: 139–151.

Hartwright, C., Apperly, I. A., & Hansen, P. C., 2012. 'Multiple roles for executive control in belief-desire reasoning: Distinct neural networks are recruited for self perspective inhibition and complexity of reasoning'. *NeuroImage* 61. 4: 921–930.

Hartwright, C., Apperly, I. A., & Hansen, P. C., 2014. 'Representation, control or reasoning? Distinct functions for Theory of Mind within the medial prefrontal cortex'. *Journal of Cognitive Neuroscience* 26. 4: 683–698.

Hartwright, C. E., Hardwick, R., Apperly I. A., & Hansen, P., 2016. 'Structural morphology in resting state networks predict the effect of theta burst stimulation in false belief reasoning'. *Human Brain Mapping* 37: 3502–3514.

Hedge, C., Powell, G., & Sumner, P., 2018. 'The reliability paradox: Why robust cognitive tasks do not produce reliable individual differences'. *Behavior Research Methods* 50. 3: 1166–1186.

Hess, T. M., 2006. 'Adaptive aspects of social cognitive functioning in adulthood: age–related goal and knowledge influences'. *Social Cognition* 24. 3: 279–309.

Hess, T. M., 2014. 'Selective engagement of cognitive resources: Motivational influences on older adults' cognitive functioning'. *Perspectives on Psychological Science* 9. 4: 388–407.

Heyes, C., 2014. 'Submentalizing: I am not really reading your mind'. *Perspectives on Psychological Science* 9. 2: 131–143.

Keysar, B., Lin, S., & Barr, D. J., 2003. 'Limits on theory of mind use in adults'. *Cognition* 89. 1: 25–41.

Keysar, B., Barr, D. J., Balin, J. A., & Brauner, J. S., 2000. 'Taking perspective in conversation: The role of mutual knowledge in comprehension'. *Psychological Science* 11. 1: 32–38.Koster-Hale, J., Dodell-Feder, D., & Saxe, R., 2012. [Unpublished instrument].

Kovács, Á. M., Téglás, E., & Endress, A. D., 2010. 'The social sense: Susceptibility to others' beliefs in human infants and adults'. *Science* 330: 1830–1834.

Lane, L. W., & Liersch, M. J., 2012. 'Can you keep a secret? Increasing speakers' motivation to keep information confidential yields poorer outcomes'. *Language and Cognitive Processes* 27. 3: 462–473.

Lin, S., Keysar, B., & Epley, N., 2010. 'Reflexively mindblind: Using theory of mind to interpret behavior requires effortful attention'. *Journal of Experimental Social Psychology* 46. 3: 551–556.

Low, J. Apperly, I. A., Butterfill, S. A., & Rakoczy, H., 2016. 'Cognitive architecture of belief reasoning in children and adults: A primer on the two-systems account'. *Child Development Perspectives* 10. 3: 184–189.

Markus, H., & Wurf, E., 1987. 'The dynamic self-concept: A social psychological perspective'. *Annual Review of Psychology* 38. 1: 299–337.

Markus, H. R., & Kitayama, S., 1991. 'Culture and the self: Implications for cognition, emotion, and motivation'. *Psychological Review* 98. 2: 224.Marr, D. 1982. *Vision: A Computational Investigation into the Human Representation and Processing of Visual Information*. Henry Holt and Co. Inc.

McCleery, J. P., Surtees, A. D., Graham, K. A., Richards, J. E., & Apperly, I. A., 2011. 'The neural and cognitive time course of theory of mind'. *Journal of Neuroscience* 31. 36: 12849–12854.

McKinnon M. C., & Moscovitch, M., 2007. 'Domain-general contributions to social reasoning: Theory of mind and deontic reasoning re-explored'. *Cognition* 102: 179–218.

Meert, G., Wang, J., & Samson, D., 2017. 'Efficient belief tracking in adults: The role of task instruction, low-level associative processes and dispositional social functioning'. *Cognition* 168: 91–98.

Meins, E., Fernyhough, C., & Harris-Waller, J., 2014. 'Is mind-mindedness trait-like or a quality of close relationships? Evidence from descriptions of significant others, famous people, and works of art'. *Cognition* 130. 3: 417–427.

Meins, E., Fernyhough, C., Russell, J., & Clark-Carter, D., 1998. 'Security of attachment as a predictor of symbolic and mentalising abilities: A longitudinal study'. *Social Development* 7. 1: 1–24.

Montag, C., Dziobek, I., Richter, I. S., Neuhaus, K., Lehmann, A., Sylla, R., ... & Gallinat, J., 2011. 'Different aspects of theory of mind in paranoid schizophrenia: Evidence from a video-based assessment'. *Psychiatry Research* 186. 2–3: 203–209.

Nielsen, M. K., Slade, L., Levy, J. P., & Holmes, A., 2015. 'Inclined to see it your way: Do altercentric intrusion effects in visual perspective taking reflect an intrinsically social process?' *Quarterly Journal of Experimental Psychology* 68. 10: 1931–1951.

Nilsen, E. S., & Duong, D., 2013. 'Depressive symptoms and use of perspective taking within a communicative context'. *Cognition & Emotion* 27. 2: 335–344.

Nisbett, R. E., & Miyamoto, Y., 2005. 'The influence of culture: Holistic versus analytic perception'. *Trends in Cognitive Sciences* 9. 10: 467–473.

Qureshi, A., Apperly, I. A., & Samson, D., 2010. 'Executive function is necessary for perspective-selection, not Level-1 visual perspective-calculation: Evidence from a dual-task study of adults'. *Cognition* 117. 2: 230–236.

Qureshi, A. W., Monk, R. L., Samson, D., & Apperly, I. A., 2020. 'Does interference between self and other perspectives in Theory of Mind Tasks reflect a common underlying process? Evidence from individual differences in theory of mind and inhibitory control'. *Psychonomic Bulletin and Review* 27. 1: 178–190.

Rice, K., & Redcay, E., 2015. 'Spontaneous mentalizing captures variability in the cortical thickness of social brain regions'. *Social Cognitive and Affective Neuroscience* 10. 3: 327–334.

Ryskin, R. A., Brown-Schmidt, S., Canseco-Gonzalez, E., Yiu, L. K., & Nguyen, E. T., 2014. 'Visuospatial perspective-taking in conversation and the role of bilingual experience'. *Journal of Memory and Language* 74: 46–76.

Samson, D., Houthuys, S., & Humphreys, G. W., 2015. 'Self- perspective inhibition deficits cannot be explained by general executive control difficulties'. *Cortex* 70: 189e201.

Samson, D., Apperly, I. A., Kathirgamanathan, U., & Humphreys, G. W., 2005. 'Seeing it my way: A case of selective deficit in inhibiting self-perspective'. *Brain* 128: 1102–1111.

Samson, D., Apperly, I. A., Braithwaite, J. J., Andrews, B. J., & Bodley Scott, S. E., 2010. 'Seeing it their way: Evidence for rapid and involuntary computation of what other people see'. *Journal of Experimental Psychology: Human Perception and Performance* 36. 5: 1255.

Savitsky, K., Keysar, B., Epley, N., Carter, T., & Swanson, A., 2011. 'The closeness-communication bias: Increased egocentrism among friends versus strangers'. *Journal of Experimental Social Psychology* 47. 1: 269–273.

Stiller, J., & Dunbar, R. I., 2007. 'Perspective-taking and memory capacity predict social network size'. *Social Networks* 29. 1: 93–104.

Surtees, A. Samson, D., & Apperly, I. A., 2016. 'Unintentional perspective-taking calculates whether something is seen, but not how it is seen'. *Cognition* 146: 97–105.

van der Wel, R. P., Sebanz, N., & Knoblich, G., 2014. 'Do people automatically track others' beliefs? Evidence from a continuous measure'. *Cognition* 130. 1: 128–133.

Wagner, A. D., Maril, A., Bjork, R. A., & Schacter, D. L., 2001. 'Prefrontal contributions to executive control: fMRI evidence for functional distinctions within lateral prefrontal cortex'. *NeuroImage* 14. 6: 1337–1347.

Wang, J. J., Ciranova, N., Woods, B., & Apperly, I. A., submitted. 'Why are listeners sometimes (but not always) egocentric? Making inferences about using others' perspective in referential communication'. *PloS One* 15. 10: e0240521.

Wang, J. J., Tseng, P., Juan, C-H., Frisson, S., & Apperly, I. A., 2019. 'Perspective-taking across cultures: Shared biases in Taiwanese and British adults'. *Royal Society Open Science* 6. 11: 190540.

Warnell, K. R., & Redcay, E., 2019. 'Minimal coherence among varied theory of mind measures in childhood and adulthood'. *Cognition* 191: 103997.

Wellman, H. M. 2014. *Making Minds: How Theory of Mind Develops*. Oxford University Press.

Wu, S., & Keysar, B., 2007. 'The effect of culture on perspective taking'. *Psychological Science* 18. 7: 600–606.

Wu, S., Barr, D. J., Gann, T. M., & Keysar, B., 2013. 'How culture influences perspective taking: Differences in correction, not integration'. *Frontiers in Human Neuroscience* 7: 822.Zhang, X., Lecce, S., Ceccato, I., Cavallini, E., Zhang, L., & Chen, T., 2018. 'Plasticity in older adults' theory of mind performance: The impact of motivation'. *Aging & Mental Health* 22. 12: 1592–1599.

6
Social Interactions in Old Age

Victoria E. A. Brunsdon*, Elisabeth E. F. Bradford*, and Heather J. Ferguson

6.1 Introduction

The world's population is ageing. In 1980, the global population aged 60 years or over was 382 million. By 2017, this had tripled to 962 million and it is projected to double again to nearly 2.1 billion by 2050. It is expected that there will be more people aged 60 and over than aged 10 to 24 years old in 2050, largely due to increased life expectancies worldwide (Office for National Statistics, 2018; Department of Economic and Social Affairs, Population Division, 2017). It is critical to understand the challenges faced by ageing populations in maintaining and improving quality of life—for instance, our social relationships and experiences are crucial for healthy ageing, with research indicating that the quantity and quality of social interactions are associated with better mental and physical health outcomes (Bailey et al., 2008; Sullivan & Ruffman, 2004a; Strang et al., 2012). Given this, a better understanding of the behaviour and cognition in older people relating to social interactions is required (e.g. in terms of characterization of the cognitive processes underlying social interactions in healthy ageing), to allow us to be better able to meet the needs of an ageing population on a global scale.

During social interactions, we need to understand other people's emotions, thoughts, and intentions to successfully predict and interpret their behaviour. Thus, everyday social experiences rely on our social-cognitive capacities, such as understanding mental states, empathic accuracy, and recognition of others' emotions. Yet, social cognition—the cognitive processes utilized to understand social agents and social interactions—may be reduced in older age, resulting in impaired social functioning (Bailey et al., 2008; Henry et al., 2013; Moran et al., 2012; Martin et al., 2019). The majority of social cognition research has been conducted on younger adults, or on the development of social cognition in children, with much less focus on older people, and even less on middle-aged adults. Social cognition research can help us to understand cognitive continuity and change, and how to improve our social interactions as we get older. This is necessary because impairments in understanding others' mental states or emotional states could have widespread impacts on social interactions, with clear consequences for a person's health and well-being. For example, there is a strong relationship between

---

* Denotes both of these authors were first authors of this chapter.

social interaction and physical and mental health in older adults, with social isolation in older age leading to more adverse outcomes (Unger et al., 1997; Gheysen et al., 2018; Zhu et al., 2016). Studies have shown that older people with more social contacts live longer, irrespective of health status, socio-economic status, smoking, drinking, physical activity, or obesity (Berkman & Syme, 1979). Furthermore, social interactions have been shown to alleviate some of the learning and memory problems experienced by older people (e.g. Derksen et al., 2015). Thus, there are clear benefits to further building our understanding of social cognition in older life, allowing for insights into how social cognition abilities, such as being able to accurately represent others' minds, correctly identify complex emotions, and be empathic towards other people, may improve social interactions; how this in turn may relate to health and life satisfaction outcomes at different ages; and whether there is scope for enhancing social cognition abilities in individuals experiencing difficulties with these capacities.

In this chapter, we will review what is currently known about the ageing trajectories of different components of social cognition, including social cognition in older age (see Box 6.1 for an overview of how the onset of 'old age' may be defined). We focus on several social processes that have been examined behaviourally in healthy ageing populations, namely: Theory of Mind (ToM), empathy, emotion recognition, action understanding, and imitation. We also describe other aspects of social cognition that are less well established in cognitive ageing research, along with considerations of potential future directions of ageing research in the field of social interactions and social cognition.

Box 6.1 When is 'old age'?

This chapter discusses social interactions in old age—but when is the onset of old age? Old age is defined as the last stage in life development. In modern Western societies, the onset of old age in human beings is typically conceptualized as 60 or 65 years old. However, there is no universally accepted age that defines when 'old age' begins.

The definition of old age differs depending on the historical and societal context. For example, the Friendly Societies Act 1875 in the UK defined old age as any age after 50. In African countries, the World Health Organization defines 50+ as old age. In Western countries, 65–68 years old is commonly used as defining when old age begins, because of this being reflective of 'pension' age. However, 65-year-olds in the future will have longer life expectancies, higher levels of education, and better cognitive functioning than 65-year-olds today. Categorizing over 65 years old as 'old age' may no longer be appropriate because of increasing life expectancies.[1] To add, there has been a rise in the maximum

---

[1] Sanderson, W. C., & Scherbov, S., 2015. 'Faster increases in human life expectancy could lead to slower population aging'. *PLoS One* 10. 4: e0121922.

age at death[2], with a doubling of the number of centenarians in the UK from 2002 to 2016.[3] If the onset of old age is defined as 65 years old, then old age spans more than 35 years. There are different issues that are important at different stages of old age—for example, compare a 65-year-old adjusting to retired life and awaiting the arrival of their first grandchild with a 100-year-old suffering from increasing ailments with limited mobility[4].

The definition of old age has implications for ageing research. There is a case for considering different stages in old age—for example, young–old (65–74-years-old), middle–old (75–84-years old), and old–old adults (85 years old and over).

A note about 'middle' age
Of the studies that examine ageing effects in social cognition abilities, most focus on young- versus old-age adults. But what about middle-age? There are currently not many studies that include middle-age adults in research samples, yet it is essential to include middle-age adults if seeking to pinpoint when problems with social cognition may arise, and what the predictors of successful ageing may be. Importantly, it is noted that biological ageing and chronological ageing are distinct concepts: different individuals age at different rates. This further highlights that, in seeking to understand ageing effects on social cognition abilities, it is important to include longitudinal rather than cross-sectional studies, whenever possible, to allow measures of individual differences across different time points in predicting performance on measures of social cognition.

6.2 How do aspects of social cognition change with age?

Cognitive ageing is the decline in cognitive processes as people get older. These cognitive processes play an important role in our everyday life, allowing us to focus attention on specific tasks, to remember key information, to engage in successful problem solving, and to plan for the future. In 1930, a seminal study reported declines in perceptual, motor, and cognitive abilities from 30 years of age (Miles, 1933). Another example of the pioneering work into cognitive ageing by Rabbitt (1965) reported that older adults have greater difficulties ignoring irrelevant information. Since these early studies, there have been major advances in our theoretical

---

[2] Dong, X., Milholland, B., & Vijg, J., 2016. 'Evidence for a limit to human lifespan'. *Nature* 538: 257–259.

[3] Siddique, H., 2017, September 27. 'Centenarians are fastest growing age group in UK, figures show'. *The Guardian*. Available at: https://www.theguardian.com/society/2017/sep/27/rise-in-uk-life-expectancy-slows-significantly-figures-show

[4] Jopp, D. S., Boerner, K., & Rott, C., 2016. 'Health and disease at age 100. Findings from the second Heidelberg Centenarian Study'. *Deutsches Arzteblatt International* 113. 12: 203–210.

understanding of cognitive ageing (Anderson & Craik, 2017). Older age is associated with declines in many cognitive processes, including speed of processing, working memory, reasoning ability, face processing, fluid intelligence, crystallized intelligence, verbal and visuospatial memory, long-term memory, inhibitory control, planning ability, and cognitive flexibility (Salthouse, 1996; Schaie, 2000; Kramer & Willis, 2002). These age-related declines in cognitive processes have been attributed to changes in brain structure and function (e.g. Raz et al., 2005).

Research into the ageing trajectories of the cognitive processes underlying social interactions has been sparser. Much of the literature focuses on the development of social-cognitive skills from infancy through childhood, such as joint attention and false belief understanding (Flavell, 1999), or on its impairment in neurodevelopmental or psychiatric disorders, such as autism (e.g. Senju, 2013) and schizophrenia (e.g. Penn et al, 1997). Furthermore, the term 'social cognition' encapsulates many overlapping socio-cognitive processes, such as ToM, empathy, emotion recognition, and action understanding, with no clearly defined taxonomy for social cognition (Beer & Ochsner, 2006; Happé et al., 2017). Here, we define social cognition as the cognitive processes used to understand the social world. These are important, yet complex, cognitive processes that could be particularly vulnerable to ageing. In the following section, we will discuss what is currently known about the ageing trajectories of the putative components (as outlined by Happé and colleagues, 2017) of social cognition.

6.2.1 Theory of Mind

The term 'Theory of Mind' (ToM) was coined by Premack and Woodruff (1978) to refer to the ability to infer one's own and other people's mental states (i.e. beliefs, desires, intentions) in order to understand and predict behaviour in social interactions. ToM is also known as 'mindreading', 'mentalizing', and 'mental state attribution'. Many studies have conceptualized ToM and social cognition as the same function. However, social cognition encompasses a wider set of cognitive functions that underlie social interactions and includes ToM as a core component. ToM is crucial for regulating social interactions and for maintaining social relationships, with a proficient ToM preceding more effective interpersonal relationships and social interactions (Lecce et al., 2019; Frith & Frith, 2003; Begeer et al., 2010). Indeed, failures in ToM abilities can lead to miscommunication and misunderstandings during social interactions (Maylor et al., 2002; Phillips et al., 2011).

The trajectory of ToM development in childhood has been extensively studied (e.g. Frith & Frith, 2003; Onishi & Baillargeon, 2005; Perner & Lang, 1999). A crucial developmental milestone in ToM is widely agreed to occur at age 4 years, when a child begins to be able to understand that another person can have beliefs that are not true and that are different from their own, as demonstrated by passing tests of explicit false belief understanding (Wimmer & Perner, 1983). This ability to attribute false beliefs precedes the development of more complex forms of ToM later in childhood, such as second-order false belief understanding (Perner & Wimmer, 1985). Development of ToM continues into late childhood and even adolescence, with further developments in the recognition of more complex emotional states and in the ability to consider another person's perspective (Dumontheil et al., 2010, Vetter et al., 2013). By adulthood, neurotypical individuals are argued to be in possession of fully developed ToM abilities, although studies have shown that, despite this, they still sometimes fail to implement these abilities in social interactions (e.g. Keysar et al., 2003; Apperly, 2012; Samson et al., 2010). Furthermore, studies have reported that adults are biased towards their own beliefs, desires, and feelings, and sometimes neglect to consider other people's perspectives unless explicitly prompted to do so (e.g. Samson et al., 2010; Bradford et al., 2015). Most ageing research has focused on this component of social cognition (ToM abilities) and has used paradigms that are broadly concerned with three types of tasks: story tasks (Happé, 1994), false belief tasks (Wimmer & Perner, 1983), and faux pas tasks (Baron-Cohen et al., 1999), which will be discussed in turn below.

6.2.1.1 Strange Stories task

Early work into the effect of ageing on ToM abilities focused on tasks that measure mentalistic inferences about the intentions of story protagonists. A pioneering study by Happé and colleagues (1998) into older people's ToM abilities utilized the Strange Stories task, which includes stories about double bluffs, mistakes, persuasions, and white lies (Happé, 1994). To perform well, accurate inferences need to be made about the characters in the story based on their thoughts, feelings, and intentions. Using this task, Happé and colleagues found that older adults showed *better* ToM abilities than younger adults, indicating that ToM ability is preserved or even enhanced in older age. Happé discussed this finding in terms of the notion that 'with age comes wisdom': in other words, greater life experience may enhance ToM. However, research that has attempted to replicate these findings has not been successful. Instead, studies using story-based ToM tasks that compare performance in younger and older age groups have indicated an age-related *decline* in ToM abilities (Maylor et al., 2002; Sullivan and Ruffman, 2004b; Rakoczy et al., 2012; Wang & Su, 2013). Given these findings, Cavallini and colleagues (2013) attempted to establish whether declines in ToM task performance such as these are related to declines in other cognitive factors, such as executive function abilities, or whether these declines are specific to ToM abilities. Results from Cavallini et al. suggested that declines in performance on the Strange Stories task were independent of working memory and inhibitory control abilities, and that this specific impairment in ToM begins at 60 years of age. However, it is noted that Cavallini et al.'s study did not have a middle-aged group included to support these claims; that is, participants in this study were split into three groups—young (20–30 years), young–old

(59–70 years), and old–old (71–82 years) adults—and given that the youngest 'old' participants were 59 years, it is difficult to ascertain whether declines in ToM abilities begin at an earlier age than this.

In general, middle-aged adults are often overlooked in social cognition research, with studies focusing on comparing dichotomous groups of young versus older adults. Baksh and colleagues (2018) reported a decline in ToM abilities from 18 to 85 years of age, but did not use a continuous age sample, instead comparing younger-, middle,- and older-aged groups of adults. Another study compared a young adult group with middle- and older-aged adult groups and revealed a non-linear increase in false belief (egocentric) bias across adulthood that is more pronounced between young- and middle-age than in older adulthood (Bernstein et al., 2011): in other words, ToM abilities were superior among young adults but were relatively stable between middle and old age. These studies provide some insights into changes in ToM abilities as a function of age, indicating the presence of a decline in abilities with advancing age, but the group-based comparison approach does not allow the detection of the developmental trajectories of ToM across the entire lifespan. Very few studies have used a continuous lifespan approach to examine ToM development. One study, by Charlton et al. (2009), examined age-related differences in ToM across middle to older age, testing a cohort of participants aged 50–90 years; they found a linear decline in ToM abilities from middle to older age. Further, studies that have included a continuous age range from adolescence to older age have indicated that ToM ability continues to improve from adolescence through to adulthood, with a peak at 30 years old, a decline to 70 years old, and no further change in older age (Brunsdon et al., 2019). Importantly, Brunsdon et al.'s results also show that this age effect is specific to social inferences, and does not reflect a general decline in memory in these story-based tasks.

6.2.1.2 False belief tasks

False belief tasks tap the ability to understand other people in terms of their internal mental states such as their beliefs and intentions, and are considered a litmus test of ToM. Overall, data suggests that false belief understanding declines in older age (German & Hehman, 2006; McKinnon & Muscovitch, 2007; Bailey & Henry, 2008; Phillips et al., 2011). In particular, older adults are able to adopt the perspective of one other person (as in first-order false belief understanding), but have difficulties when they need to adopt the perspective of two people simultaneously (as in second-order false belief understanding; McKinnon & Muscovitch, 2007). This decline in false belief understanding abilities is apparent from 65 (Phillips et al., 2011) to 70 years of age (Duval et al., 2011). Interestingly, even though older adults show these objective declines in false-belief understanding, subjectively they consider themselves to be proficient mindreaders, and rarely complain about experiencing 'real-world' ToM issues, indicating that older individuals may either not have insights into their impairments (Duval et al., 2011), or may perform better in real-world scenarios compared with experimental settings (Johansson Nolaker et al., 2018).

It is noted that a large number of studies into false-belief understanding in older adults have used group comparisons rather than continuous samples. There are a number of reasons for this, including funding limitations and accessibility to participants. However, it should be kept in mind when considering ageing literature regarding social cognition abilities, because it limits the conclusions that can be drawn regarding, for example, the age at which changes in social cognition capacities are first observed. In addition, most false-belief tasks require a categorical response, which may produce floor or ceiling effects when using a lifespan approach. In a typical false-belief paradigm, a character places an object in location X that is moved to location Y in the character's absence. Participants are then required to indicate where the character will look for the object: in location Y (where the object is currently located) or location X (where the character thinks the object is). Thus, there are only two responses supposing an all-or-nothing approach to ToM. To address these issues, Bernstein and colleagues (2017) used a continuous measure of false-belief understanding—the 'Sandbox' task—with individuals aged from 3- to 92-years old. False-belief understanding was found to be stable from the preschool years, through to older childhood, until younger adulthood, followed by a small decline in false-belief understanding from young to older adulthood. These results indicate that older adults therefore do not lose the capacity to understand another person's beliefs as age advances, but do experience difficulties representing another person's beliefs when they have to suppress their own beliefs.

6.2.1.3 Faux pas tasks

Faux pas tasks test the understanding of multiple mental states in everyday social situations. A 'faux pas' is a social gaffe in which there is an embarrassing or inconsiderate action or comment made in a social situation. Some studies have suggested that older adults, when compared with younger adults, are less able to discriminate when someone has committed a faux pas or has acted inappropriately towards others (Halberstadt et al., 2011). Conversely, Bottiroli and colleagues (2016) did not find any age-related differences in the ability to detect if someone had committed a faux pas or not. One reason for these apparently contradictory findings in ToM studies investigating differences between younger and older age groups may relate to varying education levels of participants included in these studies. For example, Li et al. (2013) found that older adults with lower levels of education were less able to detect faux pas as compared with younger adults and older adults with higher levels of education. This supports the hypothesis of the 'cognitive reserve' of ageing, in which it is suggested that higher levels of intelligence and education may act as protective factors against potential negative effects of ageing (e.g. Peters, 2006; Berkman & Syme, 1979; Dufouil et al., 2003). For instance, Stern (2012) states that the risk of developing Alzheimer's disease is reduced in individuals with higher educational or occupational attainment. A number of other studies have further supported these assertions, indicating that ToM changes as a result of advancing age may be modulated by education level, intelligence level, occupational attainment, and physical activity levels (see Peters, 2006).

6.2.1.4 Perspective taking

Another important part of successful social interactions is our ability to take other people's perspectives to assess what they can see and how they can see it (Flavell et al., 1981). Perspective-taking is an important component of ToM because it reflects our ability to reason about other people's viewpoints—that is, to understand scenes from both the self-viewpoint (egocentric) and from another location/person's viewpoint (allocentric). Martin and colleagues (2019) conducted a study to examine visual perspective-taking abilities in younger- and older-aged participants, looking at performance on both Level-1 perspective taking (i.e. whether something can be seen) and Level-2 perspective taking (i.e. how something looks to someone else/from a different position, such as viewing a '6' as a '9'). Results showed that older individuals were slower to switch to the allocentric viewpoint for both Level-1 and Level-2 perspective taking, indicating an overall reduction in the ability to inhibit the egocentric perspective and adopt the allocentric perspective with advancing age. These results have been further supported by other studies examining visual-perspective taking in older age, which have found that older-aged participants show a prioritization of the self-perspective (egocentric viewpoint) and a diminished role for consideration of other people's perspectives (Mattan et al., 2017).

Long and colleagues (2018) demonstrated that older adults are less able to switch to alternative perspectives during interactive discourse, which was strongly predicted by their cognitive-flexibility ('switching') abilities (i.e. better performance on measures of cognitive-flexibility led to better performance on the perspective-shifting aspect of the social cognition task). Charlton et al. (2009) suggest that older adults, when compared with younger adults, may have a reduced capacity to represent the mental states of other people (Henry et al., 2013; Rakoczy et al., 2012). Taken together, these results indicate that older adults experience difficulties in perspective taking, with advancing age related to declines in perspective-taking abilities, including greater focus on the egocentric perspective (Mattan et al., 2017) and taking longer to switch from the 'self' perspective to the perspective of another person (Martin et al., 2019). Given the critical role that perspective-taking plays in social interactions—in regards to both understanding the 'other' perspective *and* to being able to rapidly switch between different perspectives to successfully engage in social exchanges of information—these declines seen in perspective-taking abilities with advancing age could result in reduced social functioning, potentially leading to reduced quality of life and independence (Bailey et al., 2008; Henry et al., 2013; Martin et al., 2019). It is therefore important that we continue to further our understanding of visual perspective-taking abilities in terms of how they are influenced by advancing age, as well as examining factors that may underlie these changes; for instance, does a decline in these abilities reflect deficits in perspective-taking/social cognition *per se*, or is it reflective of declines in other abilities, such as executive functioning capacities?

6.2.1.5 Theory of Mind: summary

A meta-analysis by Henry et al. (2013), combining studies using a variety of ToM tasks, found that older adults have poorer ToM abilities as compared to younger adults regardless of the type of task (stories, eyes, videos, false-belief tasks), domain (affective, cognitive, mixed), or modality (verbal, visual-static, visual-dynamic, verbal and visual-static, verbal and visual-dynamic). Results indicated that, on the whole, older adults find it more difficult to understand complex mental states experienced by other people. However, this meta-analysis, along with much of the literature, is hampered by the use of group comparisons. Because of this limitation, it is difficult to fully establish when the beginning of this decline in ToM abilities is, and what pattern the decline follows in later life. This has potential implications for everyday social interactions as a decline in ToM mediates a substantial decline in social participation (Bailey et al., 2008). Consequently, there is a need for development of interventions that aid improvement in older adults' social functioning to try and alleviate some of the negative effects of this decline in social cognition abilities (e.g. social withdrawal).

6.2.2 Empathy

Empathy is generally defined as the 'capacity to understand others and experience their feelings in relation to oneself' (Decety & Jackson, 2004). Emotional empathy refers to the ability to respond to the emotional state of others, while cognitive empathy refers to the ability to understand another person's feelings (Decety & Jackson, 2004; Hall & Schwartz, 2019). Empathy is generally measured in terms of a trait level (self-report questionnaires), a state emotional response (stimuli to evoke an empathic state), or as a behavioural response. Lower levels of trait empathy have been associated with less satisfaction in relationships (Davis & Oathout, 1987), increased loneliness (Beadle et al., 2012), and higher levels of depression (Tully et al., 2016). The ability to empathize begins at an early age: studies have shown that even newborns and infants are able to display distressed reactions (e.g. reflexive/reactive crying) in response to stimuli, such as being exposed to the sound of another infant crying (Martin & Clark, 1982). During the second and third years of life, toddlers show empathic concern and helping behaviours with a greater awareness of the experience of others in the context of a social interaction. From age 4, there are significant developments in cognitive empathy with a developmental shift in understanding of others' minds. Following this, research suggests that there is continued development of empathy during adolescence, with the stability of empathy as a trait being reached in early adulthood (McDonald & Messinger, 2011). Empathy capacities in older adulthood are less clear, with separate components showing differential trajectories, as discussed below.

6.2.2.1 Emotional empathy

Emotional empathy may be preserved in older age: studies have reported no age-related differences between younger and older adults on trait measures of emotional empathy (Phillips et al., 2002; Bailey et al., 2008; Beadle et al., 2012; Bailey et al., 2020). Further, using a continuous age sample, Brunsdon et al. (2019) showed a linear increase in trait empathy from 10 to 90 years old. However, Chen et al. (2014) found that older adults reported *lower* trait empathic concern than both younger and middle-aged adults. In contrast, no studies have reported lower *state* emotional empathy in older adults as compared to younger adults. In fact, there may be an increase in state emotional empathy with age (Beadle et al., 2015). For instance, when watching distressing films, older adults reported higher state empathic concern than younger and middle-aged adults, which preceded more donations to charity (Sze et al., 2012). Similarly, when watching emotional films, older women reported greater empathic concern than younger women (Weick & Kunzmann, 2015) and, when watching videos of physical pain, younger and older adults reported similar levels of empathic concern (Bailey et al., 2020).

6.2.2.2 Cognitive empathy

In contrast to emotional empathy, cognitive empathy is reported to decline in older age. Older adults report lower levels of trait cognitive empathy than younger adults, and this age-related decline in cognitive empathy has been related to reduced social functioning (Bailey et al., 2008). O'Brien et al. (2013) assessed lifespan change in both emotional and cognitive trait empathy. They found evidence for an inverse U-shaped pattern across age in both components of empathy, with middle-aged adults reporting higher empathy than both younger and older adults. Empathy seems to increase from young adulthood to a peak in middle age due to the accumulation of life experiences, with declines in older age. However, cognitive empathy is strongly linked to ToM and much of the research in this domain overlaps, with many studies using the 'Reading the Mind in the Eyes' test (RMET) to assess state cognitive empathy (described in section 6.2.3), broadly reporting declines in cognitive empathy (e.g. Khanjani et al., 2015).

6.2.2.3 Empathy: summary

Contradictory findings into ageing effects on empathy may be due to diverse methods used to assess empathy, and a lack of consensus on the taxonomy of empathy. For example, age-related declines that use self-report measures of empathy may reflect the influence of cohort effects. Addressing this, Grühn and colleagues (2008) assessed change in both emotional and cognitive empathy across the lifespan. Participants (aged 10–87 years at the start of the study) were tested 4 times across a 12-year period, allowing cross-sectional and longitudinal associations of age with empathy to be examined. Results showed that, at each time point, empathy ability decreased from adolescence to old age. However, this finding was due to cohort differences, with younger adults reporting higher levels of empathy than older adults. Overall, results indicated that empathy was stable across adulthood. In addition, studies have highlighted that, when predicting empathy levels, the empathic context is important (Blanke et al., 2015)—For instance, Richter & Kunzmann (2011) reported that, when watching film clips portraying a younger or older adult, older individuals only showed age-related declines in cognitive empathy when the situation was less relevant to them (i.e. in the video clips of younger adults), with no significant deficits in the ability to perceive another's emotions when the actor was an older adult, and thus 'relevant' to the participant.

As described in sections 6.2.2.1 and 6.2.2.2, research indicates that ageing can have a differential impact on cognitive and affective empathy, with lower levels of cognitive empathy but preserved or increased emotional empathy in older age. These differences in findings may be due to cohort effects when assessing trait empathy or contextual effects when assessing state empathy. There is a need for more converging methods to investigate empathy using self-report, behavioural, physiological, and neuroimaging techniques, allowing more accurate quantification of the influence of advancing age on each of these abilities.

6.2.3 Emotion recognition

Emotion recognition is defined as the process of identifying affective states from facial expressions, body posture and movement, and verbal expressions. Basic emotion recognition involves the ability to identify six fundamental emotions: happiness, sadness, surprise, disgust, anger, and fear (Ekman et al., 1969; Elfenbein & Ambady, 2002; Keltner et al., 2019). Complex emotion recognition involves identification of both emotional and cognitive states (Sander et al., 2007). Emotional expressions relay important social information for successful social interactions— that is, social functioning requires emotion recognition from faces, voices, and bodily cues, allowing accurate detection of another person's emotional state during interaction, which in turn can guide communication strategies. This is important for maintenance of successful relationships and for well-being (e.g. Carton et al., 1999) and is related to overall life satisfaction (Ciarrochi et al., 2000). Research has indicated that infants as young as 4 to 9 months are able to discriminate facial displays of happiness, sadness, fear, and surprise (Rump et al., 2009). Across early childhood, performance increases for correctly recognizing and labelling various emotions. Some research suggests that basic emotion recognition abilities reach adult-like levels by 10 years of age (e.g. Lawrence et al., 2015). However, other research indicates that emotion recognition continues to develop across adolescence, peaking in adulthood (Thomas et al., 2007).

6.2.3.1 Basic emotion recognition

Research has suggested that, in adulthood, advancing age leads to declines in the ability to recognize even basic emotions. For instance, Sullivan and Ruffman (2004a) found that healthy older adults were impaired at recognizing negative emotions such as anger and sadness, across visual and audio modalities, although they did not find ageing effects for positive emotions such as happiness. For trials in which a decline in emotion recognition was found, Sullivan and Ruffman stated that this change was independent of general perceptual abilities, processing speed, or face-processing abilities. Two meta-analyses by Ruffman et al. (2008) and Gonçalves et al. (2018) examined 30 years of studies that have compared basic emotion recognition in younger versus older adults. The combined results support Sullivan and Ruffman's findings, indicating that older adults are less accurate at identifying basic emotions, with particular difficulties with negative emotions such as anger and sadness, when compared with younger adults. These declines in abilities were found across multiple modalities, including ratings of faces, voices, and body language, as well as face-voice matching. Taken together, results reveal a pattern in which, across both different emotions and different presentation modalities, advancing age is associated with a decline in basic emotion recognition abilities.

6.2.3.2 Complex emotion recognition

The ability to decode more complex emotions in older age has been less widely studied when compared with recognition of basic emotions. However, studies have shown that older adults are less able to decode shame and guilt from facial expressions (Stanley & Blanchard-Fields, 2008), distinguish contempt from sadness (MacPherson et al., 2002), and understand sarcasm (Phillips et al., 2015), each of which hold potential negative consequences for social interactions. Complex emotion recognition has typically been behaviourally investigated using the RMET (Baron-Cohen et al., 2001), in which complex mental states are matched to an image of an eye region. Using this task, older adults have been found to perform significantly worse when compared with young (Bailey et al., 2008; Duval et al., 2011; Phillips et al., 2002; Slessor et al., 2007) and middle-aged (Pardini & Nichelli, 2009) adults, regardless of intelligence or education (Phillips et al., 2002).

It is noted, however, that a handful of studies have not replicated these findings (e.g. Castelli et al., 2010; Li et al., 2013). Castelli et al. reported that, when engaging with the RMET task, behavioural results indicated similar levels of task success between older and younger adults, although fMRI recordings revealed different patterns of brain activation underlying older versus younger adults' task performance. Despite Castelli et al.'s findings, studies that examine RMET performance across adulthood have indicated the presence of a linear decrease in task success, and suggest that this decline may be the result of brain structural and functional changes, grey matter tissue loss, and microstructural changes in white matter areas (Cabinio et al., 2015). When considering a fuller developmental profile of emotion recognition from late childhood through to old age, RMET performance has been shown to improve from adolescence through to adulthood with a peak at 35 years old, and a decline through middle age to 70 years old; from 70 years old, task performance plateaus, with no further changes into older age (Brunsdon et al., 2019).

6.2.3.3 Emotion recognition: summary

Emotion recognition plays an important role in social interactions. Evidence indicates that there are age-related declines in both basic and complex emotion recognition. However, an issue with research into emotion recognition is that a majority of studies assess both basic and complex emotion recognition using discrete, static, prototypical expressions, which are arguably not representative of more dynamic emotions that individuals are exposed to in their daily lives. Addressing this issue, new tasks have been developed to try and create more dynamic stimuli. For instance, the Cambridge Mindreading Face-Voice Battery uses both audio clips and silent video clips involving actors from different age groups, each presented with four emotion words from which the participant is asked to select the most appropriate description of the emotion being depicted in either the video or audio clip (see Mahy et al., 2013). This more dynamic presentation of stimuli still allows recording of a behavioural response (i.e. calculation of emotion recognition accuracy), allowing assessment of complex emotion recognition abilities while including stimuli that are more aligned with real-world experiences. Results have shown that, even when using this more ecologically valid task, older adults still perform worse than younger adults in the labelling of complex emotions.

While dynamic tasks help take a step towards creating tasks that are more ecologically valid, the extent to which these lab-based measures of emotion recognition relate to everyday experiences is uncertain. For instance, the tasks used to measure emotion recognition rely on the explicit labelling of an emotion. In real-life social interactions, we do not always have to verbally label an emotion: more than one emotion may be expressed in an unravelling social interaction, and body posture, body movement, and tone of voice are also used to decode emotions. Further, relatively little is currently understood about the implicit processes used to decode emotions and how these processes may change with age. To further develop our understanding of how emotion recognition may change with advancing age, more ecologically valid measures need to be developed, allowing assessment of changes in these abilities, the implicit processes underlying changes, and how reported changes relate to social interaction success in everyday life.

6.2.4 Action recognition, observation, and imitation

Understanding the movements and actions of other people is crucial for successful social interactions. Our ability to understand others' actions involves understanding *what* action is being performed, *how* an action is being performed, and *why* the action is being performed. There are numerous processes described in the literature that are involved in the perception and understanding of an action someone else is performing, and in the reproduction of that same action, and many of these processes overlap. Here, we focus on the age-related changes in biological motion perception (also referred to as 'action recognition'), action observation, and action imitation, as identified by Happé and colleagues (2017) as crucial for social interactions. This topic remains largely understudied from an ageing or lifespan perspective, and so we also discuss gaps in the literature in relation to ageing effects in these areas.

6.2.4.1 Action recognition

Biological motion perception is the ability of the visual system to extract information from a moving human body. Successful social interactions rely on our ability to accurately detect and interpret biological motion, such as walking, dancing, or kicking. Biological motion perception is typically studied using point-light displays, in which only a few dots are placed on the main joints of an otherwise invisible human body against a dark background. Studies have demonstrated that even human infants aged 2 months are sensitive to these point-light displays, showing a preference (looking longer) towards lights depicting a human form when compared with dots moving in an independent, random direction (Fox & McDaniel, 1982). Initial studies into the effect of age on biological motion perception indicated that these abilities were relatively well preserved in older age (Billino et al., 2008; Norman et al., 2004). However, studies using a wider range of movements, and incorporating measures of emotion detection abilities, have more recently indicated that biological motion perception deteriorates with advancing age (Grainger et al., 2019; Insch et al., 2012). Grainger et al.'s study found that older age was associated with reduced ability to detect biological motion cues and, importantly, this difficulty mediated age-related variances in ToM abilities assessed in this study. Grainger and colleagues suggest that declines in biological motion detection may reflect declines in the ability to detect and efficiently process even basic cues about social agency (Frith & Frith, 2003); this in turn could have a knock-on effect, leading to impairments of more complex higher-order social cognition skills such as ToM abilities (Grainger et al., 2019; Insch et al., 2012; Ruffman et al., 2008; Phillips et al., 2011).

6.2.4.2 Action observation

One dominant theory proposes that, when we see someone else performing an action, a specialized system in the sensorimotor cortex fires to 'mirror' this action as if we were executing it (Fox et al., 2016; Kilner & Lemon, 2013). Action goals are therefore understood by the mapping of the observed action onto the corresponding internal action representation in the person's motor repertoire. The activation of this mirror system to the observation of other peoples' actions is argued to be largely preserved in older adults (Farina et al., 2017; Nedelko et al., 2010), although Diersch et al. (2016) report that this activation becomes less distinct in older age due to less precise mappings between observed actions and the corresponding internal action representations in the person's motor repertoire (Diersch et al., 2012; Diersch et al., 2013). In comparison, Brunsdon et al. (2019) report that the reactivity of the sensorimotor cortex to the observation of others' actions continues to increase from late childhood through to old age. This continued development could be reflective of the use of compensatory strategies (Ward, 2006) or enhanced specialization of the mirror neuron system (i.e. effects of 'expertise'/experience; Brunsdon et al., 2019; Calvo-Merino et al., 2006). However, further research is required to tease these two explanations apart. Overall, there is a paucity of research in action observation processes in older age, although the studies that have been conducted have revealed interesting, and conflicting, findings. Future studies, particularly using continuous ageing samples (rather than dichotomous age groups) would allow more insight into changes in action observation capacities across the lifespan, and the factors that may influence these changes.

6.2.4.3 Action imitation

Imitation is the intentional copying of an observed action, whereas automatic imitation is the unintentional copying of an observed action (see Cracco et al., 2018, for a recent meta-analysis). Automatic imitation is a key part of social interactions because it strengthens social bonds (van Baaren et al., 2009; Spengler et al., 2010) and is mediated by the mirror system (Catmur et al., 2009). A study by Léonard and Tremblay (2007) compared patterns of motor modulation when younger and older adults were asked to either *imitate* or *imagine* engaging in an observed action seen via a video. Results indicated that automatic imitation, as seen in young adult participants, was largely preserved in older adults (i.e. retaining the capacity to both explicitly imitate an action and implicitly imagine an action, as assessed by motor-evoked potentials). Interestingly, however, Léonard & Tremblay report that this distinction between overt (imitation) and covert (imagination) actions was less selective for older adults than younger ones, suggesting more overlap in activations recorded for older participants. To date, there is limited research that has focused on action imitation abilities from an ageing or lifespan perspective. Given the key role that imitation plays in the development of key social abilities during infancy and childhood (Meltzoff, 2002; Meltzoff & Decety, 2003; Want & Harris, 2002), it would be interesting in future research to further examine the role that action imitation abilities may play in predicting social outcomes with advancing age.

6.2.4.4 Action recognition, observation, and imitation: summary

As stated above, the ability to understand the movements and actions of other people plays an important role in successful social interactions. The ability to extract information about an individual's actions can provide insight into the identity of a person, their personality, and their current psychological/emotional state (Vrigkas et al., 2015). Happé and colleagues (2017) identify action recognition ('biological motion perception'), action observation, and action imitation as crucial elements of social interaction. Currently, there is limited research into how each of these capacities may change—or stay the same—across the lifespan. Of the research that has attempted to address this gap in the literature, results have indicated declines in each of these abilities with advancing age. While further research is required to more fully inform our understanding of how these capacities change and develop across the lifespan, this suggestion that deficits may be present in older age may have important repercussions for social interactions in older-aged individuals. If, as research has indicated, action recognition, observation, and imitation play a critical role in predicting social interaction abilities, deficits in these abilities may in turn lead to impairments in more general social cognition skills that are underlined by these abilities, such as advanced ToM capacities (Grainger et al., 2019; Ruffman et al., 2008; Phillips et al., 2011; Frith & Frith, 2003).

6.2.5 Agent recognition

Vogeley (2017) suggests that a fundamental aspect of social interactions is the ability to distinguish between inanimate objects (whose behaviour can be explained by physical forces) and people (who have inner experiences, such as thoughts, feelings, and intentions). This occurs through complex perceptual processing, including face processing, emotion processing, body posture and language, and voice (Arioli et al., 2018). We gather vast amounts of social information from faces, including a person's identity, what emotions they are experiencing, and what their intentions may be. Face recognition is therefore a crucial social function that is distinct from object recognition (McKone et al., 2007). Studies have indicated that face recognition improves until the early thirties, distinct from changes in other general factors, followed by a decline in this ability into older age (Germine et al., 2011). The effects of advancing age on these abilities, and how they relate to real-world social experiences, are lacking in research evidence. It could be, for instance, that, as a consequence of a decline in face recognition abilities, older individuals may experience challenges in engaging in social interactions, whether as a result of reduced confidence in social abilities or other factors. Further research is required to more accurately examine these claims, exploring the effect of advancing age on agent recognition, and how changes in these abilities may influence social interaction success.

6.2.6 Social motivation and attention

6.2.6.1 Social motivation

Social motivation is the process that biases an individual to initiate, seek, and take pleasure in social interactions, and to work to foster and maintain positive social behaviours (Chevallier et al., 2012). According to the socioemotional selectivity theory, older age involves a shift in motivation towards the quality of social relationships, and away from seeking new social experiences (Carstensen et al., 2003). In other words, as people reach older ages, they become more selective in their social interactions and interact less with others, instead focusing their attention on a limited number of individuals (Fredrickson & Carstensen, 1990). Evidence suggests that older age involves an active reduction in the number of social partners, pruning out less important social contacts and potentially negative social relationships, selecting instead to focus attention and maintenance on meaningful social relationships (Carstensen et al., 2003; Fredrickson & Carstensen, 1990; Finchum & Weber, 2000). These meaningful social relationships tend to be with close social partners (i.e. spouses, parents, and siblings), and studies suggest that older adults have more interactions with, and derive greater satisfaction from experiences with, these close partners (Ertel et al., 2009). In addition, older adults show a greater preference than younger adults to spend time with these close social partners (Birditt & Fingerman, 2003; Charles & Piazza, 2007; Schnittker, 2007). However, it is notable that, with an overall reduced number of social partners, there will consequently be less variability in the types of social exchanges and conversations experienced by older adults, with less exposure to different viewpoints. This reduced exposure to the social world in older age could lead to diminished expertise in social cognition, particularly across different, unfamiliar contexts.

According to the selective engagement hypothesis (Hess, 2006), older people tend to avoid cognitively demanding tasks due to an increase in the costs of cognitive engagement, adjusting focus of activities and goal priorities to reflect current levels of functioning. These costs result in more selectivity in the allocation of their limited cognitive resources and a reduction in motivation to engage in cognitively demanding activities (Hess, 2014). Relating to this suggestion, research has indicated that, when the level of 'social motivation' is manipulated, older adults are able to selectively engage their limited cognitive resources to the point that declines in social cognition are no longer evident (Hess, 2006). For instance, Stanley and Isaacowitz (2015) argue that socioemotional motivation plays an important role in alleviating social cognition task declines, as illustrated by their study in which older adults were better able to identify facial expressions of a familiar romantic partner (where socioemotional motivation is high) than those of a stranger (low socioemotional motivation)—that is to say, when motivated to identify emotions due to the presented face being a familiar 'other', older adults' performance was not differentiable from that of younger adults' performance. In contrast, when the face presented was of a stranger, ageing effects were present, with older adults less likely to correctly identify the facial expression compared with younger adults.

Zhang and colleagues (2013) also examined how perspective-taking abilities may be altered based on social motivation, finding that older adults showed less of a deficit in perspective-taking abilities when the person whose perspective they were tasked with considering was a familiar other. Zhang et al. argue that these results indicate that, as the closeness of the 'other' is increased, older adults are able to enhance their performance, performing at comparable levels to younger adults, thus supporting the importance of social motivation when considering ageing effects in social cognition abilities. Lecce et al. (2019) support these suggestions, arguing that older adults need to be socially motivated to put their social skills into action. Taken together, these results highlight the importance of good and supportive friendships in older age, which encourage individuals to interact with a network of friends (i.e. social motivation), potentially alleviating some of the social cognition declines experienced with advancing age.

6.2.6.2 Social attention

Social attention is the degree of visual attention given to social stimuli. Some basic attentional processes (e.g. visual search tasks) decline with advancing age (Madden, 2007). Much less is known about how social attention changes across the lifespan. Older adults are thought to use different visual scanning patterns for emotional faces compared with young adults (Circelli et al., 2013; Noh & Isaacowitz, 2013) and are not as sensitive to social gaze cues as young adults (Kuhn et al., 2015; Slessor et al., 2010). Given the importance of the face in communicating—from aiding identification of how someone is feeling to aiding interpretation of what someone is saying—these differences might impair older adults' ability to interpret others' mental states appropriately and therefore identify socially relevant information to guide communication (Langton et al., 2000).

Two key ageing studies (Grainger et al., 2019; Vicaria et al., 2015) have sought to examine changes in social attention, by proxy of eye gaze patterns, and how these may change across the lifespan, using dynamic social interactions as stimuli (i.e. videos) rather than static images. Results highlight that older adults appear to attend less to social information, such as faces, during a social interaction when compared with younger adults (Grainger et al., 2019; Vicaria et al., 2015). In Grainger et al.'s study, half of the video stimuli shown to participants were 'enriched', with additional visual and verbal contextual cues present in these trials to aid the participant's understanding of utterances within the scene. It was expected, in line with prior research that had found emotion perception abilities enhanced in older adults when additional contextual cues are provided (e.g. Noh & Isaacowitz, 2013), that enriched social contexts in this context would facilitate older adults' task performance. Interestingly, Grainger et al. found that older adults were *impeded* in their interpretation of social interactions when engaging with enriched social contexts. This could be indicative that the enriched scenes became too complex for older adults to process effectively, placing greater demands on higher-level mental state reasoning processes, and reducing their ability to filter out extraneous background information.

Taken together, these findings suggest that older adults' reduced attention towards social stimuli may reflect a difficulty filtering out non-social background information. Older adults have difficulties detecting, integrating, and processing multiple social cues during social interactions (Grainger et al., 2019). This is an important consideration for the impact of social attention on social interaction abilities in older age. Social interactions often involve the continuous processing of many subtle social cues that emerge and evolve over time, and can involve more than one conversational partner, requiring consideration of multiple social cues concurrently.

6.3 Enhancing social cognition in older age

Despite evidence that advancing age leads to declines in various facets of social cognition abilities, Salthouse (2012) comments that it is interesting that greater consequences of these declines are not reflected in everyday behaviour. Salthouse argues that this may be indicative that older-aged individuals make use of established knowledge in conducting their everyday life, such as relying on 'scripts' of prior interactions to inform current interactions, as well as indicating that everyday levels of functioning may not require 'maximal' levels of performance, allowing for flexibility in changes in ability (Hess, 2014). However, despite consequences of these declines in cognitive function not being as extreme as may be expected, these declines *do* have an impact on individuals as well as their families, particularly in terms of reducing independence, quality of life, daily functional abilities, and even life expectancy (Gheysen et al., 2018; Wilson et al., 2013; Zhu et al., 2016). It has been suggested that retained plasticity in the brain in later life may allow some aspects of cognitive decline to be prevented, or at least delayed (Reuter-Lorenz & Park, 2010), through use of intervention protocols, which in turn may help alleviate some of these issues.

Lecce and colleagues (2015) developed a form of ToM training for older adults. In this training protocol, adult participants engage in questions and discussions about the explicit understanding of mental states and characters' behaviour, with queries about how they can resolve various different social situations. Engagement in this ToM training was shown to enhance older adults' general ToM abilities (Cavallini et al., 2015; Lecce et al., 2015; Rosi et al., 2016), indicating measurable benefits of explicit conversations about mental states for older people. It is not clear as yet whether these task-based improvements in ToM abilities translate into improvements in everyday social interactions and increased quality of life for older individuals: further research into how results relate to everyday experiences are required. Nonetheless, these findings provide a promising avenue for research into developing interventions aimed at alleviating age-related declines in ToM.

Another approach to cognitive decline intervention is increased engagement in physical activity, particularly aerobic and strength exercise, which have been shown to benefit cognitive abilities (e.g. Colcombe et al., 2006; Erickson et al., 2011; Voss et al., 2010). Importantly, these benefits are argued to be selective, with studies showing that increased physical activity specifically leads to an improvement in executive control processes (Colcombe & Kramer, 2003; Kramer & Willis, 2002). There is significant research that indicates a strong link between social cognition abilities and executive functioning capacities (e.g. Bailey & Henry, 2008; Cane et al., 2017; Bradford et al., 2015; Bernstein et al., 2017; German & Hehman, 2006). Given this link, improvements in executive functioning as a result of engagement in physical activity could ultimately also support improvements in social cognition abilities in older age. Other studies have also suggested that cognitive function in older adults can be enhanced by engagement in cognitively challenging activities; for instance, Park and colleagues (2013) found that, when older adults committed to learning a new skill over the course of three months (such as learning to quilt or learning digital photography), episodic memory increased from pre- to post-intervention stages. Toril et al. (2014) reported a meta-analysis looking at the benefits of engaging in video game training interventions for older individuals, with results highlighting benefits of this training on attention and memory abilities. These results suggest that both physical activity and cognitive activities can have a positive impact on cognitive functioning in older age, although it is noted by Kramer & Willis (2002) that these training effects are often narrow, in terms of being focused on tasks and skills similar to the directly trained skill. Gheysen et al. (2018) suggest that the optimum intervention for mediating cognitive declines seen in older age may be to combine *both* physical activity and cognitive interventions, with the key component of interventions being that they challenge the individual to allow positive cognitive effects to be achieved (see also Zhu et al., 2016).

This prior research suggests that some cognitive abilities, such as executive functions, can be enhanced in older age by engaging in different intervention strategies, whether physical activity or cognitive-based tasks. These interventions could be used as a preventative measure, before declines are apparent, in addition to being used as a treatment for individuals experiencing declines in cognitive abilities (Zhu et al., 2016; Gheysen et al., 2018). It is important to note that it is not currently clear whether these established training effects are able to induce far transfer effects. However, given the well-established link between social cognition and executive functioning, it may be that improvements in one of these abilities leads to enhancement in the other. It remains to be seen how these interventions may specifically relate to social-cognitive abilities in older age and, further, the extent to which these intervention outcomes may be generalizable to everyday functioning (Noack et al., 2014). Together, however, these studies provide an exciting and promising focus for future research, to examine the extent to which physical exercise and cognitive training interventions may be developed as a means for addressing declines in social cognition abilities seen in older age, in turn providing the potential for alleviating difficulties experienced as a result of these declines.

6.4 Conclusion

Throughout this chapter, we have reviewed evidence examining ageing trajectories across different social cognition components, including ToM, empathy, emotion recognition, action understanding, and imitation. The studies reported have demonstrated evidence of declines in each of these abilities with advancing age, but have also highlighted the significant gaps in the literature as it currently stands, particularly in terms of the need for longitudinal ageing studies that include not only younger versus older adults, but also examine the timings and stages of changes in social-cognitive abilities by examining the full lifespan, including middle-aged adults. As it stands, research suggests that advancing age is associated with a reduction in the efficient use of social cognition abilities. There is promising evidence that interventions, including physical exercise and challenging cognitive tasks, may enhance these abilities, although further research is required to clarify these outcomes and whether these improvements translate to real-world experiences.

As discussed in this chapter, social interactions play a critical role in daily life, including predicting mental and physical health. Given the rapidly expanding global ageing population, research focusing on furthering our understanding of the behaviour and cognition associated with healthy ageing has an important role, including examining how social cognition abilities change in older age (e.g. which capacities may be spared), factors that may influence these changes, and how intervention protocols may be utilized to alleviate declines experienced as a result of advancing age.

References

Anderson, N. D., & Craik, F. I. M., 2017. '50 years of cognitive aging theory'. *Journals of Gerontology: Psychological Sciences* 72. 10: 1–6.

Apperly, I., 2012. 'What is "theory of mind"? Concepts, cognitive processes and individual differences'. *Quarterly Journal of Experimental Psychology* 65. 5: 825–839.

Arioli, M., Crespi, C., & Canessa, N., 2018. 'Social cognition through the lens of cognitive and clinical neuroscience'. *BioMed Research International*, 13 September, 4283427.

Bailey, P. E., & Henry, J. D., 2008. 'Growing less empathic with age: Disinhibition of the self-perspective'. *Journals of Gerontology: Series B* 63. 4: 219–226.

Bailey, P. E., Henry, J. D., & Von Hippel, W., 2008. 'Empathy and social functioning in late adulthood'. *Aging & Mental Health* 12. 4: 499–503.

Bailey, P. E., Brady, B., Ebner, N. C., & Ruffman, T., 2020. 'The effects of age on emotion regulation, emotional empathy, and prosocial behaviour'. *Journals of Gerontology: Series B* 75. 4: 802–810.

Baksh, R. A., Abrahams, S., Auyeung, B., & MacPherson, S. E., 2018. 'The Edinburgh Social Cognition Test (ESCoT): Examining the effects of age on a new measure of theory of mind and social norm understanding'. *PLoS One* 13. 4: e0195818.

Baron-Cohen, S., O'Riordan, M., Stone, V., Jones, R., & Plaisted, K., 1999. 'A new test of social sensitivity: Detection of faux pas in normal children and children with Asperger syndrome'. *Journal of Autism and Developmental Disorders* 29. 5: 407–418.

Baron-Cohen, S., Wheelwright, S., Hill, J., Raste, Y., & Plumb, I., 2001. 'The "Reading the Mind in the Eyes" Test revised version: A study with normal adults, adults with Asperger syndrome or high-functioning autism'. *Journal of Child Psychology and Psychiatry* 42. 2: 241–251.

Beadle, J. N., Sheehan, A. H., Dahlben, B., & Gutchess, A. H., 2015. 'Aging, empathy, and prosociality'. *Journals of Gerontology: Series B* 70. 2: 213–222.Beadle, J. N., Brown, V., Keady, B., Tranel, D., & Paradiso, S., 2012. 'Trait empathy as a predictor of individual differences in perceived loneliness'. *Psychological Reports* 110. 1: 3–15.

Beer, J. S., & Ochsner, K. N., 2006. 'Social cognition: A multi-level analysis'. *Brain Research* 1079. 1: 98–105.

Begeer, S., Malle, B. F., Nieuwland, M. S., & Keysar, B., 2010. Using theory of mind to represent and take part in social interactions: Comparing individuals with high-functioning autism and typically developing controls. *European Journal of Developmental Psychology* 7. 1: 104–122.

Berkman, L. F., & Syme, S. L., 1979. 'Social networks, host resistance, and mortality: A nine-year follow-up study of Alameda County residents'. *American Journal of Epidemiology* 109. 2: 186–204.

Bernstein, D. M., Thornton, W. L., & Sommerville, J. A., 2011. 'Theory of mind through the ages: Older and middle-aged adults exhibit more errors than do younger adults on a continuous false belief task'. *Experimental Aging Research* 37, 5: 481–502.

Bernstein, D. M., Coolin, A., Fischer, A. L., Thornton, W. L., & Sommerville, J. A., 2017. 'False-belief reasoning from 3 to 92 years of age'. *PLoS One* 12. 9: e0185345.

Billino, J., Bremmer, F., & Gegenfurtner, K. R., 2008. 'Motion processing at low light levels: Differential effects on the perception of specific motion types'. *Journal of Vision* 8. 3: 14.

Birditt, K. S., & Fingerman, K. L., 2003. 'Age and gender differences in adults' descriptions of emotional reactions to interpersonal problems'. *Journals of Gerontology: Series B: Psychological Sciences and Social Sciences*, 58. 4: P237–P245.

Blanke, E. S., Rauers, A., & Riediger, M., 2015. 'Nice to meet you—adult age differences in empathic accuracy for strangers'. *Psychology and Aging* 30. 1: 149–159.

Bottiroli, S., Cavallini, E., Ceccato, I., Vecchi, T., & Lecce, S., 2016. 'Theory of mind in aging: Comparing cognitive and affective components in the faux pas test'. *Archives of Gerontology and Geriatrics* 62: 152–162.

Bradford, E. E. F., Jentzsch, I., & Gomez, J.-C., 2015. 'From self to social cognition: Theory of Mind mechanisms and their relation to executive functioning'. *Cognition* 138: 21–34.

Brunsdon, V. E. A., Bradford, E. E. F., & Ferguson, H., 2019. 'Sensorimotor mu rhythm during action observation changes across the lifespan independently from social cognitive processes'. *Developmental Cognitive Neuroscience* 38: 100659.

Cabinio, M., Rossetto, F., Blasi, V., Savazzi, F., Castelli, I., Massaro, D., ... & Baglio, F., 2015. 'Mind-reading ability and structural connectivity changes in aging'. *Frontiers in Psychology* 6: 1808.

Calvo-Merino, B., Grèzes, J., Glaser, D. E., Passingham, R. E., & Haggard, P., 2006. 'Seeing or doing? Influence of visual and motor familiarity in action observation'. *Current Biology* 16. 19: 1905–1910.

Cane, J. E., Ferguson, H. J., & Apperly, I. A., 2017. 'Using perspective to resolve reference: The impact of cognitive load and motivation'. *Journal of Experimental Psychology: Learning, Memory, and Cognition* 43. 4: 591–610.

Carstensen, L. L., Fung, H. H., & Charles, S. T., 2003. 'Socioemotional selectivity theory and the regulation of emotion in the second half of life'. *Motivation and Emotion* 27. 2: 103–123.

Carton, J. S., Kessler, E. A., & Pape, C. L., 1999. 'Nonverbal decoding skills and relationship well-being in adults'. *Journal of Nonverbal Behavior* 23. 1: 91–100.

Castelli, I., Baglio, F., Blasi, V., Alberoni, M., Falini, A., Liverta-Sempio, O., Nemni, R., & Marchetti, A., 2010. 'Effects of aging on mindreading ability through the eyes: An fMRI study'. *Neuropsychologia* 48. 9: 2586–2594.

Catmur, C., Walsh, V., & Heyes, C., 2009. 'Associative sequence learning: the role of experience in the development of imitation and the mirror system'. *Philosophical Transactions of the Royal Society B* 364. 1528: 2369–2380.

Cavallini, E., Lecce, S., Bottiroli, S., Palladino, P., & Pagnin, A., 2013. 'Beyond false belief: Theory of mind in young, young-old, and old-old adults'. *International Journal of Aging and Human Development* 76. 3: 181–198.

Cavallini, E., Bianco, F., Bottiroli, S., Rosi, A., Vecchi, T., & Lecce, S., 2015. 'Training for generalization in Theory of Mind: A study with older adults'. *Frontiers in Psychology* 6: 1123.

Charles, S. T., & Piazza, J. R., 2007. 'Memories of social interactions: Age differences in emotional intensity'. *Psychology and Aging* 22. 2: 300–309.

Charlton, R. A., Barrick, T. R., Markus, H. S., & Morris, R. G., 2009. 'Theory of mind associations with other cognitive functions and brain imaging in normal aging'. *Psychology and Aging* 24. 2: 338–348.

Chen, Y. C., Chen, C. C., Decety, J., & Cheng, Y., 2014. 'Aging is associated with changes in the neural circuits underlying empathy'. *Neurobiology of Aging* 35. 4: 827–836.

Chevallier, C., Kohls, G., Troiani, V., Brodkin, E. S., & Schulz, R. T., 2012. 'The social motivation theory of autism'. *Trends in Cognitive Sciences* 16. 4: 231–239.

Ciarrochi, J. V., Chan, A. Y. C., & Caputi, P., 2000. 'A critical evaluation of the emotional intelligence construct'. *Personality and Individual Differences* 28. 3: 539–561.

Circelli, K. S., Clark, U. S., & Cronin-Golomb, A., 2013. 'Visual scanning patterns and executive function in relation to facial emotion recognition in aging'. *Aging, Neuropsychology, and Cognition* 20. 2: 148–173.

Colcombe, S., & Kramer, A.F., 2003. 'Fitness effects on the cognitive function of older adults: a meta-analytic study'. *Psychological Science* 14. 2: 125–130.

Colcombe, S. J., Erickson, K. I., Scalf, P. E., Kim, J. S., Prakash, R., McAuley, E., ... & Kramer, A. F., 2006. 'Aerobic exercise training increases brain volume in aging humans'. *Journals of Gerontology: Series A: Biological Sciences and Medical Sciences* 61. 11: 1166–1170.

Cracco, E. Bardi, L., Desmet, C., Genschow, O, Rigoni, D., De Coster, L., Radkova, I., ... & Brass, M., 2018. 'Automatic imitation: A meta-analysis'. *Psychological Bulletin* 144. 5: 453–500.

Davis, M. H., & Oathout, H. A., 1987. 'Maintenance of satisfaction in romantic relationships: Empathy and relational competence'. *Journal of Personality and Social Psychology* 53. 2: 397–410.

Decety, J., & Jackson, P.L., 2004. 'The functional architecture of human empathy'. *Behavioral and Cognitive Neuroscience Reviews* 3. 2: 71–100.

Department of Economic and Social Affairs, Population Division, 2017. World Population Ageing 2017—Highlights. United Nations. https://www.un.org/en/development/desa/population/publications/pdf/ageing/WPA2017_Highlights.pdf

Derksen, B. J., Weldon, D. K., Zhang, J., Zamba, K. D., Tranel, D., & Denburg, N. L., 2015. 'Older adults can catch up to younger adults on a learning and memory task that involves collaborative social interaction'. *Memory* 23. 4: 612–624.

Diersch, N., Jones, A. L., & Cross, E. S., 2016. 'The timing and precision of action prediction in the aging brain'. *Human Brain Mapping* 37. 1: 54–66.

Diersch, N., Cross, E. S., Stadler, W., Schütz-Bosback, S., & Rieger, M., 2012. 'Representing others' actions: the role of expertise in the aging mind'. *Psychological Research* 76. 4: 525–541.

Diersch, N., Mueller, K., Cross, E. S., Stadler, W., Riger, M., & Schütz-Bosbach, S., 2013. 'Action prediction in younger versus older adults: neural correlates of motor familiarity'. *PLoS One* 8. 5: e64195.

Dufouil, C., Alperovitch, A., & Tzourio, C., 2003. 'Influence of education on the relationship between white matter lesions and cognition'. *Neurology* 60. 5: 831–836.

Dumontheil, I., Apperly, I. A., & Blakemore, S. J., 2010. 'Online usage of theory of mind continues to develop in late adolescence'. *Developmental Science* 13. 2: 331–338.

Duval, C., Piolino, P., Bejanin, A., Eustache, F., & Desgranges, B., 2011. 'Age effects on different components of theory of mind'. *Consciousness and Cognition* 20. 3: 627–642.

Ekman, P., Sorenson, E. R., & Friesen, W. V., 1969. Pan-cultural elements in facial displays of emotions. *Science* 164: 86–88.

Elfenbein, H. A., & Ambady, N., 2002. 'Is there an in-group advantage in emotion recognition?' *Psychological Bulletin* 128. 2: 243–249.

Erickson, K. I., Voss, M. W., Prakash, R. S., Basak, C., Szabo, A., Chaddock, L., ... & Wojcicki, T. R., 2011. 'Exercise training increases size of hippocampus and improves memory'. *Proceedings of the National Academy of Sciences* 108. 7: 3017–3022.

Ertel, K. A., Glymour, M. M., & Berkman, L. F., 2009. 'Social networks and health: A life course perspective integrating observational and experimental evidence'. *Journal of Social and Personal Relationships* 26. 1: 73–92.

Farina, E. Baglio, F., Pomati, S., D'Amico, A., Campini, I. C., Di Tella, S., Belloni, G., & Pozzo, T., 2017. 'The mirror neurons network in aging, mild cognitive impairment, and Alzheimer disease: a functional MRI study'. *Frontiers in Aging Neuroscience* 9: 371.

Finchum, T., & Weber, J. A., 2000. 'Applying continuity theory to older adult friendships'. *Journal of Aging and Identity* 5. 3: 159–168.

Flavell, J. H., 1999. 'Cognitive development: Children's knowledge about the mind'. *Annual Review of Psychology* 50: 21–45.

Flavell, J. H., Everett, B. A., Croft, K., & Flavell, E. R., 1981. 'Young children's knowledge about visual perception: Further evidence for the Level 1–Level 2 distinction'. *Developmental Psychology* 17. 1: 99–103.

Fox, N. A., Bakermans-Kranenburg, M. J., Yoo, K. H., Bowman, L. C., Cannon, E.N., Vanderwert, R. E., ... & Van IJzendoorn, M.H., 2016. 'Assessing human mirror activity with EEG mu rhythm: A meta-analysis'. *Psychological Bulletin* 142. 3: 291–313.

Fox, R., & McDaniel, C., 1982. 'The perception of biological motion by human infants'. *Science* 218. 4571: 486–487.

Fredrickson, B. L., & Carstensen, L. L., 1990. 'Choosing social partners: How old age and anticipated endings make people more selective'. *Psychology and Aging* 5. 3: 335–347.

Frith, U., & Frith, C. D., 2003. 'Development and neurophysiology of mentalizing'. *Philosophical Transactions of the Royal Society B* 358. 1431: 459–473.

German, T. P., & Hehman, J. A., 2006. 'Representational and executive selection resources in 'theory of mind': Evidence from compromised belief-desire reasoning in old age'. *Cognition* 101. 1: 129–152.

Germine, L. T., Duchaine, B., & Nakayama, K., 2011. 'Where cognitive development and aging meet: Face learning ability peaks after age 30'. *Cognition* 118. 2: 201–210.

Gheysen, F., Poppe, L., DeSmet, A., Swinnen, S., Cardon, G., De Bourdeaudhuij, I., ... & Fias, W., 2018. 'Physical activity to improve cognition in older adults: Can physical activity programs enriched with cognitive challenges enhance the effects? A systematic review and meta-analysis'. *International Journal of Behavioural Nutrition and Physical Activity* 15. 1: 63.

Gonçalves, A. R., Fernandes, C., Pasion, R., Ferriera-Santos, F., Barbosa, F., & Marques-Teixeira, J., 2018. 'Effects of age on the identification of emotions in facial expressions: a meta-analysis'. *PeerJ* 6: e5278.

Grainger, S. A., Steinvik, H. R., Henry, J. D., & Phillips, L. H., 2019. 'The role of social attention in older adults' ability to interpret naturalistic social scenes'. *Quarterly Journal of Experimental Psychology* 72. 6: 1328–1343.

Grühn, D., Rebucal, K., Diehl, M., Lumley, M., & Labouvie-Vief, G., 2008. 'Empathy across the adult lifespan: Longitudinal and experience-sampling findings'. *Emotion* 8. 6: 753–765.

Halberstadt, J., Ruffman, T., Murray, J., Taumoepeau, M., & Ryan, M., 2011. 'Emotion perception explains age-related differences in the perception of social gaffes'. *Psychology and Aging* 26. 1: 133–136.

Hall, J. A., & Schwartz, R., 2019. 'Empathy present and future'. *Journal of Social Psychology* 159. 3: 225–243.

Happé, F., Cook, J. L., & Bird, G., 2017. 'The structure of social cognition: In(ter)dependence of sociocognitive processes'. *Annual Review of Psychology* 68: 243–267.

Happé, F. G. E., 1994. 'An advanced test of theory of mind: Understanding of a story characters' thoughts and feelings by able autistic, mentally handicapped, and normal children'. *Journal of Autism and Developmental Disorders* 24. 2: 129–154.

Happé. F. G. E., Winner, E., & Brownell, H., 1998. 'The getting of wisdom: Theory of mind in old age'. *Developmental Psychology* 34. 2: 358–362.

Henry, J. D., Phillips, L. H., Ruffman, T., & Bailey, P. E., 2013. 'A meta-analytic review of age differences in theory of mind'. *Psychology and Aging* 28. 3: 826–839.

Hess, T. M., 2006. 'Adaptive aspects of social cognitive functioning in adulthood: Age-related goal and knowledge influences'. *Social Cognition* 24. 3: 279–309.

Hess, T. M., 2014. 'Selective engagement of cognitive resources: Motivational influences on older adults' cognitive functioning'. *Perspectives on Psychological Science* 9. 4: 388–407.

Insch, P. M., Bull, R., Phillips, L. H., Allen, R., & Slessor, G., 2012. 'Adult aging, processing style, and the perception of biological motion'. *Experimental Aging Research* 38. 2: 169–185.

Johansson Nolaker, E., Murray, K., Happé, F., & Charlton, R. A., 2018. 'Cognitive and affective associations with an ecologically valid test of theory of mind across the lifespan'. *Neuropsychology* 32. 6: 754–763.

Keltner, D., Sauter, D., Tracy, J., & Cowen, A., 2019. 'Emotional expression: Advances in basic emotion theory'. *Journal of Nonverbal Behaviour* 43. 2: 133–160.

Keysar, B., Lin, S., & Barr, D. J., 2003. 'Limits on theory of mind use in adults'. *Cognition* 89. 1: 25–41.

Khanjani, Z., Mosanezhad Jeddi, E., Hekmati, I., Khalilzade, S., Etemadi Nia, M., Andalib, M., & Ashrafian, P., 2015. 'Empathy and social functioning'. *Australian Psychologist* 50: 80–85.

Kilner, J. M., & Lemon, R. N., 2013. 'What we know currently about mirror neurons'. *Current Biology* 23. 23: R1057–R1062.

Kramer, A. F., & Willis, S. L., 2002. 'Enhancing the cognitive vitality of older adults'. *Current Directions in Psychological Science* 11. 5: 173–177.

Kuhn, G., Pagano, A., Maani, S., & Bunce, D., 2015. 'Age-related decline in the reflexive component of overt gaze following'. *Quarterly Journal of Experimental Psychology* 68. 6: 1073–1081.

Langton, S. R., Watt, R. J., & Bruce, V., 2000. 'Do the eyes have it? Cues to the direction of social attention'. *Trends in Cognitive Sciences* 4. 2: 50–59.

Lawrence, K., Campbell, R., & Skuse, D., 2015. 'Age, gender, and puberty influence the development of facial emotion recognition'. *Frontiers in Psychology* 6: 761.

Lecce, S., Ceccato, I., & Cavallini, E., 2019. 'Theory of mind, mental state talk and social relationships in aging: The case of friendship'. *Aging & Mental Health* 23. 9: 1105–1112.

Lecce, S., Bottiroli, S., Bianco, F., Rosi, A., & Cavallini, E., 2015. 'Training older adults on Theory of Mind (ToM): transfer on metamemory'. *Archives of Gerontology and Geriatrics* 60. 1: 217–226.

Léonard, G., & Tremblay, F., 2007. 'Corticomotor facilitation associated with observation, imagery and imitation of hand actions: A comparative study in young and old adults'. *Experimental Brain Research* 177. 2: 167–175.

Li, X., Wang, K., Wang, F., Tao, Q., Xie, Y., & Cheng, Q., 2013. 'Aging of theory of mind: The influence of educational level and cognitive processing'. *International Journal of Psychology* 48. 4: 715–727.

Long, M. R., Horton, W. S., Rohde, H., & Sorace, A., 2018. 'Individual differences in switching and inhibition predict perspective-taking across the lifespan'. *Cognition* 170: 25–30.

MacPherson, S. E., Phillips, L. H., & Della Sala, S., 2002. 'Age, executive function, and social decision making: A dorsolateral prefrontal theory of cognitive aging'. *Psychology and Aging* 17. 4: 598–609.

Madden, D. J., 2007. 'Aging and visual attention'. *Current Directions in Psychological Science* 16. 2: 70–74.

Mahy, C. E. V., Vetter, N., Kühn-Popp, N., Löcher, C., Krautschuk, S., & Kliegel, M., 2013. 'The influence of inhibitory processes on affective theory of mind in young and old adults'. *Aging, Neuropsychology, and Cognition* 21. 2: 129–145.

Martin, A. K., Perceval, G., Davies, I., Su, P., Huang, J., & Meinzer, M., 2019. 'Visual perspective taking in young and older adults'. *Journal of Experimental Psychology: General*. 148. 11: 2006–2026.

Martin, G. B., & Clark, R. D., 1982. 'Distress crying in neonates: Species and peer specificity'. *Developmental Psychology* 18. 1: 3–9.

Mattan, B. D., Quinn, K. A., Acaster, S. L., Jennings, R. M., & Rotshtein, P., 2017. 'Prioritization of self-relevant perspectives in ageing', *Quarterly Journal of Experimental Psychology* 70. 6: 1033–1052.

Maylor, E. A., Moulson, J. M., Muncer, A. M., & Taylor, L. A., 2002. 'Does performance on theory of mind tasks decline with age?' *British Journal of Psychology* 93. 4: 465–485.

McDonald, N. M., & Messinger, D. S., 2011. 'The development of empathy: How, when, and why'. In *Moral Behaviour and Free Will: A Neurobiological and Philosophical Approach*, edited by J. J. Sanguieneti, A. Acerbi, & J. A. Lombo. Rome: IF-Press, pp. 341–368.

McKinnon, M. C., & Muscovitch, M., 2007. 'Domain-general contributions to social reasoning: Theory of mind and deontic reasoning re-explored'. *Cognition* 102. 2: 179–218.

McKone, E., Kanwisher, N., & Duchaine, B. C., 2007. 'Can generic expertise explain special processing for faces?'. *Trends in Cognitive Sciences* 11. 1: 8–15.

Meltzoff, A. N. (2002). Imitation as a mechanism of social cognition: Origins of empathy, theory of mind, and the representation of action. In *Blackwell handbook of childhood cognitive development*, edited by U. Goswami. Oxford: Blackwell Publishers, pp. 6–25.

Meltzoff, A. N., & Decety, J., 2003. 'What imitation tells us about social cognition: A rapprochement between developmental psychology and cognitive neuroscience'. *Philosophical Transactions of the Royal Society of London: Series B: Biological Sciences* 358. 1431: 491–500.

Miles, W. R., 1933. 'Age and human ability'. *Psychological Review* 40: 99–123.

Moran, J. M., Jolly, E., & Mitchell, J. P., 2012. 'Social-cognitive deficits in normal aging'. *Journal of Neuroscience* 32. 16: 5553–5561.

Nedelko, V., Hassa, T., Hamzei, F., Weiller, C., Binkofski, F., Schoenfeld, M. A., ... & Dettmers, C., 2010. 'Age-independent activation in areas of the mirror neuron system during action observation and action imagery. A fMRI study'. *Restorative Neurology and Neuroscience* 28. 6: 737–747.

Noack, H., Lövdén, M., & Schmiedek, F., 2014. 'On the validity and generality of transfer effects in cognitive training research'. *Psychological Research* 78. 6: 773–789.

Noh, S. R., & Isaacowitz, D. M., 2013. 'Emotional faces in context: Age differences in recognition accuracy and scanning patterns'. *Emotion* 13. 2: 238.

Norman, J. F., Payton, S. M., Long, J. R., & Hawkes, L. M., 2004. 'Aging and the perception of biological motion'. *Psychology and Aging* 19. 1: 219–225

O'Brien, E., Konrath, S. H., Grühn, D., & Hagen A. L., 2013. 'Empathic concern and perspective taking: linear and quadratic effects of age across the adult life span'. *Journals of Gerontology: Series B* 68. 2: 168–175.

Office for National Statistics, 2018, August 13. *Living Longer: How our Population is Changing and Why it Matters*. UK Statistics Authority. Available at: https://www.ons.gov.uk/peoplepopulationandcommunity/birthsdeathsandmarriages/ageing/articles/livinglongerhowourpopulationischangingandwhyitmatters/2018-08-13#how-do-changes-in-the-uk-population-compare-with-the-rest-of-the-world

Onishi, K. H., & Baillargeon, R., 2005. 'Do 15-month-old infants understand false beliefs?' *Science* 308. 5719: 255–258.

Pardini, M., & Nichelli, P. F., 2009. 'Age-related decline in mentalizing skills across the life span'. *Experimental Aging Research* 35. 1: 98–106.

Park, D. C., Lodi-Smith, J., Drew, L., Haber, S., Hebrank, A., Bischof, G. N., & Aamodt, W., 2013. 'The impact of sustained engagement on cognitive function in older adults: the synapse project'. *Psychological Science* 25. 1: 103–112.

Penn, D. L., Corrigan, P. W., Bentall, R. P., Racenstein, J. M., & Newman, L., 1997. 'Social cognition in schizophrenia'. *Psychological Bulletin* 121. 1: 114–132.

Perner, J., & Lang, B., 1999. 'Development of theory of mind and executive control'. *Trends in Cognitive Sciences* 3. 9: 337–344.

Perner, J., & Wimmer, H., 1985. '"John thinks that Mary thinks that … "': Attribution of second-order beliefs by 5- to 10-year-old children'. *Journal of Experimental Child Psychology* 39. 3: 437–471.

Peters, R., 2006. 'Ageing and the brain'. *Postgraduate Medical Journal* 82. 964: 84–88.

Phillips, L. H., MacLean, R. D., & Allen, R., 2002. 'Age and the understanding of emotions: neuropsychological and sociocognitive perspectives'. *Journals of Gerontology: Series B* 57. 6: 526–530.

Phillips, L. H., Allen, R., Bull, R., Hering, A., Kliegel, M., & Channon, S., 2015. 'Older adults have difficulty in decoding sarcasm'. *Developmental Psychology* 51. 2: 1840–1852.

Phillips, L. H., Bull, R., Allen, R., Insch, P., Burr, K., & Ogg, W., 2011. 'Lifespan aging and belief reasoning: Influences of executive function and social cue decoding'. *Cognition* 120. 2: 236–247.

Premack, D., & Woodruff, G., 1978. 'Does the chimpanzee have a theory of mind?' *Behavioral and Brain Sciences* 1. 4: 515–526.

Rabbitt, P., 1965. 'An age-decrement in the ability to ignore irrelevant information'. *Journal of Gerontology* 20: 233–238.

Rakoczy, H., Harder-Kasten, A., & Sturm, L., 2012. 'The decline of theory of mind in old age is (partly) mediated by developmental changes in domain-general abilities'. *British Journal of Psychology* 103. 1: 58–72.

Raz, N., Lindenberger, U., Rodrigue, K. M., Kennedy, K. M., Head, D., Williamson, A., ... & Acker, J. D., 2005. 'Regional brain changes in aging healthy adults: General trends, individual differences and modifiers'. *Cerebral Cortex* 15. 11: 1676–1689.

Reuter-Lorenz, P. A., & Park, D. C., 2010. 'Human neuroscience and the aging mind: A new look at old problems'. *Journals of Gerontology: Series B* 65. 4: 405–415.

Richter, D., & Kunzmann, U., 2011. 'Age differences in three facets of empathy: Performance-based empathy'. *Psychology and Aging* 26. 1: 60–70.

Rosi, A., Cavallini, E., Bottiroli, S., Bianco, F., & Lecce, S., 2016. 'Promoting theory of mind in older adults: Does age play a role?'. *Aging and Mental Health* 20. 1: 22–28.

Ruffman, T., Henry, J. D., Livingstone, V., & Phillips, L. H., 2008. 'A meta-analytic review of emotion recognition and aging: Implications for neuropsychological models of aging'. *Neuroscience & Biobehavioral Reviews* 32. 4: 863–881.

Rump, K. M., Giovannelli, J. L., Minshew, N. J., & Strauss, M. S., 2009. 'The development of emotion recognition in individuals with autism'. *Child Development* 80. 5: 1434–1447.

Salthouse, T., 2012. 'Consequences of age-related cognitive declines'. *Annual Review of Psychology* 63: 201–226.

Salthouse, T. A., 1996. 'The processing-speed theory of adult age differences in cognition'. *Psychological Review* 103. 3: 403–428.

Samson, D., Apperly, I. A., Braithwaite, J. J., Andrews, B. J., & Bodley Scott, S. E., 2010. 'Seeing it their way: Evidence for rapid and involuntary computation of what other people see'. *Journal of Experimental Psychology: Human Perception and Performance* 36. 5: 1255–1266.

Sander, D., Grandjean, D., Kaiser, S., Wehrle, T., & Scherer, K. R., 2007. 'Interaction effects of perceived gaze direction and dynamic facial expression: Evidence for appraisal theories of emotion'. *European Journal of Cognitive Psychology* 19. 3: 470–480.

Schaie, K. W., 2000. 'The impact of longitudinal studies on understanding development from young adulthood to old age'. *International Journal of Behavioral Development* 24. 3: 257–266.

Schnittker, J., 2007. 'Look (closely) at all the lonely people: Age and the social psychology of social support'. *Journal of Aging and Health* 19. 4: 659–682.

Senju, A., 2013. 'Atypical development of spontaneous social cognition in autism spectrum disorders'. *Brain Development* 35. 2: 96–101.

Slessor, G., Phillips, L. H., & Bull, R., 2007. 'Exploring the specificity of age-related differences in theory of mind tasks'. *Psychology and Aging* 22. 3: 639–643.

REFERENCES 145

Slessor, G., Laird, G., Phillips, L. H., Bull, R., & Filippou, D., 2010. 'Age-related differences in gaze following: Does the age of the face matter?'. *Journals of Gerontology: Series B: Psychological Sciences and Social Sciences* 65. 5: 536–541.

Spengler, S., von Cramon, D. Y., & Brass, M., 2010. 'Resisting motor mimicry: Control of imitation involves processes central to social cognition in patients with frontal and temporo-parietal lesions'. *Social Neuroscience* 5. 4: 401–416.

Stanley, J. T., & Blanchard-Fields, F., 2008. 'Challenges older adults face in detecting deceit: The role of emotion recognition'. *Psychology and Aging* 23. 1: 24–32.

Stanley, J. T., & Isaacowitz, D. M., 2015. 'Caring more and knowing more reduces age-related differences in emotion perception'. *Psychology and Aging* 30. 2: 383–395.

Stern, Y., 2012. 'Cognitive reserve in ageing and Alzheimer's disease'. *Lancet Neurology* 11. 11: 1006–1012.

Strang, J. F., Kenworthy, L., Daniolos, P., Case, L., Wills, M. C., Martin, A., & Wallace, G. L., 2012. 'Depression and anxiety symptoms in children and adolescents with autism spectrum disorders without intellectual disability'. *Research in Autism Spectrum Disorders* 6. 1: 406–412.

Sullivan, S., & Ruffman, T., 2004a. 'Emotion recognition deficits in the elderly'. *International Journal of Neuroscience* 114. 3: 403–432.

Sullivan, S., & Ruffman, T., 2004b. 'Social understanding: How does it fare with advancing years?'. *British Journal of Psychology* 95. 1: 1–18.

Sze, J. A., Gyurak, A., Goodkind, M. S., & Levenson, R. W., 2012. 'Greater emotional empathy and prosocial behaviour in late life'. *Emotion* 12. 5: 1129–1140.

Thomas, L. A., De Bellis, M. D., Graham, R., & LaBar, K. S., 2007. 'Development of emotional facial recognition in late childhood and adolescence'. *Developmental Science* 10. 5: 547–558.

Toril, P., Reales, J. M., & Ballesteros, S., 2014. 'Video game training enhances cognition of older adults: a meta-analytic study'. *Psychology and Aging* 29. 3: 706–716.

Tully, E. C., Ames, A. M., Garcia, S. E., & Donohue, M. R., 2016. 'Quadratic associations between empathy and depression as moderated by emotion dysregulation'. *Journal of Psychology* 150. 1: 15–35.

Unger, J. B., Johnson, C. A., & Marks, G., 1997. Functional decline in the elderly: Evidence for direct and stress-buffering protective effects of social interactions and physical activity. *Annals of Behavioral Medicine* 19. 2: 152–160.

van Baaren, R., Janssen, L., Chartran, T. L., & Dijksterhuis, A., 2009. 'Where is the love? The social aspects of mimicry'. *Philosophical Transactions of the Royal Society B* 364. 1528: 2381–2389.

Vetter, N. C., Weigelt, S., Döhnel, K., Smolka, M. N., & Kliegel, M., 2013. 'Ongoing neural development of affective theory of mind in adolescence'. *Social, Cognitive & Affective Neuroscience* 9. 7: 1022–1029.

Vicaria, I. M., Bernieri, F. J., & Isaacowitz, D. M., 2015. 'Perceptions of rapport across the life span: Gaze patterns and judgment accuracy'. *Psychology and Aging* 30. 2: 396–406.

Vogeley, K., 2017. 'Two social brains: Neural mechanism of intersubjectivity', *Philosophical Transactions of the Royal Society: Series B* 372. 1727: 20160245.

Voss, M. W., Prakash, R. S., Erickson, K. I., Basak, C., Chaddock, L., Kim, J. S., ... & Wójcicki, T. R., 2010. 'Plasticity of brain networks in a randomized intervention trial of exercise training in older adults'. *Frontiers in Aging Neuroscience* 2. 32.

Vrigkas, M., Nikou, C., & Kakadiaris, I. A., 2015. 'A review of human activity recognition methods'. *Frontiers in Robotics and AI* 2. 28.

Wang, Z., & Su, Y., 2013. 'Age-related differences in the performance of theory of mind in older adults: A dissociation of cognitive and affective components'. *Psychology and Aging* 28. 1: 284–291.

Want, S. C., & Harris, P. L., 2002. 'How do children ape? Applying concepts from the study of non-human primates to the developmental study of "imitation" in children'. *Developmental Science* 5. 1: 1–14.

Ward, N. S., 2006. 'Compensatory mechanisms in the aging motor system'. *Ageing Research Reviews* 5. 3: 239–254.

Weick, C., & Kunzmann, U., 2015. 'Age differences in empathy: Multidirectional and context-dependent'. *Psychology and Aging* 30. 2: 407–419.

Wilson, R. S., Boyle, P. A., Yu, L., Barnes, L. L., Schneider, J. A., & Bennett, D. A., 2013. 'Life-span cognitive activity, neuropathologic burden, and cognitive aging'. *Neurology* 81. 4: 314–321.

Wimmer, H., & Perner, J., 1983. 'Beliefs about beliefs: Representation and constraining function of wrong beliefs in young children's understanding of deception'. *Cognition* 13. 1: 103–128.

Zhang, X., Fung, H. H., Stanley, J. T., Isaacowitz, D. M., & Ho, M. Y., 2013. 'Perspective taking in older age revisited: A motivational perspective'. *Developmental Psychology* 49. 10: 1848–1858.

Zhu, X., Yin, S., Lang, M., He, R., & Li, J., 2016. The more the better? A meta-analysis on effects of combined cognitive and physical intervention on cognition in healthy older adults. *Ageing Research Reviews* 31: 67–79.

7
Understanding Atypical Social Behaviour Using Social Cognitive Theory

Lessons from Autism

Lucy A. Livingston and Francesca Happé

7.1 Introduction

This chapter addresses atypical social communication, taking lessons learned from a neurodevelopmental condition characterized by atypical social behaviour, namely Autism Spectrum Disorder (ASD). In this chapter, we will lay out the most prominent and compelling social cognitive models of atypical social behaviour in ASD. We will introduce and discuss evidence for each, and make conclusions about their explanatory power. We will pay particular attention to the 'Theory of Mind' (ToM) theory, and, in line with the aims of this book, use a lifespan lens by considering evidence for developmental trajectories and age-dependent changes where relevant. This will be followed by critical consideration for how individual differences and heterogeneity in ASD constrain our understanding of the social cognitive basis of ASD. Finally, we will reflect on the ongoing methodological and theoretical challenges and debates in the field, and recommend directions for future research.

Given the specific aims of this chapter in addressing social cognitive theories, we omit discussion of major biological models of ASD including genetic (see Bourgeron, 2016), and brain structure and function (see Ecker et al., 2015), as well as cognitive explanations of the non-social behavioural features of ASD—for example, the 'Weak Central Coherence' theory (Happé & Frith, 2006), Bayesian accounts (Pellicano & Burr, 2012), and atypical sensory perception (Robertson & Baron-Cohen, 2017). Although some of these non-social theories can in part explain social features of ASD—for instance, atypical prior expectations in ASD have been shown to be linked with autistic social behaviours (e.g. Lawson et al., 2017)—we will focus primarily on social cognitive theories. Furthermore, in order to enable sufficient depth in our analysis, we omit, and direct readers elsewhere to, the vast literature on face processing (e.g. Webb et al., 2011) and emotion recognition (e.g. Black et al., 2017) in ASD. Throughout the chapter, we will primarily draw on research comparing individuals with and without diagnosed autism (i.e. case-control studies) although, because it is widely acknowledged that autism lies at the end of a continuum of normally distributed autistic traits (Lundström et al., 2012), we will also highlight research using trait-wise approaches in the general population, when appropriate. On a final note, we will use multiple terms to describe observable social features of ASD interchangeably, including social skills, social behaviours, social communication, and social interaction. We also use the term 'neurotypical' to describe individuals who are not autistic.

7.2 Autism spectrum disorder

ASD refers to a set of lifelong neurodevelopmental conditions, diagnosed by the presence of behavioural impairments in social communication and interaction, and repetitive and restricted behaviours and interests (American Psychiatric Association [APA], 2013). Growing evidence suggests that these social and non-social symptoms may be underpinned by distinct genetic and neurocognitive aetiology (see Happé et al., 2006; Warrier et al., 2019). As such, this chapter will focus purely on the former, which includes, but is not limited to, difficulties in social reciprocity (e.g. turn-taking), expression and integration of verbal and non-verbal communication, and context-dependent adjustment of social behaviour. A best-estimate diagnosis of ASD is typically made after collating evidence for such atypical behaviours across multiple contexts from early in development, including parental (and often teacher) reports of behaviour, and direct observation by an experienced clinician. Critically, for diagnosis, these symptoms must cause significant impairment to the individual,—for example, in social and occupational settings (APA, 2013).

Around 1% of the general population is thought to meet criteria for ASD (e.g. Baird et al., 2006), with males being three times as likely to receive a diagnosis than females (Loomes et al., 2017), although these estimates differ by country and are largely derived from high-income countries only (de Leeuw et al., 2020). In the past 15 years, there has been a substantial worldwide rise in the number of autistic children entering adulthood, as well as individuals receiving an autism diagnosis for the first time in adulthood (L. Jones et al., 2014; Mukaetova-Ladinska et al., 2012). This latter observation has been largely attributed to increased autism awareness among the public and medical professionals, and widening of diagnostic criteria over time, rather than there being a genuine increase in the prevalence of ASD (Rutter, 2005; Simonoff, 2012). This means that ASD is now less likely to be misdiagnosed or missed (at least in males) than several decades ago—for example, due to diagnostic over-shadowing by other conditions (i.e. diagnosis of a co-occurring disorder, such as anxiety, without further assessment and diagnosis of ASD). Notwithstanding this, there is growing consensus that autism has and continues to be under-diagnosed in females; they are less likely than their male counterparts to receive a diagnosis despite equivalent autistic characteristics (Carpenter et al., 2019; Lai et al., 2015; Ratto et al., 2018). It is unclear yet whether this is due to male-biased diagnostic tools, differential manifestations of autism in females—for instance, restricted interests in females may be more subtle or social in nature (e.g. music bands; Sutherland et al., 2017)—or enhanced ability and/or societal pressure of females to 'camouflage' or 'compensate for' their autistic features (Hull et al., 2020; Livingston & Happé, 2017).

Because of this underdiagnosis in females, cognitive autism research over the past 50 years has been heavily skewed towards autistic males (Happé & Frith, 2020). Additionally, although around 50% of autistic individuals also have an intellectual disability (Charman et al., 2011), a recent meta-analysis estimated that over 90% of autism research studies excludes this subgroup (Russell et al., 2019a). Taking this into consideration, it is worth noting that many of the research findings presented in this chapter may be more easily generalized to intellectually able autistic males.

7.2.1 What are we trying to explain?

ASD is diagnosed by behaviour alone and there are currently no reliable biological markers for the condition (Loth et al., 2016). Consequently, one of the most successful approaches for explaining ASD has been cognitive theories, which aim to bridge the gap between lower-level biology (e.g. genes, neurons) and higher-level complex autistic behaviour. Morton and Frith (1995) suggested that, in neurodevelopmental conditions such as ASD, an array of biological factors—for example, genetic atypicalities leading to brain alterations—promote atypicalities in discrete mental or cognitive processes, which in turn contribute to the constellation of observed behavioural symptoms. In this way, cognitive models of ASD help to give more parsimonious explanations of complex phenomena observed at biological and behavioural levels (Frith, 2012). Further, cognitive insights can: a) give a window into the numerous and diverse features of the autistic mind that may not be immediately evident at the behavioural surface (Frith, 2019); b) guide future in-depth research towards possible underlying genetic and biological systems; and c) have important translatable implications for clinical and educational professionals. Generally speaking, an effective cognitive theory should aim to maximize universality and specificity—that is, account for the specific social behavioural profile seen in most autistic people (and not in other clinical groups). Several such social cognitive theories have been proposed, the most prominent and compelling of which will be addressed in this chapter.

7.2.2 Lifespan perspective

Viewing and investigating social behaviour and cognition in ASD through a lifespan perspective is crucial for a number of reasons. First, lifespan approaches to autism, and neurodevelopmental conditions more generally, help to delineate causal mechanisms. In autism research, this has been demonstrated most successfully by infant sibling studies, whereby younger siblings of autistic children are studied prospectively from the first few months of life (see Szatmari et al., 2016, for an overview). Such studies have facilitated clearer understanding of the dynamic developmental unfolding of autism and helped disentangle causal and correlational effects. For example, it is now well understood that, while behavioural indicators of autism may not be present until 12 months, there are early neurocognitive markers and more subtle features of parent–child interaction in the first year of life that predict a later autism trajectory (for reviews, see E. J. Jones et al., 2014, and Wan et al., 2019). Such research has therefore been able to inform early interventions that seek to target prodromal autistic symptoms and thereby steer young infants at increased genetic likelihood of autism onto an improved developmental trajectory (see Green & Garg, 2018, for review).

Second, as autism is a lifelong condition (see Happé & Frith, 2020), lifespan approaches are fundamental for delineating sensitive developmental periods, trajectories, and outcomes. Studies tracking behavioural and cognitive change over autistic childhood, adolescence and early adulthood have highlighted numerous important findings. For instance, research converges to suggest that the majority of autistic people's social difficulties persist into adulthood and, equally, that this may be underpinned by persistent social cognitive difficulties (e.g. Cantio et al., 2018; Pellicano, 2013), although there is evidence that a small subgroup of individuals may show improvement in their symptoms and have a so-called 'optimal outcome' (Fein et al., 2013). Additionally, such studies facilitate understanding of how age-dependent processes, such as cognitive decline, may or may not be altered in autism. For example, evidence thus far suggests that older autistic adults (50+ years old) experience cognitive decline across multiple domains (e.g. verbal memory, social cognition) at a similar rate compared to non-autistic adults, and but may experience slower cognitive decline in visual memory (Lever & Geurts, 2016) and ToM (Zıvralı Yarar et al., in press). This latter finding suggests that ASD may in fact protect against some age-related cognitive decline, although the putative underlying mechanisms are yet to be fully understood. Such findings will necessarily feed into age-specific interventions and support structures for autistic people across the lifespan.

Finally, there is a rapidly increasing requirement for autism research through a lifespan lens because most autistic people are adults, and there are increasing numbers now entering middle and late adulthood (Happé & Charlton, 2012), yet the majority of cognitive autism research, including investigation of trajectories and outcomes, has been carried out in children and, to a lesser degree, adolescents (Mukaetova-Ladinska et al., 2012). Therefore, it is unclear if predominant cognitive theories of ASD, largely derived from childhood data, will necessarily be able to explain adult profiles of ASD. Further, childhood research does not necessarily translate to individuals who receive a later first diagnosis in adulthood. Very little is known about how these individuals differ—in behaviour, cognition, or support needs—from those diagnosed in earlier life. Therefore, taken together, cross-sectional and longitudinal research into social behaviour and cognition across the whole autistic lifespan is seriously warranted.

7.3 Social cognitive theories of autism spectrum disorder

Social cognition is a domain-specific system that serves the processing of stimuli relevant to understanding agents (Happé et al., 2017). ASD is often viewed as *the* condition of atypical social cognition. Indeed, over the past 50 years, many social cognitive theories of ASD have been proposed. More recently, however, it has been acknowledged that there are numerous sub-components of social cognition that may be differentially impaired or intact in ASD and that other conditions with social impairments (e.g. Williams syndrome, social anxiety disorder) may be explained by a pattern of atypical social cognition distinct from ASD (see Happé & Frith, 2014). For example, there is no evidence to suggest that attachment is atypical in ASD (e.g. Teague et al., 2017) or that autistic people are not susceptible to forming social stereotypes—that is, linking particular social groups to certain attributes—similar to neurotypical people (Hirschfeld et al., 2007; Birmingham et al., 2015). There may even be some social abilities that are enhanced in ASD. For example, recent studies showed that greater autistic traits in the neurotypical population are linked with greater knowledge of social phenomena (e.g. social loafing, group think; Gollwitzer et al., 2019; Taylor et al., 2019).

There is no one accepted structure of social cognition and its sub-components. Indeed, there is ongoing debate, even in the neurotypical literature, surrounding the exact number of sub-components of social cognition, their relationship to one another, and the extent to which overlapping terminology is used in the literature to describe a single process (see Happé et al., 2017, for an in-depth review). Here, instead of following a strict 'map' of social cognition, we will focus on a handful of predominant theories of atypical social cognition in ASD, ranging from basic social perception (e.g. social attention) to higher-order social cognition (e.g. ToM). We will evaluate their explanatory power in accounting for social impairments in ASD and consider any evidence of a lifespan approach.

7.3.1 Social attention and social motivation

Behaviourally speaking, autistic people tend to engage less readily in the social world (e.g. reduced social interaction, eye contact) and more in the non-social world (e.g. restricted circumscribed interests) compared to neurotypical people (Kanner, 1943). Unsurprisingly then, researchers have investigated whether individuals with ASD have fundamental differences in social attention (the extent to which social stimuli capture attention), and/or social motivation (the extent to which social information is rewarding).

7.3.1.1 Social attention
In their seminal paper, Dawson and colleagues (1998) showed that autistic children paid significantly less attention to social stimuli (e.g. calling the child's name), but not non-social stimuli (e.g. shaking a rattle) than neurotypical children and children with Down syndrome. This led to the social orienting hypothesis of ASD, which posits that autistic people have a primary specific deficit in attentional capture by social information, which subsequently leads to reduced opportunities to engage in the social world, with knock-on effects on acquisition of social skills. However, subsequent evidence for this hypothesis has been mixed. In particular, the prospective study of infants at heightened genetic probability of ASD (i.e. with an older sibling with ASD) has shown that infants who subsequently develop ASD show no significant attentional deficits in orienting to faces, gaze, and/or body movements in the first year of life (see E. J. Jones et al., 2014, for review). One plausible explanation for this is that involuntary and subcortical social attentional systems may be intact in ASD, whereas later developing voluntary social attention, subserved by cortical regions, may be atypical, or perhaps become increasingly atypical over development (see Elsabbagh & Johnson, 2016). For example, W. Jones and Klin (2013) showed that 2-month-old infants who later go on to develop ASD fixate on an agent's eyes just as much as those who did not show an autism outcome. Interestingly, between 2 and 6 months, there was a decrease in fixation to the eyes, suggesting that specialization of cortical social processes may be reduced in those who go on to receive a diagnosis of ASD.

In line with this distinction between subcortical and cortical social attention in ASD, intact involuntary social orienting has been found in both autistic children (Fischer et al., 2014) and adults (Shah et al., 2013). Shah and colleagues showed that autistic adults show robust orienting to social (in this case, face-like) stimuli, akin to neurotypical individuals, even when these stimuli are not relevant to the task at hand. They concluded that, although basic, involuntary social orienting may be intact in ASD, a range of top-down cortical processes may modulate autistic individuals' attention to social stimuli after initial orienting, contributing to the other social cognitive deficits seen in ASD. Notwithstanding this, a recent study found evidence for atypicalities in early social processing mechanisms in ASD. Gray et al.

(2018) showed that, when experimentally presented very briefly with social and non-social scenes below conscious awareness, autistic adults were equally fast in detecting the social compared to non-social stimuli, whereas neurotypical participants showed faster detection for social stimuli.

Studies examining more endogenous forms of social attention (e.g. visual scanning of social scenes) show a more mixed pattern of results, with some studies finding deficits in autistic infants (e.g. Chawarska & Shic, 2009), children (e.g. Rice et al., 2012), adolescents and adults (e.g. Fletcher-Watson et al., 2009), and others not (e.g. Dijkhuis et al., 2019; New et al., 2010). Additionally, a review of eye-tracking studies of social attention in ASD from infancy to adulthood concluded that, although individual studies have found decreased visual attention to social stimuli (e.g. faces) in autistic individuals, these effects appear to be dependent on the context (e.g. videos versus static images versus real-life interaction), rather than generalized across all social stimuli (Guillon et al., 2014, although see Chita-Tegmark, 2016). For example, Chawarska and colleagues (2012) found that autistic infants only showed atypical scanning of a social scene when dyadic cues were introduced (e.g. child-directed speech from an adult), compared to other non-social distractions. This suggests that social attention difficulties in ASD may only arise in particular contexts. Studies of real-life interaction between autistic adults and an experimenter support this idea that numerous factors modulate social attention in ASD. For example, Freeth and Bugembe (2019) showed that autistic adults attend less to the experimenter's face compared to neurotypical participants only when the experimenter makes direct, but not averted, eye gaze. It is also noteworthy that atypical social attention is not specific to ASD. For example, one prospective study of infants who have an older sibling with ASD showed that more social attention to the mouth versus the eyes predicted later language difficulties, and not autism per se (Elsabbagh et al., 2013). Interestingly, this mouth-eyes gaze pattern also did not hold up as a specific feature in ASD in the aforementioned review (Elsabbagh et al., 2013).

Overall, evidence for altered social attention in ASD is mixed. Of less contention is the notion that subcortical social attentional mechanisms are intact in ASD and are evident in the first few months of life. This has led to the 'demise of the innate social orienting hypothesis' (Johnson, 2014). This intact orienting may be evident in autistic adults who otherwise show social cognitive and behavioural impairments. However, the extent to which, and the mechanisms by which, higher-order social attentional processes may be atypical and bias social cognition remains unclear. It is possible that particular subgroups of autistic individuals may be more likely to experience altered social attention. For example, there is some evidence for sex-specific atypicalities, whereby autistic females show fewer social attention deficits (e.g. Harrop et al., 2018; Kleberg et al., 2019). Whether this contributes to differential expression of autistic characteristics in some females (e.g. less severely affected social skills), requires further rigorous empirical analysis.

Of note, there is, to our knowledge, no research into developmental trajectories of social attention beyond childhood, and, additionally, no research into social attention generally in middle or late autistic adulthood. Knowledge of how social attention atypicalities contribute to social skills across the lifespan in ASD is sparse and further research is much needed.

7.3.1.2 Social motivation

Building on the theory of reduced social attention in ASD, it has been proposed that autistic people's atypical social behaviour can be explained in terms of reduced social motivation. Chevallier and colleagues (2012a) proposed that, as well as social stimuli not capturing autistic people's attention, social stimuli may be: a) fundamentally less rewarding than for neurotypical individuals, and that this leads to b) reduced propensity for social approach and to seek acceptance and avoid rejection (e.g. reputation management). In terms of atypical social reward, a recent meta-analysis of functional magnetic resonance imaging studies of reward processing in ASD found that neural activity associated with both social *and non-social* reward processing was atypical in ASD (Clements et al., 2018). The notion of atypical reward processing more generally, rather than a specific deficit in the social domain, is also supported by another systematic review of behavioural-cognitive studies (Bottini, 2018). Taken together, there is limited support for specifically reduced social reward, which is a fundamental component of the social motivation hypothesis of ASD.

A more mixed picture is found for evidence of reduced reputation management. Chevallier and colleagues (2012b) found that children with ASD were less likely to engage in flattery to manage their reputation compared with neurotypical children. However, other research suggests that autistic people have a reduced propensity, but not necessarily reduced ability, to manage their reputation. For example, Cage and colleagues (2013) found that although autistic individuals did not show the neurotypical effect when donating money to charity—i.e. donating more when being observed by another person than when alone—they did donate more money when they knew that the money was going to the observer and that the observer would also have the opportunity to donate to them. This suggests that, when prompted in some way, autistic people *do* have the ability to consider their reputation, although this may not come spontaneously to them. Instead, it has been suggested that it is fundamental difficulties in ToM or mentalizing—i.e. in understanding the mental states of others—that may constrain autistic individuals' propensity to demonstrate reputation management. Indeed, Izuma and colleagues (2011) showed, using a control task, that autistic people still show a typical audience effect—i.e. perform better on a task in the presence of another person than on their own—when there are no mentalizing demands.

More recently, the social motivation theory has come under scrutiny by Jaswal and Akhtar (2019), who proposed that core social atypicalities in ASD can be explained in terms of factors other than social motivation, thus reducing the explanatory power of the theory. They argued, for example, that low levels of eye contact in ASD may be an adaptive response to anxiety and/or cognitive load, rather than a sign of reduced social motivation. This is supported by evidence showing that eye contact among autistic people towards a neurotypical conversation partner is modulated by task difficulty. For example, autistic children make better modulated eye contact when the topic of conversation is their special interest versus a general topic (Nadig et al., 2010) or non-emotional versus emotional in content (Hutchins & Brien, 2016). Jaswal and Akhtar also noted that lack of social motivation does not align with anecdotal reports from autistic people who are motivated to 'fit in' socially. Indeed, there is evidence to suggest that many autistic people use 'compensatory strategies' to disguise their autistic social difficulties—for example, pre-planning conversations before they happen—in order to make social connections and avoid bullying and ostracism (Livingston, et al., 2019a; 2020a). Livingston et al. (2019b) speculated that a subset of autistic individuals may in fact have heightened social motivation, since they choose to use these strategies, which are cognitively demanding and stressful to implement, to the detriment of their own well-being (see also, Livingston et al., 2019c).

Overall, the social motivation theory of autism lacks universality because it fails to account for social atypicalities across all autistic individuals, and so-called 'lack' of social motivation may be better explained in terms of social cognitive deficits—for example, in ToM. More generally, there is little consensus about the optimal method (e.g. objective versus subjective methods, and in which context) to measure social motivation in autism research, which may account for the mixed findings in the existing literature (Dubey et al., 2018). It is also worth noting that no studies have assessed social motivation over the autistic lifespan, with the majority of the literature focused on children and adolescents (e.g. Bos et al., 2019). It is particularly unclear whether autistic individuals diagnosed in adulthood differ from those diagnosed earlier in life, potentially due to enhanced social motivation and desire to compensate to fit in to the social world.

7.3.2 Imitation

Imitation, the ability to observe and mirror another's behaviour, was originally proposed to be an important social cognitive process that precedes the development of higher-level abilities such as empathy and ToM. Given this putative link, and observations of a lack of imitative behaviours in young autistic children and autistic adults (see Williams et al., 2004, for a review), imitation difficulties were theorized to be a core feature driving the social symptoms of ASD (Rogers & Pennington, 1991). This led researchers to speculate whether the mirror neuron system—inferior frontal and inferior parietal regions of the brain activated during both the production and observation of an action (Rizzolatti & Craighero, 2004), and therefore the proposed neural basis of imitation—was affected in ASD. This became known as the 'broken mirror' theory of autism.

Initial support for the theory came from studies finding under-activation of the inferior frontal gyrus, a key component of the mirror neuron system, in autistic people during imitation tasks (e.g. Dapretto et al., 2006). However, more recent meta-analyses conclude very little evidence for atypical mirror neuron system functioning in ASD (see Hamilton, 2013). Furthermore, studies investigating automatic imitation—for example, a tendency to produce an action while/after seeing the same action performed by another person—have shown that the process is intact in ASD (Cook & Bird, 2013; Sowden et al., 2016). Impaired voluntary imitation in ASD may also be best explained by other cognitive difficulties in ASD, such as attention and memory (see Leighton et al., 2008). More generally, studies have called into question whether imitation plays a specific role in social cognition (e.g. ToM) or, instead, whether it is best conceptualized as a feature of broader domain-general learning (see Cook et al., 2014). Finally, from a developmental perspective, longitudinal data also suggests that children who show few imitative behaviours at 2 years of age show social abilities in the typical range 6 years later (McEwen et al., 2007), thus suggesting that imitation does not play a causal role in later social behaviour.

Overall, there is little evidence to suggest that difficulties in basic automatic or non-automatic imitation or a 'broken' mirror system can account for atypical social behaviours seen in autism. When imitative behaviour atypicalities are seen in autism, these may be due to non-social cognitive difficulties.

7.3.3 Empathy

One long-standing theory of social atypicalities in ASD proposes deficits in empathy (see Harmsen, 2019, for review), that is, the ability to experience and understand the affective state of another person (Lockwood, 2016). Indeed, the empathizing-systemizing hypothesis of ASD proposes that autistic people (or people with high autistic traits) tend towards a processing style of analysing rule-based systems, rather than empathizing with others (Lawson et al., 2004). This finding has most recently been replicated in a sample of half a million people (Greenberg et al., 2018), although the extent to which the self-report measures (e.g. Empathy Quotient; Baron-Cohen & Wheelwright, 2004) and cognitive tasks (e.g. 'Reading the Mind in the Eyes' task; Baron-Cohen et al., 2001) used in this body of research reflect valid measures of empathy is contentious (see Shah et al., 2019). Moreover, there have been some mixed findings and ongoing debates as to whether empathy is universally affected in ASD. Indeed, recent psychological literature suggests that empathy can be dissociated into two components: *affective* empathy, which is the ability to *feel* what others are feeling, and *cognitive* empathy, which is the ability to *know* what others are feeling (i.e. identify their affective state; see Yang et al., 2018). It is worth noting that the use of differing terms to explain similar phenomena (e.g. cognitive empathy and ToM) has also potentially led to discrepancies in the literature (see Happé et al., 2017). Overall, studies have tended to suggest that people with ASD have difficulties with cognitive, but not affective, aspects of empathy (e.g. Rueda et al., 2015) and, in this way, ASD empathy profiles can be distinguished from those of individuals with psychopathy, who show the reverse pattern (e.g. A. P. Jones et al., 2010).

Additional evidence for intact (affective) empathy in ASD comes from studies of alexithymia—the inability to recognize and label one's own emotions—in autism (for review, see Kinnaird et al, 2019). A number of studies suggest that, when empathy deficits are found in autism, these are due to co-occurring alexithymia, rather than autism per se (see Bird & Cook, 2013). Alexithymia is estimated to affect 50% of autistic adults (compared with 10% in the general population; Hill et al., 2004), and is also found at high frequencies in other clinical groups, including those with depression and eating disorders. Among autistic individuals without alexithymia, a range of empathy-relevant processes have been found to be intact, including empathy for others' pain (Bird et al., 2010), and the abilities to detect emotional expressions (Cook et al., 2013) and one's internal states (i.e. interoception; Shah et al., 2016). However, a recent study of autistic traits and alexithymia in a general population (not diagnosed) sample found that self-reported empathy difficulties were better predicted by self-reported autistic, rather than alexithymic, traits (Shah et al., 2019). Further, by separating self-report affective versus cognitive empathy, which many studies fail to do, the authors found that autistic traits were a better predictor of *lower cognitive* empathy (while statistically controlling for affective empathy). This fits with other studies finding that alexithymia only partially mediates empathy difficulties in ASD (e.g. Mul et al., 2018). More generally, these findings stress the importance of considering affective and cognitive empathy separately in ASD and studies of autistic traits in typically developing populations.

Overall, the extent to which empathy difficulties characterize ASD remains unclear. While there is considerable evidence to suggest that cognitive empathy is impaired in ASD, affective empathy deficits, and the role of co-occurring alexithymia for these in autism, remain a focus of much research. So far, this has largely relied on self-report questionnaires. Moving forward, experimental measures may play an important role in clarifying the nature and context of any empathy difficulties in ASD (Mackes et al., 2018). Greater understanding is also required of developmental trajectories of empathy and alexithymia in ASD (see Livingston & Livingston, 2016), although the developmental study of empathy and alexithymia may be limited by inaccessibility of these self-report measures to young children (see Hobson et al., 2019).

7.3.4 Theory of Mind

The previous social cognitive theories of autism are limited to varying degrees in their ability to fully explain social difficulties observed in ASD. Arguably, the most compelling account to date has been the ToM theory of autism, which postulates specific difficulties in representing the mental states (e.g. beliefs, desires) of others (Baron-Cohen, 2000; Happé, 2015). In their early seminal work, Baron-Cohen and colleagues (1985) showed, using the now classic Sally-Anne task, that autistic children failed to represent the false belief of a protagonist, a task that was passed by typically developing 3- or 4-year-olds and ability-matched children with Down syndrome. In the past 40 years, a range of first-order false belief tasks have been used to demonstrate ToM deficits in autistic children (see Tager-Flusberg, 2007), as well as 'advanced' tasks that quantify ToM ability in older children, adolescents, and adults (see Livingston et al., 2019d, for overview). For example, tasks have included inferring characters' mental states from verbal vignettes (Happé, 1994), images of the eye region (Baron-Cohen et al., 2001), videoclips of natural social interactions (e.g. Murray et al., 2017) and interacting animations (e.g. White et al., 2011). Despite relatively clear-cut findings of ToM difficulties in autistic children (although see White et al., 2009; Scheeren et al., 2013), including links between ToM performance and severity of social difficulties (see Brunsdon & Happé, 2014), findings in autistic adults have been far more equivocal (see Livingston et al., 2019d, for overview). Moreover, ToM task performance rarely predicts the extent of real-life difficulties, over and above general intelligence (Sasson et al., 2020).

One explanation for this is that our ToM tasks are unsuitable for adult populations. First, many were adapted from tasks for children and therefore demonstrate ceiling effects in adults. Second, many are heavily reliant on other cognitive and emotional abilities and therefore do not isolate ToM dis/ability specifically (see Olderbak et al., 2015). For example, performance on the Reading the Mind in the Eyes Test (Baron-Cohen et al., 2001) correlates highly with verbal ability (Baker et al., 2014) and education level (Dodell-Feder et al., 2020). This may help explain why performance on one ToM task does not necessarily correlate with performance on another (Warnell & Redcay, 2019). Finally, some tasks can be solved via learned 'compensatory strategies' and therefore may not be capturing the severity of real social processing difficulties experienced by autistic adults in their everyday lives. Promisingly, new methodological developments are underway. For example, Livingston and colleagues (submitted) showed that a response-time sensitive measurement of ToM ability—whereby slower non-social cognitive strategies used to 'hack' the task rather than intuitive ToM ability can be detected—and statistically controlling for non-ToM cognitive abilities, reveals clear-cut difficulties for autistic adults compared with their neurotypical counterparts.

A second explanation for mixed findings in autistic adults is that there may be multiple forms of ToM, which are differentially affected in ASD. It has been proposed that there is: a) a rapid, implicit form of ToM whereby mental states of others (e.g. false beliefs) can be tracked, without explicit mental reasoning, and b) a slower, explicit form of ToM, which requires deliberate reasoning about others' mental states (Apperly & Butterfill, 2009). Evidence for this has come from a range of studies showing that implicit ToM may be present already in young infants (e.g. Onishi & Baillargeon, 2005), whereas explicit ToM is not achieved until around 3–4 years of age. Infants as young as 15 months can track false beliefs as evidenced by anticipatory looking patterns and looking times, and also show early precursors to ToM ability, such as joint attention, which is the ability to coordinate one's own attention with another individual's (Mundy, 2018). The ToM tasks discussed so far fall into the category of explicit ToM. However, Senju and colleagues (2009) showed that autistic adults who can solve explicit ToM tasks, such as the Sally-Anne false belief test, still show difficulties in implicit ToM: their anticipatory looking behaviour suggests that they do not implicitly track the false belief of a protagonist (although see Kulke et al., 2018, for critique of the task). Similarly, in autistic infants, deficits in joint attention (e.g. Nyström et al., 2019) have been found, before the age at which explicit ToM can be reliably tested. Proponents of distinct explicit and implicit forms of ToM would therefore argue that mixed evidence for ToM difficulties in autistic adults is due to reliance on tasks that tap explicit, rather than implicit forms of ToM. Greater uptake of implicit ToM measures is therefore required when studying autistic adults, and particularly those in middle and older adulthood.

Despite these limitations, we propose that atypical ToM is still the most parsimonious explanation of wide-ranging atypical social behaviours observed in ASD. A recent meta-analysis of studies comparing autistic and non-autistic individuals 16+ years old found the largest group difference was in ToM, compared with a range of other social (e.g. emotion processing) and non-social cognitive abilities (e.g. working memory; Velikonja et al., 2019). The ToM theory of ASD not only accounts for difficulties in social communication and interaction, but also allows for areas of intact social processing, such as attachment and affective empathy. Further, ToM difficulties also help to explain why autistic children may be set on a different learning trajectory, with consequences for a range of other developmental milestones and abilities. For example, Happé (2015) described how having a mind that is less sensitive to the mental states of others might have an impact on understanding one's own mind, and the extent to which knowledge and skills are acquired from others through 'social osmosis'. Because ToM is such an important and early-developing gateway function, this might explain why later ToM training interventions have had little success/generalization in affecting social behaviour in ASD (see Fletcher-Watson et al., 2014). Indeed, differences in implicit ToM from infancy are likely set in motion a trajectory for autistic children that cannot simply be 'undone' through explicit later intervention.

There is also a compelling set of studies that have shown the explanatory power of ToM theory over other cognitive theories (e.g. executive dysfunction), thus supporting the notion of ToM being the single most important cognitive explanation of ASD. For example, Cantio and colleagues (2016, 2018) found that, across a range of cognitive difficulties, ToM difficulties were the most prominent and pervasive in characterizing autistic versus neurotypical individuals during adolescence. They concluded that ToM difficulties 'may after all prove to be universal in autism given more sensitive cognitive measures' (Cantio et al., 2016, p. 1336; although see Moessnang et al., 2020). Two other studies have also found that atypical ToM is the best predictor of autistic social symptoms, compared with a number of other cognitive abilities, such as executive function (Berenguer et al., 2018; C. R. Jones et al., 2018). For example, C. R. Jones et al. (2018) found that, among a large sample of autistic adolescents, a latent variable for ToM (derived from four ToM tasks), but not executive function (derived from six wide-ranging executive function tasks) predicted the extent of social symptoms.

What remains more contentious is the extent to which autistic individuals differ in their ToM abilities and the contexts in which these differences are most clearly seen. The possibility remains that some autistic people genuinely experience milder ToM difficulties than others, whereby mentalizing is manageable in explicit contexts, but much less so in fast-paced, ambiguous social interaction (e.g. group interaction at a busy party). Surprisingly little research has been conducted into how ToM ability alters across contexts and varying degrees of complexity of social interaction. This may in part explain why there is not always a clear-cut relationship between ToM task performance in the lab and severity of observable social symptoms (see Brunsdon & Happé, 2014), such as those measured on the Autism Diagnostic Observation Schedule (Lord et al., 2000). There is also much to be learned about how ToM abilities might alter over the lifespan. In cross-sectional studies, Lever and Geurts (2016) and Zıvralı Yarar et al. (in press), have found age-related decreases in ToM difficulties, with adults 50+ years old showing no impairments in ToM compared with matched controls. This hints at the possibility for improved ToM ability from younger to older adulthood, or at least less susceptibility to decline in this ability, although longitudinal studies are required to test this empirically.

Overall, the ToM theory of social behaviours in ASD is one of the most compelling and has, to a certain degree, stood the test of time compared with other theories. Empirical evidence for ToM difficulties in autistic children is fairly convincing. However, there is a serious dearth of research examining how ToM dis/ability either persists or improves moving into adulthood and later life. We propose that fundamental improvements are required in our ToM tasks in order to improve their specificity to the measurement of ToM, independent of other cognitive abilities (e.g. executive function), and their capacity to quantify genuine ToM ability, independent of compensatory non-social strategies that can be used to 'hack' task performance. Further examination of ToM in relation to other closely related mechanisms and constructs—for example, shifting between self/other perspective taking (see Bradford et al., 2019)—is also required. Such methodological improvement will enable a more detailed investigation into ToM ability, its relationship with autistic social symptoms, and potential age-related changes.

7.4 Beyond social cognition: double empathy

Traditional social cognitive models of ASD, such as those highlighted so far, tend to place emphasis on autistic individuals' own social cognitive abilities driving their social difficulties. An alternative viewpoint is that, because social interaction is dynamic and involves multiple agents, it is possible that an autistic person's social skills reflect the social cognitive abilities of, and match with, their interaction partner(s). This is most commonly referred to as the 'double empathy' problem (Milton, 2012; see also Davis & Crompton, in press), which postulates that, while autistic people may have difficulties in reading the minds of non-autistic people, non-autistic people equally struggle to read autistic people's minds, and this can subsequently lead to mis-interpretation, misunderstanding, and breakdown in social interaction. Indeed, there are an increasing number of studies now showing that non-autistic people are poorer at inferring the mental states of autistic versus non-autistic individuals and that autistic people have a mind that is 'harder to read' (Sheppard et al., 2016; Alkhaldi et al., 2019).

Additionally, it is possible that some autistic characteristics—for example, deep interest in a niche topic—are viewed and responded to negatively by non-autistic people, thereby diminishing these individuals' motivation to interact. Indeed, Sasson et al. (2017) found that neurotypical people tend to rate autistic people, as presented through brief video clips, as people they are less likely to be friends with, compared with neurotypical people. Furthermore, qualitative studies have shown that autistic people tend to report their interactions with other autistic people as less stressful than those with non-autistic people, because their interaction styles are better matched (Livingston et al., 2019a; Crompton et al., 2020). For example, one individual in Livingston et al.'s (2019a) study said, 'with autistic people, who speak my language ... [social interaction] goes fantastically well most of the time'. Yet, empirical evidence that autistic people understand other autistic people better than neurotypical people, beyond qualitative reports, is currently lacking. Brewer et al. (2016) found that autistic adults were no better at recognizing the emotional expressions of other autistic versus neurotypical people. Additionally, DeBrabander and colleagues (2019), using the same paradigm as Sasson et al (2017), found that autistic adults tend to rate other autistic individuals unfavourably, to the same degree that neurotypical people do. Further experimental research will be critical to address the validity of the double empathy phenomenon.

The double empathy model builds on the wider, and increasingly popular, neurodiversity model of autism (see Baron-Cohen, 2017), whereby autistic characteristics can be viewed as differences or preferences, rather than deficits. Indeed, there are many social characteristics of autistic people that can be viewed as strengths. For example, autistic people are often thought to be fair, honest, and not as susceptible to social conformity (Russell et al., 2019). The broader implication of this change of view is that, rather than attempting to intervene to change autistic individuals' social skills (through, for example, social skills training), we might aim to maximize successful social interaction between autistic and non-autistic people. This may involve non-autistic people making active accommodations for the social styles and preferences of autistic people. For example, we recently suggested that 'neurotypical individuals could engage in compensatory efforts, perhaps by reducing their reliance on social niceties, to improve interactions with autistic people' (Livingston et al., 2019a, p. 775). Additionally, there are other features of our social environments that could be adapted to better suit autistic people. Indeed, autistic people often report that it is the sensory aspects of social spaces (e.g. bright lights, loud sounds) that can prevent them from being their best social selves (see Livingston et al., 2019a).

Taken together, the double empathy and neurodiversity models suggest that social cognitive theories of atypical social behaviour in ASD may be underestimating the contributions of aspects of social interaction that are external to the autistic individual (e.g. non-autistic interaction partners, the environment). Further integration of these various models, therefore, is required to fully understand autistic people's social cognition and behaviour. Some promising lines of research involve measuring ToM ability in more naturalistic, interactive settings (e.g. using virtual-reality technology; Pan & Hamilton, 2018) and directly measuring two-way interactions between autistic and non-autistic people (Crompton et al., 2019).

7.5 Individual differences

In this chapter, we have focused on social cognitive theories of ASD, and, in particular, placed emphasis on the explanatory power of the ToM theory of ASD. However, one social cognitive theory may not be sufficient to account for the full range of atypical social behaviours observed in ASD (Happé et al., 2006). For example, some studies find subgroups of autistic people who, despite meeting the diagnostic criteria for ASD, show typical ToM ability on a range of tasks (e.g. Brunsdon et al., 2015; White et al., 2009, 2014). Therefore, there are important considerations for individual differences within the autistic population, which we will briefly address here.

7.5.1 Heterogeneity

It is now widely acknowledged that there is vast heterogeneity in ASD, across all levels of analysis—cognitive, neural, genetic, and behavioural (Lombardo et al.,

2019; Müller & Fishman, 2018). This has led to the notion of the 'autisms', whereby there are multiple different forms of autism that fall under the broader 'autism spectrum' category (see Happé & Frith, 2020). Different constellations of cognitive factors (including non-social factors such as executive function, attentional atypicalities, and detail-focused cognitive style) may contribute to various autistic presentations. There are now serious efforts to determine smaller, homogenous subgroups from the heterogenous autistic population (see Wolfers et al., 2019)—for example, by investigating various genetic, biological, cognitive, or behavioural markers. Given this, it is entirely possible that ToM difficulties may only characterize a certain number of these smaller subgroups, with important consequences for the support requirements of these individuals. For example, ToM 'training' or strategies may be entirely unhelpful for certain subgroups. There is also promise in 'big data' approaches, in which, for example, unsupervised machine learning can begin to parse heterogeneity within very large autistic samples (e.g. Lombardo et al., 2019) although, as it stands, it is unclear whether any meaningful subgroups will be established beyond basic distinctions between autistic subgroups with and without intellectual disability or language impairment.

7.5.2 Co-occurring conditions

Another source of individual differences is variability in conditions that frequently co-occur with autism. It is well established that ASD rarely exists in isolation. Instead, individuals with ASD are at risk for a number of other neurodevelopmental and psychiatric conditions (e.g. Attention Deficit Hyperactivity Aisorder [ADHD], depression, anxiety disorders, personality disorders; see Lai et al., 2019, for recent meta-analysis). As such, it remains imperative to be able to distinguish which aspects of atypical social cognition are specific to ASD and which may occur transdiagnostically (e.g. Cotter et al., 2018). For example, rates of social anxiety—a condition also characterised by social cognitive difficulties—are particularly high in ASD populations (see Spain et al., 2018 for review). Nevertheless, dealing with co-occurring conditions in ASD research can be problematic, because many studies of social cognition will exclude autistic participants who present with additional diagnoses. This means that our 'autism group' in case-control studies may not be sufficiently representative of the wider autistic population, in which many have co-occurring conditions. Even when co-occurring conditions are allowed in autistic recruitment, many studies exclude individuals with mental health conditions, such as anxiety and depression, which are extremely common in autism, from control comparison groups. Variability in exclusion criteria may have contributed to some of the discrepancies in findings in the social cognitive literature in ASD. For example, ToM and executive function appear to be closely related (see Apperly, 2012), yet autistic individuals are much more likely to present with ADHD, a condition with executive function difficulties at its core (Hart et al., 2013). We suggest that deeper phenotyping of autistic participants is required and further research using a cognition-first, rather than diagnosis-first, approach to explore how social cognitive abilities/difficulties may in fact span a number of different conditions. This is in line with the Research Domain Criteria framework, which proposes the studying of domains (e.g. social, cognitive) and levels (e.g. molecular, circuitry) of functioning rather than specific mental disorders.

7.5.3 Compensatory ability

Finally, there is a small but growing literature on the prevalence of 'compensation' among certain autistic people, whereby some individuals can show improvements in their social skills, despite ongoing social cognitive difficulties (see Livingston & Happé, 2017, for in-depth review). In particular, intellectual and executive function abilities, which vary widely across the autistic population, have been shown to be associated with this compensatory profile (Livingston et al., 2019c; Lai et al., 2017). Therefore, compensatory trajectories represent an important source of heterogeneity in autism and variability in social skills. For example, compensatory abilities may enable an individual to 'pass' as neurotypical at certain stages of their development or in certain environments, while appearing characteristically autistic in others. Further, certain environments/cultures at certain points in the lifespan may serve to facilitate compensation. An individual may find themselves in an environment or culture in which social rules are particularly explicit, and less requirement is placed on their own ability to reason about mental states; for instance, a structured work setting versus less structured post-retirement life. Measurement and consideration of compensation, and its moderating internal and external factors, are therefore critical to advancing knowledge of variability in social skills in ASD, particularly from a lifespan perspective. As previously mentioned, many of our social cognitive and ToM tasks do not isolate ToM independent of compensatory strategies, and more sensitive measures are required going forward.

Overall, beyond the ToM account of autism, there are multiple sources of individual differences among autistic people, which may explain why no single social cognitive theory accounts for the wide-ranging social difficulties observed in ASD.

7.6 Ongoing debates and conclusions

7.6.1 Debates

There are several ongoing debates in the literature that require critical consideration in future research. First, the structure of social cognition—that is, the extent to which different social cognitive abilities rely on similar or distinct systems, and their interrelationships across development—continues to be poorly understood (Happé et al., 2017). For example, there remain ongoing debates as to whether empathy has distinct sub-components (e.g. Heyes, 2018), and whether or not ToM and cognitive empathy are the same or different processes. Moreover, even less is known about how social cognition may be atypically structured in ASD. For example, general cognitive functioning and certain social cognitive abilities may become increasingly closely linked in ASD over development, given the potential compensatory role of executive and intellectual processes to supersede social cognitive abilities.

Second, there are issues pertaining to how ToM is conceptualized and measured. As we have previously highlighted, many self-report questionnaires and experimental tasks used to measure an array of social cognitive abilities do not isolate specific abilities and confounds—for example, empathy and ToM. Additionally, these questionnaires and tasks, validated in neurotypical populations, are often applied to autistic populations without verifying that their factor structure and psychometric properties in ASD are similar to those in neurotypical people. Furthermore, what exactly ToM is and is not, and the best way to measure it, is still contested by some researchers. Indeed, Quesque and Rossetti (2020) recently noted that multiple terms (e.g. ToM, mindreading, mentalizing, empathy) are often used to describe the ability to understand others' mental states, and, equally, tasks claiming to measure this ability may actually be measuring other sub-components of social cognition. Such heterogeneity in terminology and tasks may in part be contributing to mixed evidence and confusion in the literature. On a final note, there is an increasing need to understand ToM in autism outside the lab, in interactive 'real-world' contexts (Schilbach et al., 2013). New video-based tasks, which require participants to predict characters' mental states within a social interaction (e.g. Brewer et al., 2017; Murray et al., 2017), as well as tasks that enable direct observation of real two-way social interactions (e.g. Crompton et al., 2019) or interactions with virtual others (e.g. Schilbach et al., 2013), are showing promise.

Third, while the social cognitive models propose domain-specific mechanisms underlying social cognitive processing, critics continue to propose that some so-called 'social' abilities may in fact be explained by domain-general processes. For example, Heyes (2014) has argued that 'implicit' ToM tasks may actually be measuring domain-general processes that can simulate everyday mentalizing and, therefore, that domain-specific ToM ability may not always be required in social scenarios. Such theories require ongoing empirical testing.

Fourth, there are ongoing debates as to whether certain ToM tasks, widely used in autism research, necessarily capture ToM ability, or rather ToM propensity (i.e. tendency to mentalize). This distinction is particularly important when understanding atypical social ability in ASD because it is plausible that, while some autistic people have the *ability* to mentalize—for example, when tested in the laboratory—they may not necessarily demonstrate the propensity to mentalize in everyday life. Broadly speaking, ToM tasks so far have failed to take into account this distinction, with task performance always interpreted as reflecting ability rather than propensity, or some combination of the two.

Finally, with ongoing debates about causality of social cognitive difficulties in ASD, there is a real need for more developmentally sensitive studies of social cognition and behaviour beyond childhood. Although there is an impressive literature of longitudinal study of developmental relations between early social cognitive abilities and ASD in infancy and childhood, the same degree of detail and scrutiny has not been applied to adolescence, adulthood, and older adulthood. Furthermore, although there are some studies that have explored behavioural trajectories from childhood to adulthood (e.g. Lord et al., 2015; Pickles et al., 2020)—for example, changes in overt social skills—there is very limited understanding of how increases and decreases in social symptoms are actually underpinned by changes in social cognition. For example, the extent to which trajectories of 'optimal outcome' in ASD are necessarily due to improvements in ToM ability is very poorly understood (Livingston & Happé, 2017). There is also some evidence for sex-specific trajectories of social skills (e.g. Mandy et al., 2018) although, again, these studies have tracked social behaviour without measurement of social cognition. Additionally, while there are a handful of studies on age-dependent social cognition and behaviour in autistic adulthood (e.g. Lever & Geurts, 2016; Johansson Nolaker et al., 2018; Stewart et al., 2019; Zıvralı Yarar et al., in press), these have been cross-sectional, limiting our ability to attribute causal effects. With ongoing improvement and validation of our social cognitive tasks, as well as innovative ways of measuring a/typical social behaviour (e.g. using electronic means; Livingston et al., 2020b), it is hoped that these measures can be fruitfully used in developmentally sensitive future research to unpack how social cognition has an impact on social behaviour in ASD across the lifespan.

7.6.2 Conclusions

In this chapter, we have presented and critiqued a number of social cognitive theories (social attention, social motivation, imitation, empathy, and ToM) proposed to explain atypical social behaviour in ASD. We suggest that the ToM theory of ASD has the best explanatory power and also holds the greatest promise, with ongoing improvements in our ToM tasks for understanding social skills in ASD in future research. The theory should continue to be critically considered alongside heterogeneity, co-occurring conditions, and compensatory ability in ASD. We highlight that there is a serious dearth of research tracking social cognitive and behavioural change across the lifespan, but that such research is required to better understand aetiology, diverse outcomes, and trajectories in ASD. Such research will inform better interventions and support systems for autistic people and their changing needs across the lifespan.

References

Alkhaldi, R. S., Sheppard, E., & Mitchell, P., 2019. 'Is there a link between autistic people being perceived unfavorably and having a mind that is difficult to read?'. *Journal of Autism and Developmental Disorders* 49. 10: 3973–3982.

American Psychiatric Association (APA). 2013. *Diagnostic and Statistical Manual of Mental Disorders*. 5th edn. American Psychiatric Association.

Apperly, I. A., 2012. 'What is "theory of mind"? Concepts, cognitive processes and individual differences'. *Quarterly Journal of Experimental Psychology* 65. 5: 825–839.

Apperly, I. A., & Butterfill, S. A., 2009. 'Do humans have two systems to track beliefs and belief-like states?'. *Psychological Review* 116. 4: 953–970.

Baird, G., Simonoff, E., Pickles, A., Chandler, S., Loucas, T., Meldrum, D., & Charman, T., 2006. 'Prevalence of disorders of the autism spectrum in a population cohort of children in South Thames: The Special Needs and Autism Project (SNAP)'. *Lancet* 368. 9531: 210–215.

Baker, C. A., Peterson, E., Pulos, S., & Kirkland, R. A., 2014. 'Eyes and IQ: A meta-analysis of the relationship between intelligence and "Reading the Mind in the Eyes"'. *Intelligence* 44: 78–92.

Baron-Cohen, S., 2000. 'Theory of Mind and autism: A fifteen year review'. In *Understanding other minds: Perspectives from developmental cognitive neuroscience*, edited by S. Baron-Cohen, H. Tager-Flusberg, & D. J. Cohen. Oxford University Press.

Baron-Cohen, S., 2017. 'Editorial perspective: Neurodiversity—a revolutionary concept for autism and psychiatry'. *Journal of Child Psychology and Psychiatry* 58. 6: 744–747.

Baron-Cohen, S., & Wheelwright, S., 2004. 'The empathy quotient: An investigation of adults with Asperger syndrome or high functioning autism, and normal sex differences'. *Journal of Autism and Developmental Disorders* 34. 2: 163–175.

Baron-Cohen, S., Leslie, A. M., & Frith, U., 1985. 'Does the autistic child have a "theory of mind"?'. *Cognition* 21. 1: 37–46.

Baron-Cohen, S., Wheelwright, S., Hill, J., Raste, Y., & Plumb, I., 2001. 'The "Reading the Mind in the Eyes" Test revised version: A study with normal adults, and adults with Asperger syndrome or high-functioning autism'. *Journal of Child Psychology and Psychiatry and Allied Disciplines* 42. 2: 241–251.

Berenguer, C., Miranda, A., Colomer, C., Baixauli, I., & Roselló, B., 2018. 'Contribution of theory of mind, executive functioning, and pragmatics to socialization behaviors of children with high-functioning autism'. *Journal of Autism and Developmental Disorders* 48. 2: 430–441.

Bird, G., & Cook, R., 2013. 'Mixed emotions: The contribution of alexithymia to the emotional symptoms of autism'. *Translational Psychiatry* 3. 7: e285.

Bird, G., Silani, G., Brindley, R., White, S., Frith, U., & Singer, T., 2010. 'Empathic brain responses in insula are modulated by levels of alexithymia but not autism'. *Brain* 133. 5: 1515–1525.

Birmingham, E., Stanley, D., Nair, R., & Adolphs, R., 2015. 'Implicit social biases in people with autism'. *Psychological Science* 26. 11: 1693–1705.

Black, M. H., Chen, N. T., Iyer, K. K., Lipp, O. V., Bölte, S., Falkmer, M., ... & Girdler, S., 2017. 'Mechanisms of facial emotion recognition in autism spectrum disorders: Insights from eye tracking and electroencephalography'. *Neuroscience & Biobehavioral Reviews* 80: 488–515.

Bos, D. J., Silver, B. M., Barnes, E. D., Ajodan, E. L., Silverman, M. R., Clark-Whitney, E., ... & Jones, R. M., 2019. 'Adolescent-specific motivation deficits in autism versus typical development'. *Journal of Autism and Developmental Disorders* 50. 1: 364–372.

Bottini, S., 2018. 'Social reward processing in individuals with autism spectrum disorder: A systematic review of the social motivation hypothesis'. *Research in Autism Spectrum Disorders* 45: 9–26.

Bourgeron, T., 2016. 'Current knowledge on the genetics of autism and propositions for future research'. *Comptes Rendus Biologies* 339. 7–8: 300–307.

Bradford, E. E., Gomez, J. C., & Jentzsch, I., 2019. 'Exploring the role of self/other perspective-shifting in theory of mind with behavioural and EEG measures'. *Social Neuroscience* 14. 5: 530–544.

Brewer, N., Young, R. L., & Barnett, E., 2017. 'Measuring theory of mind in adults with autism spectrum disorder'. *Journal of Autism and Developmental Disorders* 47. 7: 1927–1941.

Brewer, R., Biotti, F., Catmur, C., Press, C., Happé, F., Cook, R., & Bird, G., 2016. 'Can neurotypical individuals read autistic facial expressions? Atypical production of emotional facial expressions in autism spectrum disorders'. *Autism Research* 9. 2: 262–271.

Brunsdon, V. E., & Happé, F., 2014. 'Exploring the "fractionation" of autism at the cognitive level'. *Autism* 18. 1: 17–30.

Brunsdon, V. E., Colvert, E., Ames, C., Garnett, T., Gillan, N., Hallett, V., ... & Happé, F., 2015. 'Exploring the cognitive features in children with autism spectrum disorder, their co-twins, and typically developing children within a population-based sample'. *Journal of Child Psychology and Psychiatry* 56. 8: 893–902.

Cage, E., Pellicano, E., Shah, P., & Bird, G., 2013. 'Reputation management: Evidence for ability but reduced propensity in autism'. *Autism Research* 6. 5: 433–442.

Cantio, C., Jepsen, J. R. M., Madsen, G. F., Bilenberg, N., & White, S. J., 2016. 'Exploring "The autisms" at a cognitive level"'. *Autism Research* 9. 12: 1328–1339.

Cantio, C., White, S., Madsen, G. F., Bilenberg, N., & Jepsen, J. R. M., 2018. 'Do cognitive deficits persist into adolescence in autism?' *Autism Research* 11. 9: 1229–1238.

Carpenter, B., Happé, F., & Egerton, J. 2019. *Girls and Autism: Educational, Family and Personal Perspectives*. Routledge.

Charman, T., Pickles, A., Simonoff, E., Chandler, S., Loucas, T., & Baird, G., 2011. 'IQ in children with autism spectrum disorders: Data from the Special Needs and Autism Project (SNAP)'. *Psychological Medicine* 41. 3: 619–627.

Chawarska, K., & Shic, F., 2009. 'Looking but not seeing: Atypical visual scanning and recognition of faces in 2 and 4-year-old children with autism spectrum disorder'. *Journal of Autism and Developmental Disorders* 39. 12: 1663–1672.

Chawarska, K., Macari, S., & Shic, F., 2012. 'Context modulates attention to social scenes in toddlers with autism'. *Journal of Child Psychology and Psychiatry* 53. 8: 903–913.

Chevallier, C., Molesworth, C., & Happé, F., 2012a. 'Diminished social motivation negatively impacts reputation management: Autism spectrum disorders as a case in point'. *PloS One* 7. 1: e31107.

Chevallier, C., Kohls, G., Troiani, V., Brodkin, E. S., & Schultz, R. T., 2012b. 'The social motivation theory of autism'. *Trends in Cognitive Sciences* 16. 4: 231–239.

Chita-Tegmark, M., 2016. 'Social attention in ASD: A review and meta-analysis of eye-tracking studies'. *Research in Developmental Disabilities* 48: 79–93.

Clements, C. C., Zoltowski, A. R., Yankowitz, L. D., Yerys, B. E., Schultz, R. T., & Herrington, J. D., 2018. 'Evaluation of the social motivation hypothesis of autism: a systematic review and meta-analysis'. *JAMA Psychiatry* 75. 8: 797–808.

Cook, R., & Bird, G., 2013. 'Do mirror neurons really mirror and do they really code for action goals?'. *Cortex* 49. 10: 2944–2945.

Cook, R., Brewer, R., Shah, P., & Bird, G., 2013. 'Alexithymia, not autism, predicts poor recognition of emotional facial expressions'. *Psychological Science* 24. 5: 723–732.

Cook, R., Bird, G., Catmur, C., Press, C., & Heyes, C., 2014. 'Mirror neurons: From origin to function'. *Behavioral and Brain Sciences* 37. 2: 177–192.

Cotter, J., Granger, K., Backx, R., Hobbs, M., Looi, C. Y., & Barnett, J. H., 2018. 'Social cognitive dysfunction as a clinical marker: A systematic review of meta-analyses across 30 clinical conditions'. *Neuroscience & Biobehavioral Reviews* 84: 92–99.

Crompton, C. J., Fletcher-Watson, S., & Ropar, D., 2019. 'Autistic peer-to-peer information transfer is highly effective'. *Autism* 1362361320919286.

Crompton, C. J., Hallett, S., Ropar, D., Flynn, E., & Fletcher-Watson, S., 2020. '"I never realised everybody felt as happy as I do when I am around autistic people": A thematic analysis of autistic adults' relationships with autistic and neurotypical friends and family'. *Autism* 24: 1438–1448.

Dapretto, M., Davies, M. S., Pfeifer, J. H., Scott, A. A., Sigman, M., Bookheimer, S. Y., & Iacoboni, M., 2006. 'Understanding emotions in others: Mirror neuron dysfunction in children with autism spectrum disorders'. *Nature Neuroscience* 9. 1: 28–30.

Davis, R., & Crompton, C. J., in press. What do new findings about social interaction in autistic adults mean for neurodevelopmental research?. *Perspectives on Psychological Science*.

Dawson, G., Meltzoff, A. N., Osterling, J., Rinaldi, J., & Brown, E., 1998. 'Children with autism fail to orient to naturally occurring social stimuli'. *Journal of Autism and Developmental Disorders* 28. 6: 479–485.

DeBrabander, K. M., Morrison, K. E., Jones, D. R., Faso, D. J., Chmielewski, M., & Sasson, N. J., 2019. 'Do first impressions of autistic adults differ between autistic and nonautistic observers?' *Autism in Adulthood* 1. 4: 250–257.

de Leeuw, A., Happé, F., & Hoekstra, R., 2020. 'A conceptual framework for understanding the cultural and contextual factors on autism across the globe'. *Autism Research* 13. 7: 1029–1050.

Dijkhuis, R., Gurbuz, E., Ziermans, T., Staal, W., & Swaab, H., 2019. 'Social attention and emotional responsiveness in young adults with autism'. *Frontiers in Psychiatry 10*: 426.

Dodell-Feder, D., Ressler, K. J., & Germine, L. T., 2020. Social cognition or social class and culture? On the interpretation of differences in social cognitive performance. *Psychological Medicine* 50. 1: 133–145.

Dubey, I., Ropar, D., & Hamilton, A., 2018. 'Comparison of choose-a-movie and approach–avoidance paradigms to measure social motivation'. *Motivation and Emotion* 42. 2: 190–199.

Ecker, C., Bookheimer, S. Y., & Murphy, D. G., 2015. 'Neuroimaging in autism spectrum disorder: brain structure and function across the lifespan'. *The Lancet Neurology* 14. 11: 1121–1134.

Elsabbagh, M., & Johnson, M. H., 2016. 'Autism and the social brain: The first-year puzzle'. *Biological Psychiatry* 80. 2: 94–99.

Elsabbagh, M., Fernandes, J., Webb, S. J., Dawson, G., Charman, T., Johnson, M. H., & British Autism Study of Infant Siblings Team, 2013. 'Disengagement of visual attention in infancy is associated with emerging autism in toddlerhood'. *Biological Psychiatry* 74. 3: 189–194.

Fein, D., Barton, M., Eigsti, I. M., Kelley, E., Naigles, L., Schultz, R. T., ... & Troyb, E., 2013. 'Optimal outcome in individuals with a history of autism'. *Journal of Child Psychology and Psychiatry* 54. 2: 195–205.

Fischer, J., Koldewyn, K., Jiang, Y. V., & Kanwisher, N., 2014. 'Unimpaired attentional disengagement and social orienting in children with autism'. *Clinical Psychological Science* 2. 2: 214–223.

Fletcher-Watson, S., McConnell, F., Manola, E., & McConachie, H., 2014. 'Interventions based on the Theory of Mind cognitive model for autism spectrum disorder (ASD)'. *Cochrane Database of Systematic Reviews* 3: CD008785.

Fletcher-Watson, S., Leekam, S. R., Benson, V., Frank, M. C., & Findlay, J. M., 2009. 'Eye-movements reveal attention to social information in autism spectrum disorder'. *Neuropsychologia* 47. 1: 248–257.

Freeth, M., & Bugembe, P., 2019. 'Social partner gaze direction and conversational phase; factors affecting social attention during face-to-face conversations in autistic adults?'. *Autism* 23. 2: 503–513.

Frith, U., 2012. 'Why we need cognitive explanations of autism'. *Quarterly Journal of Experimental Psychology* 65. 11: 2073–2092.

Frith, U., 2019. 'Flux of life'. *Developmental Cognitive Neuroscience* 38: 100669.

Gollwitzer, A., Martel, C., McPartland, J. C., & Bargh, J. A., 2019. 'Autism spectrum traits predict higher social psychological skill'. *Proceedings of the National Academy of Sciences* 116. 39: 19245–19247.

Gray, K. L., Haffey, A., Mihaylova, H. L., & Chakrabarti, B., 2018. 'Lack of privileged access to awareness for rewarding social scenes in autism spectrum disorder'. *Journal of Autism and Developmental Disorders* 48. 10: 3311–3318.

Green, J., & Garg, S., 2018. 'Annual Research Review: The state of autism intervention science: Progress, target psychological and biological mechanisms and future prospects'. *Journal of Child Psychology and Psychiatry* 59. 4: 424–443.

Greenberg, D. M., Warrier, V., Allison, C., & Baron-Cohen, S., 2018. 'Testing the empathizing–systemizing theory of sex differences and the extreme male brain theory of autism in half a million people'. *Proceedings of the National Academy of Sciences* 115. 48: 12152–12157.

Guillon, Q., Hadjikhani, N., Baduel, S., & Rogé, B., 2014. 'Visual social attention in autism spectrum disorder: Insights from eye tracking studies'. *Neuroscience & Biobehavioral Reviews* 42: 279–297.

Hamilton, A., 2013. 'Reflecting on the mirror neuron system in autism: a systematic review of current theories'. *Developmental Cognitive Neuroscience* 3: 91–105.

Happé, F., 1994. 'An advanced test of theory of mind: Understanding of story characters' thoughts and feelings by able autistic, mentally handicapped, and normal children and adults'. *Journal of Autism and Developmental Disorders* 242: 129–154.

Happé, F., 2015. 'Autism as a neurodevelopmental disorder of mind-reading'. *Journal of the British Academy* 3: 197–209.

Happé, F., & Charlton, R. A., 2012. 'Aging in autism spectrum disorders: A mini-review'. *Gerontology* 58. 1: 70–78.

Happé, F., & Frith, U., 2006. 'The weak coherence account: Detail-focused cognitive style in autism spectrum disorders'. *Journal of Autism and Developmental Disorders* 36. 1: 5–25.

Happé, F., & Frith, U., 2014. 'Annual Research Review: Towards a developmental neuroscience of atypical social cognition'. *Journal of Child Psychology and Psychiatry* 55. 6: 553–577.

Happé, F., & Frith, U., 2020. 'Annual Research Review: Looking back to look forward– changes in the concept of autism and implications for future research'. *Journal of Child Psychology and Psychiatry* 61. 3: 218–232.

Happé, F., Cook, J. L., & Bird, G., 2017. 'The structure of social cognition: In(ter) dependence of sociocognitive processes'. *Annual Review of Psychology* 68: 243–267.

Happé, F., Ronald, A., & Plomin, R., 2006. 'Time to give up on a single explanation for autism'. *Nature Neuroscience* 9. 10: 1218–1220.

Harmsen, I. E., 2019. 'Empathy in autism spectrum disorder'. *Journal of Autism and Developmental Disorders* 9. 10: 3939–3955.

Harrop, C., Jones, D., Zheng, S., Nowell, S. W., Boyd, B. A., & Sasson, N., 2018. 'Sex differences in social attention in autism spectrum disorder'. *Autism Research* 11. 9: 1264–1275.

Hart, H., Radua, J., Nakao, T., Mataix-Cols, D., & Rubia, K., 2013. 'Meta-analysis of functional magnetic resonance imaging studies of inhibition and attention in attention-deficit/hyperactivity disorder: exploring task-specific, stimulant medication, and age effects'. *JAMA Psychiatry* 70. 2: 185–198.

Heyes, C., 2014. False belief in infancy: A fresh look. *Developmental Science* 17. 5: 647–659

Heyes, C., 2018. 'Empathy is not in our genes'. *Neuroscience and Biobehavioral Reviews* 95: 499–507.

Hill, E., Berthoz, S., & Frith, U., 2004. 'Brief report: Cognitive processing of own emotions in individuals with autistic spectrum disorder and in their relatives'. *Journal of Autism and Developmental Disorders* 34. 2: 229–235.

Hirschfeld, L., Bartmess, E., White, S., & Frith, U., 2007. 'Can autistic children predict behavior by social stereotypes?'. *Current Biology* 17. 12: R451–R452.

Hobson, H., Brewer, R., Catmur, C., & Bird, G., 2019. 'The role of language in alexithymia: Moving towards a multiroute model of alexithymia'. *Emotion Review* 11. 3: 247–261.

Hull, L., Lai, M-C., Baron-Cohen, S., Allison, C., Smith, P., Petrides, K. V., & Mandy, W., 2020. 'Gender differences in self-reported camouflaging in autistic and non-autistic adults'. *Autism* 24. 2: 352–363.

Hutchins, T. L., & Brien, A., 2016. 'Conversational topic moderates social attention in autism spectrum disorder: Talking about emotions is like driving in a snowstorm'. *Research in Autism Spectrum Disorders* 26: 99–110.

Izuma, K., Matsumoto, K., Camerer, C. F., & Adolphs, R., 2011. 'Insensitivity to social reputation in autism'. *Proceedings of the National Academy of Sciences* 108. 42: 17302–17307.

Jaswal, V. K., & Akhtar, N., 2019. 'Being versus appearing socially uninterested: Challenging assumptions about social motivation in autism'. *Behavioral and Brain Sciences* 42: e82.

Johansson Nolaker, E., Murray, K., Happé, F., & Charlton, R. A., 2018. 'Cognitive and affective associations with an ecologically valid test of theory of mind across the lifespan'. *Neuropsychology* 32. 6: 754–763.

Johnson, M. H., 2014. 'Autism: Demise of the innate social orienting hypothesis'. *Current Biology* 24. 1: R30–R31.

Jones, A. P., Happé, F. G., Gilbert, F., Burnett, S., & Viding, E., 2010. 'Feeling, caring, knowing: different types of empathy deficit in boys with psychopathic tendencies and autism spectrum disorder'. *Journal of Child Psychology and Psychiatry* 51. 11: 1188–1197.

Jones, C. R., Simonoff, E., Baird, G., Pickles, A., Marsden, A. J., Tregay, J., ... & Charman, T., 2018. 'The association between theory of mind, executive function, and the symptoms of autism spectrum disorder'. *Autism Research* 11. 1: 95–109.

Jones, E. J., Gliga, T., Bedford, R., Charman, T., & Johnson, M. H., 2014. 'Developmental pathways to autism: a review of prospective studies of infants at risk'. *Neuroscience & Biobehavioral Reviews* 39: 1–33.

Jones, L., Goddard, L., Hill, E. L., Henry, L. A., & Crane, L., 2014. 'Experiences of receiving a diagnosis of autism spectrum disorder: A survey of adults in the United Kingdom'. *Journal of Autism and Developmental Disorders* 44. 12: 3033–3044.

Jones, W., & Klin, A., 2013. 'Attention to eyes is present but in decline in 2–6-month-old infants later diagnosed with autism'. *Nature* 504. 7480: 427–431.

Kanner, L., 1943. 'Autistic disturbances of affective contact'. *Nervous Child* 2. 3: 217–250.

Kinnaird, E., Stewart, C., & Tchanturia, K., 2019. 'Investigating alexithymia in autism: A systematic review and meta-analysis'. *European Psychiatry* 55: 80–89.

Kleberg, J. L., Nyström, P., Bölte, S., & Falck-Ytter, T., 2019. 'Sex differences in social attention in infants at risk for autism'. *Journal of Autism and Developmental Disorders* 49. 4: 1342–1351.

Kulke, L., von Duhn, B., Schneider, D., & Rakoczy, H., 2018. 'Is implicit theory of mind a real and robust phenomenon? Results from a systematic replication study'. *Psychological Science* 29. 6: 888–900.

Lai, M-C., Lombardo, M. V., Auyeung, B., Chakrabarti, B., & Baron-Cohen, S., 2015. 'Sex/gender differences and autism: Setting the scene for future research'. *Journal of the American Academy of Child & Adolescent Psychiatry* 54. 1: 11–24.

Lai, M-C., Kassee, C., Besney, R., Bonato, S., Hull, L., Mandy, W., ... & Ameis, S. H., 2019. 'Prevalence of co-occurring mental health diagnoses in the autism population: A systematic review and meta-analysis'. *The Lancet Psychiatry* 6. 10: 819–829.

Lai, M-C., Lombardo, M. V., Ruigrok, A. N., Chakrabarti, B., Auyeung, B., Szatmari, P., ... & MRC AIMS Consortium, 2017. 'Quantifying and exploring camouflaging in men and women with autism'. *Autism* 21. 6: 690–702.

Lawson, J., Baron-Cohen, S., & Wheelwright, S., 2004. 'Empathising and systemising in adults with and without Asperger syndrome'. *Journal of Autism and Developmental Disorders* 34. 3: 301–310.

Lawson, R. P., Mathys, C., & Rees, G., 2017. 'Adults with autism overestimate the volatility of the sensory environment'. *Nature Neuroscience* 20. 9: 1293–1299.

Leighton, J., Bird, G., Charman, T., & Heyes, C., 2008. 'Weak imitative performance is not due to a functional 'mirroring' deficit in adults with Autism Spectrum Disorders'. *Neuropsychologia* 46. 4: 1041–1049.

Lever, A. G., & Geurts, H. M., 2016. 'Age-related differences in cognition across the adult lifespan in autism spectrum disorder'. *Autism Research* 9. 6: 666–676.

Livingston, L. A., & Happé, F., 2017. 'Conceptualising compensation in neurodevelopmental disorders: Reflections from autism spectrum disorder'. *Neuroscience & Biobehavioral Reviews* 80: 729–742.

Livingston, L. A., & Livingston, L. M., 2016. 'Commentary: alexithymia, not autism, is associated with impaired interoception'. *Frontiers in Psychology* 7: 1103.

Livingston, L. A., Ashwin, C., & Shah, P. 2020b. 'Electronic communication in autism spectrum conditions'. *Molecular Autism* 11. 1: 1–3.

Livingston, L. A., Carr, B., & Shah, P., 2019d. 'Recent advances and new directions in measuring theory of mind in autistic adults'. *Journal of Autism and Developmental Disorders* 49. 4: 1738–1744.

Livingston, L. A., Shah, P., & Happé, F., 2019a. 'Compensatory strategies below the behavioural surface in autism: A qualitative study'. *Lancet Psychiatry* 6. 9: 766–777.

Livingston, L. A., Shah, P., & Happé, F., 2019b. 'Compensation in autism is not consistent with social motivation theory'. *Behavioral and Brain Sciences* 42: e99.

Livingston, L. A., Shah, P., & Happé F., submitted. 'Integrating speed and accuracy to quantify theory of mind ability: Evidence from autistic and neurotypical adults'.

Livingston, L. A., Shah, P., Milner, V., & Happé F., 2020a. 'Quantifying compensatory strategies in adults with and without diagnosed autism'. *Molecular Autism* 11. 1: 15.

Livingston, L. A., Colvert, E., Social Relationships Study Team, Bolton, P., & Happé, F., 2019c. 'Good social skills despite poor theory of mind exploring compensation in autism spectrum disorder. *Journal of Child Psychology and Psychiatry* 60. 1: 102–110.

Lockwood, P. L., 2016. 'The anatomy of empathy: Vicarious experience and disorders of social cognition'. *Behavioural Brain Research* 311: 255–266.

Lombardo, M. V., Lai, M-C., & Baron-Cohen, S., 2019. 'Big data approaches to decomposing heterogeneity across the autism spectrum'. *Molecular Psychiatry* 24. 10: 1435–1450.

Loomes, R., Hull, L., & Mandy, W., 2017. 'What is the male-to-female ratio in autism spectrum disorder? A systematic review and meta-analysis'. *Journal of the American Academy of Child & Adolescent Psychiatry* 56. 6: 466–474.

Lord, C., Bishop, S., & Anderson, D., 2015. 'Developmental trajectories as autism phenotypes'. *American Journal of Medical Genetics Part C: Seminars in Medical Genetics* 169. 2: 198–208.

Lord, C., Risi, S., Lambrecht, L., Cook, E. H., Leventhal, B. L., DiLavore, P. C., ... & Rutter, M., 2000. 'The Autism Diagnostic Observation Schedule—Generic: A standard measure of social and communication deficits associated with the spectrum of autism'. *Journal of Autism and Developmental Disorders* 30. 3: 205–223.

Loth, E., Spooren, W., Ham, L. M., Isaac, M. B., Auriche-Benichou, C., Banaschewski, T., ... & Charman, T., 2016. 'Identification and validation of biomarkers for autism spectrum disorders'. *Nature Reviews Drug Discovery* 15. 1: 70–73.

Lundström, S., Chang, Z., Råstam, M., Gillberg, C., Larsson, H., Anckarsäter, H., & Lichtenstein, P., 2012. 'Autism spectrum disorders and autistic like traits: similar etiology in the extreme end and the normal variation'. *JAMA Psychiatry* 69. 1: 46–52.

Mackes, N. K., Golm, D., O'Daly, O. G., Sarkar, S., Sonuga-Barke, E. J., Fairchild, G., & Mehta, M. A., 2018. 'Tracking emotions in the brain—Revisiting the Empathic Accuracy Task'. *NeuroImage* 178: 677–686.

Mandy, W., Pellicano, L., St Pourcain, B., Skuse, D., & Heron, J., 2018. 'The development of autistic social traits across childhood and adolescence in males and females'. *Journal of Child Psychology and Psychiatry* 59. 11: 1143–1151.

McEwen, F., Happé, F., Bolton, P., Rijsdijk, F., Ronald, A., Dworzynski, K., & Plomin, R., 2007. 'Origins of individual differences in imitation: Links with language, pretend play, and socially insightful behavior in two-year-old twins'. *Child Development* 78. 2: 474–492.

Milton, D. E., 2012. On the ontological status of autism: The 'double empathy problem'. *Disability & Society* 27. 6: 883–887.

Moessnang, C., Baumeister, S., Tillmann, J., Goyard, D., Charman, T., Ambrosino, S., ... & Crawley, D., 2020. 'Social brain activation during mentalizing in a large autism cohort: the Longitudinal European Autism Project'. *Molecular Autism* 11. 1: 17.

Morton, J., & Frith, U., 1995. 'Causal modelling: Structural approaches to developmental psychopathology'. In *Developmental Psychopathology Vol. 1: Theory and Methods*, edited by D. Cicchetti & D. Cohen. John Wiley & Sons. Inc.

Mukaetova-Ladinska, E. B., Perry, E., Baron, M., Povey, C., & Autism Ageing Writing Group, 2012. 'Ageing in people with autistic spectrum disorder'. *International Journal of Geriatric Psychiatry* 27. 2: 109–118.

Mul, C. L., Stagg, S. D., Herbelin, B., & Aspell, J. E., 2018. 'The feeling of me feeling for you: Interoception, alexithymia and empathy in autism'. *Journal of Autism and Developmental Disorders* 48. 9: 2953–2967.

Müller, R. A., & Fishman, I., 2018. 'Brain connectivity and neuroimaging of social networks in autism'. *Trends in Cognitive Sciences* 22. 12: 1103–1116.

Mundy, P., 2018. 'A review of joint attention and social-cognitive brain systems in typical development and autism spectrum disorder'. *European Journal of Neuroscience* 47. 6: 497–514.

Murray, K., Johnston, K., Cunnane, H., Kerr, C., Spain, D., Gillan, N., ... & Happé, F., 2017. 'A new test of advanced theory of mind: The "Strange Stories Film Task" captures social processing differences in adults with autism spectrum disorders'. *Autism Research* 10. 6: 1120–1132.

Nadig, A., Lee, I., Singh, L., Bosshart, K., & Ozonoff, S., 2010. 'How does the topic of conversation affect verbal exchange and eye gaze? A comparison between typical development and high-functioning autism'. *Neuropsychologia* 48. 9: 2730–2739.

New, J. J., Schultz, R. T., Wolf, J., Niehaus, J. L., Klin, A., German, T. C., & Scholl, B. J., 2010. 'The scope of social attention deficits in autism: Prioritized orienting to people and animals in static natural scenes'. *Neuropsychologia* 48. 1: 51–59.

Nyström, P., Thorup, E., Bölte, S., & Falck-Ytter, T., 2019. 'Joint attention in infancy and the emergence of autism'. *Biological Psychiatry* 86. 8: 631–638.

Olderbak, S., Wilhelm, O., Olaru, G., Geiger, M., Brenneman, M. W., & Roberts, R. D., 2015. 'A psychometric analysis of the reading the mind in the eyes test: toward a brief form for research and applied settings'. *Frontiers in Psychology* 6: 1503.

Onishi, K. H., & Baillargeon, R., 2005. 'Do 15-month-old infants understand false beliefs?' *Science* 308. 5719: 255–258.

Pan, X., & Hamilton, A., 2018. 'Why and how to use virtual reality to study human social interaction: The challenges of exploring a new research landscape'. *British Journal of Psychology* 109. 3: 395–417.

Pellicano, E., 2013. 'Testing the predictive power of cognitive atypicalities in autistic children: Evidence from a 3-year follow-up study'. *Autism Research* 6. 4: 258–267.

Pellicano, E., & Burr, D., 2012. 'When the world becomes "too real": A Bayesian explanation of autistic perception'. *Trends in Cognitive Sciences* 16. 10: 504–510.

Pickles, A., McCauley, J. B., Pepa, L. A., Huerta, M., & Lord, C., 2020. 'The adult outcome of children referred for autism: Typology and prediction from childhood'. *Journal of Child Psychology and Psychiatry* 61. 7: 760–767.

Quesque, F., & Rossetti, Y., 2020. 'What do theory-of-mind tasks actually measure? Theory and practice'. *Perspectives on Psychological Science* 15. 2: 384–396.

Ratto, A. B., Kenworthy, L., Yerys, B. E., Bascom, J., Wieckowski, A. T., White, S. W., ... & Anthony, L. G., 2018. 'What about the girls? Sex-based differences in autistic traits and adaptive skills'. *Journal of Autism and Developmental Disorders* 48. 5: 1698–1711.

Rice, K., Moriuchi, J. M., Jones, W., & Klin, A., 2012. 'Parsing heterogeneity in autism spectrum disorders: Visual scanning of dynamic social scenes in school-aged children'. *Journal of the American Academy of Child & Adolescent Psychiatry* 51. 3: 238–248.

Rizzolatti, G., & Craighero, L., 2004. 'The mirror-neuron system'. *Annual Review of Neuroscience* 27: 169–192.

Robertson, C. E., & Baron-Cohen, S., 2017. 'Sensory perception in autism'. *Nature Reviews Neuroscience* 18. 11: 671–684.

Rogers, S. J., & Pennington, B. F., 1991. 'A theoretical approach to the deficits in infantile autism'. *Development and Psychopathology* 3. 2: 137–162.

Rueda, P., Fernández-Berrocal, P., & Baron-Cohen, S., 2015. 'Dissociation between cognitive and affective empathy in youth with Asperger Syndrome'. *European Journal of developmental Psychology* 12. 1: 85–98.

Russell, G., Kapp, S. K., Elliott, D., Elphick, C., Gwernan-Jones, R., & Owens, C., 2019. 'Mapping the autistic advantage from the accounts of adults diagnosed with autism: A qualitative study'. *Autism in Adulthood* 1. 2: 124–133.

Russell, G., Mandy, W., Elliott, D., White, R., Pittwood, T., & Ford, T., 2019a. 'Selection bias on intellectual ability in autism research: A cross-sectional review and meta-analysis'. *Molecular Autism* 10. 1: 9.

Rutter, M., 2005. 'Incidence of autism spectrum disorders: Changes over time and their meaning'. *Acta Paediatrica* 94. 1: 2–15.

Sasson, N. J., Morrison, K. E., Kelsven, S., & Pinkham, A. E., 2020. 'Social cognition as a predictor of functional and social skills in autistic adults without intellectual disability'. *Autism Research* 13: 259–270.

Sasson, N. J., Faso, D. J., Nugent, J., Lovell, S., Kennedy, D. P., & Grossman, R. B., 2017. 'Neurotypical peers are less willing to interact with those with autism based on thin slice judgments'. *Scientific Reports* 7: 40700.

Scheeren, A. M., de Rosnay, M., Koot, H. M., & Begeer, S., 2013. 'Rethinking theory of mind in high-functioning autism spectrum disorder'. *Journal of Child Psychology and Psychiatry* 54. 6: 628–635.

Schilbach, L., Timmermans, B., Reddy, V., Costall, A., Bente, G., Schlicht, T., & Vogeley, K., 2013. 'Toward a second-person neuroscience'. *Behavioral and Brain Sciences* 36. 4: 393–414.

Senju, A., Southgate, V., White, S., & Frith, U., 2009. 'Mindblind eyes: An absence of spontaneous theory of mind in Asperger syndrome'. *Science* 325. 5942: 883–885.

Shah, P., Gaule, A., Bird, G., & Cook, R., 2013. 'Robust orienting to protofacial stimuli in autism'. *Current Biology* 23. 24: R1087–R1088.

Shah, P., Hall, R., Catmur, C., & Bird, G., 2016. 'Alexithymia, not autism, is associated with impaired interoception'. *Cortex* 81: 215–220.

Shah, P., Livingston, L. A., Callan, M. J., & Player, L., 2019. 'Trait autism is a better predictor of empathy than alexithymia'. *Journal of Autism and Developmental Disorders* 49. 10: 3956–3964.

Sheppard, E., Pillai, D., Wong, G. T. L., Ropar, D., & Mitchell, P., 2016. 'How easy is it to read the minds of people with autism spectrum disorder?' *Journal of Autism and Developmental Disorders* 46. 4: 1247–1254.

Simonoff, E., 2012. 'Autism spectrum disorder: Prevalence and cause may be bound together'. *The British Journal of Psychiatry* 201. 2: 88–89.

Sowden, S., Koehne, S., Catmur, C., Dziobek, I., & Bird, G., 2016. 'Intact automatic imitation and typical spatial compatibility in autism spectrum disorder: Challenging the broken mirror theory'. *Autism Research* 9. 2: 292–300.

Spain, D., Sin, J., Linder, K. B., McMahon, J., & Happé, F., 2018. 'Social anxiety in autism spectrum disorder: A systematic review'. *Research in Autism Spectrum Disorders* 52: 51–68.

Stewart, G. R., Wallace, G. L., Cottam, M., & Charlton, R. A., 2019. 'Theory of mind performance in younger and older adults with elevated autistic traits'. *Autism Research* 13. 5: 751–762.

Sutherland, R., Hodge, A., Bruck, S., Costley, D., & Klieve, H., 2017. 'Parent-reported differences between school-aged girls and boys on the autism spectrum'. *Autism* 21. 6: 785–794.

Szatmari, P., Chawarska, K., Dawson, G., Georgiades, S., Landa, R., Lord, C., ... & Halladay, A., 2016. 'Prospective longitudinal studies of infant siblings of children with autism: lessons learned and future directions'. *Journal of the American Academy of Child & Adolescent Psychiatry* 55. 3: 179–187.

Tager-Flusberg, H., 2007. 'Evaluating the theory-of-mind hypothesis of autism'. *Current Directions in Psychological Science* 16. 6: 311–315.

Taylor, E. C., Livingston, L. A., Callan, M. J., & Shah, P., 2019. 'Divergent contributions of autistic traits to social psychological knowledge'. *Proceedings of the National Academy of Sciences* 116. 51: 25378–25379.

Teague, S. J., Gray, K. M., Tonge, B. J., & Newman, L. K., 2017. 'Attachment in children with autism spectrum disorder: A systematic review'. *Research in Autism Spectrum Disorders* 35: 35–50.

Velikonja, T., Fett, A. K., & Velthorst, E., 2019. 'Patterns of nonsocial and social cognitive functioning in adults with autism spectrum disorder: A systematic review and meta-analysis'. *JAMA Psychiatry* 76. 2: 135–151.

Wan, M. W., Green, J., & Scott, J., 2019. 'A systematic review of parent–infant interaction in infants at risk of autism'. *Autism* 23. 4: 811–820.

Warnell, K. R., & Redcay, E., 2019. 'Minimal coherence among varied theory of mind measures in childhood and adulthood'. *Cognition* 191: 103997.

Warrier, V., Toro, R., Won, H., Leblond, C. S., Cliquet, F., Delorme, R., ... & Grove, J., 2019. 'Social and non-social autism symptoms and trait domains are genetically dissociable'. *Communications Biology* 2. 1: 328.

Webb, S., Faja, S., & Dawson, G., 2011. 'Face processing in autism'. In *Oxford Handbook of Face Perception*, edited by G. Rhodes et al. Oxford University Press.

White, S. J., Coniston, D., Rogers, R., & Frith, U., 2011. 'Developing the Frith-Happé animations: A quick and objective test of Theory of Mind for adults with autism'. *Autism Research* 4. 2: 149–154.

White, S. J., Hill, E., Happé, F., & Frith, U., 2009. 'Revisiting the strange stories: Revealing mentalizing impairments in autism'. *Child Development* 80. 4: 1097–1117.

White, S. J., Frith, U., Rellecke, J., Al-Noor, Z., & Gilbert, S. J., 2014. 'Autistic adolescents show atypical activation of the brain's mentalizing system even without a prior history of mentalizing problems'. *Neuropsychologia* 56: 17–25.

Williams, J. H., Whiten, A., & Singh, T., 2004. 'A systematic review of action imitation in autistic spectrum disorder'. *Journal of Autism and Developmental Disorders* 34. 3: 285–299.

Wolfers, T., Floris, D. L., Dinga, R., van Rooij, D., Isakoglou, C., Kia, S. M., ... & Peng, H., 2019. 'From pattern classification to stratification: Towards conceptualizing the heterogeneity of Autism Spectrum Disorder'. *Neuroscience & Biobehavioral Reviews* 104: 240–254.

Yang, C. C., Khalifa, N., & Völlm, B., 2018. 'The effects of repetitive transcranial magnetic stimulation on empathy: a systematic review and meta-analysis'. *Psychological Medicine* 48. 5: 737–750.

Zıvralı Yarar, E., Howlin, P., Charlton, R., & Happé, F., in press. Age-related effects on social cognition in adults with Autism Spectrum Disorder: A possible protective effect on theory of dind. *Autism Research*.

8
The Ageing Brain in Context
Towards a Refined Understanding of Social Cognition in Ageing and Dementia

Muireann Irish and Siddharth Ramanan

8.1 Introduction

Successful social interactions hinge upon our capacity to infer the thoughts, beliefs, emotions, and perspectives of others, enabling us to anticipate and predict subsequent behaviour, and to respond appropriately. A large corpus of research explores the foundational building blocks of these processes in childhood, with rigorous investigation of atypical social interactions in developmental disorders such as autism. In contrast, social cognitive function at the opposite end of the lifespan has received comparatively less attention. This gap in the literature is surprising given that older age is a time of immense biological, psychological, and social change. Moreover, the establishing and maintenance of social bonds in later years has been linked to a number of important adaptive outcomes including cognitive reserve, resilience, and improved mood and wellbeing. As such, it is imperative to understand the unique profiles of social cognitive functioning through the lens of healthy and pathological ageing. Here, we take a mechanistic approach to understanding how alterations in Theory of Mind and empathy arise as a natural consequence of healthy ageing, with important caveats regarding how we construct and assess these processes in older adults. Then, we consider how pathological disturbances of the brain networks specialized for social cognition have an impact on social functioning in dementia syndromes. Our aim is to provide a road map to study social cognitive function in older age, and to reorient the discourse to consider new ways of promoting social interaction in healthy and pathological ageing.

8.1.1 Sociocognitive versus socioaffective processes

Despite being fundamental to human interpersonal function, there currently remains no firm consensus on how best to define or accurately measure social cognition. It is generally accepted that, in order to successfully navigate within the social milieu, humans must engage in a process known as 'mentalizing', wherein we infer the thoughts, beliefs, and perspectives of others. Through this process of mentalizing, we can have a 'Theory of Mind' (ToM) (Premack & Woodruff, 1978), conferring an awareness that others will have beliefs and intentions distinct from our own, which in turn will govern their behaviour. ToM has been suggested to underwrite a range of social processes including empathy, forming judgements of trust, and recognizing communicative intentions or non-verbal behaviours (Frith, 2007). In clinical and experimental settings, mentalizing/ToM capacity is typically captured using behavioural assessments requiring perspective taking, belief inference of story characters (i.e. false belief tasks), detection of social faux-pas, reading emotional cues from face and/or eye expressions, and/or attributing intentions and emotions to characters in cartoons or videos (reviewed in detail by Duclos et al., 2018; Christidi et al., 2018; Elamin et al., 2012; Adenzato et al., 2010). While ToM can be subdivided into cognitive (inferring thoughts, beliefs) versus affective (inferring emotions, feelings) elements, we will focus here on the *cognitive* component of ToM, which enables us to understand and appreciate the perspectives of others (i.e. mentalizing).

To complement the cognitive aspect of ToM, we will consider the related, but distinct, construct of empathy, a multifaceted process enabling us to share the emotions or the affective experience of others (Lamm et al., 2007; Zaki & Ochsner, 2012). While the capacity for empathy has been suggested to rely upon a number of core underlying processes, the modulating role of domain-specific mechanisms remains a source of contention. Not unlike ToM, empathy can be deconstructed into cognitive (understanding the other person's experience) and affective (sharing the emotional experience of the person) components (Zaki & Ochsner, 2012). Here, we focus on the experience-sharing processing stream of *affective* empathy. By considering how *sociocognitive* (cognitive ToM) and *socioaffective* (affective empathy) processes are altered in healthy and pathological ageing, we aim to provide a comprehensive overview of the fate of the social brain across the adult lifespan in health and disease.

8.1.2 The social brain

It is now widely accepted that the human brain comprises a discrete set of neural regions specialized for enabling us to interact with other people, to anticipate and predict behaviour, and to configure our own behaviour accordingly (Frith, 2007). This so-called 'social brain' enables us to mentalize, to infer the mental states of others, and to use this information to understand and predict behaviour (Fig. 8.1). Central to the ToM/mentalizing network is the medial prefrontal cortex (mPFC) and anterior cingulate-fronto-insular (ACC/fIN) cortices, regions that may

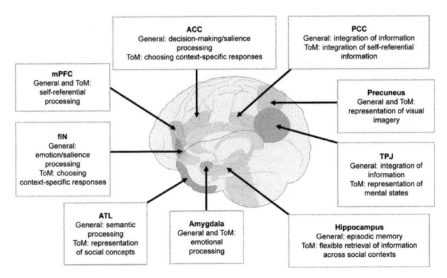

Fig. 8.1 Functional neuroimaging studies of healthy individuals engaged in social reasoning

Functional neuroimaging studies of healthy individuals engaged in various forms of social reasoning consistently reveal the importance of a distributed network—dubbed 'the social brain'—centred on the medial prefrontal cortex, and including fronto-insular, lateral and medial temporal, as well as lateral and medial posterior parietal cortices. Many of the core regions of this network support Theory of Mind-specific (indicated with 'ToM') and domain-general functions (indicated with 'General'), and overlap with the brain's Default Mode and Salience Networks, both of which play important modulating roles in social cognitive functioning.

Image reproduced with permission from Strikwerda-Brown, C., Ramanan, S. & Irish, M., 2019. 'Neurocognitive mechanisms of Theory Of Mind impairment in neurodegeneration: a transdiagnostic approach'. *Neuropsychiatric Disease and Treatment* 15: 557-573.

facilitate the tagging and integration of incoming salient information to guide appropriate behavioural and social responses with social context in mind (reviewed by Menon & Uddin, 2010). Within the ACC/fIN cortices are a special class of rare, large neurons, not found anywhere else in the brain, called 'von Economo neurons'. These neurons are suggested to have evolved specifically to tag and process socially salient information, expediting the relaying of this information from the ACC/fIN to other regions in the brain, and guiding the selection of appropriate responses to rapidly adjust to changing social contexts (Seeley et al., 2012; Allman et al., 2010). Beyond the frontal cortex, anterior temporal regions support the integration of perceptual and emotional responses with personal knowledge of social concepts (reviewed by Olson et al., 2007). The hippocampus has further been suggested to facilitate the dynamic updating of flexible representations of social information based on personal experience (Montagrin et al., 2017), whereas the amygdala is frequently implicated in behaviours that involve recognition of complex emotional characteristics and responses to socially salient stimuli (Gallagher & Frith, 2003). More posteriorly, the temporo-parietal junction (TPJ) has been implicated in representing information that is key to belief inference, with TPJ activity increasing when incongruencies between a character's mental state and social background are detected (Saxe & Wexler, 2005). Finally, there is emerging evidence for a role for the precuneus and posterior cingulate cortices in ToM processing, potentially reflecting the recruitment of mental imagery to represent perspectives of other people (reviewed by Cavanna & Trimble, 2006).

8.2 Ageing and the social brain

A perplexing motif within the ageing literature is the largely pessimistic picture that is painted, typically emphasizing loss of functional brain network integrity. This standard view of ageing is referred to as the 'loss of integrity, loss of function (LILF)' view (reviewed by Andrews-Hanna et al., 2019), and implies widespread disruption of complex cognitive processes and the underlying neural networks that mediate these processes. Cross-sectional studies of changes in cortical thickness in ageing, however, reveal conflicting findings, with some reporting age-related thinning of anterior medial prefrontal cortices of the brain, whereas others report thickening (reviewed in Fjell et al., 2009). A critical look at the literature further reveals that the standard LILF view in normal ageing may not necessarily hold with respect to complex socially oriented cognitive functions such as pro-social behaviour and empathy (Beadle & de la Vega, 2019; Sze et al., 2012). In fact, there is growing consensus that many internally guided processes are preserved or *enhanced* in cognitively healthy older adults. Differences in motivational, contextual, and physiological factors between young and older adults must be considered when interpreting cognitive and neuroimaging findings (Andrews-Hanna et al., 2019; Irish et al., 2019). Rather than viewing normal ageing as a concatenation of degradation and decline, ageing can be viewed as a series of adaptive *alterations* that promote socio-emotional well-being and stability in a stage of life noted for change (Park & Reuter-Lorenz, 2009).

8.3 Theory of Mind, empathy, and healthy ageing

8.3.1 Sociocognitive processing

At first glance, the available evidence suggests a diminished capacity to infer the perspectives of others via ToM/mentalizing in healthy ageing. Such impairments in mental state attribution have been suggested to relate to reduced social participation, poorer self-reported social skills, and smaller social networks in later adulthood (Laillier et al., 2019). Importantly, however, social neuroscience research increasingly emphasizes the importance of distinguishing between cognitive and affective routes of social understanding, which are posited to operate relatively independently from one another (Kanske et al., 2016). In the context of healthy ageing, sociocognitive processes are disproportionately affected, leading to compromised performance on classic ToM/mentalizing tasks where mental state inference or perspective taking is required (Reiter et al., 2017). Despite progressive difficulties on cognitive ToM tasks in older age, affective ToM performance remains relatively intact (Laillier et al., 2019; Reiter et al., 2017).

The nature of the tasks used to assess ToM in ageing is of critical importance in this case and significantly influences the resultant profiles (see Duclos et al., 2018, for a comprehensive overview of commonly used social cognitive tasks). Notably, age-related changes in ToM capacity are typically observed on sociocognitive tasks with high loading on memory and executive function (Moran, 2013). Individual differences in executive function have been shown to, at least partially, account for age-related deficits on both experimental and naturalistic sociocognitive tasks (Johansson Nolaker et al., 2018). Task modality must also be considered because ageing effects on affective ToM tasks are only evident when visual paradigms requiring emotion decoding are used (Slessor et al., 2007). When verbal reasoning tools are deployed, older adults appear adept at harnessing their superior vocabulary to complete the task.

Dynamic ToM tasks, which more closely approximate the everyday social scenarios that we typically encounter, have further been shown to attenuate age-related effects in social cognitive performance (Krendl & Ambady, 2010; Slessor et al., 2007). The use of naturalistic task design is increasingly acknowledged as critical in studying age-related changes in social functioning with many studies lacking appropriate control conditions, and employing self-report or age-irrelevant scenarios. A recent study using a naturalistic and tightly controlled paradigm suggests that ageing is associated with deficits in metacognitive abilities in the context of preserved empathic responding and enhanced compassion (Reiter et al., 2017). The authors interpret these findings in terms of a differential effect of ageing exclusively for sociocognitive function, potentially mediated by the selective redeployment of cognitive resources on socio-emotional content rather than self- and future-oriented goals (Reiter et al., 2017). This finding parallels a recent study from our own group in which we observed a shift from self- and future-oriented spontaneous thought to more past- and other-focused forms of thinking in older adults (Irish et al., 2019), suggesting that, on deliberate cognitive tasks and during periods of quiet contemplation, older adults default towards socio-emotional forms of processing.

8.3.2 Socioaffective reasoning

The importance of task dimensions and individual differences is amplified when we consider the literature on socioaffective reasoning—i.e. tasks that probe the *emotional* aspects of social cognition. Shifts in motivational priorities towards reflective and interpersonal processes have been suggested to manifest in stable or even improved socio-emotional well-being in older age (Scheibe & Carstensen, 2010) and may contribute to the 'positivity effect' in ageing, whereby older adults allocate more attentional resources to positive versus negative information (Mather & Carstensen, 2005). Consistent with this proposal, numerous studies reveal comparable or even *enhanced* performance on affective ToM tasks (Reiter et al., 2017; Wang & Su, 2013) and trait empathy questionnaires (Bailey et al., 2008) in older relative to younger adults. Moreover, older adults have been shown to display heightened affective state empathy, elevated levels of compassion, and increases in prosocial behaviour, relative to their younger counterparts (reviewed by Beadle & de la Vega, 2019). An open question in the literature pertains to positive empathy in older adults—i.e. the capacity to share the *positive* emotions of others, rather than displaying compassion and prosocial behaviour on tasks where another person is in need or suffering. According to the socio-emotional selectivity theory of ageing (Carstensen et al., 1999), a bias towards positive emotions and the prioritizing of attention towards such emotions would be predicted in older age. However, formal testing of these proposals is required (Reiter et al., 2017).

8.3.3 Neural substrates of age-related changes

To date, only a handful of studies have explored age-related changes in mentalizing capacity using functional magnetic resonance imaging (fMRI). One study by Moran et al. (2012) varied the working memory demands of three mentalizing tasks and reported that, irrespective of executive and verbal processing demands, older adults were less likely to take intentions into account when making moral permissibility judgements, and displayed poorer accuracy in false belief judgements. Collectively, these age-related decrements in sociocognitive reasoning were associated with down-regulation of the dorsomedial prefrontal cortex (Moran et al., 2012), one of the core nodes of the social brain. It must be noted, however, that these findings stand in contrast with fMRI studies of socioaffective processing in older adults. For example, a study employing the 'Reading the Mind in the Eyes' task observed comparable performance in older and younger adults on the behavioural level, but this was mediated by common and divergent profiles of neural activity. Whereas older adults displayed decreases in ACC activity, they were observed to recruit lateral temporal regions to a comparable degree as younger adults, and demonstrated *enhanced* age-related activity in the left inferior frontal gyrus, an area not traditionally associated with social cognition (Castelli et al., 2010). Additional recruitment of prefrontal regions in older versus younger adults has been noted in other studies where, despite comparable behavioural ratings, older adults displayed increased cingulate activity in response to ratings of unpleasantness for images of pain (Chen et al., 2014). Finally, in a third study, older female adults displayed reduced fIN activity compared with their younger counterparts when making empathy judgements towards pleasant and unpleasant touch conditions (Riva et al., 2018).

Together, these findings suggest a shift in the functional recruitment of frontal brain regions in older age when engaging in sociocognitive and socioaffective reasoning, irrespective of behavioural performance. This recruitment of additional prefrontal regions has been interpreted as 'compensatory scaffolding', denoting an adaptive response to widespread neural changes that are characteristic of ageing (Park & Reuter-Lorenz, 2009). Compensatory recruitment of temporoparietal brain regions has also been observed during social evaluations of others. Despite common recruitment of mPFC and parietal regions across younger and older age groups when socially evaluating other individuals (Cassidy et al., 2012), age-related *increases* in right temporal pole activation were reported during social versus non-social evaluations, with further increases in the left inferior frontal gyrus and bilateral posterior cingulate cortex when making socially meaningful evaluations (Cassidy et al., 2012). It is important to note that these studies assessed socioaffective processing—i.e. the *sharing* of the affective state of others—which may account for the finding of increased neural activation in older adults. Age-related increases in neural activation during social reasoning tasks may reflect changes to socio-emotional goals and/or the utilization of compensatory strategies to augment task performance. However, formal investigation of these proposals is lacking. As such, the few functional differences that have been reported in the literature to date may reflect non-specific reductions in executive functioning, enhanced socioaffective processing, changes in social motivation and goals, or a combination of these factors, with increasing age (Andrews-Hanna et al., 2019).

8.3.4 Conclusions on ageing

In summary, we do not find compelling evidence to support a global decline in social cognition in older adults. Rather, healthy ageing is associated with alterations on tasks assessing cognitive aspects of mentalizing, in the context of preserved or even enhanced capacity to share the affective dimensions of another's experience. Studies demonstrating age-related stability of self-referential cognition and the intimate connection between self and emotion converge to support a model of preserved socio-emotional functioning in healthy ageing (Scheibe & Carstensen, 2010; Gutchess & Kensinger, 2018). The question remains, however, whether currently available tests of social cognition are sufficient to index the types of social interaction and social judgements that older adults prioritize. In this regard, researchers must balance the 'purity' of the ToM measure, from a conceptual standpoint, with the cognitive demands imposed by the task. For example, second-order ToM measures, where participants predict what a character thinks about what another person is thinking, are widely accepted as reliable assessments of ToM, yet they impose heavy demands on executive function and working memory. On the other hand, when ToM task demands are reduced (e.g. via cartoon or line drawing stimuli), they may suffer from a lack of contextual information to communicate the intensity and veracity of the emotions and intentions of the protagonists. As mentioned previously, one solution is to use naturalistic paradigms, wherein actors enact social situations with age-appropriate information. Such approaches may offer greater contextual support and provide more accurate measures of ToM capacity in ageing. Finally, looking beyond task-related performance, evidence suggests that older adults value maintaining a small number of existing or high-quality relationships rather than developing larger, but less meaningful, social networks (Mather & Carstensen, 2005). Whether healthy ageing is associated with a concomitant shift in social motivation (Moran et al., 2012) is an intriguing proposal that we suggest warrants serious empirical investigation in the future.

8.4 The other side of the coin: pathological ageing

Dementia represents a marked departure from the trajectory of healthy ageing, due to underlying pathological insult that propagates along neural pathways in a targeted and predictable fashion. Of interest here is the reliable observation of neurodegeneration affecting the structural and functional integrity of key nodes of the brain's Default Mode Network (DMN) and Salience Network, both of which are implicated in complex socio-emotional processes (Ahmed et al., 2016). These large-scale network perturbations give rise to distinct clinico-anatomical presentations. However, a feature held in common across dementia syndromes is the disruption of foundational processes essential for perspective taking and interpersonal functioning (Irish et al., 2012). We next consider how sociocognitive and socioaffective processes are differentially disrupted in two dementia syndromes—Alzheimer's disease (AD) and the behavioural variant of frontotemporal dementia (bvFTD)—and the underlying neurocognitive mediators of these deficits. We specifically focus on these two syndromes because they commonly display divergent profiles of social functioning, with the preservation of social graces and comportment in AD contrasting sharply with emotional blunting and socially inappropriate behaviour characteristic of bvFTD (reviewed by Strikwerda-Brown et al., 2019). By synthesizing the evidence to date, we hope to provide new insights on differentiating healthy from pathological ageing, and to provide an accurate picture of the ageing brain in health and disease.

8.5 Degeneration of the social brain

8.5.1 Alzheimer's disease

While memory difficulties represent one of the cardinal features of AD, over time the cognitive profile evolves to encompass visuospatial and executive dysfunction, culminating in widespread cognitive decline (Ramanan et al., 2017a). On the neural level, medial temporal and posterior parietal nodes of the DMN are vulnerable from early in the disease trajectory (see Fig. 8.2) (Sperling et al., 2010). Tau deposition and neural atrophy typically affect the entorhinal cortex before spreading to adjacent medial temporal regions (hippocampus and parahippocampal cortex), parietal regions, and thereon to the frontal and temporal cortices (Braak & Braak, 1991). Hypometabolism and significant amyloid deposition in the posterior cingulate cortex of the DMN has also been documented as a potential early marker of prodromal AD (Buckner et al., 2005). Collectively, these disturbances have been suggested to precipitate a cascade of changes throughout the DMN, which ultimately affect the integrity of other large-scale networks in the brain (Jones et al., 2016).

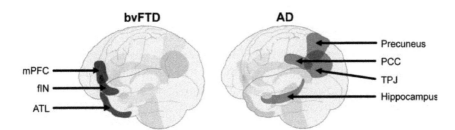

Fig. 8.2 Vulnerability of key nodes of the social brain in neurodegenerative disorders BvFTD primarily targets the fronto-insular nodes of the Salience Network, which supports the tagging and processing of salient information in the external environment. AD mainly affects medial temporal and posterior parietal nodes of the Default Mode Network, which is implicated in introspection and representation of contextually rich and detailed information. bvFTD = behavioural variant of frontotemporal dementia; AD = Alzheimer's disease; mPFC = medial prefrontal cortex; fIN = fronto-insular cortex; ATL = anterior temporal lobe; PCC = posterior cingulate cortex; TPJ = temporoparietal junction.

Image reproduced with permission from Strikwerda-Brown, C., Ramanan, S. & Irish, M., 2019. 'Neurocognitive Mechanisms of Theory Of Mind impairment in neurodegeneration: a transdiagnostic approach'. *Neuropsychiatric Disease and Treatment* 15: 557-573.

8.5.2 Sociocognitive Theory of Mind in Alzheimer's disease

Anecdotal reports from carers and clinicians converge to suggest that socio-emotional functioning is largely preserved in early stages of AD. Patients are typically described as showing preserved social graces, remaining affable, engaged, and socially appropriate. When present, ToM/mentalizing difficulties are typically attributed to increasing cognitive and executive dysfunction (Fortier et al., 2018, Strikwerda-Brown et al., 2019). Mounting evidence demonstrates that AD patients show relatively preserved task performance when inferring mental states from cartoon scenarios despite significant difficulties in comprehending the control non-ToM cartoons (Irish et al., 2014). AD patients further show relatively intact performance on first-order ToM tasks that impose low demands on higher-order cognitive abilities (Fernandez-Duque et al., 2009; Fortier et al., 2018). On the other hand, deficits are noted on second-order ToM tasks and second-order non-ToM control questions that place greater demands on working memory, and attentional and executive abilities. ToM performance on second-order belief tasks further correlates with memory, executive functioning, and language decline in AD (Zaitchik et al., 2006). Data-driven studies using two independent AD samples demonstrate that 50%–70% of variance in ToM performance in AD (as measured by the social faux-pas task), can be explained by attention, executive, and episodic memory decline (Ramanan et al., 2017b).

The provision of situational context is further important to consider as a recent study suggests that ambiguous or abstract stimuli may impede ToM performance in AD (Synn et al., 2018). Using the Frith-Happé animations task, which attempts to minimize cognitive load by using simple animations of triangles moving in 'interacting' or non-interacting patterns, Synn and colleagues demonstrated that AD patients could successfully recognize goal-directed physical interactions. By contrast, AD patients performed remarkably poorly in correctly labelling random movements or ToM interactions between the stimuli, suggesting an inability to interpret ambiguous movement of the stimuli when divorced from an appropriate social context (Synn et al., 2018). A number of caveats, however, warrant consideration in relation to the Frith-Happé animations used in this study. Although widely held as a simplified task of social cognition, participants nevertheless must hold the various elements of the story in mind as the scenario unfolds, integrate these elements into a coherent narrative across the 40-second clip, and then remember the story sufficiently to answer the questions that follow. Indeed, Synn et al. (2018) reported that ToM impairments in AD correlated with episodic memory dysfunction on a standard neuropsychological test. Together, these findings suggest that task performance in AD is mediated by a number of underlying, and potentially interacting, cognitive processes. Finally, it may be that such pared back tasks prevent participants from drawing on contextual information or schemas regarding what is considered socially acceptable in certain scenarios, as well as their own previous autobiographical experiences to guide their responses (see, for example, Wilson et al., 2020). As such, there appears to be a delicate balance between simplifying social cognitive tasks to circumvent cognitive difficulties, but not to the point where the stimuli are so abstract or ambiguous as to render the tasks meaningless for participants.

8.5.2.1 Neural substrates of Theory of Mind impairments in Alzheimer's disease

To date, only a handful of studies have explored the underlying neural bases of ToM impairments in AD. Using positron emission tomography, Le Bouc et al. (2012) found that impaired performance on a false belief task in a combined cohort of AD and bvFTD patients correlated with hypometabolism of the left inferior parietal cortex and TPJ. The aggregating of two disease groups, however, prevents us from drawing inferences regarding brain-behaviour associations specific to AD. More recently, Synn et al. (2018) found that poor overall performance on the Frith-Happé task in AD correlated with episodic memory dysfunction, and was associated with grey matter intensity decrease of the right hippocampus and bilateral cerebellum. The hippocampal contribution to impaired mental state inference was interpreted as reflecting a breakdown in the representational flexibility and online processing of complex configurations, coupled with hallmark episodic memory impairments in this syndrome. The observation of a significant cerebellar contribution to ToM impairments in AD is noteworthy and may reflect its contribution to mentalizing in conditions where the level of abstraction is high (Van Overwalle et al., 2014). Accordingly, the encroachment of AD pathology into cerebellar cortices may compound ToM difficulties, particularly when the task requires the coordination of multiple higher-order cognitive processes under highly abstract de-contextualized conditions (Synn et al., 2018).

8.5.3 Socioaffective empathy in Alzheimer's disease

The evidence to date converges to suggest that socioaffective processes remain largely intact in AD, and alterations, if present, typically do not emerge until much later in the disease course (Kumfor et al., 2014). Evidence for preserved affective empathy in AD predominantly stems from studies using the Interpersonal Reactivity Index (IRI; Davis, 1983), a trait measure of empathy that probes discrete facets of sociocognitive (i.e. perspective taking) and socioaffective (i.e. empathic concern) functioning. Using ratings on the Empathic Concern subscale as a proxy for affective empathy, carers consistently report preserved levels of empathy in the AD patient, mirroring their pre-morbid levels (Nash et al., 2007; Dermody et al., 2016; Rankin et al., 2006; Rankin et al., 2005; Hsieh et al., 2013; Bartochowski et al., 2018). Notably, AD patients also self-rate their capacity for empathy at pre-morbid levels, resulting in a close correspondence between patient and carer ratings. This convergence is notable because it suggests that AD patients have insight into their socioaffective comportment, which, coupled with their preserved empathy, may bolster intimacy and interpersonal connection between the individual and their family (Hsieh et al., 2013).

When experimental tasks probing affective empathy are used (e.g. animated scenarios depicting acts of intentional or accidental harm), the role of context must again be considered. Emerging evidence suggests that AD patients display near-normal empathy responses on experimental videos only when the emotions depicted are non-ambiguous (Fernandez-Duque et al., 2010). In contrast, when the emotional states to be inferred are abstract or variable in nature, this produces marked impairments in decoding the emotional state of a protagonist. These findings have been tentatively interpreted as reflecting a reliance on schemas or generalized semantic accounts of how the experimental scenarios would typically unfold, whereby AD participants default to the global feelings associated with a particular situational context (e.g. positive feelings in motherhood), rather than decoding the specific emotional reactions displayed by the protagonist in the videos (Fernandez-Duque et al., 2010). The tendency to focus on general rather than specific aspects of socio-emotional processing in AD resonates with well-established shifts towards producing over-general, well-rehearsed narratives during autobiographical memory retrieval (Irish et al., 2011; Irish & Piguet, 2013). When social processing is concerned, reliance on gist or schemas may serve the AD patient well, particularly for social interactions with familiar people and in familiar settings. When making inferences about social interactions in abstract, dynamic, or novel contexts, however, the AD patient cannot default to the familiar and instead would be predicted to experience difficulties. While this proposal can account for many of the conflicting findings in the AD literature, we note that it will be crucial to formally test these predictions to understand fluctuations in empathic processing across different contexts in AD.

Findings of relatively intact socioaffective empathy in a patient population characterized by widespread cognitive impairment and neural insult are intriguing, yet the precise mechanisms mediating this preservation of affective empathy in AD remain unclear (Fischer et al., 2019). Of the few neuroimaging studies exploring affective empathy in AD, no significant associations have been documented between structural integrity of grey matter regions and spared capacity for empathic concern (Dermody et al., 2016; Rankin et al., 2006). Task-based fMRI studies could offer important insights in this regard, enabling us to observe which brain regions not initially targeted by the AD pathology in earlier stages of the disease are recruited during socioaffective reasoning. Candidate regions include the mPFC, which modulates the emotional enhancement of memory in AD (Kumfor et al., 2013b) and the ACC/fIN cortices of the Salience Network, which coactivate in response to emotionally salient ambient stimuli and events, have been shown to be intact in AD (Seeley et al., 2012). Determining the mechanisms of preserved empathy in AD could offer important insights in treating neurodegenerative disorders with marked socio-emotional dysfunction, as will be considered in the next section.

8.5.4 Behavioural variant of frontotemporal dementia

Of all the neurodegenerative syndromes, bvFTD represents the canonical example of the social brain in disarray (O'Callaghan & Irish, 2018; Wong et al., 2018). Characterized as a younger-onset dementia, bvFTD typically strikes individuals under the age of 65 years, resulting in pervasive behavioural and executive dysfunction, changes in personality, emotion decoding difficulties and blunted affect, in the context of apathy, disinhibition, loss of insight, and rigid or stereotypical behaviours. Central to the bvFTD syndrome is a profound lack of social comportment, alongside a progressively egocentric world view and an apparent lack of concern for others, all of which contribute to a general decline in personal and interpersonal conduct (Irish & van Kesteren, 2018). That patients have little or no insight into these changes further compounds the problem for carers, who often struggle to adjust to the seemingly cold-hearted demeanour of their formerly affectionate spouse (Hsieh et al., 2013). The flagrant violation of social norms is a further challenge to manage, with bvFTD patients more likely to commit crimes of an antisocial and disinhibited nature, such as shoplifting, harassing strangers, sexual advances, theft from others' purses, and urinating in public (Liljegren et al., 2015).

8.5.5 Degeneration of the Salience Network

As the name suggests, the underlying pathological changes in bvFTD initially target the prefrontal cortices, although widespread atrophy is evident from early in the disease trajectory affecting the dorsal mPFC, ACC/fIN, amygdala, thalamus, and striatum (see Fig. 8.2). The most striking alterations occur in the brain's Salience Network, a functional brain network posited to process emotionally salient information in the external environment, and to facilitate the dynamic switching between internally and externally focused cognition (Menon & Uddin, 2010). Anchored on the orbitofrontal cortices, dorsal ACC and fIN regions, the Salience Network benefits from robust connections to subcortical and limbic structures, and is recruited in response to attention-orienting changes in the external environment. Notably, bvFTD pathology appears to preferentially target the Salience Network (Fig. 8.2) and this network-specific vulnerability has been suggested to underpin the constellation of socio-emotional disturbances typically seen in this syndrome (Seeley et al., 2012).

8.5.6 Sociocognitive dysfunction: impaired Theory of Mind in the behavioural variant of frontotemporal dementia

The evidence to date overwhelmingly points to pervasive mentalizing difficulties in bvFTD. Indeed, aberrant social cognitive functioning is a hallmark diagnostic feature of this syndrome (Bora et al., 2015; Henry et al., 2014; Wong et al., 2018). Irrespective of the experimental task or the nature of the stimuli employed, bvFTD patients display a host of sociocognitive reasoning impairments including, but not limited to, first- and second-order belief interpretation (Eslinger et al., 2007; Gregory et al., 2002), faux pas detection (Bertoux et al., 2015; Torralva et al., 2007; Ramanan et al., 2017b), and drawing mental state inferences from verbal and pictorial stimuli (Irish et al., 2014; Shany-Ur et al., 2012; Lough et al., 2006).

While it has been suggested that executive dysfunction is a key driver of ToM impairments in bvFTD (Poletti et al., 2012), conflicting findings exist in the literature (Roca et al., 2011; Johnen & Bertoux, 2019). On the one hand, data-driven cluster-based and regression analyses suggest almost no shared statistical variance between ToM impairments and co-occurring executive, memory, and general cognitive decline in bvFTD (Ramanan et al., 2017b; Bertoux et al., 2015). Moreover, other studies have demonstrated that bvFTD patients display ToM difficulties on simple first-order false belief tasks but not on their counterpart first-order control questions, which involve comparable cognitive and executive demands devoid of the mentalizing component (Lough et al., 2001; Gregory et al., 2002; Adenzato et al., 2010). These findings reinforce the proposal that ToM deficits in bvFTD emerge independently from cognitive dysfunction. ToM disturbances in bvFTD may reflect a primary socio-emotional impairment given the characteristic early and pervasive emotional blunting and diminished autonomic responses towards emotional stimuli (Joshi et al., 2014). Nevertheless, evidence of co-occurring and comparable levels of sociocognitive and socioaffective disturbances in bvFTD (Henry et al., 2014), would suggest that emotion-processing difficulties do not fully account for ToM impairments in this syndrome.

A further proposal is that mentalizing difficulties in bvFTD may stem, in part, from a person's inability to inhibit their own perspective, rather than an exclusive deficit in the inference of mental states in general (Le Bouc et al., 2012). Mentalizing not only requires the ability to introspect to consider the perspective of another person, it also relies upon our capacity to inhibit the prepotent tendency to take one's own viewpoint and to differentiate our own sense of self from that of others (Amodio & Frith, 2006). Mounting evidence of an impaired capacity for introspection and self-referential processing (Wong et al., 2017, Strikwerda-Brown, Grilli, Andrews-Hanna, & Irish, 2019) in bvFTD, as well as a profound inability to disengage from the immediate sensorium (O'Callaghan et al., 2019), suggest that any number of candidate mechanisms may underlie the sociocognitive disturbances characteristic of this syndrome.

8.5.7 Socioaffective disturbances: loss of empathy in the behavioural variant of frontotemporal dementia

In parallel with marked ToM and emotion decoding difficulties, a reduction in empathy represents one of the earliest diagnostic markers of bvFTD (Carr & Mendez, 2018). Carer ratings of empathic concern on the IRI consistently reveal a stark loss of empathy in the bvFTD patient relative to their premorbid personality (Eslinger et al., 2011; Hsieh et al., 2013; Hutchings et al., 2015; Shdo et al., 2018). Notably, bvFTD patients commonly rate their current levels of empathy as within the normal range (Eslinger et al., 2011; Hutchings et al., 2015) or even *overestimate* their capacity for empathic concern (Sollberger et al., 2014), suggesting a profound lack of insight into their socio-emotional difficulties. Loss of empathy in bvFTD has far-reaching consequences, with studies suggesting it relates to reduced prosocial behaviour (Sturm et al., 2017) but also increased rates of infidelity and relationship dissolution (Takeda et al., 2019). Such associations are unsurprising given that the pervasive lack of empathy is reported by carers as particularly difficult to adjust to, with the seemingly 'cold-hearted' and 'callous' nature of patients compounding the social and marital stress endemic to bvFTD (Hsieh et al., 2013).

Socioaffective empathy disturbances in bvFTD have also been documented on experimental tasks incorporating ecologically valid stimuli, in which misfortune or harm is observed to befall the protagonist. For example, bvFTD patients demonstrate clear difficulties in inferring and empathizing with the emotional state of protagonists in naturalistic film clips (Fernandez-Duque et al., 2010) and on cartoons that depict misfortunes (Cerami et al., 2014). The intentionality of the harm appears to play a crucial role in modulating the response of bvFTD patients. When watching animated scenarios where protagonists are subjected to intentional harm, bvFTD patients display less empathy compared with healthy controls (Baez et al., 2014). By contrast, when harm is depicted as accidental (e.g. the protagonist trips over a carpet edge), bvFTD patients display a comparable empathic response to controls (Baez et al., 2014). Disrupted capacity for empathy may also relate to the propensity to engage in normative social behaviours, as has recently been demonstrated using a neuroeconomic task in bvFTD. Reduced levels of empathy in bvFTD were associated with the tendency to reject unfair offers on the Ultimatum Game, in violation of normative social expectations (O'Callaghan et al., 2016). The authors suggest that normative social behaviours on the Ultimatum Game may serve as a useful surrogate for everyday expressions of empathy, a proposal that will be important to test in future studies exploring complex social behaviours such as punishment and prosociality (O'Callaghan et al., 2016).

Turning to the cognitive mechanisms underpinning socioaffective disturbances in bvFTD, the most intuitive proposal is that reductions in empathic concern reflect a fundamental disruption in the recognition and labelling of emotions, particularly negative emotions (Kumfor et al., 2013a). As previously discussed in relation to AD, context plays an important role in modulating the empathic response of bvFTD patients. For example, in conditions of low contextual support, bvFTD patients display diminished empathic responses (Ibanez & Manes, 2012; Baez et al., 2017), as is typically observed on experimental paradigms in which the intentionality of a harmful action must be inferred. In contrast, bvFTD patients tend to display appropriate levels of empathy when witnessing accidental harm or when actors in videos explicitly display their emotional states (Fernandez-Duque et al., 2010; Baez et al., 2014). Whether manipulating contextual information to accentuate the intentionality of the act, or the emotional response of the protagonist, may improve empathic responses in bvFTD is an important question for future studies to explore.

8.5.8 Neural substrates of sociocognitive and socioaffective disturbances in the behavioural variant of frontotemporal dementia

Up until recently, the pervasive ToM impairment in bvFTD was ascribed predominantly to degeneration of the mPFC, a key node of the brain's DMN (Amodio & Frith, 2006). Neurodegenerative disorders, however, rarely target single brain regions in isolation and are better conceptualized as network phenomena (Ahmed et al., 2016; Irish et al., 2012). Deficits in higher-level sociocognitive abilities in bvFTD reflect the aberrant functioning of prefrontal *and* temporoparietal nodes of the 'social brain' (Figs 8.1 and 8.2) and, more macroscopically, the abnormal modulation of the DMN by the Salience Network (Chiong et al., 2013). A key region of interest in this context is the ACC/fIN, a core node of the Salience Network that appears particularly vulnerable to the bvFTD pathological process. The degeneration of ACC/fIN regions is consistently implicated in sociocognitive ToM difficulties in both verbal and non-verbal mentalizing tasks in bvFTD, suggesting a fundamental role in interpersonal difficulties in this syndrome. We caution, however, that ACC/fIN involvement is observed in parallel with mPFC/OFC, lateral temporal, and posterior parietal contributions (Irish et al., 2014; Synn et al., 2018; Brioschi Guevara et al., 2015), underscoring the importance of adopting a network approach to understanding the nature of social dysfunction in bvFTD.

The same argument can be made in relation to the neural substrates of socioaffective empathy disturbances in bvFTD. For example, emotional attribution deficits in bvFTD have been linked to atrophy in the Salience Network as well as resting state abnormalities in dorsomedial prefrontal cortices of the DMN (Caminiti et al., 2015). Notably, carer-rated decline in Empathic Concern on the IRI has been associated with grey matter intensity decrease in orbitofrontal and prefrontal, ACC/fIN, and inferior parietal cortices (Dermody et al., 2016). While the prefrontal and ACC/fIN contributions to empathy performance are well established in bvFTD (Baez et al., 2016, Rankin et al., 2006, Eslinger et al., 2011), we note mounting evidence for a disease-specific vulnerability of ACC/fIN *and* temporoparietal regions (Cerami et al., 2014), the accumulation of which likely gives rise to the widespread sociocognitive and socioaffective disturbances in this syndrome.

8.6 The ageing brain—future directions

We conclude this chapter at an important juncture in research on social cognition in ageing and dementia. Where healthy ageing is concerned, we see clear evidence of stability and improvements in socio-emotional functioning in older adults, accompanied by shifts in motivational priorities and life goals that may account for the discrepant findings in the literature. Couching ageing solely in terms of *loss* of function neglects a host of adaptive and potentially compensatory processes that enable older adults to prioritize socio-emotional information (Reiter et al., 2017), which in turn may augment socioaffective processes such as empathy. The extant research strongly suggests differential age-related changes in social cognition, with difficulties emerging on cognitively demanding sociocognitive ToM tasks, in the context of *adaptive* changes by which socioaffective processing is enhanced. These changes likely serve to promote well-being in an otherwise challenging stage of life (Andrews-Hanna et al., 2019), but their relationship to shifts in overall task engagement, perceived difficulty, and social motivation remain unclear. There is increasing awareness that many of the currently available social cognitive tasks are poor surrogates for real-world behaviour given their de-contextualized nature, high cognitive demand, and failure to use age-appropriate stimuli. Future research incorporating naturalistic paradigms that are attuned to the social and motivational goals of older adults will be crucial to ensure that we accurately capture the intricacies of social processing across the lifespan (see, for example, Johansson Nolaker et al., 2018).

Where pathological ageing is concerned, the evidence to date suggests a transdiagnostic disruption of sociocognitive reasoning (i.e. ToM) in dementia (Strikwerda-Brown et al., 2019), the mechanisms of which are likely to be multifactorial. While important insights have been gleaned from neuroimaging studies, it is important to note that these brain-behavioural associations are correlational and limit our understanding of causal mechanisms. To that end, longitudinal studies tracking the evolution of social cognitive disturbances will be important to gain a thorough understanding of how the progressive degeneration of large-scale functional networks has differential impacts on distinct aspects of interpersonal functioning.

Dementia represents the ultimate test of social cognition and interpersonal bonds. When viewed in this context, older adults in caring roles occupy a precipitous position. An individual living with AD will face difficulties in cognitive perspective taking and ToM/mentalizing, yet may display preserved warmth and affability to those around them. In contrast, the profound changes in ToM and empathy in bvFTD can prove extremely challenging for carers, and have a negative impact on the carer–patient relationship (Hsieh et al., 2013). Trying to view the changing perspective of the individual with dementia, to understand thoughts and beliefs that may be incongruent with current contextual information, and to empathize and remain compassionate in the face of blunted affect or seemingly callous behaviour, is extremely challenging. It is not surprising, therefore, that carers of bvFTD patients are particularly vulnerable to stress, burnout, and depression. Given the cognitive and neural changes associated with normal ageing, older adults tend to focus on smaller and more valuable social friendships, leading to a narrowing of their social groups. When placed in a caring role, these adaptive changes may progressively lead to social isolation. One of the great challenges of the coming decades, therefore, will be to optimize healthy ageing and to minimize the burden of carer roles, while ensuring that individuals with dementia and their families can continue to live meaningful and socially engaged lives.

References

Adenzato, M., Cavallo, M., & Enrici, I., 2010. 'Theory of mind ability in the behavioural variant of frontotemporal dementia: An analysis of the neural, cognitive, and social levels'. *Neuropsychologia* 48. 1: 2–12.

Ahmed, R. M., Devenney, E. M., Irish, M., Ittner, A., Naismith, S., ... & Kiernan, M. C., 2016. 'Neuronal network disintegration: Common pathways linking neurodegenerative diseases'. *Journal of Neurology, Neurosurgery & Psychiatry* 87. 11: 1234–1241.

Allman, J. M., Tetreault, N. A., Hakeem, A. Y., Manaye, K. F., Semendeferi, K., Erwin, J., ... & Hof, P. R., 2010. 'The von economo neurons in the frontoinsular and anterior cingulate cortex in great apes ans humans'. *Brain Structure and Function* 214. 5–6: 59–71.

Amodio, D. M., & Frith, C. D., 2006. 'Meeting of minds: The medial frontal cortex and social cognition'. *Nature Reviews Neuroscience* 7. 4: 268–277.

Andrews-Hanna, J. R., Grilli, M. D., & Irish, M., 2019. 'A review and reappraisal of the default network in normal ageing and dementia'. In *Oxford Encyclopedia of Psychology and Ageing*, edited by R. T. Knight et al., Oxford University Press, pp. 725–741

Baez, S., Garcia, A. M., & Ibanez, A., 2017. 'The social context network model in psychiatric and neurological diseases'. In *Social Behavior from Rodents to Humans. Current Topics in Behavioral Neurosciences*, vol. 30, edited by M. Wöhr & S. Krach, Springer.

Baez, S., Manes, F., Huepe, D., Torralva, T., Fiorentino, N., Richter, F., ... & Ibanez, A., 2014. 'Primary empathy deficits in frontotemporal dementia'. *Frontiers in Aging Neuroscience* 6: 262.

Baez, S., Morales, J. P., Slachevsky, A., Torralva, T., Matus, C., Manes, F., & Ibanez, A., 2016. 'Orbitofrontal and limbic signatures of empathic concern and intentional harm in the behavioral variant frontotemporal dementia'. *Cortex* 75: 20–32.

Bailey, P. E., Henry, J. D., & Von Hippel, W., 2008. 'Empathy and social functioning in late adulthood'. *Aging and Mental Health* 12. 4: 499–503.

Bartochowski, Z., Gatla, S., Khoury, R., Al-Dahhak, R., & Grossberg, G. T., 2018. 'Empathy changes in neurocognitive disorders: A review'. *Annals of Clinical Psychiatry* 30. 3: 220–232.

Beadle, J. N., & de la Vega, C. E., 2019. 'Impact of aging on empathy: Review of psychological and neural mechanisms'. *Frontiers in Psychiatry 10*: 331.

Bertoux, M., O'Callaghan, C., Dubois, B., & Hornberger, M., 2015. 'In two minds: Executive functioning versus theory of mind in behavioural variant frontotemporal dementia'. *Journal of Neurology, Neurosurgery & Psychiatry* 87. 3: 231–234.

Bora, E., Walterfang, M., & Velakoulis, D., 2015. 'Theory of mind in behavioural-variant frontotemporal dementia and Alzheimer's disease: a meta-analysis'. *Journal of Neurology, Neurosurgery & Psychiatry* 86. 7: 714–719.

Braak, H., & Braak, E., 1991. 'Neuropathological stageing of Alzheimer-related changes'. *Acta Neuropathologica* 82. 4: 239–259.

Brioschi Guevara, A., Knutson, K. M., Wassermann, E. M., Pulaski, S., Grafman, J., & Krueger, F., 2015. 'Theory of mind impairment in patients with behavioural variant fronto-temporal dementia (bv-FTD) increases caregiver burden'. *Age and Ageing* 44. 5: 891–895.

Buckner, R. L., Snyder, A. Z., Shannon, B. J., Larossa, G., Sachs, R., Fotenos, A. F., . . . & Mintun, M. A., 2005. 'Molecular, structural, and functional characterization of Alzheimer's disease: Evidence for a relationship between default activity, amyloid, and memory'. *Journal of Neuroscience* 25. 34: 7709–7717.

Caminiti, S. P., Canessa, N., Cerami, C., Dodich, A., Crespi, C., Iannaccone, S., . . . & Cappa, S. F., 2015. 'Affective mentalizing and brain activity at rest in the behavioral variant of frontotemporal dementia'. *NeuroImage: Clinical* 9: 484–497.

Carr, A. R., & Mendez, M. F., 2018. 'Affective empathy in behavioral variant frontotemporal dementia: a meta-analysis'. *Frontiers in Neurology* 9: 417.

Carstensen, L. L., Isaacowitz, D. M., & Charles, S. T., 1999. 'Taking time seriously. A theory of socioemotional selectivity'. *American Psychologist* 54. 3: 165–181.

Cassidy, B. S., Shih, J. Y., & Gutchess, A. H., 2012. 'Age-related changes to the neural correlates of social evaluation'. *Social Neuroscience* 7. 6: 552–564.

Castelli, I., Baglio, F., Blasi, V., Alberoni, M., Falini, A., Liverta-Sempio, O., Nemni, R., & Marchetti, A., 2010. 'Effects of aging on mindreading ability through the eyes: an fMRI study'. *Neuropsychologia* 48. 9: 2586–2594.

Cavanna, A. E., & Trimble, M. R., 2006. 'The precuneus: A review of its functional anatomy and behavioural correlates'. *Brain* 129. 3: 564–583.

Cerami, C., Dodich, A., Canessa, N., Crespi, C., Marcone, A., Cortese, F., . . . & Cappa, S. F., 2014. 'Neural correlates of empathic impairment in the behavioral variant of frontotemporal dementia'. *Alzheimer's & Dementia* 10. 6: 827–834.

Chen, Y. C., Chen, C. C., Decety, J., & Cheng, Y., 2014. 'Aging is associated with changes in the neural circuits underlying empathy'. *Neurobiology of Aging* 35. 4: 827–836.

Chiong, W., Wilson, S. M., D'esposito, M., Kayser, A. S., Grossman, S. N., Poorzand, P., . . . & Rankin, K. P., 2013. 'The salience network causally influences default mode network activity during moral reasoning'. *Brain* 136. 6: 1929–1941.

Christidi, F., Migliaccio, R., Santamaria-Garcia, H., Santangelo, G., & Trojsi, F., 2018. 'Social cognition dysfunctions in neurodegenerative diseases: Neuroanatomical correlates and clinical implications'. *Behavioural Neurology*: 1849794.

Davis, M. H., 1983. 'Measuring individual differences in empathy: Evidence for a multidimensional approach'. *Journal of Personality and Social Psychology* 44. 1: 113–126.

Dermody, N., Wong, S., Ahmed, R., Piguet, O., Hodges, J. R., & Irish, M., 2016. 'Uncovering the neural bases of cognitive and affective empathy deficits in Alzheimer's disease and the behavioral-variant of frontotemporal dementia'. *Journal of Alzheimer's Disease* 53. 3: 801–816.

Duclos, H., Desgranges, B., Eustache, F., & Laisney, M., 2018. 'Impairment of social cognition in neurological diseases'. *Revue Neurologique (Paris)* 174. 4: 190–198.

Elamin, M., Pender, N., Hardiman, O., & Abrahams, S., 2012. 'Social cognition in neurodegenerative disorders: A systematic review'. *Journal of Neurology, Neurosurgery & Psychiatry* 83. 11: 1071–1079.

Eslinger, P. J., Moore, P., Anderson, C., & Grossman, M., 2011. 'Social cognition, executive functioning, and neuroimaging correlates of empathic deficits in frontotemporal dementia'. *Journal of Neuropsychiatry and Clinical Neurosciences* 23. 1: 74–82.

Eslinger, P. J., Moore, P., Troiani, V., Antani, S., Cross, K., Kwok, S., & Grossman, M., 2007. 'Oops! Resolving social dilemmas in frontotemporal dementia'. *Journal of Neurology, Neurosurgery & Psychiatry* 78. 5: 457–460.

Fernandez-Duque, D., Baird, J. A., & Black, S. E., 2009. 'False-belief understanding in frontotemporal dementia and Alzheimer's disease'. *Journal of Clinical and Experimental Neuropsychology* 31. 4: 489–497.

Fernandez-Duque, D., Hodges, S. D., Baird, J. A., & Black, S. E., 2010. 'Empathy in frontotemporal dementia and alzheimer's disease'. *Journal of Clinical and Experimental Neuropsychology* 32. 3: 289–298.

Fischer, A., Landeira-Fernandez, J., Sollero De Campos, F., & Mograbi, D. C., 2019. 'Empathy in Alzheimer's disease: Review of findings and proposed model'. *Journal of Alzheimer's Disease* 69. 4: 921–933.

Fjell, A. M., Westlye, L. T., Amlien, I., Espeseth, T., Reinvang, I., Raz, N., ... & Dale, A. M., 2009. 'High consistency of regional cortical thinning in aging across multiple samples'. *Cerebral Cortex* 19. 9: 2001–2012.

Fortier, J., Besnard, J., & Allain, P., 2018. 'Theory of mind, empathy and emotion perception in cortical and subcortical neurodegenerative diseases'. *Revue Neurologique (Paris)* 174. 4: 237–246.

Frith, C. D., 2007. 'The social brain?' *Philosophical Transactions of the Royal Society B: Biological Sciences* 362. 1480: 671–678.

Gallagher, H., & Frith, C., 2003. 'Functional imaging of "theory of mind"'. *Trends in Cognitive Sciences* 7. 2: 77–83.

Gregory, C., Lough, S., Stone, V., Erzinclioglu, S., Martin, L., Baron-Cohen, S., & Hodges, J. R., 2002. 'Theory of mind in patients with frontal variant frontotemporal dementia and Alzheimer's disease: Theoretical and practical implications'. *Brain* 125. 4: 752–764.

Gutchess, A., & Kensinger, E. A., 2018. 'Shared mechanisms may support mnemonic benefits from self-referencing and emotion'. *Trends in Cognitive Sciences* 22. 8: 712–724.

Henry, J. D., Phillips, L. H., & Von Hippel, C., 2014. 'A meta-analytic review of theory of mind difficulties in behavioural-variant frontotemporal dementia'. *Neuropsychologia* 56: 53–62.

Hsieh, S., Irish, M., Daveson, N., Hodges, J. R., & Piguet, O., 2013. 'When one loses empathy: its effect on carers of patients with dementia'. *Journal of Geriatric Psychiatry and Neurology* 26. 3: 174–184.

Hutchings, R., Hodges, J. R., Piguet, O., Kumfor, F., & Boutoleau-Bretonniere, C., 2015. 'Why should I care? Dimensions of socio-emotional cognition in younger-onset dementia'. *Journal of Alzheimer's Disease* 48. 1: 135–147.

Ibanez, A., & Manes, F., 2012. 'Contextual social cognition and the behavioral variant of frontotemporal dementia'. *Neurology* 78. 17: 1354–1362.

Irish, M., & Piguet, O., 2013. 'The pivotal role of semantic memory in remembering the past and imagining the future'. *Frontiers in Behavioral Neuroscience* 7: 27.

Irish, M., & Van Kesteren, M. T., 2018. 'New perspectives on the brain lesion approach—Implications for theoretical models of human memory'. *Neuroscience* 374: 319–322.

Irish, M., Hodges, J. R., & Piguet, O., 2014. 'Right anterior temporal lobe dysfunction underlies theory of mind impairments in semantic dementia'. *Brain* 137. 4: 1241–1253.

Irish, M., Piguet, O., & Hodges, J. R., 2012. 'Self-projection and the default network in frontotemporal dementia'. *Nature Reviews Neurology* 8. 3: 152–161.

Irish, M., Lawlor, B. A., O'Mara, S. M., & Coen, R. F., 2011. 'Impaired capacity for autonoetic reliving during autobiographical event recall in mild Alzheimer's disease'. *Cortex* 47. 2: 236–249.

Irish, M., Goldberg, Z. L., Alaeddin, S., O'Callaghan, C., & Andrews-Hanna, J. R., 2019. 'Age-related changes in the temporal focus and self-referential content of spontaneous cognition during periods of low cognitive demand'. *Psychological Research* 83. 4: 747–760.

Johansson Nolaker, E., Murray, K., Happe, F., & Charlton, R. A., 2018. 'Cognitive and affective associations with an ecologically valid test of theory of mind across the lifespan'. *Neuropsychology* 32. 6: 754–763.

Johnen, A., & Bertoux, M., 2019. 'Psychological and cognitive markers of behavioral variant frontotemporal dementia—A clinical neuropsychologist's view on diagnostic criteria and beyond'. *Frontiers in Neurology* 10: 594.

Jones, D. T., Knopman, D. S., Gunter, J. L., Graff-Radford, J., Vemuri, P., Boeve, B. F., … & Alzheimer's Disease Neuroimaging Initiative, 2016. 'Cascading network failure across the Alzheimer's disease spectrum'. *Brain* 139. 2: 547–562.

Joshi, A., Mendez, M. F., Kaiser, N., Jimenez, E., Mather, M., & Shapira, J. S., 2014. 'Skin conductance levels may reflect emotional blunting in behavioral variant frontotemporal dementia'. *Journal of Neuropsychiatry and Clinical Neurosciences* 26. 3: 227–32.

Kanske, P., Bockler, A., Trautwein, F. M., Parianen Lesemann, F. H., & Singer, T., 2016. 'Are strong empathizers better mentalizers? Evidence for independence and interaction between the routes of social cognition'. *Social Cognitive and Affective Neuroscience* 11. 9: 1383–1392.

Krendl, A. C., & Ambady, N., 2010. 'Older adults' decoding of emotions: Role of dynamic versus static cues and age-related cognitive decline'. *Psychology and Aging* 25. 4: 788–793.

Kumfor, F., Irish, M., Hodges, J. R., & Piguet, O., 2013a. 'Discrete neural correlates for the recognition of negative emotions: Insights from frontotemporal dementia'. *PloS One* 8. 6: E67457.

Kumfor F., Irish, M., Hodges, J. R., & Piguet, O., 2013b. 'The orbitofrontal cortex is involved in emotional enhancement of memory: Evidence from the dementias'. *Brain* 136. 10: 2992–3003.

Kumfor, F., Irish, M., Leyton, C., Miller, L., Lah, S., Devenney, E., … & Piguet, O., 2014. 'Tracking the progression of social cognition in neurodegenerative disorders'. *Journal of Neurology, Neurosurgery & Psychiatry* 85. 10: 1076–1083.

Laillier, R., Viard, A., Caillaud, M., Duclos, H., Bejanin, A., de La Sayette, V., … & Laisney, M., 2019. 'Neurocognitive determinants of theory of mind across the adult lifespan'. *Brain and Cognition 136:* 103588.

Lamm, C., Batson, C. D., & Decety, J., 2007. 'The neural substrate of human empathy: Effects of perspective-taking and cognitive appraisal'. *Journal of Cognitive Neuroscience* 19. 1: 42–58.

Le Bouc, R., Lenfant, P., Delbeuck, X., Ravasi, L., Lebert, F., Semah, F., & Pasquier, F., 2012. 'My belief or yours? differential theory of mind deficits in frontotemporal dementia and Alzheimer's disease'. *Brain* 135. 10: 3026–3038.

Liljegren, M., Naasan, G., Temlett, J., Perry, D. C., Rankin, K. P., Merrilees, J., . . . & Miller, B. L., 2015. 'Criminal behavior in frontotemporal dementia and Alzheimer disease'. *JAMA Neurology* 72. 3: 295–300.

Lough, S., Gregory, C., & Hodges, J. R., 2001. 'Dissociation of social cognition and executive function in frontal variant frontotemporal dementia'. *Neurocase* 7: 123–130.

Lough, S., Kipps, C., Treise, C., Watson, P., Blair, J., & Hodges, J., 2006. 'Social reasoning, emotion and empathy in frontotemporal dementia'. *Neuropsychologia* 44. 6: 950–958.

Mather, M., & Carstensen, L. L., 2005. 'Aging and motivated cognition: The positivity effect in attention and memory'. *Trends in Cognitive Sciences* 9. 10: 496–502.

Menon, V., & Uddin, L. Q., 2010. 'Saliency, switching, attention and control: A network model of insula function'. *Brain Structure and Function* 214. 5–6: 655–667.

Montagrin, A., Saiote, C., & Schiller, D., 2017. 'The social hippocampus'. *Hippocampus* 28. 9: 672–679.

Moran, J. M., 2013. 'Lifespan development: The effects of typical aging on theory of mind'. *Behavioural Brain Research* 237: 32–40.

Moran, J. M., Jolly, E., & Mitchell, J. P., 2012. 'Social-cognitive deficits in normal ageing'. *Journal of Neuroscience* 32. 16: 5553–5561.

Nash, S., Henry, J. D., Mcdonald, S., Martin, I., Brodaty, H., & Peek-O'leary, M. A., 2007. 'Cognitive disinhibition and socioemotional functioning in Alzheimer's disease'. *Journal of the International Neuropsychological Society* 13. 6: 1060–1064.

O'Callaghan, C., & Irish, M., 2018. 'Candidate mechanisms of spontaneous cognition as revealed by dementia syndromes'. In *The Oxford Handbook Of Spontaneous Thought: Mind-Wandering, Creativity, And Dreaming*, edited by K. Christoff & K. C. Fox. Oxford University Press.

O'Callaghan, C., Shine, J. M., Hodges, J. R., Andrews-Hanna, J. R., & Irish, M., 2019. 'Hippocampal atrophy and intrinsic brain network dysfunction relate to alterations in mind wandering in neurodegeneration'. *Proceedings of the National Academy of Sciences* 116. 8: 3316–3321.

O'Callaghan, C., Bertoux, M., Irish, M., Shine, J. M., Wong, S., Spiliopoulos, L., ... & Hornberger, M., 2016. 'Fair play: Social norm compliance failures in behavioural variant frontotemporal dementia'. *Brain* 139. 1: 204–216.

Olson, I. R., Plotzker, A., & Ezzyat, Y., 2007. 'The enigmatic temporal pole: A review of findings on social and emotional processing'. *Brain* 130. 7: 1718–1731.

Park, D. C., & Reuter-Lorenz, P., 2009. 'The adaptive brain: Ageing and neurocognitive scaffolding'. *Annual Review of Psychology* 60: 173–196.

Poletti, M., Enrici, I., & Adenzato, M., 2012. 'Cognitive and affective theory of mind in neurodegenerative diseases: Neuropsychological, neuroanatomical and neurochemical levels'. *Neuroscience & Biobehavioral Reviews* 36. 9: 2147–2164.

Premack, D., & Woodruff, G., 1978. 'Does the chimpanzee have a Theory of Mind?'. *Behavioural and Brain Sciences* 1. 4: 515–526.

Ramanan, S., Bertoux, M., Flanagan, E., Irish, M., Piguet, O., Hodges, J. R., & Hornberger, M., 2017a. 'Longitudinal executive function and episodic memory profiles in behavioral-variant frontotemporal dementia and Alzheimer's disease'. *Journal of the International Neuropsychological Society* 23. 1: 34–43.

Ramanan, S., De Souza, L. C., Moreau, N., Sarazin, M., Teixeira, A. L., Allen, Z., ... & Bertoux, M., 2017b. 'Determinants of theory of mind performance in alzheimer's disease: A data-mining study'. *Cortex* 88: 8–18.

Rankin, K. P., Kramer, J. H., & Miller, B. L., 2005. 'Patterns of cognitive and emotional empathy in frontotemporal lobar degeneration'. *Cognitive and Behavioral Neurology* 18. 1: 28–36.

Rankin, K. P., Gorno-Tempini, M. L., Allison, S. C., Stanley, C. M., Glenn, S., Weiner, M. W., & Miller, B. L., 2006. 'Structural anatomy of empathy in neurodegenerative disease'. *Brain* 129. 11: 2945–2956.

Reiter, A. M. F., Kanske, P., Eppinger, B., & Li, S. C., 2017. 'The ageing of the social mind—differential effects on components of social understanding'. *Scientific Reports* 7. 1: 1–8.

Riva, F., Tschernegg, M., Chiesa, P. A., Wagner, I. C., Kronbichler, M., Lamm, C., & Silani, G., 2018. 'Age-related differences in the neural correlates of empathy for pleasant and unpleasant touch in a female sample'. *Neurobiology of Aging* 65: 7–17.

Roca, M., Torralva, T., Gleichgerrcht, E., Woolgar, A., Thompson, R., Duncan, J., & Manes, F., 2011. 'The role of area 10 (BA10) in human multitasking and in social cognition: a lesion study'. *Neuropsychologia* 49. 13: 3525–3531.

Saxe, R., & Wexler, A., 2005. 'Making sense of another mind: The role of the right temporoparietal junction'. *Neuropsychologia* 43. 13: 1391–1399.

Scheibe, S., & Carstensen, L. L., 2010. 'Emotional aging: Recent findings and future trends'. *Journals of Gerontology: Series B* 65. 2: 135–144.

Seeley, W. W., Zhou, J., & Kim, E. J., 2012. 'Frontotemporal dementia: What can the behavioral variant teach us about human brain organization?' *Neuroscientist* 18. 4: 373–385.

Shany-Ur, T., Poorzand, P., Grossman, S. N., Growdon, M. E., Jang, J. Y., Ketelle, R. S., ... & Rankin, K. P., 2012. 'Comprehension of insincere communication in neurodegenerative disease: Lies, sarcasm, and theory of mind'. *Cortex* 48. 10: 1329–1341.

Shdo, S. M., Ranasinghe, K. G., Gola, K. A., Mielke, C. J., Sukhanov, P. V., Miller, B. L., & Rankin, K. P., 2018. 'Deconstructing empathy: Neuroanatomical dissociations between affect sharing and prosocial motivation using a patient lesion model'. *Neuropsychologia* 116: 126–135.

Slessor, G., Phillips, L. H., & Bull, R., 2007. 'Exploring the specificity of age-related differences in theory of mind tasks'. *Psychology and Aging* 22. 3: 639–643.

Sollberger, M., Rosen, H. J., Shany-Ur, T., Ullah, J., Stanley, C. M., Laluz, V., ... & Rankin, K. P., 2014. 'Neural substrates of socioemotional self-awareness in neurodegenerative disease'. *Brain and Behavior* 4. 2: 201–214.

Sperling, R. A., Dickerson, B. C., Pihlajamaki, M., Vannini, P., Laviolette, P. S., Vitolo, O., ... & Johnson, K. A., 2010. 'Functional alterations in memory networks in early Alzheimer's disease'. *Neuromolecular Medicine* 12. 1: 27–43.

Strikwerda-Brown, C. Grilli, M.D., Andrews-Hanna, J.R., & Irish, M. 2019. "All is not lost" – Rethinking the nature of memory and the self in dementia. *Ageing Research Review* 54: 100932.

Strikwerda-Brown, C., Ramanan, S., & Irish, M., 2019. 'Neurocognitive mechanisms of theory of mind impairment in neurodegeneration: A transdiagnostic approach'. *Neuropsychiatric Disease and Treatment* 15: 557–573.

Sturm, V. E., Perry, D. C., Wood, K., Hua, A. Y., Alcantar, O., Datta, S., ... & Kramer, J. H., 2017. 'Prosocial deficits in behavioral variant frontotemporal dementia relate to reward network atrophy'. *Brain and Behavior* 7. 10: e00807.

Synn, A., Mothakunnel, A., Kumfor, F., Chen, Y., Piguet, O., Hodges, J. R., & Irish, M., 2018. 'mental states in moving shapes: Distinct cortical and subcortical contributions to theory of mind impairments in dementia'. *Journal of Alzheimer's Disease* 61. 2: 521–535.

Sze, J. A., Gyurak, A., Goodkind, M. S., & Levenson, R. W., 2012. 'Greater emotional empathy and prosocial behavior in late life'. *Emotion* 12. 5: 1129–1140.

Takeda, A., Sturm, V. E., Rankin, K. P., Ketelle, R., Miller, B. L., & Perry, D. C., 2019. 'Relationship turmoil and emotional empathy in frontotemporal dementia'. *Alzheimer Disease and Associated Disorders* 33. 3: 260–265.

Torralva, T., Kipps, C., Hodges, J. R., Clark, L., Bekinschtein, T., Roca, M., ... & Manes, F., 2007. 'The relationship between affective decision-making and theory of mind in the frontal variant of fronto-temporal dementia'. *Neuropsychologia* 45. 2: 342–349.

Van Overwalle, F., Baetens, K., Marien, P., & Vandekerckhove, M., 2014. 'Social cognition and the cerebellum: A meta-analysis of over 350 fMRI studies'. *NeuroImage* 86: 554–572.

Wang, Z., & Su, Y., 2013. 'Age-related differences in the performance of theory of mind in older adults: A dissociation of cognitive and affective components'. *Psychology and Aging*: 28. 1: 284–291.

Wilson, N. A., Ahmed, R., Hodges, J. R., Piguet, O., & Irish, M., 2020. 'Constructing the social world: Evidence for a core constructive deficit in frontotemporal dementia'. *Cognition* 202: 104321.

Wong, S., Irish, M., & Hornberger, M., 2018. 'Behavioural-variant frontotemporal dementia: A unique window into the disrupted self: Reply to Genon & Salmon'. *Cortex* 104: 130–132.

Wong, S., Irish, M., Leshikar, E. D., Duarte, A., Bertoux, M., Savage, G., ... & Hornberger, M., 2017. 'The self-reference effect in dementia: differential involvement of cortical midline structures in alzheimer's disease and behavioural-variant frontotemporal dementia'. *Cortex* 91: 169–185.

Zaitchik, D., Koff, E., Brownell, H., Winner, E., & Albert, M., 2006. 'Inference of beliefs and emotions in patients with alzheimer's disease'. *Neuropsychology* 20. 1: 11–20.

Zaki, J., & Ochsner, K. N., 2012. 'The neuroscience of empathy: Progress, pitfalls and promise'. *Nature Neuroscience* 15. 5: 675–680.

9
The Future of Research on Social Interaction

Elisabeth E. F. Bradford, Martina De Lillo, and Heather J. Ferguson

9.1 Introduction

Social cognition, or social interaction, abilities have been the topic of a significant amount of research across past decades, examining questions such as when and how social cognition abilities first emerge in infants, how social cognition capacities develop throughout childhood, and the implications of deficits in social cognition abilities that can be seen with advancing age in neurotypical ageing. Difficulties in social cognition capacities are associated with detrimental effects for individuals, including declines in social well-being and social motivation, and reports of higher levels of loneliness, depressive symptoms, and anxiety (e.g. Bailey et al., 2008; Sullivan & Ruffman, 2004; Strang et al., 2012). Given these findings, the importance of developing our understanding of social cognition is highlighted as an extremely important area of research to continue to focus on. However, current research is limited in its applications due to a number of constraints, including focus on lab-based measures that reduce our ability to assess the impact of social cognition capacities on everyday life; focus on specific populations, most commonly Western, white, undergraduate individuals; and limited collaborative approaches to studying social cognition that would allow a wider understanding of social cognition abilities 'in situ'.

Beyond examining the development and declines seen in social communication capacities across the lifespan, there remains many open questions regarding so-called 'mindreading' abilities when examining individuals who are in possession of fully developed social cognition concepts. For instance, what makes some individuals better mindreaders than other people? Does having an 'enhanced' Theory of Mind (henceforth, ToM) necessarily lead to better social abilities? Due to the intrinsically private nature of mental states, individuals often have to make inferences as to the mental states of another individual—that is, social cognition often involves inference of the best explanation of what an individual is experiencing (i.e. their beliefs/knowledge/visual perspective), based on the information available, which may be incomplete (Hartwright et al., 2014; Schneider et al., 2015). Prior research has indicated that social cognition is not a 'have or have not' ability, but rather is subject to a variety of individual differences, and these individual differences in both social and cognitive skills can predict success on social cognitive tasks (e.g. Bradford et al., 2015; Cane et al., 2017; Converse et al., 2008; Ferguson et al., 2015a). There also remains open-ended research questions as to *when* individuals engage their social cognition capacities. Are we constantly evaluating other people's mental states, or is it only when required? How do we use our belief-reasoning/mental state understanding to guide our everyday communication? To successfully engage in social interactions, we use our understanding of other people's mental states—their knowledge of different events or topics—to guide our communication, and there remains many open-ended questions about how efficiently we are able to do this, to what extent this varies on an individual basis, and whether differences in social cognitive abilities can predict social success (Apperly, 2012; Bradford et al., Submitted; Cutting & Dunn, 2002).

In addition to questions regarding social cognition in neurotypical individuals, evidence has highlighted that social cognition deficits are often associated with a number of different disorders, including autism spectrum disorder (Baron-Cohen et al., 1985; Bradford et al., 2018a; Hutchins et al., 2012), schizophrenia (Brüne, 2004; Couture et al., 2006; Herold et al., 2002), and different forms of dementia (Kemp et al., 2012; Lough et al., 2001; Lough et al., 2006). Milward and Sebanz (2016) suggest that social cognition deficits in certain psychiatric conditions, such as schizophrenia, may be related to aspects of self-representation. While social cognition research often focuses on how well an individual can understand and process the mental states of the 'other', equally important, as a result of this, is an individual's ability to distinguish between 'self' and 'other' perspectives, understanding which mental states belong to oneself versus another person. Alongside a distinction between 'self' and 'other', the ability to *integrate* these two perspectives is also required in order to optimally balance understanding of each perspective, so as to allow successful social interaction to occur (i.e. accurate identification of both one's own and someone else's mental state, which may be aligned or different from each other). Liepelt et al. (2012) found that patients with schizophrenia showed a marked deficit in integrating 'self' and 'other' perspectives when engaging in a task, in contrast to controls, which was associated with deficits in performance on tests of social cognition abilities. These results could be due to the lack of self/other integration, or indeed a failure to represent the 'other' at all. Further research is required to tease these explanations apart (Milward & Sebanz, 2016; Liepelt et al., 2012). Combs et al. (2007) suggest that impairments in social functioning are one of the hallmark characteristics of schizophrenia, with social cognition abilities showing a stronger relationship with functional outcomes than neurocognition abilities (see also Pinkham & Penn, 2006). These findings highlight the need to consider research into social cognition as a target of intervention for patients with schizophrenia, and further illustrate the importance of furthering our understanding of the mechanisms underlying ToM abilities.

Taken together, it is clear that there is still substantial research to be done to further inform our understanding of social cognition abilities, across a number of populations. First, examining the developmental routes of social cognition capacities, ensuring that developmental research is able to clearly define what it is that different tasks used with infants and young children are measuring specifically (e.g. Apperly (2012) states that it is not clear what false belief tasks, for instance, are measuring—possession of concepts? Capacity to pass a task? Motivation to pass a task?). Second, establishing how social cognition continues to develop throughout childhood and into adolescence: when are 'peak' social cognition abilities reached? In adulthood, how do we sensitively and accurately measure 'mindreading' abilities in individuals who clearly *do* possess mindreading concepts? How can we assess individual differences in social interaction abilities, and are these reflective of underlying social cognition capacities? What leads to differences in social cognition abilities across individuals (e.g. different levels of egocentrism), and do these differences predict social success? When examining social cognition deficits in different disorders, how do we establish the impact of social cognition capacities as an underlying factor in reported difficulties? For disorders in which a link between social interaction abilities and reported symptoms is established, to what extent can social cognition abilities act as an intervention target for reducing social difficulties, when relevant?

These questions—and many more—highlight the importance of continuing to study social interaction abilities across a number of different contexts and populations. Further, prior research has demonstrated a positive link between successful social cognition abilities and social well-being (Bailey et al., 2008; Sullivan & Ruffman, 2004). However, in order to address key research questions into social interaction abilities, it is important to identify some key challenges that are present within the social cognition literature, providing targets for change to further enhance our understanding of social cognition capacities across different contexts and, importantly, with 'real-world' implications.

9.1.1 Putting the 'social' back into social cognition research

A core issue with social interaction research is its inherent lack of *social experience*—that is, a majority of studies examining social cognition abilities require participants to complete a computerized task in a lab, under well-controlled conditions, often observing and responding to static stimuli (Parsons et al., 2017). While this set-up typically allows for insight into how efficiently—speed- and accuracy-wise—individuals can engage with social cognition abilities in a particular, controlled situation, it removes a core part of human sociality. In everyday life, social interactions are much less organized than when presented in lab-based tasks. Indeed, they can often be seen as 'messy', involving overlapping talk, fast-paced interactions, and multiple mental states to consider in a group conversation. Zaki and Ochsner (2012) define real-life social exchanges as multimodal, requiring interactive, dynamic, and contextually embedded social cues to be integrated together to allow perceivers to flexibly interpret another individual's internal state relevant to current social goals. Lab-based studies face an issue therefore, because they may fail to capture the nuances of real-world social interactions and may not be representative of real-life social encounters. To address this issue, research needs to develop 'bridges' between *observation* and *communication* (e.g. Laidlaw et al., 2011; Samson & Apperly, 2010). By constructing these so-called bridges, studies aim to retain experimental control while conducting studies that are more akin to real-world scenarios.

Typically, social interactions involve two or more individuals, and it is important therefore that, when we are measuring social interaction in the lab context, we consider key differences between data collection scenarios and their real-world—likely much more complex—equivalents. For instance, considering the 'mental state' of a virtual avatar is arguably very different from considering mental states of conversational partners in dyads, triads, or any number of larger groups. One way of attempting to address this issue has been to use video clips to present dynamic social stimuli in a controlled setting, thus increasing engagement with stimuli compared with presentation of static scenes. However, although this allows participants to passively observe the social interactions of others, and therefore may provide further insight into how an individual processes a social interaction as an observer, it still does not allow participants to actively engage with and experience the social interaction itself. This is an important consideration for social cognition research going forward: how to create more ecologically valid situations in which to assess social cognition capacities in more 'real-world' scenarios, allowing results to be more generalizable to the types of social cognition processes involved in interactions throughout our daily lives (Ochsner, 2004; Schilback et al., 2006; Schilback et al., 2013; Schilback, 2015).

Throughout this chapter, we will discuss some of the approaches adopted by researchers to address these issues, including focusing on (1) methods for studying social cognition abilities, (2) some of the core topics within the field of social interaction research and how these research topics may be addressed, and (3) research on factors that may influence social interaction abilities, and how these may be used to develop intervention protocols for improving social cognition abilities.

9.2 Methods for studying social cognition

9.2.1 Virtual reality

The availability of virtual reality (VR) technology is becoming more and more accessible for research purposes, offering many advantages to traditional lab-based tasks. VR paradigms provide a stepping stone towards more real-life social situations, allowing the creation of customizable and interactive conditions in more embodied and interactive settings than traditional computerized tasks, while retaining experimental control to limit the influence of potential extraneous variables (Froese et al., 2014). In this way, VR methods offer an alternative research approach between studying live social interactions (e.g. observational research or research involving more than one participant engaging in a task), and use of simple cognitive trials requiring a button-press response as often used in key research tasks. It is worth noting that both these research approaches provide valuable insights into mechanisms involved in social interaction processes, but come with their own issues in measurements. Pan and Hamilton (2018), for instance, highlight how studies using static stimuli button-press response tasks, although allowing for detection of subtle differences between performance across different task conditions (e.g. measuring small but significant response time differences across trial types), come with low ecological validity, making it harder to ascertain how performance may relate to or predict behaviour in real-world situations involving more complex stimuli and a wider range of response options. As a result, interest has grown in studies that present more interactive dynamic stimuli, allowing more accurate assessment of the integrative processes carried out by perceivers over time when engaged in social interaction tasks. Use of VR methodologies offers significant advantages in experimental control, reproducibility, and ecological validity, by allowing researchers to test the effect of various social cues in a systematic and independent manner (Parsons et al., 2017). For example, a significant benefit of VR technology is the ability to manipulate a variable (e.g. race or gender of an avatar) with full experimental control (i.e. controlling other potentially influential variables such as facial expressions or height), allowing examination of how these changes may influence different social cognitive abilities (e.g. perspective taking, empathy ratings).

Prior research has established that virtual environments are able to activate a sense of 'presence' in participants, including emotional experiences (Diemer et al., 2015), and there is a growing body of evidence suggesting that perceptions of human-like avatars in a VR setting do not differ significantly from the perception of real human beings, in terms of triggering comparable behavioural and neuronal activations (Parsons et al., 2017; de Borst & de Gelder, 2015). This further highlights the usefulness of VR in providing a 'bridge' between traditional lab-based studies and observations of live social interactions that lack experimental control, and indicates that participant responses within VR scenarios may well be representative and generalizable from the VR experience to 'real-world' social cognitions (Parsons et al., 2017). For instance, one particular application that has utilized VR technology is in assessing the capacity of VR as a training intervention aimed at enhancing social cognition abilities in individuals with high-functioning autism. Kandalaft et al. (2013) conducted a study in which young adults with high-functioning autism completed a series of 10 VR training sessions across a five-week period with the aim of enhancing social skills, social cognition, and social functioning. The training sessions involved participants engaging in role-playing scenarios of different social situations within a VR environment. These training scenarios varied in goals and difficulty, including interactions with a 'friend' (i.e. someone with common interests), negotiating with a salesman, and attending a job interview. Participants were tested on a number of different measures of social cognition (e.g. emotion recognition, ToM, conversation abilities) pre- and post-training intervention. Results showed that young adults who completed the training interventions showed improved social cognition task performance following the training, and improved self-reported real-world conversation skills, indicating a significant effect of this VR training approach. These results highlight the promising scope of VR as a tool for not only assessing social cognition abilities, but also in utilizing this methodology as a form of intervention when aiming to enhance social cognition capacities with real-world behavioural outcomes (Kandalaft et al., 2013; Strickland et al., 1996; Whyte et al., 2015). These outcomes are particularly important when considering that social cognition is argued to be compromised in a number of neuropsychiatric disorders, in patients with traumatic brain injury (e.g. following stroke), as well as in autism. Pilot results such as Kandalaft et al.'s may indicate that rehabilitation of social cognition capacities in contexts such as these may at least be partially approached via use of VR training protocols (Maggio et al., 2019).

Evidently, VR studies offer a promising approach to studying social cognition abilities in scenarios more akin to real-world situations, although more research is required to establish the extent to which outcomes can really be generalized to real-world experiences. Given this, caution in interpretation of VR study outcomes, and how these may be indicative of social cognition capacities in daily life, must currently be retained.

9.2.2 Second-person neuroscience

Human beings are inherently social, possessing dedicated social-cognitive abilities (e.g. biological motion perception, action understanding, mental state attribution; Blakemore, 2008; Brunsdon et al., 2019; Naughtin et al., 2017; Frith & Frith, 2003). Given this, it is important that, when examining social communication abilities, we use dyads, triads, and even larger groups to examine these 'interactive brains', allowing insight into the neural and cognitive mechanisms of two- (or more) person social interactions. Konvalinka and Roepstorff (2012) argue that, currently, social interaction research often focuses on an individual, social observation approach. However, in order to gain a better understanding of social interactions, research needs to turn towards two-person, active interaction approaches, which are more akin to everyday experiences (e.g. Dumas, 2011; Schilbach, 2015). Indeed, second-person neuroscience has seen a recent rise in popularity (e.g. Froese et al., 2014; Konvalinka & Roepstorff, 2012), and focuses on engagement of 'two-person' (or 'second-person') paradigms, both behaviourally—in which studies are conducted using, for instance, dyads of participants—and using neuroscientific measures, in which studies look at the brain activity of two (or more) individuals involved in a real-time interaction, rather than a single individual engaging in a computerized task.

The aim of second-person neuroscience is to study real-time interactive behaviour, which will allow research to further build our understanding of the 'social brain' both in neurotypical individuals (e.g. changes across the lifespan) and in psychiatric disorders (Pinti et al., 2020; Konvalinka & Roepstorff, 2012; Frith, 2007). Some approaches to examining the second-person problem in research has been to use electroencephalography (EEG) and functional near-infrared spectroscopy (fNIRS) methods to assess inter-brain synchronization when undertaking different tasks in real-time interactions, rather than a single individual completing a computerized task. In this way, results can measure the effect of interpersonal coordination using a neurofeedback two-brain task, providing much more subtle measures than explicit behavioural measures such as response times. In using this approach, data can also be collected to examine whether differences in dyads influence underlying responses—for instance, does synchronization differ when engaging in a task with a familiar other, a friend or spouse, versus a stranger? Does the gender of the dyads—same versus different—affect neural responses? This second-person neuroscience approach has begun to reveal some promising results, including identification of neural mechanisms that are specifically active during social encounters (e.g. Froese et al., 2014; Schilbach, et al., 2013; Dumas, 2011), using both EEG and fNIRS technology, as will be detailed below.

9.2.3 Electrophysiological data

EEG refers to the technique of measuring electrical brain activity in a non-invasive manner, at the surface level of the scalp (Millett, 2001; Dale & Sereno, 1993). EEG records brain activity with high temporal resolution, allowing assessment of the timings of neurocognitive processes to within a range of milliseconds (Dale & Halgren, 2001; Debener et al., 2006). In this way, functional and neural processes can be seen unfolding in real time, providing valuable information about the temporal factors that may influence processing under different conditions. The main limitation of EEG is its inability to specify localized brain regions, with limited spatial detail available (Saxe et al., 2009). EEG has been used in a number of studies examining social cognition abilities. In particular, it is often used to capture event-related potential (ERP) information. ERPs use time-locked stimuli presentation to allow key moments in a task to be identified and directly compared across different task conditions, allowing insight into neural responses to different stimuli (Kang et al., 2018; Liu et al., 2004; Sabbagh & Taylor, 2000; Kühn-Popp et al., 2013; Meinhardt et al., 2012).

Ferguson and colleagues (2015b) recorded neural responses from adult participants who read a series of short narratives in which a character held a true or false belief about the location of an object, before responding in a manner that was consistent or inconsistent with this belief-state. Results highlighted a classic N400 effect in true belief scenarios, with a more negative-going N400 following outcomes that violated the story character's belief-state. However, for false belief scenarios, this effect was reversed, with more a negative-going N400 when the character's actions were consistent with their belief-state. Taken together, these results indicate that participants interpreted the stories in an egocentric manner, failing to integrate the character's perspective when following the stories (i.e. processing the stories based on their own belief-state, in which they knew the location of the moved object in the stories). Further research has supported these findings and extended them to populations across the lifespan, revealing prolonged egocentric interference in older adults (e.g. Bradford et al., 2020). It has also highlighted the information that EEG methods can provide in examining the neural substrates of social cognition processing, providing insight into the underlying mechanisms of social interaction (Balconi et al., 2015).

The use of EEG methods also provides the opportunity to conduct two-person EEG studies to capture inter-brain processes while two individuals are interacting (Dumas, 2011). Konvalinka and Roepstorff (2012) highlight that this is a relatively new opportunity due to newly available technology that allows quantification of between-brain effects to be ascertained, and thus provides scope for future studies to examine the neural markers of social interaction in contexts involving mutual exchanges of information (rather than a single individual taking part in a computerized task, when they often take the role of 'observer' rather than 'interactor'). Astolfi et al. (2010) conducted a study in which four individuals were playing a card game while EEG was recorded; focusing on selected regions of interest, a measure of inter-brain functional connectivity was established. Importantly, within this card game, participants were playing with a paired partner, with one pair competing against the other pair. Results showed coherence between activity in the anterior cingulate cortex in the brain of the 'leader' of the group (i.e. the individual who started the game) and their paired partner. Konvalinka and Roepstorff (2012) speculate potential reasons for this alignment, including that the leaders may be more actively engaged in working out their partner's strategy in the game by representing their partner's intentions. However, it is difficult to specify what may be causing this coherence across the paired participants without further research.

This approach to looking at multi-person EEG recordings highlights the importance of examining social interactions in more active paradigms. In doing so, we will gain further insight into neural processes that underlie social interactions as they unfold in real time—including factors leading to successful social coordination—and provide scope for future research to explore social cognition at both the behavioural and neuronal level across groups of participants.

9.2.4 Functional near-infrared spectroscopy

Over the past few decades in the field of cognitive neuroscience, there has been a significant increase in the number of studies using fNIRS to examine the neural basis of social cognition abilities. fNIRS has gained in popularity because of its flexible usage, particularly over other neuroimaging modalities such as fMRI and EEG methods. Pinti et al. (2020) describe fNIRS as: 'harmless, tolerant to bodily movements, and highly portable, being suitable for all participant populations, from new-borns to the elderly, and experimental settings both inside and outside of the laboratory' (p. 1). fNIRS is a non-invasive optical imaging method that estimates levels of oxygenated and deoxygenated haemoglobin in brain tissue by monitoring changes in scattering of near-infrared light from the scalp (Hyde et al., 2015; Boas & Franceschini, 2009). Of particular interest, fNIRS allows for continual monitoring of brain activity across dynamic stimuli, allowing changes in brain activity to be measured across a trial duration. For instance, Hyde et al. (2015) conducted a study using fNIRS to examine whether participants track beliefs of others spontaneously (i.e. when not explicitly required to do so for the task). In their study, participants viewed a series of video clips involving two characters interacting with an object in a goal-directed manner. There were two conditions: one in which the target character knew the location of the object (i.e. possession of a true belief) and one in which the target character was in possession of a false belief about the position of an object. While these videos were played, participants were free-viewing them (i.e. they did not have to respond to the recordings) and fNIRS was used to record brain activity over right parietal, temporal, and frontal regions. Results showed significant increases in brain activity for participants while watching the videos which, importantly, was modulated by the extent to which the belief-state of the target character contrasted with reality (i.e. whether they were in possession of a true versus false belief state). When the character was in possession of a false-belief, increased activity in the right temporoparietal junction (rTPJ) was found, which Hyde et al. (2015)

suggest is indicative of increased demands on the rTPJ of holding two inconsistent belief states in mind concurrently.

The flexibility in the conditions under which fNIRS methods can be used are particularly important when considering a drive to collect data that is more aligned with 'real-world' scenarios in future research into social interactions, allowing mapping of functional activation patterns while participants engage in everyday activities (Pinti et al., 2020). Data collection from, for instance, an fMRI study can provide detailed insights into patterns of brain activity when engaging in different social cognitive tasks. However, collection of fMRI data is in an environment very far removed from everyday life, both in terms of the context (e.g. restricted movement, restricted hearing due to noise of fMRI machine) and tasks completed (e.g. computer-based tasks involving a motor response, usually to static stimuli), reducing the ecological validity of the results. This is important to consider if trying to learn more about how social interactions occur successfully in everyday contexts. fNIRS can be used in contexts where researchers want to record from two or more participants simultaneously ('hyper-scanning'), rather than running single-person studies, allowing assessment of 'brain-to-brain coupling' (Hasson et al., 2012), inter-brain synchronization (Dumas, 2011; Konvalinka & Roepstorff, 2012), and new insights into the neural mechanisms of social interactions in more ecologically valid situations. In this way, data regarding social interactions can be collected in a *direct* manner, rather than requiring inference of what lab-based tasks may represent in their real-world equivalents. However, while fNIRS provides the opportunity to collect rich data in more ecologically valid contexts, the limitation of this is reduced accuracy of the recorded time course of mental activity. In contrast, while EEG methods may be less ecologically valid due to the requirements of the equipment (e.g. remaining stationary), they provide accurate and detailed information on the time course of changes in brain activity.

Both EEG and fNIRS methods have the potential to provide further insight into social cognition abilities across individuals, in particular by allowing assessment of patterns seen during different stages of social interactions, whether as a listener or speaker, and specifically by allowing 'hyper-scanning' (multi-person) experimental set-ups (e.g. Konvalinka & Roepstorff, 2012; Schilbach, 2015).

9.3 Social cognition: key research focuses

9.3.1 Neurotypical ageing research

Traditionally, research into social cognition abilities has focused on young infants and children, and the emergence of these abilities. However, as demonstrated in the earlier chapters of this book, the past few decades have seen a significant increase in interest in looking at social cognition abilities beyond their emergence, including older children, adolescents, and adults, to explore how social cognition may continue to develop and change across the lifespan (Bradford et al., submitted; Apperly, 2012; Bailey et al., 2008; Samson & Apperly, 2010; Ligneau-Hervé & Mullet, 2005). This expansion of social cognition research is extremely important in further informing our understanding of the mechanisms underlying social interaction abilities, and looking at lifespan changes that may indicate how social cognition is structured and organized (Milward & Sebanz, 2016; Phillips et al., 2011; Moran, 2013; Rakoczy et al., 2012). Further, research across the lifespan has highlighted that social cognition abilities can predict social functioning outcomes (Apperly et al., 2009; Dumontheil et al., 2010). For instance, it has been shown that age-related declines in ToM abilities can mediate a decline in social well-being and social participation by older adults, which in turn can lead to experiences of isolation, loneliness, and poor health (Bailey et al., 2008; Sullivan & Ruffman, 2004). It is therefore important that we continue to seek a fuller understanding of the cognitive mechanisms that underlie social interactions, and how these change across the lifespan, potentially allowing insight into early signs of potential cognitive decline and, resultantly, exploration of new protocols to improve social cognition abilities via training at different ages.

It is noted that one of the main challenges to examining social cognition abilities in ageing populations is how to accurately measure social cognition in people who possess fully developed abilities, while avoiding ceiling effects in tasks. Researchers have attempted to address this problem in a number of ways—first, by using tasks that are argued to test 'advanced' ToM abilities. It is suggested, for example, that tasks such as the Director Task (Keysar et al., 2003; Keysar et al., 2000), Animated Triangles (Abell et al., 2000), and the Strange Stories Task (Happé, 1994) are sensitive enough to detect subtle differences in how efficiently an individual is able to engage their social cognition, allowing assessment of individual differences in ToM abilities in adulthood. Second, relatively new methods of measuring implicit social cognition abilities, such as using EEG, fNIRS, fMRI, and eye-tracking, are providing exciting and important new insights into the structure of ToM abilities, and how these may change across different ages. Moran (2013) highlights that social cognition is dependent on the functioning of multiple basic cognitive processes (e.g. joint attention, emotion attribution, mental state attribution), and therefore research seeking to document the effect of ageing on ToM requires use of a number of different tasks and approaches that each emphasize different aspects of social cognition, allowing assessment of how different abilities may change or remain stable across the lifespan.

9.3.2 Research with clinical populations

Alongside furthering our understanding of social cognition abilities in neurotypical individuals across the lifespan, it is also important to note the importance of researching social cognition abilities in atypical populations. As discussed at the start of this chapter, research outcomes have suggested that social cognition deficits are associated with a number of different disorders, including autism spectrum disorder (Baron-Cohen et al., 1985; Baron-Cohen et al., 2001; Bradford et al., 2018a; Hutchins et al., 2012), schizophrenia (Brüne, 2004; Frith, 1992; Jardri et al., 2011; Couture et al., 2006; Herold et al., 2002), attention deficit hyperactivity disorder (Caillies et al., 2014), and different forms of dementia (Happé et al., 1999; Cuerva et al., 2001; Gregory et al., 2002; Lough et al., 2001; Lough et al., 2006). It is beyond the scope of this chapter to detail each of these in turn, but it is highlighted that research into these clinical populations can help further our understanding not only of how social cognition itself is structured and develops, but also provide potential targets of intervention for individuals who experience difficulties with social cognition abilities (Frith & Frith, 2003; Leslie & Thaiss, 1992; Kemp et al., 2012).

9.3.3 Self/other distinction

A particular research question that has emerged from studies examining social interaction processes is the consideration of 'self' versus 'other' representations (Bradford et al., 2015; Bradford et al., 2018a; Milward & Sebanz, 2016; De Guzman et al., 2016; Steinbeis, 2016). The ability to distinguish between self/other plays a crucial role in engaging in social interactions, required for engagement in imitation, perspective taking, empathy, and aiding avoidance of egocentric attributions of both cognitive and affective states to others (De Guzman et al., 2016). Prior research, most often conducted with single participants in a lab-based setting, supports the notion of a differentiation between processing of the 'self' versus 'other' perspectives across different task paradigms (e.g. Bradford et al., 2015; Bradford et al., 2018a; Ferguson et al., 2018; Ferguson et al., 2017; Samson et al., 2010; Santiesteban et al., 2015). For instance, Bradford et al. (2015) conducted a computerized false belief study in which adult participants were required to consider either their own belief-state or that of another person. Furthermore, there were some occasions within the task when participants were asked to switch between different perspectives, either from the self-perspective to the other-perspective, or from the other-perspective to the self-perspective. Results showed that participants were significantly faster and more accurate at responding to trials from the *Self*-perspective compared with the *Other*-perspective. Results also showed that participants were much more efficient (faster and more accurate) at switching from the Other-to-Self perspective than from the Self-to-Other perspective. These results indicated that, even when aligned (i.e. when both the self and other are in possession of the same belief/knowledge state), self and other perspectives are calculated and considered separately, suggesting a clear distinction between these perspectives.

Bradford et al.'s results further support claims from prior research that suggest that, in order to understand what other people are thinking or feeling across different situations, we at least partly rely on projections of what we ourselves would think/feel in similar situations, resulting in a faster perspective-shift from Other-to-Self when compared to shifting from Self-to-Other (Steinbeis, 2016).

Interestingly, it has been shown that self/other differentiation abilities, as a core part of social cognition, can be enhanced through training protocols. For instance, De Guzman et al. (2016) report a study in which adult participants were trained to increase self-other control; to achieve this, participants engaged in a training task in which they watched a video of an actor's hand and were required to perform a motor movement (lifting either their index or middle finger), which was either congruous (same finger as the actor; decreased self-other control due to low inhibitory control demands) or incongruous (opposite finger to the actor; increased self-other control due to higher inhibitory control demands on egocentric perspective) to the actor in the video. Participants in the increased self-other control condition subsequently showed increased empathy levels, indicating that enhanced self/other control may lead to increases in empathy. Self/other control plays an important role in social interaction, including in imitation, perspective taking, and empathy abilities (Santiesteban et al., 2012). De Guzman et al.'s findings have important implications for individuals who experience difficulties in social interactions, particularly due to difficulties in distinguishing between 'self' and 'other' perspectives, indicating potential scope for the development of behavioural interventions.

While there is significant evidence highlighting the importance of self/other differentiation in social interaction processes, a majority of these insights have been ascertained through lab-based studies involving single participants interacting with a computerized task. As highlighted previously in this chapter, it is important when considering social cognition abilities to consider how particular types of social interactions may affect the processes involved. For instance, in the context of a single individual versus working within a dyad, or even a larger group of individuals, self/other distinction may be processed in vastly different ways. This again highlights the need to look at social cognition abilities across different contexts, and across different social interaction settings.

9.3.4 Social cognition in group contexts

Many of the studies and research approaches cited throughout this chapter have discussed the importance of the opportunity to examine social cognition abilities in situations requiring *actual* social interaction (e.g. studying participant dyads using behavioural measures alongside fNIRS or EEG to explore inter-brain synchrony within these contexts). Over (2016) also highlights the importance of examining social cognition abilities in larger group sizes. For instance, communicating within a group of three or more individuals is likely to differ in terms of underlying processes from interacting with one other interactive partner, requiring joint attention and task co-representation with a number of different individuals, and potentially with more than one common goal in the interactive setting (Milward & Sebanz, 2016; McAuliffe & Dunham, 2016). Over (2016) argues that the purpose of using social cognition abilities in daily life (e.g. mental state understanding, empathy, joint action, cooperation) is motivated by a 'need to belong'—that is, it is suggested that, by efficiently utilizing social cognition abilities, we are better able to interact and form affiliations with other group members, an important aspect of social functioning. Interestingly, Over's argument may indicate that, unlike prior research which has emphasized the importance of being able to efficiently distinguish self/other perspectives (De Guzman et al., 2016; Bradford et al., 2015; Samson et al., 2010), in some circumstances it may be optimal to experience *less* distinction between 'self' and 'other'—other, in this case, being a social group—to aid a sense of belonging to the specific social group (Over, 2016; Milward & Sebanz, 2016; Whitehouse & Lanman, 2014). To further our understanding of the role of self/other distinctions and how social interactions differ across different contexts, from dyadic interactions to small or large group scenarios, more research is required into these different contexts and outcomes across social interaction settings.

Some studies have already started to examine the role of group settings in assessing social cognition abilities, including in fNIRS studies that allow monitoring of brain activity while individuals engage in face-to-face interactions. Importantly, this allows real-time updating of information perceived about an interactive partner when engaging in a set task. Jiang et al. (2015), for example, conducted a study in which three individuals engaged in a conversation while brain activity was monitored using fNIRS to assess interpersonal neural synchronization between participants. Results of these three-way conversations found that one person in each group tended to emerge as a leader (as judged by naïve individuals who rated the interactions from video recordings). Particularly interesting was that the results also showed that interpersonal neural synchronization in the temporoparietal junction was higher for the leader-follower pairs than for the follower-follower pairs. These results provide valuable insights into potential differences in processing of social interactions according to a number of factors, including role within a social group (e.g. leader versus follower).

Milward and Sebanz (2016) further support the need for more research into group versus dyadic interactions, suggesting that these two fields of research are currently examined independently, and that bringing together literature from each of these two fields may further inform our understanding of social cognitive abilities across different contexts. By examining the mechanisms that underlie social cognition in the lab (i.e. single-person studies), in dyads of participants, and in group scenarios, we can further our understanding of how social interactions vary across different settings, and whether underlying cognitive mechanisms differ across contexts.

9.3.5 Cross-cultural research

Henrich and colleagues (2010) highlighted a critically important issue in behavioural sciences when they stated that much of human psychology research is drawn from a very specific population: Western, Educated, Industrialized, Rich, and Democratic (WEIRD) societies. Given this reliance on a particular subpopulation of 'WEIRD' participants in a significant amount of psychological research, it is difficult to ascertain how representative this sample is of the world population, and how generalizable established results are to other cultures (Hong & Chiu, 2001; Fiske et al., 1998). A number of prior studies have shown clear cultural differences across a number of different traits, including personality traits, visual perception, and spatial reasoning (McCrae & Terracciano, 2005; Nisbett et al., 2001). In regards to social interaction capacities, research outcomes are somewhat mixed, with a majority of studies focusing on the differences and similarities in the developmental trajectories of social cognition across different cultures. Some studies reveal very similar developmental trajectories of social cognition development across a variety of cultures (e.g. Avis & Harris, 1991; Callaghan et al., 2005; Sabbagh et al., 2006). Results from a meta-analysis comparing Chinese to North American children indicated parallel developmental trajectories (i.e. the same stages undertaken in development of social cognition capacities) for children from both populations, but substantially different timelines, with Chinese children lagging behind (Liu et al., 2008). Other studies have suggested that children from different cultures—e.g. individualist versus collectivist backgrounds—may acquire specific social cognition capacities in different sequences (e.g. Lecce & Hughes, 2010; Mayer & Träuble, 2013), indicating a key influence of cultural background on development of social interaction abilities (Hughes et al., 2014).

Kobayashi and colleagues (2006) conducted a study examining social cognition abilities of adult participants, comparing performance of American English-speaking monolinguals and Japanese–English bilinguals. Using fMRI scanning, the study involved presenting participants with stories involving ToM reasoning or control stories (e.g. physical causation reasoning). Results showed comparable activation across participants in the medial pre-frontal cortex and anterior cingulate cortex when trials required social cognition reasoning, suggesting similarities in brain regions recruited for ToM processes. Interestingly, results also showed that the Japanese participants demonstrated significantly less TPJ activity than the American participants during the task, despite no differences in behavioural performance. Kobayashi et al. (2006) suggested this could be due to cultural differences between the two populations, with a reduced 'Self' versus 'Other' distinction in the Japanese participants (associated with 'collectivist' traits) compared with the American participants (associated with 'individualist' traits). Bradford and colleagues (2018b) conducted a study comparing performance of participants from China versus participants from the UK on a computerized belief-attribution task to assess how efficiently individuals could attribute beliefs to themselves and others, and how efficiently they could switch between different perspectives. Results indicated core similarities in performance across participants from both cultures, with all participants responding faster to self-oriented questions than other-oriented questions, and also demonstrating slower and less accurate abilities when shifting to another person's perspective, compared with shifting from the 'other' perspective to one's own.

Studies such as these, examining potential differences and similarities across different cultures, are important for helping to establish traits that are universal versus traits that are influenced by an individual's social and cultural surroundings (Bradford et al., 2018b; Callaghan et al., 2005; Kobayashi et al., 2006; Shahaeian et al., 2014). By exploring the presence or absence of cross-cultural differences in social cognition capacities, and reducing focus on WEIRD populations, we will be able to gain more insight into the structure of the ToM mechanism, as well as expanding our understanding of individual differences in social cognition within different populations (Sabbagh et al., 2006; Shahaeian et al., 2014; Wang et al., 2019).

9.3.6 'Real-world' interactions

As discussed throughout this chapter, there is a fine balance in social cognition research between studies conducted in lab-based settings, with high experimental control and the ability to manipulate different variables that would not be possible outside this setting (e.g. manipulation of an avatar's gender and ethnicity, and ensuring that other features remain stable), and observation studies in 'real-world' scenarios that have high ecological validity but reduce or remove experimental control. Given this, it is critically important to ensure that stimuli used when studying social interactions are appropriate for the aims of the study and, in particular, when looking to bridge the gap between lab-based data collection and real-world applications of outcomes, that the stimuli are as closely matched as possible to experiences that would occur in everyday life. One way of doing this is by ensuring that tasks provide the potential for actual social interaction and more natural communication than typical behavioural response-based tasks (Mansour & Kuhn, 2019).

To demonstrate the importance of this, Mansour and Kuhn (2019) conducted a study in which they recorded participants' eye movements while they engaged in a Skype conversation. Participants were either told they were going to be engaging in a live Skype call, or that the Skype conversation was pre-recorded, removing the opportunity for spontaneous interaction. Critically, in reality, both conversations were pre-recorded, allowing stringent experimental control of stimuli, with the key difference being between the instructions participants were given. Results showed that, despite the stimuli being the same in both conditions (i.e. same pre-recorded video played), significant differences in eye movements between the two conditions were found: in particular, when individuals believed they were engaging in a 'live' conversation, they spent less time looking at the speaker's eyes compared to when they believed they were engaging in a pre-recorded conversation. These findings highlight significant differences in participant behaviour in social situations when they believe they are interacting with an individual directly, as opposed to watching a video, and thus emphasize the importance of including *genuine* interactions in research into social interactions if we want to ascertain results that are generalizable to real-world interactions.

9.4 Can we change social cognition abilities?

9.4.1 Executive functions

Given that research indicates that social cognition continues to change across the lifespan, with evidence suggesting that, for instance, older adults experience more difficulty with social cognition than younger adults (Bradford et al., Submitted; Bailey & Henry, 2008; Phillips et al., 2011; German & Hehman, 2006), and that some individuals experience deficits in social cognition abilities as a result of clinical disorders (e.g. Hutchins et al., 2012; Brüne, 2004; Herold et al., 2002; Gregory et al., 2002), a key question in this research area has been consideration of whether social cognition abilities can be enhanced through training interventions. Training protocols could be directly targeted at social cognition mechanisms themselves, although successful outcomes may also be accomplished by focusing on more than just direct training of social cognition abilities (Kloo & Perner, 2003; Santiesteban et al., 2012). For instance, there is significant evidence of a strong relationship between social cognition and executive functioning abilities, particularly in early childhood (Ozonoff et al., 1991; Ozonoff & McEvoy, 1994; Sabbagh et al., 2006). Executive functions refer to a set of cognitive processes that regulate, control, and manage other cognitive processes. These cognitive processes include inhibitory control, working memory, cognitive flexibility, and planning abilities (Miyake et al., 2000; Miyake & Friedman, 2012). It is clear that executive functions may play a critical role in social interactions—for instance, in order to overcome an egocentric bias and consider the 'other' perspective rather than the 'self' perspective, an individual is required to inhibit the 'self' perspective, flexibly shift to an alternative perspective, and use working memory to hold different mental states belonging to 'self' and 'other' in mind.

Recent research has started to focus on the relationship between social cognition abilities and executive functions in *adulthood* (e.g. Bradford et al., submitted; Bernstein et al., 2011; Cane et al., 2017; Duval et al., 2011; Brown-Schmidt, 2009). Previous studies have documented relationships in particular between working memory, inhibitory control, and social cognition capacities (Bailey & Henry, 2008; Carlson & Moses, 2001; Phillips et al., 2011), and recent theoretical models have proposed a mediating role of executive functions in successful social interactions (Apperly & Butterfill, 2009; Butterfill & Apperly, 2013; Carruthers, 2016), highlighting the importance of furthering our understanding of the mediating role of executive functions in predicting social cognition abilities across different ages. Declines in both social cognition (Bradford et al., 2020; Bradford et al., Submitted; Bailey & Henry, 2008; Phillips et al., 2011; German & Hehman, 2006) and executive functioning (Brunsdon et al., Submitted; German & Hehman, 2006; Salthouse et al., 2003; Elderkin-Thompson et al., 2008) with advancing age have been well documented. However, the nuances of the relationship between these two key cognitive abilities, and how this relationship may change and evolve across the lifespan, remains a topic of debate. One problem with research aiming to tackle this question is that studies often aggregate data into dichotomous age groups, comparing 'young' versus 'old' participant groups, thus making it more difficult to establish when—and in what way—social cognition changes as a result of advancing age.

Some studies have attempted to address this issue by using a *continuous* ageing sample rather that dichotomous groups. A recent study by Bradford et al. (Submitted) used a continuous sample of adults aged 20–86 years to examine changes in perspective-taking abilities across adulthood, and how these abilities may relate to individual differences in executive functioning (inhibition, working memory, cognitive flexibility, and planning) capacities. Results showed a decline in social cognition (perspective-taking) abilities from ~38 years, with advancing age leading to increased egocentric errors in the task. Interestingly, mediation analyses revealed that this decline in perspective taking was at least partially independent of age-related decline in executive functions. However, other studies have suggested that declines in social cognition abilities are related to more domain-general declines in executive functions (e.g. Bailey & Henry, 2008; Duval et al., 2011; Phillips et al., 2011). This difference in findings may reflect the limited coherence among tasks measuring social cognition (e.g. Warnell & Recay, 2019; Hayward & Homer, 2017) and executive function (e.g. Miyake, et al., 2000; Testa et al., 2012) abilities that prior research has indicated. Given this, it is important for future research to use a number of different measures of both social cognition and executive functioning abilities to more accurately assess the extent of a relationship between these two cognitive processes, and how this relationship may change at different stages of the lifespan.

9.4.2 'Brain training'

Prior research has supported the notion that executive functions can be enhanced via training protocols (e.g. Dowsett & Livesey, 2000; Holmes et al., 2019; McKendrick et al., 2014). Results for improvements in social cognition are more mixed, with some studies supporting improvements in social interaction abilities following engagement in a training protocol (e.g. Lecce et al., 2014), while other studies show no significant improvements in social cognition performance following training interventions in children with Autism (Begeer et al., 2011). Based on the suggested relationship between social cognition and executive function skills, some research has attempted to examine how 'brain training' protocols aimed at enhancing executive function abilities may in turn help enhance social cognition/ToM abilities. For instance, Kloo and Perner (2003) found that when children aged 3 or 4 years old engaged in training of cognitive flexibility (using a set-shifting task), performance on a false belief task resultantly improved to a level over and above that achieved by the control group who did not undertake training. Interestingly, results also showed that training on the *false belief* task led to a significant increase in performance on the cognitive flexibility task, although this improvement was in line with improvements also seen in the control group. These results provide promising indications that training of executive function abilities may aid enhancement of social cognition abilities. However, current literature is limited in ascertaining the extent to which these training effects relate to real-world influences (i.e. does increased social cognition task performance also indicate improvements in social interactions in daily lives?), as well as which tasks may be best suited for both training and assessing of executive function and social cognition abilities (Fisher & Happé, 2005; De Lillo, 2020). This provides an exciting and promising opportunity for future research to examine the extent to which 'brain training' protocols can be utilized as a way of improving social interaction capacities.

9.4.3 Transcranial direct current stimulation

An exciting new avenue of research on the 'social brain' has involved the use of transcranial direct current stimulation (tDCS), a safe, non-invasive technique for modulating neural activity by applying a weak current to the skull (Sellaro et al., 2016; Santiesteban et al., 2015; Adenzato et al., 2017; Martin et al., 2017). Martin et al. (2017) state that excitatory 'anodal' tDCS *increases* the likelihood of neuronal firing, while inhibitory 'cathodal' stimulation *reduces* the likelihood of neuronal firing. Studies using tDCS have reported intriguing results, including the presence of sex differences in the results outcome; for instance, tDCS administered to the dorsal-medial prefrontal cortex (dmPFC) showed improved cognitive ToM performance for females only, with no improvement in male participants' performance, in emotion recognition (Martin et al., 2017) and attribution of intentions (Adenzato et al., 2017) tasks. It has also been shown that tDCS administration can enhance adaptive cognitive control in both younger (Gbadeyan et al., 2016) and older (Gbadeyan et al., 2019) adults, highlighting the potential beneficial effects of tDCS on cognitive abilities. These results provide a promising basis for future research, including examining improvements in social cognition task performance that may be encouraged by tDCS administration for individuals at different ages experiencing declines in their social cognition capacities.

9.5 Conclusions

Social cognition plays an important role in daily life, allowing successful interactions to occur. Over the past few decades, there have been significant advances in our understanding of social cognition abilities across different populations. However, many questions still remain. As highlighted throughout this chapter, there is a need to include a 'social' element in social cognition research, bridging the gap between lab-based behavioural tasks and real-world experiences in day-to-day life, allowing further insight into the underlying structure of social cognition across different contexts. Cutting-edge new methods being used for this purpose, including virtual reality methods, EEG, fNIRS, and tDCS, provide an exciting and promising way of addressing this gap, aiming at looking at social interactions across different scenarios, including dyads and groups of participants, to examine social interaction behaviours in real time. Research examining social cognition across the lifespan, in clinical populations, and in non-WEIRD participants also provides opportunity for insight into the structure of social cognition across populations, which in turn may aid in development of intervention protocols aimed at improving social cognition abilities. There remain many open-ended questions within the field of social cognition research but, with these promising avenues for future research, it remains an exciting field with much more information about social cognition processes to be gained as research methods and approaches evolve.

References

Abell, F., Happé, F., & Frith, U., 2000. 'Do triangles play tricks? Attribution of mental states to animated shapes in normal and abnormal development'. *Cognitive Development* 15. 1: 1–16.

Adenzato, M., Brambilla, M., Manenti, R., De Lucia, L., Trojano, L., Garofalo, S., . . . & Cotelli, M., 2017. 'Gender differences in cognitive Theory of Mind revealed by transcranial direct current stimulation on medial prefrontal cortex'. *Scientific Reports* 7. 1: 1–9.

Apperly, I., 2012. 'What is "theory of mind"? Concepts, cognitive processes and individual differences'. *Quarterly Journal of Experimental Psychology* 65. 5: 825–839.

Apperly, I. A., & Butterfill, S. A., 2009. 'Do humans have two systems to track beliefs and belief-like states?'. *Psychological Review* 116. 4: 953–970.

Apperly, I. A., Samson, D., & Humphreys, G. W., 2009. 'Studies of adults can inform accounts of theory of mind development'. *Developmental Psychology* 45. 1: 190–201.

Astolfi, L., Toppi, J., De Vico Fallani, F., Vecchiato, G., Salinari, S., Mattia, D., ... & Babiloni, F., 2010. 'Neuroelectrical hyperscanning measures simultaneous brain activity in humans.' *Brain Topography* 23. 3: 243–256.

Avis, J., & Harris, P. L., 1991. 'Belief-desire reasoning among Baka children: Evidence for a universal conception of mind'. *Child Development* 62. 3: 460–467.

Bailey, P. E., & Henry, J. D., 2008. 'Growing less empathic with age: Disinhibition of the self-perspective'. *Journals of Gerontology Series B: Psychological Sciences and Social Sciences* 63. 4: 219–226.

Bailey, P. E., Henry, J. D., & von Hippel, W., 2008. 'Empathy and social functioning in late adulthood'. *Aging and Mental Health* 12. 4: 499–503.

Balconi, M., Grippa, E., & Vanutelli, M. E., 2015. 'What hemodynamic (fNIRS), electrophysiological (EEG) and autonomic integrated measures can tell us about emotional processing'. *Brain and Cognition* 95: 67–76.

Baron-Cohen, S., Leslie, A. M., & Frith, U., 1985. 'Does the autistic child have a "theory of mind"?'. *Cognition* 21. 1: 37–46.

Baron-Cohen, S., Wheelwright, S., Hill, J., Raste, Y., & Plumb, I., 2001. 'The "Reading the Mind in the Eyes" test revised version: A study with normal adults, and adults with Asperger syndrome or high-functioning autism'. *Journal of Child Psychology and Psychiatry and Allied Disciplines* 42. 2: 241–251.

Begeer, S., Gevers, C., Clifford, P., Verhoeve, M., Kat, K., Hoddenbach, E., & Boer, F., 2011. 'Theory of Mind training in children with autism: A randomized controlled trial'. *Journal of Autism and Developmental Disorders* 41. 8: 997–1006.

Bernstein, D. M., Thornton, W. L., & Sommerville, J. A., 2011. 'Theory of mind through the ages: Older and middle-aged adults exhibit more errors than do younger adults on a continuous false belief task'. *Experimental Aging Research* 37. 5: 481–502.

Blakemore, S. J., 2008. 'The social brain in adolescence'. *Nature Reviews Neuroscience* 9. 4: 267–277.

Boas, D., & Franceschini, M. A., 2009. 'Near infrared imaging'. *Scholarpedia* 4. 4: 6997.

Bradford, E. E. F., Brunsdon, V. E., & Ferguson, H. J., 2020. 'The neural basis of belief-attribution across the lifespan: False-belief reasoning and the N400 effect'. *Cortex* 126: 265–280.

Bradford, E. E. F., Brunsdon, V. E., & Ferguson, H. J., submitted. 'The cognitive basis of perspective-taking across adulthood: An eye-tracking study using the Director Task'.

Bradford, E. E. F., Jentzsch, I., & Gomez, J. C., 2015. 'From self to social cognition: Theory of mind mechanisms and their relation to executive functioning'. *Cognition* 138: 21–34.

Bradford, E. E. F., Hukker, V., Smith, L., & Ferguson, H. J., 2018a. 'Belief-attribution in adults with and without autistic spectrum disorders'. *Autism Research* 11. 11: 1542–1553.

Bradford, E. E. F., Jentzsch, I., Gomez, J. C., Chen, Y., Zhang, D., & Su, Y., 2018b. 'Cross-cultural differences in adult theory of mind abilities: A comparison of native-English speakers and native-Chinese speakers on the self/other differentiation task'. *Quarterly Journal of Experimental Psychology* 71. 12: 2665–2676.

Brown-Schmidt, S., 2009. 'The role of executive function in perspective taking during on-line language comprehension'. *Psychonomic Bulletin & Review* 16. 5: 893–900.

Brüne, M., 2004. 'Schizophrenia—an evolutionary enigma?'. *Neuroscience & Biobehavioral Reviews* 28. 1: 41–53.

Brunsdon, V. E. A., Bradford, E. E. F., & Ferguson, H. J., 2019. 'Sensorimotor mu rhythm during action observation changes across the lifespan independently from social cognitive processes'. *Developmental Cognitive Neuroscience* 28: 100659.

Ferguson, H. J., Brunsdon, V. E. A., & Bradford, E. E. F., 2021. 'The developmental trajectories of executive function from adolescence to old age'. *Scientific Reports* 11: 1382.

Butterfill, S. A., & Apperly, I. A., 2013. 'How to construct a minimal theory of mind'. *Mind & Language* 28. 5: 606–637.

Caillies, S., Bertot, V., Motte, J., Raynaud, C., & Abely, M., 2014. 'Social cognition in ADHD: Irony understanding and recursive theory of mind'. *Research in Developmental Disabilities* 35. 11: 3191–3198.

Callaghan, T., Rochat, P., Lillard, A., Claux, M. L., Odden, H., Itakura, S., ... & Singh, S., 2005. 'Synchrony in the onset of mental-state reasoning: Evidence from five cultures'. *Psychological Science* 16. 5: 378–384.

Cane, J. E., Ferguson, H. J., & Apperly, I. A., 2017. 'Using perspective to resolve reference: The impact of cognitive load and motivation'. *Journal of Experimental Psychology: Learning, Memory, and Cognition* 43. 4: 591.

Carlson, S. M., & Moses, L. J., 2001. 'Individual differences in inhibitory control and children's theory of mind'. *Child Development* 72. 4: 1032–1053.

Carruthers, P., 2016. 'Two systems for mindreading?'. *Review of Philosophy and Psychology* 7. 1: 141–162.

Combs, D. R., Adams, S. D., Penn, D. L., Roberts, D., Tiegreen, J., & Stem, P., 2007. 'Social Cognition and Interaction Training (SCIT) for inpatients with schizophrenia spectrum disorders: Preliminary findings'. *Schizophrenia Research* 91. 1–3: 112–116.

Converse, B. A., Lin, S., Keysar, B., & Epley, N., 2008. 'In the mood to get over yourself: Mood affects theory-of-mind use'. *Emotion* 8. 5: 725.

Couture, S. M., Penn, D. L., & Roberts, D. L., 2006. 'The functional significance of social cognition in schizophrenia: A review'. *Schizophrenia Bulletin* 32. suppl_1: S44–S63.

Cuerva, A. G., Sabe, L., Kuzis, G., Tiberti, C., Dorrego, F., & Starkstein, S. E., 2001. 'Theory of mind and pragmatic abilities in dementia'. *Cognitive and Behavioral Neurology* 14. 3: 153–158.

Cutting, A. L., & Dunn, J., 2002. 'The cost of understanding other people: Social cognition predicts young children's sensitivity to criticism'. *Journal of Child Psychology and Psychiatry* 43. 7: 849–860.

Dale, A. M., & Halgren, E., 2001. 'Spatiotemporal mapping of brain activity by integration of multiple imaging modalities'. *Current Opinion in Neurobiology* 11. 2: 202–208.

Dale, A. M., & Sereno, M. I., 1993. 'Improved localizadon of cortical activity by combining EEG and MEG with MRI cortical surface reconstruction: A linear approach'. *Journal of Cognitive Neuroscience* 5. 2: 162–176.

Debener, S., Ullsperger, M., Siegel, M., & Engel, A. K., 2006. 'Single-trial EEG–fMRI reveals the dynamics of cognitive function'. *Trends in Cognitive Sciences* 10. 12: 558–563.

de Borst, A. W., & de Gelder, B., 2015. 'Is it the real deal? Perception of virtual characters versus humans: An affective cognitive neuroscience perspective'. *Frontiers in Psychology* 6: 576.

De Guzman, M., Bird, G., Banissy, M. J., & Catmur, C., 2016. 'Self–other control processes in social cognition: From imitation to empathy'. *Philosophical Transactions of the Royal Society B: Biological Sciences* 371. 1686: 20150079.

De Lillo, M. (2020). Social cognition across the lifespan and its relation to executive functions. University of Kent. Unpublished PhD thesis.

Diemer, J., Alpers, G. W., Peperkorn, H. M., Shiban, Y., & Mühlberger, A., 2015. 'The impact of perception and presence on emotional reactions: A review of research in virtual reality'. *Frontiers in Psychology* 6: 26.

Dowsett, S. M., & Livesey, D. J., 2000. 'The development of inhibitory control in preschool children: Effects of "executive skills" training'. *Developmental Psychobiology: The Journal of the International Society for Developmental Psychobiology* 36. 2: 161–174.

Dumas, G., 2011. 'Towards a two-body neuroscience'. *Communicative & Integrative Biology* 4. 3: 349–352.

Dumontheil, I., Apperly, I. A., & Blakemore, S. J., 2010. 'Online usage of theory of mind continues to develop in late adolescence'. *Developmental Science* 13. 2: 331–338.

Duval, C., Piolino, P., Bejanin, A., Eustache, F., & Desgranges, B., 2011. 'Age effects on different components of theory of mind'. *Consciousness and Cognition* 20. 3: 627–642.

Elderkin-Thompson, V., Ballmaier, M., Hellemann, G., Pham, D., & Kumar, A., 2008. 'Executive function and MRI prefrontal volumes among healthy older adults'. *Neuropsychology* 22. 5: 626.

Ferguson, H. J., Apperly, I., & Cane, J. E., 2017. 'Eye tracking reveals the cost of switching between self and other perspectives in a visual perspective-taking task'. *Quarterly Journal of Experimental Psychology* 70. 8: 1646–1660.

Ferguson, H. J., Brunsdon, V. E., & Bradford, E. E. F., 2018. 'Age of avatar modulates the altercentric bias in a visual perspective-taking task: ERP and behavioral evidence'. *Cognitive, Affective, & Behavioral Neuroscience* 18. 6: 1298–1319.

Ferguson, H. J., Cane, J. E., Douchkov, M., & Wright, D., 2015b. 'Empathy predicts false belief reasoning ability: Evidence from the N400'. *Social Cognitive and Affective Neuroscience* 10. 6: 848–855.

Ferguson, H. J., Apperly, I., Ahmad, J., Bindemann, M., & Cane, J., 2015a. 'Task constraints distinguish perspective inferences from perspective use during discourse interpretation in a false belief task'. *Cognition* 139: 50–70.

Fisher, N., & Happé, F., 2005. 'A training study of theory of mind and executive function in children with autistic spectrum disorders'. *Journal of Autism and Developmental Disorders* 35. 6: 757.

Fiske, A. P., Kitayama, S., Markus, H. R., & Nisbett, R. E., 1998. 'The cultural matrix of social psychology'. In *The Handbook of Social Psychology*, edited by D. T. Gilbert et al. McGraw-Hill.

Frith, C. D. 1992. *The Cognitive Neuropsychology of Schizophrenia*. Psychology Press.

Frith, C. D., 2007. 'The social brain?'. *Philosophical Transactions of the Royal Society B: Biological Sciences* 362. 1480: 671–678.

Frith, U., & Frith, C. D., 2003. 'Development and neurophysiology of mentalizing'. *Philosophical Transactions of the Royal Society of London. Series B: Biological Sciences* 358. 1431: 459–473.

Froese, T., Iizuka, H., & Ikegami, T., 2014. 'Embodied social interaction constitutes social cognition in pairs of humans: A minimalist virtual reality experiment'. *Scientific Reports* 4: 3672.

Gbadeyan, O., McMahon, K., Steinhauser, M., & Meinzer, M., 2016. 'Stimulation of dorsolateral prefrontal cortex enhances adaptive cognitive control: A high-definition transcranial direct current stimulation study'. *Journal of Neuroscience* 36. 50: 12530–12536.

Gbadeyan, O., Steinhauser, M., Hunold, A., Martin, A. K., Haueisen, J., & Meinzer, M., 2019. 'Modulation of adaptive cognitive control by prefrontal high-definition transcranial direct current stimulation in older adults'. *Journals of Gerontology: Series B* 74. 7: 1174–1183.

German, T. P., & Hehman, J. A., 2006. 'Representational and executive selection resources in "theory of mind": Evidence from compromised belief-desire reasoning in old age'. *Cognition* 101. 1: 129–152.

Gregory, C., Lough, S., Stone, V., Erzinclioglu, S., Martin, L., Baron-Cohen, S., & Hodges, J. R., 2002. 'Theory of mind in patients with frontal variant frontotemporal dementia and Alzheimer's disease: Theoretical and practical implications'. *Brain* 125. 4: 752–764.

Happé, F. G., 1994. 'An advanced test of theory of mind: Understanding of story characters' thoughts and feelings by able autistic, mentally handicapped, and normal children and adults'. *Journal of Autism and Developmental Disorders* 24. 2: 129–154.

Happé, F., Brownell, H., & Winner, E., 1999. 'Acquired "theory of mind" impairments following stroke'. *Cognition* 70. 3: 211–240.

Hartwright, C. E., Apperly, I. A., & Hansen, P. C., 2014. 'Representation, control, or reasoning? Distinct functions for theory of mind within the medial prefrontal cortex'. *Journal of Cognitive Neuroscience* 26. 4: 683–698.

Hasson, U., Ghazanfar, A. A., Galantucci, B., Garrod, S., & Keysers, C., 2012. 'Brain-to-brain coupling: A mechanism for creating and sharing a social world'. *Trends in Cognitive Sciences* 16. 2: 114–121.

Hayward, E. O., & Homer, B. D., 2017. 'Reliability and validity of advanced theory-of-mind measures in middle childhood and adolescence'. *British Journal of Developmental Psychology* 35. 3: 454–462.

Henrich, J., Heine, S. J., & Norenzayan, A., 2010. 'Most people are not WEIRD'. *Nature* 466. 7302: 29.

Herold, R., Tényi, T., Lénárd, K., & Trixler, M., 2002. 'Theory of mind deficit in people with schizophrenia during remission'. *Psychological Medicine* 32. 6: 1125.

Holmes, J., Woolgar, F., Hampshire, A., & Gathercole, S. E., 2019. 'Are working memory training effects paradigm-specific?'. *Frontiers in Psychology* 10: 1103.

Hong, Y. Y., & Chiu, C. Y., 2001. 'Toward a paradigm shift: From cross-cultural differences in social cognition to social-cognitive mediation of cultural differences'. *Social Cognition* 19. 3: 181–196.

Hughes, C., Devine, R. T., Ensor, R., Koyasu, M., Mizokawa, A., & Lecce, S., 2014. 'Lost in translation? Comparing British, Japanese, and Italian children's theory-of-mind performance'. *Child Development Research*, article ID 893492.

Hutchins, T. L., Prelock, P. A., & Bonazinga, L., 2012. 'Psychometric evaluation of the Theory of Mind Inventory (ToMI): A study of typically developing children and children with autism spectrum disorder'. *Journal of Autism and Developmental Disorders* 42. 3: 327–341.

Hyde, D. C., Aparicio Betancourt, M., & Simon, C. E., 2015. 'Human temporal-parietal junction spontaneously tracks others' beliefs: A functional near-infrared spectroscopy study'. *Human Brain Mapping* 36. 12: 4831–4846.

Jardri, R., Pins, D., Lafargue, G., Very, E., Ameller, A., Delmaire, C., & Thomas, P., 2011. 'Increased overlap between the brain areas involved in self-other distinction in schizophrenia'. *PloS One* 6. 3: e17500.

Jiang, J., Chen, C., Dai, B., Shi, G., Ding, G., Liu, L., & Lu, C., 2015. 'Leader emergence through interpersonal neural synchronization'. *Proceedings of the National Academy of Sciences* 112. 14: 4274–4279.

Kandalaft, M. R., Didehbani, N., Krawczyk, D. C., Allen, T. T., & Chapman, S. B., 2013. 'Virtual reality social cognition training for young adults with high-functioning autism'. *Journal of Autism and Developmental Disorders* 43. 1: 34–44.

Kang, K., Schneider, D., Schweinberger, S. R., & Mitchell, P., 2018. 'Dissociating neural signatures of mental state retrodiction and classification based on facial expressions'. *Social Cognitive and Affective Neuroscience* 13. 9: 933–943.

Kemp, J., Després, O., Sellal, F., & Dufour, A., 2012. 'Theory of Mind in normal ageing and neurodegenerative pathologies'. *Ageing Research Reviews* 11. 2: 199–219.

Keysar, B., Lin, S., & Barr, D. J., 2003. 'Limits on theory of mind use in adults'. *Cognition* 89. 1: 25–41.

Keysar, B., Barr, D. J., Balin, J. A., & Brauner, J. S., 2000. 'Taking perspective in conversation: The role of mutual knowledge in comprehension'. *Psychological Science* 11. 1: 32–38.

Kloo, D., & Perner, J., 2003. 'Training transfer between card sorting and false belief understanding: Helping children apply conflicting descriptions'. *Child Development* 74. 6: 1823–1839.

Kobayashi, C., Glover, G. H., & Temple, E., 2006. 'Cultural and linguistic influence on neural bases of "Theory of Mind": An fMRI study with Japanese bilinguals'. *Brain and Language* 98. 2: 210–220.

Konvalinka, I., & Roepstorff, A., 2012. 'The two-brain approach: How can mutually interacting brains teach us something about social interaction?'. *Frontiers in Human Neuroscience* 6: 215.

Kühn-Popp, N., Sodian, B., Sommer, M., Döhnel, K., & Meinhardt, J., 2013. 'Same or different? ERP correlates of pretense and false belief reasoning in children'. *Neuroscience* 248: 488–498.

Laidlaw, K. E., Foulsham, T., Kuhn, G., & Kingstone, A., 2011. 'Potential social interactions are important to social attention'. *Proceedings of the National Academy of Sciences* 108. 14: 5548–5553.

Lecce, S., & Hughes, C., 2010. 'The Italian job?: Comparing theory of mind performance in British and Italian children'. *British Journal of Developmental Psychology* 28. 4: 747–766.

Lecce, S., Bianco, F., Devine, R. T., Hughes, C., & Banerjee, R., 2014. 'Promoting theory of mind during middle childhood: A training program'. *Journal of Experimental Child Psychology* 126: 52–67.

Leslie, A. M., & Thaiss, L., 1992. 'Domain specificity in conceptual development: Neuropsychological evidence from autism'. *Cognition* 43. 3: 225–251.

Liepelt, R., Schneider, J. C., Aichert, D. S., Wöstmann, N., Dehning, S., Möller, H. J., . . . & Ettinger, U., 2012. 'Action blind: Disturbed self-other integration in schizophrenia'. *Neuropsychologia* 50. 14: 3775–3780.

Ligneau-Hervé, C., & Mullet, E., 2005. 'Perspective-taking judgments among young adults, middle-aged, and elderly people'. *Journal of Experimental Psychology: Applied* 11. 1: 53.

Liu, D., Sabbagh, M. A., Gehring, W. J., & Wellman, H. M., 2004. 'Decoupling beliefs from reality in the brain: An ERP study of theory of mind'. *NeuroReport* 15. 6: 991–995.

Liu, D., Wellman, H. M., Tardif, T., & Sabbagh, M. A., 2008. 'Theory of mind development in Chinese children: A meta-analysis of false-belief understanding across cultures and languages'. *Developmental Psychology* 44. 2: 523.

Lough, S. Gregory, C., & Hodges, J. R., 2001. 'Dissociation of social cognition and executive function in frontal variant frontotemporal dementia'. *Neurocase* 7: 123–130.

Lough, S., Kipps, C. M., Treise, C., Watson, P., Blair, J. R., & Hodges, J. R., 2006. 'Social reasoning, emotion and empathy in frontotemporal dementia'. *Neuropsychologia* 44. 6: 950–958.

Maggio, M. G., Latella, D., Maresca, G., Sciarrone, F., Manuli, A., Naro, A., De Luca, R., & Calabrò, R. S., 2019. 'Virtual reality and cognitive rehabilitation in people with stroke: An overview'. *Journal of Neuroscience Nursing* 51. 2: 101–105.

Mansour, H., & Kuhn, G., 2019. 'Studying "natural" eye movements in an "unnatural" social environment: The influence of social activity, framing, and sub-clinical traits on gaze aversion'. *Quarterly Journal of Experimental Psychology* 72. 8: 1913–1925.

Martin, A. K., Huang, J., Hunold, A., & Meinzer, M., 2017. 'Sex mediates the effects of high-definition transcranial direct current stimulation on "mind-reading"'. *Neuroscience* 366: 84–94.

Mayer, A., & Träuble, B. E., 2013. 'Synchrony in the onset of mental state understanding across cultures? A study among children in Samoa'. *International Journal of Behavioral Development* 37. 1: 21–28.

McAuliffe, K., & Dunham, Y., 2016. 'Group bias in cooperative norm enforcement'. *Philosophical Transactions of the Royal Society B: Biological Sciences* 371. 1686: 20150073.

McCrae, R. R., & Terracciano, A., 2005. 'Personality profiles of cultures: Aggregate personality traits'. *Journal of Personality and Social Psychology* 89. 3: 407.

McKendrick, R., Ayaz, H., Olmstead, R., & Parasuraman, R., 2014. 'Enhancing dual-task performance with verbal and spatial working memory training: Continuous monitoring of cerebral hemodynamics with NIRS'. *NeuroImage* 85: 1014–1026.

Meinhardt, J., Kühn-Popp, N., Sommer, M., & Sodian, B., 2012. 'Distinct neural correlates underlying pretense and false belief reasoning: Evidence from ERPs'. *NeuroImage* 63. 2: 623–631.

Millett, D., 2001. 'Hans Berger: From psychic energy to the EEG'. *Perspectives in Biology and Medicine* 44. 4: 522–542.

Milward, S. J., & Sebanz, N., 2016. 'Mechanisms and development of self–other distinction in dyads and groups'. *Philosophical Transactions of the Royal Society B: Biological Sciences* 371. 1686: 20150076.

Miyake, A., & Friedman, N. P., 2012. 'The nature and organization of individual differences in executive functions: Four general conclusions'. *Current Directions in Psychological Science* 21. 1: 8–14.

Miyake, A., Friedman, N. P., Emerson, M. J., Witzki, A. H., Howerter, A., & Wager, T. D., 2000. 'The unity and diversity of executive functions and their contributions to complex "frontal lobe" tasks: A latent variable analysis'. *Cognitive Psychology* 41. 1: 49–100.

Moran, J. M., 2013. 'Lifespan development: The effects of typical aging on theory of mind'. *Behavioural Brain Research* 237: 32–40.

Naughtin, C. K., Horne, K., Schneider, D., Venini, D., York, A., & Dux, P. E., 2017. 'Do implicit and explicit belief processing share neural substrates?'. *Human Brain Mapping* 38. 9: 4760–4772.

Nisbett, R. E., Peng, K., Choi, I., & Norenzayan, A., 2001. 'Culture and systems of thought: Holistic versus analytic cognition'. *Psychological Review* 108. 2: 291.

Ochsner, K. N., 2004. 'Current directions in social cognitive neuroscience'. *Current Opinion in Neurobiology* 14. 2: 254–258.

Over, H., 2016. 'The origins of belonging: Social motivation in infants and young children'. *Philosophical Transactions of the Royal Society B: Biological Sciences* 371. 1686: 20150072.

Ozonoff, S., & McEvoy, R. E., 1994. 'A longitudinal study of executive function and theory of mind development in autism'. *Development and Psychopathology* 6. 3: 415–431.

Ozonoff, S., Pennington, B. F., & Rogers, S. J., 1991. 'Executive function deficits in high-functioning autistic individuals: Relationship to theory of mind'. *Journal of Child Psychology and Psychiatry* 32. 7: 1081–1105.

Pan, X., & Hamilton, A. F. D. C., 2018. 'Why and how to use virtual reality to study human social interaction: The challenges of exploring a new research landscape'. *British Journal of Psychology* 109. 3: 395–417.

Parsons, T. D., Gaggioli, A., & Riva, G., 2017. 'Virtual reality for research in social neuroscience'. *Brain Sciences* 7. 4: 42.

Phillips, L. H., Bull, R., Allen, R., Insch, P., Burr, K., & Ogg, W., 2011. 'Lifespan aging and belief reasoning: Influences of executive function and social cue decoding'. *Cognition* 120. 2: 236–247.

Pinkham, A. E., & Penn, D. L., 2006. 'Neurocognitive and social cognitive predictors of interpersonal skill in schizophrenia'. *Psychiatry Research* 143. 2–3: 167–178.

Pinti, P., Tachtsidis, I., Hamilton, A., Hirsch, J., Aichelburg, C., Gilbert, S., & Burgess, P. W., 2020. 'The present and future use of functional near-infrared spectroscopy (fNIRS) for cognitive neuroscience'. *Annals of the New York Academy of Sciences* 1464. 1: 5.

Rakoczy, H., Harder-Kasten, A., & Sturm, L., 2012. 'The decline of theory of mind in old age is (partly) mediated by developmental changes in domain-general abilities'. *British Journal of Psychology* 103. 1: 58–72.

Sabbagh, M. A., & Taylor, M., 2000. 'Neural correlates of theory-of-mind reasoning: An event-related potential study'. *Psychological Science* 11. 1: 46–50.

Sabbagh, M. A., Xu, F., Carlson, S. M., Moses, L. J., & Lee, K., 2006. 'The development of executive functioning and theory of mind: A comparison of Chinese and US preschoolers'. *Psychological Science* 17. 1: 74–81.

Salthouse, T. A., Atkinson, T. M., & Berish, D. E., 2003. 'Executive functioning as a potential mediator of age-related cognitive decline in normal adults'. *Journal of Experimental Psychology: General* 132. 4: 566.

Samson, D., & Apperly, I. A., 2010. 'There is more to mind reading than having theory of mind concepts: New directions in theory of mind research'. *Infant and Child Development* 19. 5: 443–454.

Samson, D., Apperly, I. A., Braithwaite, J. J., Andrews, B. J., & Bodley Scott, S. E., 2010. 'Seeing it their way: Evidence for rapid and involuntary computation of what other people see'. *Journal of Experimental Psychology: Human Perception and Performance* 36. 5: 1255.

Santiesteban, I., Banissy, M. J., Catmur, C., & Bird, G., 2015. 'Functional lateralization of temporoparietal junction–imitation inhibition, visual perspective-taking and theory of mind'. *European Journal of Neuroscience* 42. 8: 2527–2533.

Santiesteban, I., White, S., Cook, J., Gilbert, S. J., Heyes, C., & Bird, G., 2012. 'Training social cognition: From imitation to theory of mind'. *Cognition* 122. 2: 228–235.

Saxe, R. R., Whitfield-Gabrieli, S., Scholz, J., & Pelphrey, K. A., 2009. 'Brain regions for perceiving and reasoning about other people in school-aged children'. *Child Development* 80. 4: 1197–1209.

Schilbach, L., 2015. 'Eye to eye, face to face and brain to brain: Novel approaches to study the behavioral dynamics and neural mechanisms of social interactions'. *Current Opinion in Behavioral Sciences* 3: 130–135.

Schilbach, L., Timmermans, B., Reddy, V., Costall, A., Bente, G., Schlicht, T., & Vogeley, K., 2013. 'Toward a second-person neuroscience 1'. *Behavioral and Brain Sciences* 36. 4: 393–414.

Schilbach, L., Wohlschlaeger, A. M., Kraemer, N. C., Newen, A., Shah, N. J., Fink, G. R., & Vogeley, K., 2006. 'Being with virtual others: Neural correlates of social interaction'. *Neuropsychologia* 44. 5: 718–730.

Schneider, D., Slaughter, V. P., & Dux, P. E., 2015. 'What do we know about implicit false-belief tracking?' *Psychonomic Bulletin & Review* 22. 1: 1–12.

Sellaro, R., Nitsche, M. A., & Colzato, L. S., 2016. 'The stimulated social brain: Effects of transcranial direct current stimulation on social cognition'. *Annals of the New York Academy of Sciences* 1369. 1: 218–239.

Shahaeian, A., Nielsen, M., Peterson, C. C., & Slaughter, V., 2014. 'Cultural and family influences on children's theory of mind development: A comparison of Australian and Iranian school-age children'. *Journal of Cross-Cultural Psychology* 45. 4: 555–568.

Steinbeis, N., 2016. 'The role of self–other distinction in understanding others' mental and emotional states: Neurocognitive mechanisms in children and adults'. *Philosophical Transactions of the Royal Society B: Biological Sciences* 371. 1686: 20150074.

Strang, J. F., Kenworthy, L., Daniolos, P., Case, L., Wills, M. C., Martin, A., & Wallace, G. L., 2012. 'Depression and anxiety symptoms in children and adolescents with autism spectrum disorders without intellectual disability'. *Research in Autism Spectrum Disorders* 6. 1: 406–412.

Strickland, D., Marcus, L. M., Mesibov, G. B., & Hogan, K., 1996. 'Brief report: Two case studies using virtual reality as a learning tool for autistic children'. *Journal of Autism and Developmental Disorders* 26. 6: 651–659.

Sullivan, S., & Ruffman, T., 2004. 'Emotion recognition deficits in the elderly'. *International Journal of Neuroscience* 114. 3: 403–432.

Testa, R., Bennett, P., & Ponsford, J., 2012. 'Factor analysis of nineteen executive function tests in a healthy adult population'. *Archives of Clinical Neuropsychology* 27. 2: 213–224.

Wang, J. J., Tseng, P., Juan, C. H., Frisson, S., & Apperly, I. A., 2019. 'Perspective-taking across cultures: Shared biases in Taiwanese and British adults'. *Royal Society Open Science* 6. 11: 190540.

Warnell, K. R., & Redcay, E., 2019. 'Minimal coherence among varied theory of mind measures in childhood and adulthood'. *Cognition* 191: 103997.

Whitehouse, H., Lanman, J. A., Downey, G., Fredman, L. A., Swann Jr, W. B., Lende, D. H., . . . & Whitehouse, H., 2014. 'The ties that bind us: Ritual, fusion, and identification'. *Current Anthropology* 55. 6: 674–695.

Whyte, E. M., Smyth, J. M., & Scherf, K. S., 2015. 'Designing serious game interventions for individuals with autism'. *Journal of Autism and Developmental Disorders* 45. 12: 3820–3831.

Zaki, J., & Ochsner, K. N., 2012. 'The neuroscience of empathy: Progress, pitfalls and promise'. *Nature Neuroscience* 15. 5: 675–680.

Index

For the benefit of digital users, indexed terms that span two pages (e.g., 52–53) may, on occasion, appear on only one of those pages.

Boxes are indicated by *b* following the page number

actor-partner interaction model (APIM) 61–62
adolescence 70–95
  defining 71
  depression 85–86
  emotion regulation 82–85
  executive functions 82–85
  face perception 77–79
  hormones 74–76
  mate-seeking behaviour 74–75
  mating intelligence (reproductive competence) 70–72, 76, 80, 81
  mentalizing 79–81
  peer evaluation 72–73
  perspective-taking 80–81
  puberty 74–76
  reward sensitivity 75
  risk-taking behaviour 75–76, 82–84
  romantic relationships 73–74, 85
  school transitions 72–73
  sexual activity 73–74
  social affect 83–84
  social brain 76–77, 79–80, 81
  social changes 72–74
  social feedback 73
  social reorientation hypothesis 73
  status preoccupation 73
adrenarche 74
adult mindreading 96–116
  individual differences 100–6
  measurement challenges 101–5
  motivation 106–11
affective (emotional) empathy 125–26, 156–57, 178, 187–89, 191–92
affective theory of mind 2–3, 9, 177–78
ageing *see* old age
agent recognition 132
alexithymia 157
altercentric interference 99, 100
Alzheimer's disease 184–89, 193–94
amygdala 82, 178–80
animated triangles task 101–2, 211
anterior cingulate cortex 73, 83–85, 182–83

anterior cingulate-fronto-insular cortices 178–80, 182–83, 188–89, 192–93
anterior temporal cortex 76–77
anticipatory looking 37, 38–39
appearance–reality tasks 35–36
attention, social
  autism spectrum disorder 152–54
  old age 134–35
attention deficit hyperactivity disorder 211–12
autism spectrum disorder (ASD) 147–76, 202–3, 211–12
  adulthood 150
  age-related cognitive decline 150
  alexithymia 157
  appropriateness of theory of mind tasks 11–12, 165–66
  big data approach 162–63
  broken mirror theory 155–56
  cognitive models 149
  compensatory ability 164
  co-occurring conditions 163–64
  diagnosis 148–49
  double empathy model 161–62
  early neurocognitive markers 150
  egocentric errors in subclinical population 102–3, 109
  empathizing-systemizing theory 156–57
  enhanced social abilities 151
  executive functions 7–8
  eye contact 154–55
  females 148–49, 153
  heterogeneity 162–63
  imitation 155–56
  individual differences 162–64
  lifespan perspective 150–51
  mindblindness 109–10
  neurodiversity model 161–62
  non-social theories 147–48
  optimal outcome 150, 166
  prevalence 148–49
  reputation management 154
  reward processing 154

autism spectrum disorder (ASD) (*cont.*)
  social attention 152–54
  social cognitive theories 151–61
  social motivation 109–10, 154–55
  social orienting hypothesis 152–53
  theory of mind 7–8, 50, 158–61
  virtual reality training 205–6
automatic imitation
  autism spectrum disorder 156
  old age 131
Awareness of Social Inference Test (TASIT) 10

behavioural variant frontotemporal dementia 184–85, 189–94
belief–desire folk psychology 31, 35–41
big data 162–63
bilinguals 215–16
biological motion 29, 137
biosocial model of status 75
brain
  action observation 130–31
  default mode network 184–85, 192–93
  dementia 184–85, 187, 188–89, 192–93
  emotion processing 82
  emotion recognition 128–29
  emotion regulation 83–84
  face processing 77–78
  mindreading 97–98, 100
  mirror neurons 130–31, 155–56
  neural substrates of age-related changes 5, 182–83
  perspective-taking 81
  romantic love 84–85
  salience network 184–85, 188–89, 192–93
  self–other interference control 100, 104–5
  social feedback in adolescence 73
  testosterone effects 74–75
  training 219
  see also social brain
broken mirror theory 155–56

Cambridge Mindreading Face-Voice Battery (CAM) 10, 129
caudate nucleus 84–85
cerebellum 187
child–caregiver turn-taking 30
childhood *see* early and middle childhood
cognitive activities 136
cognitive ageing 119–20
cognitive empathy 125–26, 156–57, 178
cognitive flexibility 7, 124–25
cognitive gadgets 6
cognitive reserve 123–24

cognitive theory of mind 2–3, 9, 177–78, 186–87, 190
collectivist cultures 215
compensatory scaffolding 183
conceptual change 36
conflict 52
context
  empathy 188, 191–92
  theory of mind 58–62
cross-cultural research 110–11, 215–16
cross-sex mind reading 79, 81

deaf children 36
default mode network 184–85, 192–93
dementia 184–85, 193–94, 202–3, 211–12
  Alzheimer's disease 184–89, 193–94
  behavioural variant frontotemporal 184–85, 189–94
depression
  adolescence 85–86
  egocentric errors 102–3
director task 97–98, 102–3, 105–8, 109, 211
dorsal striatum 85
dorsolateral prefrontal cortex 81
dorsomedial prefrontal cortex 79–80, 182–83
double empathy model of autism 161–62
Dual-Systems Model 82–83
dyadic approaches 61–62, 206–7

early and middle childhood 47–69
  development of theory of mind 47–50
  firstborn children 52
  friendships 56
  gender difference 57–58
  individual differences in theory of mind 48–50, 57
  parent–child interactions 51
  peer status 55–56
  prosocial behaviour 53–55
  sibling interactions 51–53
  social competence 53–55
  theory of mind training 61
ecological validity 13–15
EEG 207–9
egocentric interference 97, 99, 100, 102–3, 105–6, 109
electrophysiology 105, 108, 207–9
emotion
  emotional (affective) empathy 125–26, 156–57, 178, 187–89, 191–92
  quality of relationships 58–59
  recognition in old age 127–29
  regulation in adolescence 82–85

empathy 108, 178
  Alzheimer's disease 187–89
  autism spectrum disorder 156–57
  behavioural variant frontotemporal dementia 191–93
  cognitive 125–26, 156–57, 178
  double empathy 161–62
  emotional (affective) 125–26, 156–57, 178, 187–89, 191–92
  old age 125–27, 180–84
error management theory 81
event-related potentials (ERPs) 105, 108, 207–8
executive functions
  adolescence 82–85
  ageing 181, 218
  autism spectrum disorder 7–8
  behavioural variant frontotemporal dementia 190
  development 7
  laboratory task correlations 103–4
  physical activity 136
  theory of mind and 7–9, 36
  training 217–19
exercise 136
explicit theory of mind 158–59
Eyes task 61–62
eye tracking 14–15, 153, 216–17

faces
  cues for mate-seeking behaviour 74–75, 78–79
  perception in adolescence 77–79
  recognition in old age 132
  sensitivity in infancy 29
false belief tasks 7, 9–10, 35–36, 48–49, 120–21, 122–23, 158, 209–10
  replicability and validity issues 38–39
  violation-of-expectation 37, 38–39
faux pas task 10, 123–24
firstborn children 52
folk psychology 4–5
  belief–desire 31, 35–41
  perception-goal 31–35
friendships 56
Frith-Happé animations task 186–87
frontotemporal dementia, behavioural variant 184–85, 189–94
functional magnetic resonance imaging 182–83, 215–16
functional near-infrared spectroscopy 209–10, 214
fusiform gyrus 77–78

gaze following 31–32
gender difference 57–58

goals
  intentional action 32–34
  perception-goal folk psychology 31–35
  theory of mind deployment 57
gonadarche 74
group contexts 213–15

hippocampus 178–80, 187
hormones 74–76

Imbalance Model 82–83
imitation
  autism spectrum disorder 155–56
  infancy 30, 31, 33–34
  old age 131
implicit theory of mind 12–13, 158–59
individual differences
  adult mindreading 100–6
  autism spectrum disorder 162–64
  theory of mind in early and middle childhood 48–50, 57
individualist cultures 215
infancy 27–46
  biological motion sensitivity 29
  child–caregiver turn-taking (proto-conversations) 30
  early interaction 30
  emergence of first forms of theory of mind 31–35
  emergence of meta-representational theory of mind 35–41
  face sensitivity 29
  gaze following 31–32
  goal-directed intentional action 32–34
  imitation 30, 31, 33–34
  joint attention 31
  language sensitivity 30
  orienting reactions 30
  perception understanding 31–32
  perspective-taking 32, 35
  precursors to theory of mind 29–30
  shared intentionality 34–35
  triadic interactions 31
inferior frontal gyrus 100, 104–5, 182–83
inferior occipital gyrus 77–78
inferior parietal cortex 187
inhibition 7, 82–83, 104–5
insula 73, 84–85
intentionality
  goal-directed action 32–34
  shared 34–35
interaction-based paradigms 37, 38–39
Interpersonal Reactivity Index (IRI) 187–88
interventions
  brain training 219

interventions (*cont.*)
   enhancing social cognition in old age 135–37
   executive functions training 217–19
   self/other differentiation 213
   theory of mind training 61, 135–36
   virtual reality training in autism 205–6

joint attention 31

language
   infant sensitivity 30
   theory of mind and 36
life history theory 83
looking-time studies 32–33
love 84–85

ManyBabies initiative 40–41
mating cues 74–75, 78–79
mating intelligence 70–72, 76, 80, 81
medial prefrontal cortex 73, 76–77, 97–98, 178–80, 188–89
mentalizing 177–78
   adolescence 79–81
   brain networks *see* social brain
   see also mindreading; theory of mind
mental-state talk 51, 52
metaphor interpretation 56
middle age 119*b*, 122
mindblindness 109–10
mind-mindedness 109
mindreading
   altercentric interference 99, 100
   brain regions associated with 97–98, 100
   cognitive model 97–100
   cross-cultural domain 110–11
   cross-sex 79, 81
   egocentric interference 97, 99, 100, 102–3, 105–6, 109
   emotional quality of relationships 58–59
   individual differences 100–6
   inference, storage and use of information 97–99
   motivation 106–11
   one system account 5–6
   propensity 108–11
   self perspective 99
   situational incentives 106–8, 110–11
   social constructivist accounts 53
   two systems model 5
'Mind-Space' framework 6
mirror neurons 130–31, 155–56
mobile eye-tracking 14–15
monetary rewards 107

motivation
   adult mindreading 106–11
   autism spectrum disorder 109–10, 154–55
   old age 133–34, 183–84
   theory of mind deployment 57
Movie Assessment of Social Cognition 101–2

nativism 37
naturalistic observations 61–62
neurodiversity model of autism 161–62
neuroimaging 182–83, 187, 188–89, 207–10, 214, 215–16
Nicaraguan Sign Language 36
nucleus accumbens 75

oestradiol 76
old age 117–46, 210–11
   action recognition, observation and imitation 130–32
   agent recognition 132
   autism spectrum disorder 150
   cognitive activities 136
   cognitive ageing 119–20
   cognitive decline 8
   cognitive reserve 123–24
   compensatory scaffolding 183
   definition 118*b*
   emotion recognition 127–29
   empathy 125–27, 180–84
   executive function 181, 218
   face recognition 132
   frontal brain recruitment 183
   imitation 131
   interventions to enhance social cognition 135–37
   loss of integrity, loss of function view 180
   neural substrates of brain changes 5, 182–83
   perspective-taking 124–25, 134
   physical activity 136
   positivity effect 182
   selective engagement hypothesis 133–34
   social attention 134–35
   social brain 180, 182–83
   social isolation 117–18, 210–11
   social motivation 133–34, 183–84
   social relationships 133, 183–84
   socioemotional selectivity theory 133, 182
   theory of mind 4, 8–9, 120–25, 180–84, 210–11
   theory of mind training 135–36
orienting reactions 30
overmentalizing 109
ovulation cues 78–79

partner effect 61–62
peer status 55–56, 72–73
perception-goal folk psychology 31–35
perspective-taking 3, 102–3, 105, 106–7
    adolescence 80–81
    infancy 32, 35
    Level 1 and Level 2 3, 32, 35
    old age 124–25, 134
physical activity 136
planning 7
point-light displays 130
positron emission tomography 187
posterior cingulate cortex 178–80
posterior superior temporal sulcus 76–78, 79–80
precuneus 178–80
prefrontal cortex
    adolescence 76–77, 79–80, 82–83
    ageing 5, 182–83
    Alzheimer's disease 188–89
    emotion processing/regulation 82, 83–84
    mindreading 97–98
    perspective-taking 81
    social brain 76–77, 178–80
    social feedback 73
preschoolers *see* early and middle childhood
progesterone 76
propositional attitudes 31
prosocial behaviour 53–55
proto-conversations 30
psychosis, egocentric errors in subclinical population 102–3, 109
puberty 74–76
putamen 84–85

rational imitation 33–34
Reading the Mind in the Eyes task 9, 79–80, 101–2, 128–29, 158, 182–83
real-world interactions 14–15, 165–66, 203–4, 216–17
reproductive competence 70–72, 76, 80, 81
reputation management 154
rewards 75, 107, 154
risk-taking behaviour 75–76, 82–84
romantic relationships 73–74, 84–85

salience network 184–85, 188–89, 192–93
Sandbox test 123
schizophrenia 109, 202–3, 211–12
second-order false belief 122–23
second-person neuroscience 206–7, 208–9, 210
selective engagement hypothesis 133–34
self-concept 110–11
self/other differentiation and integration 202–3, 212–13

self-other interference 99–100, 102–3, 104–6
sexual activity 73–74
sexual selection 72
shared intentionality 34–35
sibling interactions 51–53
sign language 36
simulation theory 4–5
social affect 83–84
social attention
    autism spectrum disorder 152–54
    old age 134–35
social brain 178–80
    adolescence 76–77, 79–80, 81
    ageing 180, 182–83
    degeneration 185–93
social cognition 1
    structure 2, 164–65
social communication 56
social competence 53–55
social constructivism 53
social context framework 59–62
social hierarchy, as mindreading incentive 106–7
social isolation 117–18, 210–11
social motivation
    autism spectrum disorder 109–10, 154–55
    old age 133–34, 183–84
social orienting hypothesis 152–53
social relationships
    mindreading incentive 106–7, 108
    old age 133, 183–84
social reorientation hypothesis 73
socioaffective processes 177–78
    Alzheimer's disease 187–89
    behavioural variant frontotemporal dementia 191–93
    healthy ageing 182–83
sociocognitive processes 177–78
    Alzheimer's disease 186–87
    behavioural variant frontotemporal dementia 190, 192–93
    healthy ageing 180–81
socioemotional selectivity theory 133, 182
status
    adolescent preoccupation with 73
    biosocial model 75
still-face effect 30
Strange Stories task 8–9, 10, 61–62, 121–22, 211

temporoparietal junction 76–77, 81, 97–98, 178–80, 183, 187, 209–10
testosterone 74–75, 76
theory of mind (ToM) 1, 177–78
    affective 2–3, 9, 177–78
    Alzheimer's disease 186–87

theory of mind (ToM) (*cont.*)
  autism spectrum disorder 7–8, 50, 158–61
  behavioural variant frontotemporal dementia 190, 192
  cognitive 2–3, 9, 177–78, 186–87, 190
  context 58–59, 61–62
  correlations between ToM tasks 11
  development in early and middle childhood 47–50
  dual process theories 37
  emergence of first forms 31–35
  emergence of meta-representational form 35–41
  executive functions and 7–9, 36
  explicit 158–59
  family environment 50–53
  friendships 56
  goals 57
  implicit 12–13, 158–59
  individual differences 48–50, 57
  interventions 61
  language and 36
  metaphor interpretation 56
  motivation 57
  nativistic accounts 37
  old age 4, 8–9, 120–25, 180–84, 210–11
  parent–child interactions 51
  peer status 55–56
  precocious capacities 37
  precursors 29–30
  prosocial behaviour 53–55
  real-world contexts 165–66
  sibling interactions 51–53
  social communication 56
  social competence 53–55
  social context framework 59–62
  social individual differences 50, 57
  standard picture of development 35–36
  terminology issues 165
  training 61, 135–36
  transitional phase 3
  Type I and Type II processes 37
theory theory 4–5
Tourette syndrome 109
training
  brain training 219
  enhancing social cognition in old age 135–37
  executive functions 217–19
  self/other differentiation 213
  theory of mind 61, 135–36
  virtual reality training in autism 205–6
transcranial direct current stimulation 219–20

Ultimatum Game 191

ventral striatum 82
ventral tegmental area 84–85
ventrolateral prefrontal cortex 83–84
ventromedial prefrontal cortex 82
virtual reality 13–14, 205–6
visual scanning 153
von Economo neurons 178–80

WEIRD societies 215
working memory 7